LECTURES ON THE HISTORY OF MORAL PHILOSOPHY

LECTURES ON THE
HISTORY OF MORAL PHILOSOPHY

JOHN RAWLS

Edited by Barbara Herman

HARVARD UNIVERSITY PRESS
Cambridge, Massachusetts, and London, England

Copyright © 2000 by the President and Fellows of Harvard College

ALL RIGHTS RESERVED

Printed in the United States of America

Second printing, 2003

Library of Congress Cataloging-in-Publication Data

Rawls, John, 1921–
    Lectures on the history of moral philosophy/John Rawls ; edited by Barbara
Herman.
        p. cm.
    Includes bibliographical references and index.
    ISBN 0-674-00296-2 (alk. paper)—ISBN 0-674-00442-6 (pbk. : alk. paper)
    1. Ethics, Modern—17th century.   2. Ethics, Modern—18th century.
3. Ethics, Modern—19th century.   I. Herman, Barbara.   II. Title.

BJ301.R39 2000
170'.9'03'—dc21   00-031942

CONTENTS

CONTENTS

Editor's Foreword

There is little doubt that modern political philosophy was transformed in 1971 with the publication of John Rawls's *A Theory of Justice*. Its questions and method, its manner of argumentation and its range of topics, set an agenda for social and political philosophy in the last quarter of the past century and into this one. But John Rawls's contribution to philosophy is not to be measured solely in terms of the impact of *A Theory of Justice* and related published work. As a professor at Harvard from 1962 until 1991, he had a profound influence on the approach to philosophical ethics of many generations of students, and through them, on the way the subject is now understood. In particular, his teaching conveyed an unusual commitment to the history of moral philosophy. At the center of his thought about this history is the idea that in the great texts of our tradition we find the efforts of the best minds to come to terms with many of the hardest questions about how we are to live our lives. Whatever their flaws, superficial criticism of these texts is always to be resisted; it is without serious point. If in studying these figures one thinks about what *their* questions were, and how they saw their work as responsive to worries that might not be our own, a fruitful exchange of ideas across the centuries is possible. Rawls's lectures at Harvard offered a compelling example of just how much could be learned through such an engagement. Although it is obvious throughout his published work that the history of philosophy matters greatly to him, very little of the extraordinary product of his life-long study of this history is known. The present volume of Rawls's lectures on the history of moral philosophy aims to make widely available this important part of his philosophical accomplishment.

In his thirty years at Harvard, Rawls offered a variety of courses in moral and political philosophy. The one that had the greatest impact was the course he thought of as his introductory undergraduate course on ethics. Prior to 1977, it surveyed a mix of historical figures, usually including Aristotle, Kant, and Mill, but sometimes also Hume or Sidgwick or Ross. The course was sometimes called Ethics, sometimes Moral Psychology. As Rawls taught it, moral psychology was not an academic subfield of ethics, but rather the study of the role of a moral conception in human life: how it organizes moral reasoning, the conception of a person that it presupposes, and the social role of the moral conception. Along with a substantive account of the right, it completed the practical part of a moral conception, and often contained its most distinctive contribution.

The broad plan for the course involved delineating four basic types of moral reasoning: perfectionism, utilitarianism, intuitionism, and Kantian constructivism. Views from historical texts were set out within these rubrics with an eye to providing answers to such questions as: How do we deliberate—rationally and morally? What is the connection between principles of belief and motives? What are the first principles, and how do we come to desire to act on them? Essential to an adequate response was always an account of a moral conception's social role. Rawls held that the idea of social role is often wrongly restricted to finding principles for adjudicating competing claims. The wider examination of social role involves considering how and whether a moral conception can be an essential part of a society's public culture—how it supports a view of ourselves and each other as rational and reasonable persons. These were the kind of questions Rawls thought moral philosophy, as a branch of philosophy with its own methods, was in a position to answer. Other sorts of questions—about realism or about meaning, for example—were neither best investigated by moral philosophy nor necessary for making progress in the areas of moral philosophy's distinctive problems.[1]

---

1. See John Rawls, "The Independence of Moral Theory," in *John Rawls: Collected Papers* (Cambridge, Mass.: Harvard University Press, 1999).

In the mid-1970s the course changed, and Rawls began to focus primarily on Kant's ethical theory. The change coincided with the period of work leading up to his 1980 Dewey Lectures ("Kantian Constructivism in Moral Theory," delivered at Columbia University), in which Rawls was concerned to "set out more clearly the Kantian roots of *A Theory of Justice*," and to elaborate the Kantian form of constructivism, whose absence from the scene, he thought, impeded "the advance of moral theory."[2] The first time he taught the new Kant material was in a graduate seminar (in spring 1974) on Kant on the topic of Moral Goodness, and in spring 1977, Rawls delivered the first series of his "Kant lectures."

About a week and a half into the lecture course, Rawls took pity on the graduate and undergraduate students frantically trying to take verbatim notes, and offered to make his lectures available to anyone who wanted them. Copies of the first batch of handwritten notes cost 40 cents. Rawls's unpublished work had often circulated among students and friends. Either he made it available himself or, as in the 1960s, graduate student teaching assistants prepared and distributed "dittos" of their course notes. Starting in 1978, Rawls took on the regular task of preparing and updating the Kant lectures as part of the materials for his course. These lecture notes acquired something of a life of their own, passed on from one generation of Rawls's students to their own students elsewhere. The lectures in this volume are from the last offering of the course, in 1991.

The lectures went through major revisions in 1979, 1987, and 1991. (In between these years, versions would be amended and corrected, but remained substantially the same.) The organizing principle of the first version of the lectures was an interpretation of Kant's *Groundwork for the Metaphysics of Morals*. Eight of ten lectures were about the *Groundwork;* there was, in addition, an introductory lecture, sometimes about intuitionism, sometimes about Sidgwick, moral psychology, and constructivism, and a tenth lecture on the Fact of Reason. In discussing the *Groundwork*, Rawls paid considerable attention to the formulas of the categorical imperative and the well-known difficulties with it as a procedure for moral judgment. In the mid-1980s, Rawls added lectures on Hume and Leibniz (four on Hume, two on

2. John Rawls, "Kantian Constructivism in Moral Theory: The Dewey Lectures, 1980," *Journal of Philosophy* 77, 9 (1980), 515.

Leibniz), and the content of the Kant lectures underwent a shift into roughly their current form, with only four lectures on the *Groundwork*, and six other Kant lectures on the Priority of Right, Constructivism, the Fact of Reason, Freedom, the moral psychology of *Religion within the Limits of Reason Alone*, and the Unity of Reason. In 1991 a lecture on Justice as an Artificial Virtue became the fifth Hume lecture, and two lectures on Hegel were added (though Rawls produced no version of the Hegel lectures for distribution).[3]

Two ideas figured prominently in Rawls's rethinking of the Kant lectures. One was that too intense a focus on the *Groundwork* and its collection of interpretive issues gave a distorted picture of Kant's contribution to moral theory. Many central notions were present only in the *Critique of Practical Reason*, *Religion within the Limits of Reason Alone*, and the *Doctrine of Virtue*. In addition, Rawls came to believe that negotiating the details of the categorical imperative procedure didn't matter nearly as much as understanding what such a procedure was about—namely, how Kant thought a formal procedure could model a noninstrumental conception of rationality. The second large decision was to take up the subjects of freedom and Kant's constructivist solution to foundational questions.[4] Here, Rawls argues, the *Groundwork* has neither the last word nor always the best. This shift in emphasis in the Kant lectures partly motivates the inclusion of lectures on Leibniz. Leibniz was the dominant figure in German philosophy in Kant's time, and where Kant's concerns touch those of Leibniz, even when Kant developed his own distinctive views, "the fact remains that Leibniz's ideas often shape Kant's mature doctrine in striking and subtle ways" (Leibniz I, §1). This is particularly so with Leibniz's philosophical reconciliation of faith and reasonable belief, his perfectionism, and his view of freedom. For Rawls, to understand Kant's constructivism in a serious way, one has to

---

3. The Hegel lectures in this volume were compiled by the editor from Rawls's notes for those classes, and from some partial notes for lectures in his political philosophy course. Rawls read through them in 1998 and made some changes. Given Rawls's long-standing interest in Hegel, to have in print even a little of his view of Hegel's contribution to moral philosophy seemed to warrant the editorial license.

4. The new focus is evident in Rawls's one published piece on Kant's ethics: "Themes in Kant's Moral Philosophy," in *Kant's Transcendental Deductions*, ed. Eckart Förster (Stanford: Stanford University Press, 1989).

appreciate with some historical specificity the strengths and weaknesses of the rationalist thought of his day.

An extended discussion of Hume, especially of Book II of the *Treatise of Human Nature*, was always a part of the Kant lectures. While it is common to compare Kantian and Humean moral psychology (one as the foil for the other), the view of Hume in such comparisons tends to be superficial: passions as original existences and the sources of our interests and ends, the purely instrumental role of reason, and so forth. Rawls, by contrast, looks closely and at length at Hume's moral psychology (with special attention to Hume's criticisms of rational intuitionism), carefully eliciting from the text of the *Treatise* a rich and layered Humean account of deliberation and practical reasoning. It is a Humean view that is both powerful and resourceful. Nevertheless, Rawls makes it clear just what the limits of the Humean desire-based account of deliberation are, motivating the idea, central to Kant's rationalist moral psychology, of principle-dependent desires as essential to an account of practical reason (see Hume II, §5).

The rationale for the inclusion of Hegel in a series of lectures focused on Kant is obvious: Hegel's criticisms of Kant's ethics set the terms of Kant interpretation for more than 150 years. But Rawls's chief interest in Hegel was not to rebut his criticisms (by itself, for Rawls, that would probably not be enough; the careful reading of Kant would be sufficient). It is Hegel's notion of *Sittlichkeit* that interests Rawls; it is the idea that allows Hegel to elaborate the notion of a wide social role for morality (and for moral philosophy) first broached in Kant's ethical and political writings. In a sense, the Hegel lectures sketch the bridge between Kantian moral thought and the liberalism of Rawls's own work: the view of persons as "rooted in and fashioned by the system of political and social institutions under which they live" (Hegel I), the place of religion in secular society, and the role of philosophy in public ethical life. Unlike many, Rawls reads Hegel as a part of the liberal tradition, and his reading of Hegel helps us to see what the complete shape of that tradition is. Certainly, in reading the Hegel lectures one gets a full measure of Rawls's method of reading historical texts. It does not matter that one view or another may seem to us wrongheaded if there is something to be learned from understanding why a philosopher of the first order would advance it.

About his aims and method in presenting a philosophical text to students, no one is more eloquent than Rawls himself. In 1997 he wrote a marvelous description of his teaching. It occurs near the end of a reminiscence about his friend and colleague Burton Dreben.

When lecturing, say, on Locke, Rousseau, Kant, or J. S. Mill, I always tried to do two things especially. One was to pose their problems as they themselves saw them, given what their understanding of these problems was in their own time. I often cited the remark of Collingwood that "the history of political theory is not the history of different answers to one and the same question, but the history of a problem more or less constantly changing, whose solution was changing with it."[5] . . . The second thing I tried to do was to present each writer's thought in what I took to be its strongest form. I took to heart Mill's remark in his review of [Alfred] Sedgwick: "A doctrine is not judged until it is judged in its best form."[6] I didn't say, not intentionally anyway, what I myself thought a writer should have said, but rather what the writer did say, supported by what I viewed as the most reasonable interpretation of the text. The text had to be known and respected, and its doctrine presented in its best form. Leaving aside the text seemed offensive, a kind of pretending. If I departed from it—no harm in that—I had to say so. Lecturing that way, I believed, made a writer's views stronger and more convincing, and a more worthy object of study.

I always took for granted that the writers we were studying were much smarter than I was. If they were not, why was I wasting my time and the students' time by studying them? If I saw a mistake in their arguments, I supposed those writers saw it too and must have dealt with it. But where? I looked for their way out, not mine. Sometimes their way out was historical: in their day the question need not be raised, or wouldn't arise and so couldn't then be fruitfully discussed. Or there was a part of the text I had overlooked, or had not read.

5. R. G. Collingwood, *An Autobiography* (Oxford: Clarendon Press, 1939), p. 62.
6. In Mill's *Collected Works*, vol. 10, *Essays on Ethics, Religion, and Society*, ed. J. M. Robson (Toronto: University of Toronto Press, 1969), p. 52.

I assumed there were never plain mistakes, not ones that mattered anyway.

In doing this I followed what Kant says in the *Critique of Pure Reason* at B866, namely that philosophy is a mere idea of a possible science and nowhere exists *in concreto:* "[W]e cannot learn philosophy; for where is it, who is in possession of it, and how shall we recognize it? We can only learn to philosophize, that is, to exercise the talent of reason, in accordance with its universal principles, on certain actually existing attempts at philosophy, always, however, reserving the right of reason to investigate, to confirm, or to reject these principles in their very sources." Thus we learn moral and political philosophy—or indeed any part of philosophy—by studying the exemplars, those noted figures who have made cherished attempts at philosophy; and if we are lucky, we find a way to go beyond them. . . .

The result was that I was loath to raise objections to the exemplars; that's too easy and misses what is essential. However, it was important to point out difficulties that those coming later in the same tradition sought to overcome, or to point to views those in other traditions thought were mistaken. . . .

With Kant I hardly made any criticisms at all. My efforts were centered on trying to understand him so as to be able to describe his ideas to the students. Sometimes I would discuss well-known objections to his moral doctrine, such as those of Schiller and Hegel, Schopenhauer and Mill. Going over these is instructive and clarifies Kant's view. Yet I never felt satisfied with the understanding I achieved of Kant's doctrine as a whole. I never could grasp sufficiently his ideas on freedom of the will and reasonable religion, which must have been part of the core of his thought. All the great figures . . . lie to some degree beyond us, no matter how hard we try to master their thought. With Kant this distance often seems to me somehow much greater. Like great composers and great artists—Mozart and Beethoven, Poussin and Turner—they are beyond envy. It is vital in lecturing to try to exhibit to students in one's speech and conduct a sense of this, and why it is so. That can only be done by taking the thought of the text seriously, as worthy of honor and respect. This may at times be a kind of reverence, yet it is sharply distinct from adulation or uncritical acceptance of the text or author as authoritative. All true philosophy seeks fair criticism and depends on continuing reflective public judgment.[7]

Rawls never intended that his lectures be published. As he saw things, they were not serious works of scholarship, but were aimed at helping his students and himself to understand and appreciate the thought of a set of important figures in the history of moral philosophy, most prominently Kant. Too many questions remained unanswered, too much was obscure for them to be of value to anyone, he often said. It was only after many years of resistance that he finally agreed to let the project go forward. In the end, he was moved by two considerations. The first was the unfairness that some but not all who might benefit from the lectures had access to them. If you were not a friend of a friend of someone who studied ethics at Harvard, you would not have them. And second was the fact of the multiple generations of the lectures. However imperfect Rawls thought the last version was, since he also thought the lectures had improved over time, it was important that the version that would survive be the best. His own past generosity in distributing the lectures to generations of his students guaranteed that one or more of the older sets of the lectures would continue to circulate. When he agreed to let the lectures be published, Rawls did so on the condition that their format not be changed: they were to remain *lectures,* that is, retain the style and voice of the pages distributed to students. The editorial work on the lectures has, accordingly, been minor. Apart from sorting out obscure abbreviations, checking quotations, and cleaning up some of the inevitable roughness of a teaching manuscript, the lectures have been left as Rawls distributed them in 1991.[8] They are offered to students of the subject in the spirit of an earlier generation of scholarship—where the best teaching was more commonly preserved alongside the best finished work.

*   *   *

7. John Rawls, "Burton Dreben: A Reminiscence," in Juliet Floyd and Sanford Shieh, eds., *Future Pasts: Perspectives on the Place of the Analytic Tradition in Twentieth-Century Philosophy* (New York: Oxford University Press, 2000).

8. Except, that is, for the two Hegel lectures.

Textual citations throughout the lectures are given in the running text. There is one major idiosyncrasy in the method of citation to Kant's *Groundwork for the Metaphysics of Morals*. It is now standard scholarly practice to give textual citations to the relevant volume and page of the Prussian Academy edition of Kant's collected writings. The practice is followed for citations to all of Kant's work other than the *Groundwork*. For the *Groundwork*, the lectures continue Rawls's teaching practice of referring to parts of the text by chapter and paragraph number (e.g., *Gr* I:4 is the fourth paragraph of the first chapter of the *Groundwork*). The Academy number (to Volume 4) follows in brackets (so, *Gr* I:4 [394]). Although this sometimes makes for a page cluttered with numbers, since Rawls discusses arguments as they develop in a series of paragraphs, there is no way to avoid it. (In his courses, Rawls used the chapter and verse system for the *Groundwork* and for J. S. Mill's *Utilitarianism*.) Those who plan to work closely with the Kant lectures should follow Rawls's instructions to his students to prepare their copy of the *Groundwork* for study by numbering the paragraphs, starting again with "1" at the beginning of each chapter.

Translations for the most part follow the editions Rawls used for teaching. Some departures seemed clearly to be errors in transcription, and these were corrected. In other cases, most often in passages from the *Critique of Practical Reason*, it was clear that Rawls had changed the translation deliberately; these have been kept.

For help with editing and preparing the manuscript, thanks to Glenn Branch, Amanda Heller, and Donna Bouvier; thanks also to Ben Auspitz for the index.

A Note on the Texts

Unless otherwise indicated, Kant's works will be cited by volume and page of the *Gesammelte Schriften,* usually called the *Akademieausgabe.* This edition was first published starting in 1900 by the Prussian Academy of Sciences. Citations to the *Groundwork* are by chapter and paragraph as well as *Akademie* page of Volume 4; citations to the *Critique of Pure Reason* are in the customary first- and second-edition pagination.

Gr *Groundwork of the Metaphysics of Morals,* trans. H. D. Paton (New York: Harper and Row, 1964)

KP *Critique of Practical Reason,* trans. L. W. Beck (Indianapolis: Bobbs-Merrill, 1956)

KR *Critique of Pure Reason,* trans. N. Kemp Smith (New York: St. Martin's Press, 1965)

KU *Critique of Judgment,* trans. J. C. Meredith (Oxford: Oxford University Press, 1952)

MdS *Metaphysics of Morals,* pt. 2, trans. M. Gregor as *The Doctrine of Virtue* (New York: Harper and Row, 1964)

Rel *Religion within the Limits of Reason Alone,* trans. T. M. Greene and H. H. Hudson (New York: Harper and Row, 1960)

Other texts:

David Hume, *Enquiry Concerning the Principles of Morals* (= *E*), ed. L. A. Selby-Bigge (Oxford: Oxford University Press, 1975)

David Hume, *Treatise of Human Nature* (= *T*), ed. P. H. Nidditch (Oxford: Oxford University Press, 1978)

G. W. Leibniz, *Philosophical Essays,* ed. Roger Ariew and Daniel Garber (Indianapolis: Hackett, 1989)

G. W. F. Hegel, *Elements of the Philosophy of Right* (= *PR*), trans. H. B. Nisbet, ed. A. W. Wood (Cambridge: Cambridge University Press, 1991)

LECTURES ON THE HISTORY OF MORAL PHILOSOPHY

Introduction: Modern Moral Philosophy, 1600–1800

§1. A Difference between Classical and Modern Moral Philosophy

1. I begin with an apparent difference between classical and modern moral philosophy. By classical moral philosophy I mean that of ancient Greece, mainly of Athens or of the philosophers who lived there, Socrates, Plato, and Aristotle, and members of the Epicurean and Stoic schools. By modern moral philosophy I mean that of the period from 1600 to 1800, but we should include sixteenth-century writers such as Montaigne, who were major influences later on.

When Sidgwick comes in Book I of the *Methods of Ethics* to the concept of good, he remarks that until then he has been discussing rightness, which is, he says, the concept frequently used by English writers. He has treated this concept and its equivalents as implying a dictate, or an imperative, of reason. Reason is seen as prescribing certain actions unconditionally, or else with reference to some ulterior end. Yet it is possible, Sidgwick says, to see the moral ideal as attractive, as specifying an ideal good to be pursued, rather than as a dictate, or an imperative, of reason. Virtuous action, or rightness in action, is seen not as a dictate of an imperative reason, but as something good in itself, and not merely as a means to some ulterior good.

Sidgwick thinks that such was the fundamental ethical view of the Greek schools of moral philosophy:

> The chief characteristics of ancient ethical controversy as distinguished
> from modern may be traced to the employment of a generic notion
> [of good] instead of a specific one [such as rightness] in expressing

the common moral judgments on actions. Virtue or Right action is commonly regarded [by the Greeks] as only a species of the Good: and so . . . the first question . . . when we endeavour to systematise conduct, is how to determine the relation of this species of good to the rest of the genus. (*Methods*, 7th ed. [London, 1907], pp. 105–106)

We can hardly understand Greek moral philosophy, Sidgwick continues, unless we put aside the "quasi-jural," or legalistic, concepts of modern ethics and ask not "What is duty and what is its ground?" but rather "Which of the objects that people think good is truly good, or the highest good?" Alternatively, "[W]hat is the relation of the good we call virtue, the qualities of conduct and character that we commend and admire, to other good things?" But to answer this question, we need, of course, some way of estimating the relative values of different goods, some way of telling how they are related to or make up the highest good.

2. Let's agree that there is this difference between ancient and modern moral philosophy. So, to conclude, we say: the ancients asked about the most rational way to true happiness, or the highest good, and they inquired about how virtuous conduct and the virtues as aspects of character—the virtues of courage and temperance, wisdom and justice, which are themselves good—are related to that highest good, whether as means, or as constituents, or both. Whereas the moderns asked primarily, or at least in the first instance, about what they saw as authoritative prescriptions of right reason, and the rights, duties, and obligations to which these prescriptions of reason gave rise. Only afterward did their attention turn to the goods these prescriptions permitted us to pursue and to cherish.

Now, to suppose that there is this difference between ancient and modern moral philosophy is not necessarily to suppose that it is deep. Indeed, this difference may be not deep at all but simply a matter of the vocabulary used to articulate and to order the moral domain. What determined this vocabulary may have been a matter of historical accident, with further examination showing that the two families of concepts expressed by these vocabularies are equivalent in the sense that whatever moral ideas we can express in one family, we can also express in the other, even if not as naturally.

But granting this, it is possible that given the historical and cultural background with its main problems, using one family of concepts rather than another may lead us to see these problems in a particular way, and this in turn may lead to substantive differences of moral doctrine between ancient and modern moral philosophy. Or the historical context itself may point to one vocabulary as the more fitting and appropriate.

§2. The Main Problem of Greek Moral Philosophy

1. I begin with a conjecture—I shouldn't say it is more than that—about the historical and cultural context that accounts for the main problem that concerned the Greeks. I note first that when moral philosophy began, say with Socrates, Greek religion was a civic religion of public social practice, of civic festivals and public celebrations. As long as one participated in the expected way and recognized the proprieties, the details of what one believed were not of enormous importance. It was a matter of doing the done thing and being a trustworthy member of society, always ready to carry out one's civic duties as a good citizen—to serve on juries or to row in the fleet in war—when called upon to do so. It was not a religion of salvation in the Christian sense, and there was no class of priests who dispensed the necessary means of grace; indeed, the ideas of immortality and eternal salvation did not have an important role in classical culture.

Moreover, this civic religious culture was not based on a sacred work like the Bible, or the Koran, or the Vedas of Hindu religion. The Greeks celebrated Homer, and the Homeric poems were a basic part of their education, but the *Iliad* and the *Odyssey* were never sacred texts. Beginning with Socrates, Greek moral philosophy criticized Homer and rejected the Homeric ideal of the heroic warrior, the ideal of the feudal nobility that ruled in earlier times and that still had a wide influence.

It is true that in the classical world the irreligious and the atheist were feared and thought dangerous when their rejection of civic pieties was openly flaunted. This was because the Greeks thought such conduct showed that they were untrustworthy and not reliable civic friends on whom one could count. People who made fun of the gods invited rejection, but this was a matter not so much of their unbelief as such as of their manifest unwillingness to participate in shared civic practice.

To understand this, keep in mind that the Greek polis was by our standards a very small, quite homogeneous society. Athens, for instance, contained about 300,000 people, including women and children, aliens and slaves. The number who could attend the assembly and exercise political power—all adult males born into one of the recognized demes—was around 35,000. The civic religion of the polis was an essential part of its arrangements for maintaining social cohesion and rapport.

2. Thus Greek moral philosophy begins within the historical and cultural context of a civic religion of a polis in which the Homeric epics, with their gods and heroes, play a central part. This religion contains no alternative idea of the highest good to set against that of these gods and heroes. The heroes are of noble birth; they unabashedly seek success and honor, power and wealth, social standing and prestige. While they are not indifferent to the good of family, friends, and dependents, these claims have a lesser place. When Achilles is selfishly indifferent and sulks in his tent, he doesn't lose his heroic virtue; and while he returns to battle because Patroclus has been killed, it is not because he grieves for Patroclus' sake but because he is upset about the weakness he has shown in not protecting his own dependent. As for the gods, they are not, morally speaking, very different, though being immortal, their life is relatively happy and secure.

So, rejecting the Homeric ideal as characteristic of a way of life of a bygone age, and finding no guidance in civic religion, Greek philosophy must work out for itself ideas of the highest good of human life, ideas suitable for the different society of fifth-century Athens. The idea of the highest good is, then, quite naturally at the center of the moral philosophy of the Greeks: it addresses a question civic religion leaves largely unanswered.

3. To conclude: time does not permit a discussion of the philosophical moral views of the Greeks, except to note a few very general points.

They focused on the idea of the highest good as an attractive ideal, as the reasonable pursuit of our true happiness.

They were concerned largely with this good as a good for the individual. For example, Aristotle meets the criticism of acting justly not by saying that we should sacrifice our own good to the claims of justice, but by saying that we lose our own good if we reject those claims.[1] The approach of Socrates and Plato is similar.

---

1. Terence Irwin, *Classical Thought* (Oxford: Oxford University Press, 1989), p. 138.

Again, virtuous conduct they saw as a kind of good to be given a place along with other goods in the good life, and they looked for a conception of the highest good to serve as a basis for judging how this could reasonably be done.

Finally, moral philosophy was always the exercise of free, disciplined reason alone. It was not based on religion, much less on revelation, since civic religion did not offer a rival to it. In seeking moral ideals more suited than those of the Homeric age to the society and culture of fifth-century Athens, Greek moral philosophy from the beginning stood more or less by itself.

§3. The Background of Modern Moral Philosophy

1. I begin as before with the historical and cultural context. I suggest that three major historical developments account for the nature of moral philosophy in the modern period.

There is, first, the Reformation in the sixteenth century, which is fundamental in shaping the modern world. It fragmented the religious unity of the Middle Ages and led to religious pluralism, with all its consequences for later centuries. This in turn fostered pluralisms of other kinds, which were a basic and permanent feature of contemporary life by the end of the eighteenth century. As Hegel recognized, pluralism made religious liberty possible, which certainly was not Luther's and Calvin's intention. (See *Philosophy of Right* §270 [end of the long comments], pp. 302f.)

Second, there is the development of the modern state with its central administration. At first in its highly centralized form, the modern state was ruled by monarchs with enormous powers, who tried to be as absolute as they could, granting a share in power to the aristocracy and the rising middle classes only when they had to, or as suited their convenience. The development of the state took place in different ways and at different rates in the various countries of Europe. Central states were fairly well established in England, France, and Spain by the end of the sixteenth century, but not in Germany and Italy until the nineteenth. (Prussia and Austria were certainly strong states by the eighteenth century and rivals as to which would unify Germany, a question finally settled by Bismarck by 1870.)

Finally, there is the development of modern science beginning in the seventeenth century (with important roots in Greek and Islamic thought, of course). By modern science, I mean the development of astronomy by Copernicus and Kepler and Newtonian physics; and also, it must be stressed, the development of mathematical analysis (calculus) by Newton and Leibniz. Without analysis, the development of physics would not have been possible. The advances of mathematics and physics go together.

Certainly these three main developments affect one another in complicated ways and set off an immense chain of consequences impossible to follow, or even to understand, in any detail. (Consider how the desire of Henry VIII, an absolute monarch, for an heir led to the English Reformation.)

2. Now observe the contrast with the classical world with respect to religion. Medieval Christianity had *five* important features that Greek civic religion lacked:

> It was an *authoritative* religion and the authority was institutional, with the papacy, central and nearly absolute, though sometimes challenged, as in the conciliar period of the fourteenth and fifteenth centuries.
>
> It was a religion of *salvation*, a way to eternal life, and salvation required true belief as the church taught it.
>
> Hence, it was a *doctrinal* religion with a creed that was to be believed.
>
> It was a religion of *priests* with the sole authority to dispense means of grace, themselves normally essential to salvation.
>
> Finally, it was an *expansionist* religion, that is, a religion of conversion that recognized no territorial limits to its authority short of the world as a whole.

Thus, in contrast with classical moral philosophy, the moral philosophy of the medieval Church is not the result of the exercise of free, disciplined reason alone. This is not to say that its moral philosophy is not true, or that it is unreasonable; but it was subordinate to church authority and largely practiced by the clergy and the religious orders in order to fulfill the Church's practical need for a moral theology.

Moreover, the doctrine of the Church saw our moral duties and obligations as resting on divine law. They were the consequences of the laws laid

[6]

down by God who creates us all and who maintains us in being at every moment, and to whom we are everlastingly obligated. If we think of God as supremely reasonable, as Aquinas did, then these laws are dictates, or prescriptions, of the divine reason. It is from Christianity that the idea of a dictate, or imperative, of reason specifying our duties and obligations enters modern moral philosophy. Alternatively, if we take a voluntarist view, as Scotus and Ockham did, these dictates are those of divine will. We find one or another of these views not only in Suarez, Bellarmine, and Molina, and in other late scholastics, but also in the Protestant writers Grotius, Pufendorf, and Locke.

Thus the concept of obligation was widely understood in the seventeenth century as resting on the idea of natural law, or divine law. This law is addressed to us by God, who has legitimate authority over us as our creator; it is a dictate of divine reason, or of divine will, and in either case it directs us to comply with it on pain of sanctions. And while the law commands only what is in due course good for us and for human society, it is not in acting from it as for our good that we fulfill our obligation but rather in acting from it as imposed by God and in obedience to God's authority. (See, for example, Locke, *An Essay Concerning Human Understanding*, Bk. II, Ch. 28, §§4–15.)

3. The Reformation had enormous consequences. To see why, we have to ask what it is like for an authoritative, salvationist, and expansionist religion such as medieval Christianity to fragment. Inevitably this means the appearance within the same society of rival authoritative and salvationist religions, different in some ways from the original religion from which they split off, but having for a certain period of time many of the same features. Luther and Calvin were as dogmatic and intolerant as the Church had been. For those who had to decide whether to become Protestant or to remain Catholic, it was a terrible time. For once the original religion fragments, which religion then leads to salvation?

I put aside, as more relevant to political philosophy, both the controversy over toleration, one of the historical origins of liberalism, and also the efforts to establish constitutional limits on the sovereigns of nation-states, a second origin of liberalism. But these are large issues that we should recognize as lying in the background of much of the moral philosophy of this period. The Reformation gave rise to the severe conflicts of the religious wars, which the Greeks did not experience. The question it raised was not simply the Greek question of how to live, but the question of how one can live with people who are of a different authoritative and salvationist religion. That was a new question, which posed in an acute form the question of how human society was possible at all under those conditions.

§4. The Problems of Modern Moral Philosophy

1. The moral philosophy of our period, I think, like Greek moral philosophy, was deeply affected by the religious and cultural situation within which it developed, in this case, by the situation following the Reformation. By the eighteenth century, many leading writers hoped to establish a basis of moral knowledge independent of church authority and available to the ordinary reasonable and conscientious person. This done, they wanted to develop the full range of concepts and principles in terms of which to characterize autonomy and responsibility.[2]

To elaborate: as we have seen, on the one hand, there is the traditional view of the Church that, in the absence of divine revelation, we cannot know the principles of right and wrong with which we must comply and which specify our duties and obligations. Even if some of us can know them, not all can, or not all can keep in mind their consequences for particular cases. Therefore the many must be instructed by the few (who may be the clergy) and made to comply by threats of punishments. On the other hand, there is the view more congenial to the radical side of Protestantism, with its idea of the priesthood of all believers and the denial of an ecclesiastical authority interposed between God and the faithful. This view says that

2. I emphasize Protestantism because nearly all the main writers are Protestant. The leading writers in the development of natural law—Grotius and Pufendorf, Hobbes and Locke—are Protestant. If we leave out the case of Leibniz, so is the German line of Wolff and Crusius, Kant and Hegel. Crusius and Kant are Pietists and Hegel professes to be Lutheran, although certainly he was a highly unorthodox one. The English writers of the moral sense school—Shaftesbury, Butler and Hutcheson, Hume and Smith—as well as those of the rational intuitionist school—Clarke, Price, and Reid—we expect to be Protestant (at least in their upbringing) in view of the English Reformation. Of course, there is always moral philosophy done in the Catholic Church, but in this period it is done by scholar-priests—such as Suarez, Bellarmine, and Molina—and in the form of casuistry it is finally addressed to other priests who are confessors and advisers. This is very practical business, not intended for the laity, except insofar as it is part of their doctrinal instruction.

[8]

Schools of modern moral philosophy

The School of Natural Law

Francisco Suarez: 1548–1617
  On Law and God the Lawgiver: 1612
Hugo Grotius: 1583–1645
  On the Law of War and Peace: 1625
Samuel Pufendorf: 1632–1688
  On the Law of Nature and of Nations: 1672
John Locke: 1632–1704
  An Essay Concerning the Understanding: 1690
  The Reasonableness of Christianity: 1695

The German Line

Gottfried Wilhelm Leibniz: 1646–1716
  Discourse: 1686
  Theodicy: 1710
Christian Wolff: 1679–1754
  *Vernünftige Gedanken von Menschen
  Tun und Lassen:* 1720
Christian August Crusius: 1715–1775
  Anweisung vernünftig zu Leben: 1774
Immanuel Kant: 1724–1804
  Grundlegung: 1785
  Critique of Practical Reason: 1788
Georg Wilhelm Friedrich Hegel: 1770–1831
  Philosophy of Right: 1821

The Moral Sense School

Third Earl of Shaftesbury: 1671–1713
  An Inquiry Concerning Virtue or Merit: 1711
Francis Hutcheson: 1694–1746
  *An Inquiry into the Original of Our Ideas of
  Beauty and Virtue:* 1725
Joseph Butler: 1692–1752
  Fifteen Sermons: 1726
David Hume: 1711–1776
  A Treatise of Human Nature: 1739–1740
  *An Enquiry Concerning the Principles of
  Morals:* 1751

The Rational Intuitionists

Samuel Clarke: 1675–1729
  *A Discourse Concerning the Unchangeable
  Obligations of Natural Religion:* 1705
Richard Price: 1723–1791
  A Review of the Principal Questions of Morals:
  1758
Thomas Reid: 1710–1796
  *Essays on the Active Power of the Human
  Mind:* 1788

moral principles and precepts are accessible to normal reasonable persons generally—various schools explain this in different ways—and hence that we are fully capable of knowing our moral duties and obligations and also fully capable of being moved to fulfill them.

2. In the contrast stated in the above paragraph, three questions may be distinguished:

First: Is the moral order required of us derived from an external source, or does it arise in some way from human nature itself (as reason or feeling or both), and from the requirements of our living together in society?

Second: Is the knowledge or awareness of how we are to act directly accessible only to some, or to a few (the clergy, say), or is it accessible to every person who is normally reasonable and conscientious?

Third: Must we be persuaded or compelled to bring ourselves in line with the requirements of morality by some external motivation, or are we so constituted that we have in our nature sufficient motives to lead us to act as we ought without the need of external inducements?[3]

Of course, the terms I use here are both vague and ambiguous. It is unclear what is meant by such terms as "external motivation," or "human nature itself," or "normally reasonable and conscientious person," and the like. These terms gain their sense from how they are interpreted or rejected by the various traditions of moral philosophy that develop within the modern period, as we will see in due course in our examination of particular texts.

Here I think of the tradition of moral philosophy as itself a family of traditions, such as the traditions of natural law and of the moral sense schools, and of the schools of rational intuitionism and of utilitarianism. What makes these traditions all part of one inclusive tradition is that they use a commonly understood vocabulary and terminology. Moreover, they reply and adjust to one another's views and arguments so that exchanges between them are, in part, a reasoned discussion that leads to further development.

3. Looking at the three questions above, one should note that the writers of this period more or less agree on what in fact is right and wrong, good and bad. They do not differ about the content of morality, about what its first principles of rights, duties and obligations, and the rest, really are. None

---

3. In the last two paragraphs above, I follow J. B. Schneewind, *Moral Philosophy from Montaigne to Kant: An Anthology* (Cambridge: Cambridge University Press, 1990), intro. to vol. 1, p. 18.

of them doubted that property ought to be respected; all of them affirmed the virtues of fidelity to promises and contracts, of truthfulness and beneficence and charity, and much else. The problem for them was not the content of morality but its basis: How we could know it and be moved to act from it. Particular moral questions are examined for the light they throw on those matters. The moral sense school of Shaftesbury, Butler, and Hutcheson gave one answer; the rational intuitionists Clarke, Price, and Reid another; Leibniz and Crusius yet another.

To refer again to the three questions above, Hume and Kant both in their different ways affirm in each case the second alternative. That is, they believe that the moral order arises in some way from human nature itself and from the requirements of our living together in society. They also believe that the knowledge or awareness of how we are to act is directly accessible to every person who is normally reasonable and conscientious. And finally, they believe that we are so constituted that we have in our nature sufficient motives to lead us to act as we ought without the need of external sanctions, at least in the form of rewards bestowed and punishments imposed by God or the state. Indeed, both Hume and Kant are about as far as one can get from the view that only a few can have moral knowledge and that all or most people must be made to do what is right by means of such sanctions.[4]

§5. The Relation between Religion and Science

1. The writers we study are each much concerned (in their own ways) with the relation between modern science and Christianity and accepted moral beliefs. Here, of course, modern science means, as I have said, Newtonian physics. The problem was how the discoveries of Copernicus and Galileo, of Newton and Huyghens and others, were to be understood in relation to religion and morals.

Spinoza, Leibniz, and Kant answer this question in different ways, but they face a common problem. In some respects, of these three Spinoza's way is the most radical: his pantheism incorporates the new scientific and

---

4. Schneewind says this of Kant (ibid., p. 29), but I believe it holds of Hume as well.

deterministic view of the world while preserving important elements of a religious (but heterodox) doctrine. His view is one that neither Leibniz nor Kant can accept, and they are on guard against falling into Spinozism, so-called, something then to be avoided at all costs. (Likewise, in the late seventeenth century, falling into Hobbism was to be similarly avoided.) Leibniz was particularly worried about this, and some think that he did not succeed in avoiding Spinozism and that there are deep Spinozistic elements in his view.

Of the writers we study, Leibniz is the great conservative in the best sense of the term. That is, he fully accepts orthodox Christianity and its moral view, and he confronts and masters—and indeed contributes to— the new science of his day, making use of it in his philosophical theology. He is a great conservative in the way Aquinas was in the thirteenth century: Aquinas confronted the new Aristotelianism and used it for his own aims and purposes in his magnificent *Summa Theologica,* his restatement of Christian theology. Similarly, Leibniz incorporates modern science into traditional philosophical theology; and in this enlarged and revised scheme he tries to resolve all the outstanding problems. Thus, for example, he uses the new science in his definition of truth, in his distinction between necessary and contingent truths, in his account of free will and God's foreknowledge, and in his vindication of God's justice in the *Theodicy.* From our standpoint, Leibniz's moral philosophy—his metaphysical perfectionism, as I shall call it—is less original than the others are, but it nevertheless represents an important doctrine and one particularly instructive in contrast to Hume's and Kant's.

2. Hume may seem to be an exception to the idea that the writers we study are concerned with the relation between modern science and religion. Now, it is true that Hume is different in that he tries to get along entirely without the God of religion. Hume believes in the Author of Nature; but his Author is not the God of Christianity, not the object of prayer or worship. Spinoza, by contrast, presented his view as pantheism—certainly a religious view, though very different from Christian and Jewish orthodoxy. But Hume does without the God of religion altogether, and he does this without lament or a sense of loss. It is characteristic of Hume that he has no need for religion; moreover, he thinks religious belief does more harm than good, that it is a corrupting influence on philosophy and a bad influ-

ence on one's moral character. A good use of philosophy is that it tends to moderate our sentiments and to keep us from those extravagant opinions that disrupt the course of our natural propensities. He says (T:272 [near the end of the last section of Book I]): "Generally speaking, the errors in religion are dangerous; those in philosophy only ridiculous."

In the *Enquiry Concerning the Principles of Morals*, Hume has a particularly harsh passage on the Christian virtues. He has argued that every quality that is either useful or agreeable to us or to others is in our common life allowed to be a part of personal merit, of good character. No other qualities will be recognized as virtuous when we "judge of things by their natural unprejudiced reason, without the delusive glosses of superstition and false religion." He then lists as what he calls "the monkish virtues . . . celibacy, fasting, penance, mortification, self-denial, humility, silence [and] solitude." These are rejected by people of sense, he says, because they serve no purpose: they advance no one's fortune in the world, nor do they make us better members of society; they do not make us more entertaining in the company of others, nor do they increase our powers of self-enjoyment. The monkish virtues are in effect vices. He then concludes: "A gloomy, hare-brained enthusiast, after his death may have a place in the calendar; but will scarcely ever be admitted, when alive, into intimacy and society, except by those who are as delirious and dismal as himself" (E:II:270).

I suggest that while Hume's view seems completely nonreligious (in the traditional sense), he is always conscious of its nonreligious character. In Calvinist Scotland he could hardly be otherwise; he is fully aware that he is going against his surrounding culture. In this sense his view is secular by intention. Raised in a Calvinist lowland gentry family, at an early age (circa twelve?) he abandoned the religion he was instructed in: that's one solution to the problem of the age.

3. In support of what I have been saying, note that we today often feel a need for the reflections of moral philosophy in view of the profound disagreements and great variety of opinions in our pluralist democratic society. Our disagreements extend to the political sphere, where we must vote on legislation that affects all. Our task is to find and elaborate some public basis of mutually shared understanding. But this is not how Hume sees the problem (nor how Kant sees it, for that matter).

Hume's skepticism in morals does not arise from his being struck by the diversity of the moral judgments of mankind. As I have indicated, he thinks that people more or less naturally agree in their moral judgments and count the same qualities of character as virtues and vices; it is rather the enthusiasms of religion and superstition that lead to differences, not to mention the corruptions of political power. Further, Hume's moral skepticism is not based on an alleged contrast between moral judgments and judgments in science. His is not a typical modern (often positivistic) view that science is rational and based on sound evidence whereas morals is nonrational (even irrational) and simply an expression of feeling and interest. To be sure (as we shall discuss), Hume thinks that moral distinctions are not based on reason, and, in the famous provocative and exaggerated remark, says that "[r]eason is and ought only to be the slave of the passions" (T:415). But something parallel to this is true, Hume thinks, of science: his skepticism extends to reason, to the understanding, and to the senses. His moral skepticism is part of what I shall call his fideism of nature.

Now, as I shall note briefly next time, Hume believes that reason and the understanding, when proceeding on their own and not moderated by custom and the imagination—that is, by the benign principles of our nature—destroy themselves. We cannot live in accordance with the ensuing skepticism; fortunately, when we leave our study, we inevitably act from our natural beliefs engendered by custom and imagination. He pursues his skeptical reflections—that is, philosophy—because when we leave our study, not *all* our beliefs return. In particular, our fanaticisms and superstitions (our traditional religious beliefs) don't return; and we are morally better and happier for it. The point, then, is that Hume's skepticism, of which his moral skepticism is but one part, belongs to skepticism as part of a way of life—a way of life that Hume quite explicitly sees in contrast to that of traditional religion. Thus Hume does not simply abandon that religion: he has a way of life to replace it, which, it seems, he never abandoned. It seems to have suited him perfectly.

§6. Kant on Science and Religion

1. Hume, then, along with Spinoza, adopts a radical solution to the problem of the relation between modern science and traditional religion and ac-

cepted moral beliefs. Kant can't accept Hume's solution any more than he can accept Spinoza's. However, with respect to the points I just noted about Hume, Kant and Hume are somewhat alike. Kant is also not troubled by the diversity and conflicts between our moral judgments; he supposes that what he calls "common human reason" *(gemein Menschenvernunft)*, which we all share, judges in more or less the same way; even the philosopher can have no (moral) principles different from those of ordinary human reason *(Gr* I:20[415]; *KP* 5:404).

And again like Hume, for Kant science and morals stand on a par: if for Hume they both involve forms of sensation and feeling, for Kant they are both forms of reason, one theoretical, the other (pure) practical reason. Of course, this is in fundamental opposition to Hume's skepticism; but, the point is that, in contrast to modern views—the logical positivism of Vienna, for example—that count science as rational but morals as not, Kant, like Hume, does not elevate science to the detriment of moral thought and judgment. Of course, Kant's way of reconciling science with traditional religion and accepted moral beliefs is basically opposed to Hume's. His attempted solution is found in the three *Critiques* and supplemented by various of his writings in moral philosophy. I shall not try to characterize it today, but I will comment on the three topics in Kant's moral philosophy we will be studying.

2. You will observe first that while we begin with the categorical imperative as found in the *Groundwork,* this short work is only one of the three parts of our study of Kant. Now certainly the *Groundwork* is important, but it fails to give an adequate account of Kant's moral doctrine as a whole. What it does provide is a reasonably full analytic account of the moral law by developing "the concept of morality" implicit in our commonsense moral judgments. As Kant says *(Gr* II:90[445]), Chapter II of the *Groundwork,* like Chapter I, is "merely analytic." What he means in saying this is that it still remains to be shown that the moral law has "objective reality": that is, that it is not a *mere* concept but actually can and does apply to us. In Chapter III of the *Groundwork,* Kant does try to show this; but I believe that he later abandons the kind of argument he attempts in that chapter and replaces it in the second *Critique* with his doctrine of the fact of reason: it is this fact which shows that the moral law has objective reality. And what this fact amounts to is our second topic.

The third topic, that of practical faith, can be explained roughly as follows. Kant is always concerned with human reason as a form of human self-consciousness: in the first *Critique,* the self-consciousness of a human subject acquiring knowledge of given objects and investigating the order of nature; in the second *Critique,* the self-consciousness of a human subject deliberating and acting to produce objects in accordance with a conception of the objects. He thinks that in addition to spelling out analytically the content of the moral law and to showing its objective reality, we must also examine certain beliefs intimately connected with acting from that law, beliefs that are necessary to sustain our devotion to it. At places in the second *Critique,* he refers to these beliefs as postulates, which are three in number: of freedom, of God, and of immortality. The nature of these beliefs, and how Kant thinks they are essential to our moral self-consciousness, is part of our third topic.

The other part of this third topic is that of the "unity of reason" and the "primacy of the practical" in the constitution of reason. This involves the questions of how the theoretical point of view and the practical point of view fit together and how the legitimate claims of each form of reason are adjusted in a reasonable (and of course consistent) way. Kant believes that at bottom there is only one reason, which issues into different ideas and principles according to its application: whether to the knowledge of given objects or to the production of objects according to a conception of those objects (*Gr* Pref:11[391]; *KP* 5:119ff.). This is his doctrine of the unity of reason. An aspect of this unity is the primacy of the practical: the discussion of this leads to the idea of philosophy as defense. Kant, like Leibniz, wants to reconcile science and practical faith—to defend each against the other.

Thus, in sum, I hope to cover the three main parts of Kant's moral philosophy and to consider how the point of view of practical reason connects with the point of view of theoretical reason to give a coherent conception of reason as a whole. I believe that excessive concentration on the *Groundwork* obscures the importance to Kant's view of these larger questions; and in our study of them the exact details of the Categorical Imperative don't much matter. So long as the account of that imperative meets certain conditions, it can serve to illustrate the doctrine of the Fact of Reason and the Unity of Reason and the Primacy of the Practical, which brings us to the center of Kant's critical philosophy as a whole.

§7. On Studying Historical Texts

1. If (a) we viewed philosophy as specified by a more or less fixed family of problems or questions (which might be added to over time); and if (b) we agreed about the criteria for deciding when these problems are satisfactorily resolved; and if (c) we saw ourselves as making steady progress over time in resolving these problems, then we would have rather little philosophical interest in the history of philosophy. I say philosophical interest because certainly we might have an interest in knowing about the great figures in philosophy, just as mathematicians have an interest in knowing about Gauss and Riemann, and physicists about Newton and Einstein. But we would not suppose the study of these figures helps us much now with our problems, although of course it might. We would still read about the subject's history to celebrate its progress and to give us courage to go on, and also to honor the people who have made philosophical progress, since this is essential to sustain and encourage philosophy as an ongoing collective enterprise. Yet none of this would be essential to our philosophical reflection itself.

However, the idea that philosophy is specified by a fixed family of problems with agreed criteria for deciding when they are resolved, and that there is a clear sense in which progress has been made and an established doctrine arrived at, is itself in dispute. For one thing, even if there were a more or less fixed family of philosophical problems and answers—marked out roughly by its leading topics—these problems and answers would take on a different cast depending on the general scheme of thought within which a writer approaches them. This scheme of thought imposes its own requirements on acceptable solutions to the allegedly standard problems, so there will not be agreed criteria of philosophical progress so long as there are diverse schemes of philosophical thought, as is now the case. Thus, one of the benefits of studying historical texts—and of trying to get a sense of the writer's view as a whole—is that we come to see how philosophical questions can take on a different cast from, and are indeed shaped by, the scheme of thought from within which they are asked. And this is illuminating, not only in itself, as it discloses to us different forms of philosophical thought, but also because it prompts us to consider by contrast our own scheme of thought, perhaps still implicit and not articulated, from within which we now ask our questions. And this self-clarification helps us to decide which questions we really want to resolve, which ones we can reasonably expect to settle, and much else.

2. It is hard to talk sensibly about these matters when talking so generally, and without illustrating one's points with detailed examples. Therefore I shall not do so. As we proceed, we shall look in some detail at how a writer's background scheme of thought and basic aim affect not only the way questions get posed but also the reasons people have for being concerned with the questions in the first place. I have already suggested that Hume's, Leibniz's, and Kant's reasons for being concerned with moral philosophy are quite different from ours. But showing this convincingly is a matter of going into the details, and this must wait.

A final caveat: I shall try to suggest a general interpretation for each of the writers we look at. While I do the best I can at this, I don't think for a moment that my interpretations are plainly correct; other interpretations are surely possible, and some are almost certainly better. It's just that I don't know what they are. Part of the wonderful character of the works we study is the depth and variety of ways they can speak to us. I don't want to do anything to interfere with their doing that. So if I present an interpretation, it is not only to try to illuminate the writer's background scheme of thought but also to encourage you to work out a better interpretation, one that is sensitive to more features of the text than mine, and makes better sense of the whole.

HUME

HUME I

Morality Psychologized and the Passions

§1. Background: Skepticism and the Fideism of Nature

1. I shall not say much about Hume's life. His dates are 1711–1776, the last coinciding with the Declaration of Independence and the publication of Adam Smith's *Wealth of Nations*. He was born of a lowland gentry Scottish family in Berwickshire, just across the Scottish border from the east coast of England. By any standard he was precocious. After being tutored at home, he entered the University of Edinburgh at age twelve and left when he was fourteen or fifteen without taking a degree, as was then quite customary. That completed his formal education. His family wanted him to enter the law, but at eighteen in 1729 he dropped all pretense of doing that and began to work on what became the *Treatise of Human Nature*.

Hume says that the work was projected before he left the university at fifteen in 1726, it was planned before he was twenty-one in 1732, and it was composed before he was twenty-five in 1736. These dates are probably not entirely accurate but are extraordinary nonetheless. The *Treatise* was finally written, after a year at Reims in France in 1735, at La Flèche in Anjou in 1736–37, with further revisions made for the next year or so after Hume's return to England by late 1737. These astounding facts leave one speechless. (Volumes I and II appeared in 1739, Volume III in 1740.)

2. As with other leading writers in philosophy, Hume has not been easy to interpret, and at different times he has been read very differently. In the later part of the nineteenth century, Green and Bradley (among the English

Idealists) led the way (following Hume's eighteenth-century Scottish critics Reid and Beattie) in understanding him as a radical skeptic and saw his views as the *reductio ad absurdum* of empiricism. In this century the logical positivists of the Vienna Circle (including Schlick and Carnap) saw Hume as their great predecessor, while Kemp Smith, in his very important study *The Philosophy of David Hume* (1941), which has made a lasting contribution to the reading of Hume, gave pride of place to Hume's psychological naturalism and de-emphasized his skepticism.

More recently several writers, among them Burnyeat and Fogelin, have tried to right the balance and to present an interpretation that emphasizes both the skepticism and the naturalism, and indeed sees them as complementary and working together. Since both skepticism and naturalism are prominent in Hume's text, an interpretation that succeeds in making them work in tandem is to be preferred, other things being equal. Today I begin with a brief sketch of this interpretation.[1] The view that results I shall sometimes refer to as Hume's fideism of nature, for reasons that will become clear as we proceed.

3. Let's begin by distinguishing several kinds of skepticism as follows. In each case, the meaning and point are given in part by the contrast:[2]

(a) theoretical in contrast with normative skepticism
(b) epistemological in contrast with conceptual skepticism

To explain: theoretical skepticism calls into question on various grounds the soundness or basis of some scheme of beliefs or system of thought. Radical skepticism holds that the beliefs in question have no reasoned support; they are completely ungrounded. Moderate skepticism holds them to be less well grounded than is usually thought. By contrast, normative skepticism (established perhaps on the basis of theoretical skepticism, but possibly on other grounds) enjoins us to suspend belief altogether, or more moderately, to give less credence to them than is usually done. A person who follows a form of normative skepticism is a practicing skeptic.

Epistemological skepticism accepts a scheme of beliefs as meaningful and intelligible but questions the grounds and reasons for them. Conceptual

---

1. See Robert J. Fogelin, *Hume's Skepticism in the Treatise of Human Nature* (London: Routledge and Kegan Paul, 1985).
2. Ibid., pp. 5–12.

skepticism denies that they are meaningful and intelligible. (It was in part because there are places where Hume expresses a conceptual skepticism concerning certain concepts that the Vienna Circle saw him as a predecessor; note what Hume says about substance and attributes and about primary and secondary qualities.) To illustrate: Hume's skepticism about induction is epistemological; he doesn't doubt that inductive inferences are meaningful. Similarly, in his philosophical theology Hume's arguments may undermine the familiar proofs for the existence of God, but he doesn't doubt that the idea of God is sufficiently intelligible so that the merits of those proofs can be examined. He thinks that the evidence for the God of Religion (as opposed to the evidence for an Author of Nature) is negligible, but nevertheless the question has sense.

4. In view of these distinctions, let me make the following points. Hume seems to affirm a theoretical and epistemological skepticism that is radical, wholly unmitigated: this is his Pyrrhonism. Only our immediate impressions and ideas are immune from doubt. Whereas Hume's normative skepticism is moderate: it is part of his psychological naturalism that it is not in our power to control our beliefs by acts of mind and will, for our beliefs are causally determined largely by other forces in our nature. He urges us to try to suspend our beliefs only when they go beyond those generated by the natural propensities of what he calls custom and imagination (custom here is often a stand-in for the laws of association of ideas). Only beliefs that go beyond these can be undermined by skeptical reflection. What is crucial for Hume is that the beliefs that go beyond custom and imagination are not reinvigorated—do not come back—when we leave our study and return to everyday social life. We may, in fact, find ourselves purged of the religious enthusiasms that corrupt our reason and support the monkish virtues which render us unfit for society.

This sketch gives an idea of how radical, unmitigated theoretical and epistemological skepticism works in tandem with Hume's psychological naturalism in his fideism of nature. The fact that such skepticism, however correct its reasoning may be, cannot be sustained except by solitary philosophical reflection, and then not for long, reveals to us that for the most part other psychological forces such as custom and imagination regulate our everyday beliefs and conduct (paragraph 8 of E:iv:1 at T:183). But, as I've noted, Hume believes that this radical skepticism has a salutary effect on our moral character and enables us to live peaceably in society and to accept without resignation or lament the conditions of human life—mortal and fragile though our life may be. The upshot of this philosophical pilgrim's progress, as it were, is someone who shares the beliefs of ordinary people on everyday matters, and who when going beyond this does so with circumspection guided by probability and the weight of the evidence. As for matters beyond experience, belief is suspended.

It is important to observe here that this view is not itself said by Hume to be the result of reasoned argument. Rather it is the outcome of the psychological interplay of two kinds of forces: those of his skeptical philosophical reflections on the one hand and those of his natural psychological propensities of custom and imagination on the other. Hume does not, then, defend his view by using his reason: it is rather his happy acceptance of the upshot of the balance between his philosophical reflections and the psychological propensities of his nature. This underlying attitude guides his life and regulates his outlook on society and the world. And it is this attitude that leads me to refer to his view as a fideism of nature. (See T:179, 183, 184, 187.)

§2. Classification of the Passions

1. So much for a few background remarks about how Hume's skepticism and his psychological naturalism work in tandem. I now turn to his moral philosophy. He proceeds by trying to show that reason alone cannot be a motive that influences our conduct; rather it has only a secondary role limited to correcting false beliefs and identifying effective means to given ends (in II:iii:3). He then tries to show that it is not reason but moral sense that is the (epistemological) basis of moral distinctions (in III:i). He offers several quite brief knockout arguments to try to establish these claims. I postpone considering these arguments until the fourth and fifth meetings on Hume. Today I discuss what I shall call his official view of rational deliberation (in II:iii:3) and then raise some questions about it, which we shall pursue next time. For while in his official view Hume's skepticism seems radical and unmitigated with regard to reason, we should ask how far this is really so, and how exactly he characterizes rational deliberation.

2. I begin with Hume's classification of the passions. At the outset of the *Treatise* (1–8; and later 275ff.), Hume classifies the items of experience, which he calls "perceptions," as follows:

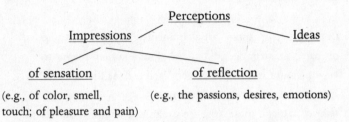

Perceptions

Impressions — Ideas

of sensation — of reflection

(e.g., of color, smell, touch; of pleasure and pain)   (e.g., the passions, desires, emotions)

In Hume's theory, impressions both of sensation and of reflection strike us with greater force and violence than do the ideas that derive from them; impressions are both prior to and more lively and vivid than ideas.

Impressions of reflection, however, may derive from impressions of sensation indirectly via ideas. Hume gives this account (*T*:7f.): the impression of sensation, say of a pleasure or a pain, gives rise to a corresponding idea of pleasure or pain, which is "a copy taken by the mind" (*T*:8). Then this idea of a pleasure or pain, when it returns upon the soul (as Hume says), produces a new impression of reflection, a reflexive impression of a desire or an aversion, a hope or a fear, as the case may be. These impressions of reflection may themselves be copied by memory or imagination, and in this way they give rise to further ideas. Impressions of reflection are antecedent to the ideas derived from them, but they are posterior to impressions of sensation from which they may be indirectly derived via an idea of pleasure or pain, this idea itself arising from an antecedent impression of pleasure or pain (*T*:8). Thus all ideas originate from antecedent impressions of sensation somewhere down the line; the same holds for impressions of reflection, which derive from pleasures and pains. Hume's concern is not with natural philosophy—mechanics and astronomy—but with moral philosophy, with the science of human nature (see the Introduction to the *Treatise*, xvii–xix). Since "the examination of our sensations belongs more to anatomists and natural philosophers than to moral" (*T*:8), it is impressions of reflection (passions, desires, and emotions) that are the focus of his attention (*T*:8).

3. In II:i:1 Hume gives a classification of impressions of reflection, which include the passions. His arrangement is not altogether clear, but I think the following fits his intentions.

First, Hume distinguishes the passions according to how they arise, so we get:

(i) *Direct passions:* these arise immediately from pleasure or pain, or from good or evil. Hume often seems to view pleasure and pain, and good and evil, as the same (*T*: 276, 399, 438, most explicitly at 439).

(ii) *Indirect passions:* these arise from pleasure and pain but require more complicated conditions that involve what Hume describes as "this double relation of ideas and impressions" (*T*:286). Examples of indirect passions are pride and humility, ambition, vanity, and love and hate, as well as envy, pity, and malice (*T*:276).

(iii) *Original passions* (implanted instincts): these do not arise from pleasure and pain, either directly or indirectly, although when acted upon they produce pleasure and pain (or good or evil: *T*:439).

Second, Hume distinguishes passions according to their turbulence and felt intensity (*T*:276). This distinction, Hume thinks, is not very exact: the degrees of turbulence vary widely within passions of the same kind, and there is much overlap. But we can still distinguish:

(i) *calm* passions (*T*:276, 417ff., 437f.)
(ii) *violent* passions (ibid.)

Third and finally, Hume distinguishes the *strong* and *weak* passions (*T*:419). This distinction refers to the (causal) influence that a passion exerts. A central point here is that certain calm passions may also be strong, that is, exert a steady and controlling influence on our deliberation and conduct. This may be so of the very important secondary passion which he calls "the general appetite to good and aversion to evil" (*T*:417). As we shall see, it is because this and other calm passions may be strong that we wrongly suppose, when acting from them, that we are acting from reason (alone).

We mistake the calm, steady, and controlling influence of these passions for the operations of reason (T:417f., 437f.).

4. Putting all this together, we get (T:275ff., 417ff., 437ff.):

(a) *Original (primary) passions* (implanted instincts [T:417])
  (i) Often violent: the desire to punish our enemies or to give happiness to our friends; hunger, thirst, bodily appetites
  (ii) Often calm: benevolence, resentment, love of life, kindness to children

(b) *Secondary (nonoriginal) passions*
  (i) *Direct* (arise directly from pleasure and pain)
    1. Often violent: desire and aversion, joy and grief, hope and fear, despair and sense of security
    2. Often calm: general appetite to good and aversion to evil (T:417; as mistaken for reason T:437)
  (ii) *Indirect* (not directly arising from pleasure and pain but requiring in addition a double relation of ideas and impressions [T:286])
    1. Often violent: pride and humility; love and hate; also ambition, vanity, envy, malice, pity, and generosity (T:276f.)
    2. Often calm: moral approval and disapproval (T:583); sense of beauty and deformity

Note that the distinction between the strong and weak passions applies to all three main kinds of passions, since for the most part whether a passion is strong or weak is a matter of its possessor's character (the particular configuration of someone's passions as a whole).

§3. Outline of Section 3 of Part III of Book II

I now turn to II:iii:3. This section has ten paragraphs (T:413–418), some of which I comment on in order to get Hume's view before us. After doing this, I sketch a general summary of his official view in II:iii:3. As stated above, I shall not critically assess Hume's arguments here until later; for the moment we focus on his account of rational deliberation.

(Paragraph One) Hume states the rationalist view as he understands it: that all rational creatures are *obliged* to regulate their actions by reason. And this view he will oppose by holding that:

> (a) Reason *alone* can never be the motive to any action of the will.
>
> (b) Reason *alone* can never oppose passion in the direction of the will.

(Paragraph Two) The two functions of *reason* that Hume recognizes are stated as follows:

> (a) Reason may establish *demonstrative truths* founded on the abstract relations among our ideas. These we may think of as the truths of logic and mathematics and the like. (This is a fair enough rendering for our purposes.)
>
> (b) Reason may also establish, on the basis of experience, the *relations of cause and effect* between objects and events.

The point he emphasizes is that the effectiveness of demonstrative reasoning presupposes some desired end or purpose: it influences our actions only insofar "as it directs our judgment concerning cause and effects" (T:414).

(Paragraph Three) The effectiveness of reasoning showing the relations of cause and effect likewise presupposes some desired end. We want to ascertain the means to our ends only because we desire to achieve these ends. The impulse to reason about means and to adopt them does not "arise from reason but is only directed by it." By a psychological *principle of transfer,* as we may call it, our concern with ends spreads backward to the appropriate means and forward to their consequences. Without concern for ends, we would be indifferent to means and to the consequences of their use. In the practical sphere, reasoning from experience is simply the attempt to discover the causal and other relations between means and the ends we desire for their own sake, as well as the true qualities and features of those ends.

(Paragraph Four) So far Hume takes himself to have sketched the argument for the first point of paragraph 1, that reason alone can never be a motive of an action. He now contends that the second point—that reason alone cannot oppose passions in guiding the will—is the other side of the first. For reason by itself could oppose the passions only if it could generate an impulse contrary to those passions. But Hume's first point is that there can be no such impulse. Nothing can oppose a passion except a contrary passion; and no passion, or impulse, can arise from reason alone. Thus there is no struggle between reason and the passions. The appearance of such comes from mistaking the struggle between the violent passions and the calm passions, such as the general appetite to good, with a struggle between reason and the passions. Hence Hume's famous provocative remark: "Reason is and ought only to be the slave of the passions, and can never pretend to any other office than to serve and obey them." A question this remark raises is: Why "ought" and not "can"? I shall come back to this remark in the fifth meeting, when we reflect on Hume's view as a whole.

(Paragraph Five) In this paragraph Hume states his knockout argument to show that the passions cannot be contrary to reason: a passion is simply an occurrent *psychological state,* an impression of reflection that occurs under certain conditions, gives rise to certain propensities, and prompts us to action. As such, a passion does not *assert* anything. Hume says that it has no representative quality since it is not a "copy of any other existence." The passions *assert* nothing, and so they cannot *contradict* a truth established by demonstrative reasoning or experience.

(Paragraph Six) In this paragraph Hume maintains, however, that a passion can be considered contrary to reason and unreasonable (his term) when it is directed in its specific present course by incorrect judgments. This can happen in two ways:

(a) Our passion is founded on a false belief, as when we are, for example, afraid of something that is not in fact dangerous or threatening.

(b) Our choice of means to our end is mistaken, as when the means we adopt are insufficient and won't have the results we expect them to have.

It is in this paragraph that Hume makes another of his famous provocative remarks (to give only part of it): " 'Tis not contrary to reason to prefer the destruction of the whole world to the scratching of my finger. 'Tis not contrary to reason for me to chuse my total ruin, to prevent the least uneasiness of an *Indian* or person wholly unknown to me. 'Tis as little contrary to reason to prefer even my own acknowledg'd lesser good to my greater, and have a more ardent affection for the former than the latter" (*T*:416).

(Paragraph Eight) This important paragraph contains Hume's explanation of the rationalists' philosophical error: namely, they confuse the pervasive and *strong influence* of the *calm passions* with the operations of reason. Recall that passions can be both *strong* and *calm*. The rationalists are misled by the absence of turbulence or violence in the way these passions work (*T*:419, 437, 470). Hume assigns a fundamental role to the calm passions, at least when they are strong, as they sometimes are. Their influence is shown in how they regulate and control our deliberation and conduct.

Comment: In section 8 (*T*:437), where Hume emphasizes the same point, he says that we commonly understand by "passion" a sensible and violent emotion when any good or evil is presented to us that is fit to excite an appetite; and by "reason" we commonly understand an affection of the very same kind that operates more calmly and occasions no disorder. So the mistake of the rationalists has its foothold in commonsense thought. Sometimes, as fits the context, I refer to reason as Hume defines it as *strict* reason, whereas the commonsense idea of reason as the steady influence of the calm passions I refer to as *calm* reason (as suggested by *T*:437, 583), but this is not Hume's term. Next time I want to ask whether the description of this so-called calm reason (the steady influence of the calm passions as Hume describes it) is compatible with his official view of rational deliberation.

(Paragraph Ten) In the concluding and very important paragraph, Hume asserts that people are guided sometimes by their calm and sometimes by their violent passions. We often act against our interests, as specified (it seems) by our general appetite to good or by the balance of all our passions together. Yet we often do manage to counteract the violent passions in pursuing our more important and permanent interests and designs; so the present promptings of the violent passions (as felt impressions of reflection) are not by any means always decisive. Whether we are moved by them depends upon what Hume calls our *general character* and *present disposition*. By this he means, I believe, the present configuration of our passions (of all kinds with their strength and turbulence) that constitutes our character.

Note that Hume defines *strength of mind* as, let's say, a more or less pervasive (permanent) present disposition in which the calm passions are usually effective in controlling our deliberations and influencing our conduct. Strength of mind enables someone to pursue long-run and larger aims in an effective manner. In doing this, the calm passions are strong as opposed to weak. Later (*T*:437f.) Hume adds that while the violent passions have a more powerful influence, often the calm ones "when corroborated by reflection, and seconded by resolution, are able to control them in their most furious moments" (*T*:437–438). This is an important remark. But how *can* the calm passions do this on Hume's account? I return to this next time.

§4. Hume's Account of (Nonmoral) Deliberation: The Official View

1. I now sum up the ground covered so far with an account of what I shall refer to as Hume's *official* view of (nonmoral) practical reasoning, or deliberation. (By nonmoral I mean that questions of duty and obligation and the like are not expressly involved; Hume does not discuss these matters until Book III, so I put them aside). My account takes Hume at his word in II:iii:3 (hence the term "official") and sets out his view in a straightforward way. Next time we see that Hume's view, once we include what he says in later sections of II:iii, is rather more complicated and raises a number of questions. Today I conclude with the official view of II:iii:3 which often passes as his doctrine: the so-called Humean view. The main points seem to be the following.

First, in deliberation every chain of reasons in means-to-ends reasoning is finite and has as its stopping point a final (or ultimate) end, which is an objective or aim of one or more of the passions as Hume specifies them. I suppose that a reason in such a chain of reasons is a *statement* (and so true or false) saying that (doing) something is an (effective) means to something desired.

> (i) Finiteness means that the chain of "in order to" clauses ("I do X in order to Y") is finite and usually has a small number of links.

He says, "Ask a man *why he uses exercise;* he will answer, *because he desires to keep his health.* If you then enquire, *why he desires health,* he will readily reply, *because sickness is painful.* If you push your enquiries further, and desire a reason *why he hates pain,* it is impossible he can ever give any. This is an *ultimate end* [my italics] and is never referred to any other object" (*Enquiry,* Appendix I, 293).

> (ii) As the quotation shows, the stopping point must be an objec-
> tive or aim of one or more of the passions. This means that
> if "I do *W* in order to have *Z*" (or to possess, secure, establish
> *Z*, and so on for many variations) is the last link in the chain
> of reasons, then the having of *Z* is an objective or aim of
> one or more of my passions (original, direct, or indirect).

I think that for Hume, all kinds of passions may specify ultimate, or final, ends; for example, benevolence and kindness to children, pride and shame, our general appetite to good as well as our sense of beauty, and much else, can all specify such ends.

2. Second, we see that there are many possible different stopping points given by the passions. The aims of the passions are many, and there is no single end, not even that of aiming at pleasure and avoiding pain.

Hume's view is not, I believe, hedonistic; nor is it egoistic (see *Enquiry,* Appendix II, 295–302, on self-love, where he essentially accepts Bishop Butler's criticism of the doctrine of self-love in *Sermons,* XI and XII [1726]). He doesn't suppose that all our passions are concerned with self-centered objectives. Benevolence and kindness to children are examples. Of course, pleasures and pains have an important psychological role: first, pleasures may enter into the causes (or the generation) of passions, and second, achieving the aims of passions generally gives pleasure, since fulfilling any passion does so; but that pleasure is not the *aim,* not the *objective,* of the passion. We must distinguish three roles of pleasures and pains: (i) as causes of passions, (ii) as resulting from fulfilling passions, and (iii) as the aims and objectives of passions. In saying that Hume's view is neither hedonistic nor egoistic, I mean the aims and objectives of passions are neither hedonistic nor egoistic.

3. Third, the process of deliberation (practical reasoning) may *correct* our existing passions in at least *two* ways:

(a) If we desire to do X in order to Y, we may be brought no longer to desire to do X when by reasoning we see that X won't bring about Y. We may then desire to do Z (something else) instead. This correction via means-to-ends reasoning subtracts one desire and adds another to what we may call the *configuration* of our passions.

(b) If we desire to run because we are worried by the grizzly bear we think we've just spotted, we may no longer worry when we later see that it is a black bear. This is correcting our beliefs about the features of things as causes or objectives of our passions.

4. Fourth, the process of deliberation may affect the system of the passions in other ways that are not merely correcting mistaken beliefs but are more constructive. There might be some question whether these are consistent with Hume's official account (he doesn't discuss them in II:iii:3), but I would count them so, given what he says later.

(a) Deliberation may render a rather indeterminate desire more determinate, as when a desire to eat arising from hunger turns into the more specific desire for a particular dish on the menu when at the table. Call this *specifying* the passions.

(b) Deliberation may schedule our activities for the fulfillment of various passions in such a way that they can all be satisfied quite effectively over a certain interval of time. Call this *scheduling*.

(c) Deliberation may also lead us to see that there are decisions in which we must decide which of our passions are more important to us. Perhaps we face a conflict between final ends and there is no way to schedule them, or to render them more determinate, so as to avoid the conflict. In this case we must assign weights, or priorities, to our ends. It seems that the general appetite (*T*:417, 437) to good must have an important role here. Call this *weighting* final ends.

On Hume's official account, then, deliberation can *affect* our system of passions in at least *five* ways. Two consist of corrections to adjust the passions to true (or well-grounded) beliefs; three others are specifying, scheduling, and weighting. We may consider these five ways of affecting the passions to be necessary (I don't say sufficient) if practical reasoning is to render our thought and conduct *rational*. Think of them as ways of achieving *rationality*, as Hume implicitly characterizes it. There are, I think, certain common features shared by different conceptions of rationality. Seeking to make the beliefs from which we act true, or well grounded, is one, and scheduling our activities in pursuit of our aims and assigning weights to those aims are others.

5. Fifth, and last, an important point: the passions specifying the final ends in deliberation (the outcome of which [our decision] is acted upon) must, it seems, be passions that we have and may be moved by *now*, at the time of the deliberation and before we carry out the action. A basic idea of Hume's seems to be that strict reason in conjunction with the calm passions, such as the general appetite to good, guides and organizes the configuration of passions that exists and moves us now. He writes as if the passions are already there, *given* to, or available to, strict reason *during deliberation*. Of course, what we later do (as a consequence of actions decided on) may change the passions; and so our decisions can affect them at a later time. Except as our desires adjust for corrections of beliefs, the passions would appear to be more or less constant *while we deliberate*, even though they can be coordinated in the last three ways surveyed: by specifying and scheduling them and by assigning them weights. Surely that the passions are in this sense given or fixed is suggested by saying, "Reason is and ought only to be the slave of the passions."

Thus reasons for action must connect, it seems, with one or more of our *existing* passions. This is one thing meant by speaking of Hume's view as *internalist:* what count as reasons for someone must link up with *that* person's currently existing motivations, in Hume's case, with that person's currently existing passions.[3]

Now this implies, for example, that the bare knowledge of our *future* passions does not move us now unless that knowledge guides, or connects with, some passion we have now. Yet on Hume's view, how *can* that bare

3. For a discussion of the internalist conception of reasons, see Bernard Williams, "Internal and External Reasons," in *Moral Luck* (Cambridge: Cambridge University Press, 1981).

knowledge move us now? Next I shall discuss this in regard to what he calls the general appetite to good and aversion to evil, considered merely as such. Then we must ask whether Hume can account for the influence of that knowledge without introducing kinds of passions that are not apparently allowed for by his classification and description of them. Doing that will bring out certain questions about his account which will force us to go into his view more fully. But that must wait.

Hume II

Rational Deliberation and the Role of Reason

§1. Three Questions about Hume's Official View

1. In the last lecture I mentioned that there are certain questions about Hume's official view of rational deliberation (as stated in II:iii:3) that call for more discussion. Today I consider three of these in order to get a better idea of his account.

The *first* question concerns the *kinds* of the possible *effects* of rational deliberation on the passions. We saw last time that Hume explicitly mentions only two effects, which arise via corrections of belief: first, beliefs about means to ends, and second, beliefs about the features of objects that arouse our passions. We added three more effects, which we labeled specifying, scheduling, and assigning weights. As we allow deliberation to affect the passions in other ways, the changes it may bring about increase. This leads us to ask what kind of *continuity*, and how much, Hume's account requires between the configuration of passions at the *beginning* of deliberation and the configuration from which we act as a *result* of it. How far can deliberation by itself—that is, without the causal effects of actions taken on the basis of decisions—transform our passions?

2. The *second* question is about the nature of the passions. Hume views them as impressions of reflection: he speaks of pride and shame, love and hate as being qualitatively distinct impressions, just as impressions of different colors are qualitatively distinct. Further, as psychological states, passions are sometimes experienced as turbulent, or violent, and as possessing a fund

of *psychic energy*, which may be gained from or lost to other passions. We are, it seems, at least *minimally* aware of passions as experienced (introspectible) impressions of some kind.

Now, does this description apply to the *calm* passions, the influence of which Hume says we mistake for the operations of reason? To make this question specific, I discuss the general appetite to good, and the question of how on Hume's view the bare knowledge of our future passions can move us now. I ask also whether the general appetite to good is what I call a principle-dependent desire, that is, a desire the content of which is given by a principle of practical reason. I conclude that it is not: Hume seems to regard it as a psychic force governed by custom, habit, and imagination, but not by judgments applying one or more principles.

This leads to a *third* question, which is whether Hume has a conception of practical reason at all. Indeed, I believe that the Hume of the *Treatise* lacks such a conception. It is of course not clear what this means, and it is by no means easy to say. But I hope to get to this by the end of the class today.

§2. Three Further Psychological Principles

1. Before taking up the first question concerning the kinds of changes that deliberation may bring about in our configuration of desires, I note three psychological principles relevant to deliberation discussed in sections 4–6 and 9 of II:iii. You will find parts of these sections very tedious, and there are passages that I feel I don't understand. Hume's psychological doctrine is enormously complicated, and it is hard to assess what it implies. Nevertheless, you really should read these sections since they show Hume seriously engaged in trying to sketch the more obvious psychological principles of his science of human nature, which of course it is the aim of the *Treatise* to do. I say the more obvious principles because Hume recognizes the severe limits of his efforts. He says (*T*:438):

Philosophy can only account for a few of the greater and more sensible events in this war [that is, the war between the turbulent passions and the calm passions]; but [philosophy] must leave all the smaller and more delicate revolutions, as dependent on principles too fine and minute for her comprehension.

Observe that he is not presenting an account of rational deliberation understood as normative. Rather, he is saying how, psychologically, we do deliberate.

2. In support of this understanding of Hume's aims, consider three psychological principles he introduces in sections 4–6 and 9. He discusses others as well but these three suffice for our purposes.

(a) The principle of the predominant passion (introduced in section 4) says that any emotion that accompanies a stronger passion may easily be converted into the stronger one. Hume writes (T:420): "The predominant passion swallows up the inferior, and converts it into itself. The spirits, when once excited, easily receive a change in their direction; and 'tis natural to imagine this change will come from the prevailing affection. The connexion is in many respects closer betwixt any two passions, than betwixt any passion and indifference." Note that this principle is contrary to what we might call a parallelogram law of psychic forces: such a law would hold that the passions influence the decision reached according to their direction (object) and strength. Instead, Hume seems to think that at times the weaker passions are excitable and unstable in the presence of dominant passions, in which case their energy may be transferred to the dominant passions, which then largely determine the action taken.

(b) The principle of custom is described in section 5. Hume believes that custom and repetition are important in increasing or diminishing our passions, and in converting pleasure into pain and pain into pleasure. Custom does so by its two original effects on us: first, it gives a *facility* in performing any action, or in forming a conception of an object; second, this facility, once acquired, causes an *inclination* to the performance, or to the conception. This inclination is, Hume says, an "infallible source of pleasure," provided the facility is "moderate," by which he means that the effort required is not too great. He writes (T:423): "The pleasure of facility does not so much consist in any ferment of the spirits, as in their orderly motion; which will sometimes be so powerful as even to convert pain into pleasure, and give us a relish in time for what at first was most harsh and disagreeable." Hume notes that the two aspects of custom (facility and inclination) tend to increase the active habits and decrease the passive. Together with the principle of the predominant passion, this means that over time the active habits tend to absorb energy from the passive, so up to a point the active habits are controlling (T:424).

(c) Finally, there is the principle of the greater influence of more particular and determinate ideas on the imagination (section 6). Hume's thought is that pleasures with which we are acquainted, and of which we have detailed and specific ideas, have more influence on us than those we conceive of under the general notion of pleasure or advantage. In fact, the more general and universal our ideas, the less their influence on the imagination and so on the passions (T:424f.).

He illustrates this principle by the story of Aristides the Just. The date is the winter of 478 B.C., when Athens and Sparta were still allies after defeating the Persians under Xerxes (in 480 B.C.), though now uneasy and suspicious of each other. Themistocles (an admiral of the fleet) told the Athenian assembly that he had a secret naval plan. This was to set fire to a Peloponnesian fleet then wintering in the Bay of Pagasai; but since the plan's success depended on secrecy, he could not make it public: the assembly should trust him. Rather than grant this, he was told to clear his plan with Aristides (also a leading military commander), in whose judgment the assembly had confidence. As Hume tells the story, Aristides consulted with Themistocles, returned to the assembly, and said that nothing could be more advantageous than the plan but at the same time nothing could be more unjust. The plan was unanimously rejected.[1]

Unlike the historian he cites, Hume sees nothing extraordinary in this rejection: he denies that it shows a great sense of justice in the Athenians. For had they been told the plan in detail, and had they held vividly before their minds the nearly certain destruction of the Peloponnesian fleet, they would have approved of it. As it was, they knew of its merits only under the general idea of advantage, and so the temptation was less violent. Hume says that otherwise (T:426) " 'tis difficult to conceive, that a whole people, unjust and violent as men commonly are, should so unanimously have adhered to justice, and rejected any considerable advantage." On this princi-

---

1. The story is told in many places. One is A. R. Burn, *Pelican History of Greece* (Harmondsworth: Penguin Books, 1965), p. 194.

ple depends the power of rhetoric and persuasion to stir the passions by describing their objects "in their strongest and most lively colors" (T:426). It shows the significance of the specific point of view from which things are seen, enabling strict reasoning and imaginative rehearsal to affect the passions during deliberation.

§3. Deliberation as Transforming the System of Passions

1. Hume mentions several other principles in these sections, but the three principles surveyed, especially when we see them as working *in concert*, suffice for discussing our question: How far can deliberation transform the passions? The following points seem clear from the foregoing three principles.

(a) Deliberation can alter the *degree* to which certain passions that we have now are *active* now and so the weight—the degree of influence—with which they affect the decision reached. Deliberation can be carried out so as to reduce or even to eliminate the present influence of some passions and increase the influence of others. The example of Aristides the Just makes this point.

(b) While Hume does not explicitly mention it, deliberation could lead us to realize that we have now certain passions of which we have been largely unaware (we cannot say they are repressed or unconscious [in Freud's sense]), not merely passions we have forgotten about or paid little attention to. We become aware of them by finding it attractive to imagine ourselves doing this or that. So as before, while throughout deliberation the final passions are viewed as fixed, deliberation can affect their *felt* vivacity and force, and so their influence on our decision and subsequent conduct.

In these two ways at least, deliberation may largely control which passions direct and influence our conduct. Hume does not deny this. Recall his saying that, in general (T:437f.), "the violent passions have a more powerful influence on the will; tho' 'tis often found that the calm ones, when corroborated by reflection and seconded by resolution, are able to control them in their most furious moments." I think that he means by resolution a virtue built up by custom and habit. On his view, it is clearly incorrect to regard the passions as already given *together with* their relative intensity and influence and as merely being directed by deliberation.

2. We must now ask: Since deliberation is an activity, how is it moved and regulated by one or more passions? After all, it cannot simply happen without some passion moving it. Hume may answer by saying (as in the passage cited above) that the calm passions, corroborated by reflection and seconded by resolution, can control the violent passions in their most furious moments. Recall that possessing such control over the passions is what Hume means by strength of mind, since this, he says, implies "the prevalence of the calm passions above the violent" (T:418). Putting these remarks together (T:437f. and 418), we might say the following:

(a) In persons of strength of mind, the calm passions have a central place in the total configuration of their passions and have taken control of the powers of rational thought, i.e., strict reason and imagination. Thus the calm passions can normally guide deliberation in the ways already described.

(b) Hume thinks also that custom, habit, and imagination, supported by the total configuration of the passions, play an important role in strength of mind. As we have seen, custom bestows a facility in performing an action, or in conceiving an object, and thereby generates an inclination to act accordingly. These two effects allow us to explain strength of mind as follows.

Deliberation, like any other activity, is something we must *learn* to do. It involves forming certain conceptions, going through various steps; it also involves the *imaginative rehearsal* of the consequences of adopting various alternatives, and so on. As we gain *practice,* we do it more easily, and the benefits of deliberating, as judged by our success in fulfilling our calm passions and more basic interests, are greater. Thus facility in deliberation is *rewarded,* and this in turn gives rise to a stronger inclination, a stronger tendency to engage in deliberation because we enjoy the moderate (not too hard or too easy) exercise of our facility. (It may be odd to speak of *enjoying* deliberation, so let's say instead that we overcome an *aversion* to it, to the mental exercises it requires.) Further, we learn *when* deliberation is called for, and we come to appreciate its advantages.

3. So far, I have assumed that passions come into and go out of existence only from the effects of actions undertaken as a result of deliberation

or from the effects of what happens to us. This means that deliberation itself cannot now change the final passions that exist now (in the interval between the beginning of deliberation and taking the action), although it can, as we have seen, greatly modify their intensity and influence, and make us fully aware of passions of which we were before largely unaware. What it apparently cannot do by itself, leaving aside the changes resulting from corrections of beliefs, is to eliminate passions altogether, or to generate new ones.

However, once the calm passions have acquired control of the powers of deliberation, they can shape our character so as to ensure strength of mind. They can lead us to perform the actions required to eliminate passions likely to challenge their dominance and to cultivate supporting passions and habits. Often our tastes and preferences can by brute force—the steady dominance of the calm passions—be changed in a short time. In "The Skeptic" (*Essays:* 170–171), where I think Hume speaks for himself, he writes:

> Habit is another powerful means of reforming the mind and implanting in it good dispositions and inclinations. A man who continues in a course of sobriety and temperance, will hate riot and disorder; if he engage in business or study, indolence will seem a punishment to him; if he constrain himself to practice beneficence and affability, he will soon abhor instances of pride and violence. Where one is thoroughly convinced that the virtuous course of life is preferable; if he have but resolution enough, for some time, to impose a *violence* [my italics] on himself; his reformation needs not be despaired of. The misfortune is, that this conviction and this resolution can never have place, unless a man be, beforehand, tolerably virtuous.

What does Hume mean here by imposing a violence on oneself? Well, when you are going on a three-month canoe trip in northern Quebec, say, you can stop smoking by dwelling on the harms it causes you, and acting from your aroused aversion to such harms, you throw away your cigarettes as you depart.

To conclude: Hume allows that, in certain circumstances, strict reason and the calm passions—which we mistake for the operations of reason—

together with custom, habit, and imagination, can shape our character over time, sometimes rather quickly. Yet this prompts a question: Why can't it happen that upon reading a play or a novel or the life of a historical figure, or listening to a talk, we are introduced to an ideal, a certain way to lead our life, and then and there, before we do anything (beyond the reading, the learning, and the listening), we are, as it were, seized by that ideal, which from then on deeply affects us?

Must the reading, the hearing, or the listening merely enliven certain passions already existing in our configuration of passion? Can't we deny this? After all, Hume insists that in advance anything may affect anything else; it's up to experience to say. Sometimes such conversions certainly seem to happen. Does Hume have a reply to this? Or must he simply postulate such passions—as pure dispositions—shown in what we actually do? Does his view then lose its special character? What is the criterion for saying, when a passion arises in the imagined kind of case, that we already had it? Do these questions have a clear answer? I shall come back to this.

§4. The General Appetite to Good

1. I turn to our second question: whether Hume's general account of the passions really applies to the calm passions (the operations of which we mistake for reason). I begin with examining how the general appetite to good allows the bare knowledge of our future passions to move us now.

Recall the problem: only the passions that exist now are supposed to move us now. So while we may know now about our future passions (say, future passions for food and drink, which will arise when we need nourishment in the future), and while we know the anguish it will cause us if we do not make provision now for satisfying them, we don't have those passions now, so *they* can't move us now. We do, however, make such provisions. Hume accounts for this by invoking the general appetite to good. I first discuss how this appetite works, and then ask whether Hume views it as a passion or as a principle-dependent desire (a term I shall explain).

2. Despite its obvious importance, Hume says little about the general

appetite to good. He counts it as a calm secondary passion (recall that the secondary passions are the passions arising from pleasure and pain). He says (T:417): "Reason . . . exerts itself without producing any sensible emotion . . . Hence . . . every action of the mind, which operates with the same calmness and tranquility, is confounded with reason by all those who judge of things from the first view and appearance. . . . There are certain calm desires and tendencies, which tho' they be real passions, produce little emotion in the mind, and are known more by their effects than by their immediate feeling or sensation." Note the calm passions produce little but still *some* emotion and are known partly by immediate feeling, though more by their effects. And further:

> These [calm] desires are of two kinds: either certain instincts originally implanted in our natures . . . benevolence . . . the love of life . . . kindness to children; or the general appetite to good, and aversion to evil, consider'd merely as such. (Ibid.)

> The mind by an *original* instinct tends to unite itself with the good, and avoid the evil, tho' they may be conceiv'd merely in idea, and be consider'd as to exist in any future period of time. (T:438)

> . . . good or evil, or in other words, pain and pleasure . . . (T:439)

> When good is certain or probable, it produces JOY. When evil is in the same situation there arises GRIEF and SORROW. (Ibid.)

3. This is not much to go on, but the answer to the question how our *present* passions prompt us to make provision for our *future* passions is clear enough. Since we now know about our future passions and how to provide for them, our present general appetite to good is sensitive now to the good (the pleasure) of satisfying our future needs and to the evil (the pain) of not doing so. It is sensitive because, as Hume says, it unites itself with good and avoids evil "tho' they be conceiv'd *merely in idea* and be consider'd as to exist in any *future period of time* [my italics]."

The answer, then, rests on a basic principle of Hume's moral psychology, the principle that an *idea* of a pleasure or pain can generate a *present passion* (a present impression of reflection). In this way the bare knowledge of our future passions (and so of our future desires and wants generally) generates, through the general appetite to good, present passions that lead us to make at least some provision for the needs that will be aroused by our future passions.

4. Of course, Hume's answer presupposes that we have a conception of our identity as distinct persons over time, so that we know *which* future persons we are and thus which passions of which persons to make provision for. But granted such a conception, the required identities are known and the background for the general appetite to good to do its work is in place. I should note in passing that the question of specifying a suitable conception of personal identity is an extremely deep matter, and so is the question of how it connects with our concern both for our own future and for that of other persons. I only mention these issues here.[2]

§5. The General Appetite to Good: Passion or Principle?

1. We have seen how the general appetite to good makes us responsive now to satisfying our future passions. Next I ask: Is the general appetite to good a passion, or a principle-dependent desire associated with a principle of practical reason? To explain this, I must say a bit about what practical reasoning is, as opposed to deliberation as Hume apparently describes it. A first statement is this:

In *practical reasoning,* our deliberations are guided by, or checked against, certain *principles* of practical reason, such as the two Hume himself seems to mention in his official view: the principle to take effective means to ends, and the principle to correct our knowledge of the features of the things we want, in the light of true, or reasonable, beliefs. These principles, among others, specify what is correct, or *valid,* in practical reasoning. In asking whether the general appetite to good is a passion or a principle-dependent desire, we are asking whether Hume describes it as working as a passion

---

2. See Thomas Nagel, *The Possibility of Altruism* (Oxford: Oxford University Press, 1970), pp. 27–76.

or as working as a principle-dependent desire associated with a principle of practical reason.

2. To answer this question, I introduce the conception of a rational agent specified as one whose general character, or whose full configuration of passions, includes desires of the following two kinds (among others):

First, *object*-dependent desires. The object of an object-dependent desire, or the state of affairs that fulfills it, can be described *without* the use of any moral conceptions, or reasonable or rational principles. This definition presupposes some way of distinguishing these conceptions and principles, but let's assume that we have some rough way of doing this with mutually agreed results.

Indefinitely many kinds of desires are object-dependent, including many if not most of Hume's passions. They include desires for food and drink and sleep, desires to engage in pleasurable activities of various kinds, and desires that depend on social life: desires for standing, power, and glory, and for property and wealth. And much else.

3. Next, there are what I shall call *principle*-dependent desires. These are of two main kinds depending on whether the principle in question is rational or reasonable.

Rational principles are those we use in practical reasoning about what we may call prudential questions. For example (read each as qualified by *ceteris paribus*):

(i)   To adopt the most effective means to our ends.
(ii) To acquire reasonable beliefs about our ends and objectives.
(iii) To select the more probable alternative.
(iv) To prefer the greater good (which helps to account for scheduling and adjusting ends to be mutually supporting).
(v)   To order our objectives (by priorities) when they conflict.

Each of these principles Sidgwick would consider a dictate of (practical) reason.

Let's take these principles to be given by enumeration and not derived from a definition of practical rationality, as there is no agreement on the best way of defining this conception, especially when uncertainty is involved. We should allow that there are different views of rationality.

Still, the general idea is that these principles specify what a *single* agent with a variety of aims—whether an individual, or association, or community, or nation, or an alliance of nations—is to be guided by, so far as practicable and reasonable, in what common sense views as rational deliberation.

We may add a *second* kind of principle-dependent desire connected with the principles of Hume's strict reason, reasoning in logic and mathematics, in weighing evidence and probable inference. After all, strict reasoning, like any other activity, has to be moved by some passion, Hume would say. Most people have these desires to some degree, since, as Aristotle says, we desire to know: we enjoy puzzles, riddles, and so on. No one could be a mathematician or physicist without these desires.

The *third* kind of principle-dependent desires are connected with *reasonable principles:* those that regulate how a plurality of agents (or a community or society of agents), whether of individual persons or groups, are to conduct themselves in their relations with one another. Principles of fairness or justice that define the fair terms of cooperation are standard examples. So are principles associated with the moral virtues recognized by common sense: truthfulness, fidelity, and so on. I put these reasonable desires and principles aside for now.[3]

4. Now what distinguishes principle-dependent desires is that the aim of the desire, or the deliberative, intellectual activity in which we desire to engage, cannot be described without using the principles, rational or reasonable as the case may be, that enter into that activity. Only a being that can understand and apply these principles—that knows how to use them—can have these desires. A rational agent is someone of just this kind.

By definition, then, a rational agent is one whose character, whose con-

3. I mention in passing that there are also conception-dependent desires. These can be described by saying that the principles we desire to follow can be connected with a desire to realize a certain rational or reasonable conception, or moral ideal. For example, we desire to conduct ourselves in a manner appropriate to our being a rational person, one whose conduct is guided by practical reasoning; and desiring to be this kind of person involves having and acting from these principle-dependent desires, and not only from object-dependent desires as governed by custom and habit. Such a conception is formed when the principles specifying the principle-dependent desires are suitably related and connected to the conception in a certain way. Thus we saw that practical reasoning concerning the future involves, let's say, a conception of ourselves as enduring over time. I won't pursue this thought here. But to speak of conception-dependent desires, we must be able to make the appropriate kind of connection.

figuration of desires (passions), contains principle-dependent desires associated with the principles of practical reason. Like all desires, these desires have a greater or lesser *strength*, which may vary from time to time. But beyond this, the principles with which these desires are associated are recognized by the agent to have *authority*, say, the authority of reason. The agent will say: "I was foolish not to spend more time being sure I was taking appropriate means to my ends," and so on. Thus, it is via principle-dependent desires that the principles of practical reason have a foothold in the agent's character.[4] Insofar as an agent is rational—satisfies the definition—the agent will be motivated to act accordingly, not always decisively, but to some significant degree.

5. Finally, we come to our question: Is the general appetite to good, as Hume describes it, literally a calm *passion*, or is it a principle-dependent desire, and if so, what is the principle?

Now, if Hume viewed the general appetite to good as a principle-dependent desire, it is likely that he would have made explicit its principle; and the principle most suggested by the text is perhaps this:

> Other things being equal, to maximize over time the net balance of good over evil in one's life, estimating these goods and evils, when appropriate, by foreseen pleasures and pains, and measuring pleasures and pains by their intensity and duration, and discounting them by their probability.

Or something like that. The principle of practical reasoning becomes: to take account of our future goods and evils according to their weight, or their degree of prospective importance or satisfaction, thus determined.

But I think that Hume never describes the general appetite to good as guided by such a principle, and so never as a principle-dependent desire. Rather, he sees it as a *psychological* principle that works in certain ways, but not as a rational principle that the agent applies in recognition of its rational

---

4. In Bernard Williams's terminology, these principle-dependent desires are contained in the agent's motivational set. See his "Internal and External Reasons," in *Moral Luck* (Cambridge: Cambridge University Press, 1981), pp. 104f. The account of a rational agent in the text follows that given by Christine Korsgaard in "Skepticism and Practical Reason," *Journal of Philosophy* (January 1986), 15–23.

authority. Some examples of passages that support this are in II:iii:9, where he discusses the direct passions. He considers how probabilities give rise to hope and fear (T:440f.), and he approaches the idea of mathematical expectation (T:444f.). But always the emphasis is on the way certain psychological principles govern the vivacity of beliefs and cause such passions as hope and fear. Moreover, Hume likes physical analogies, as when he says (T:440f.):

> If we consider the human mind, we shall find, that with regard to the passions, 'tis not of the nature of a wind-instrument of music, which in running over all the notes immediately loses the sound after the breath ceases; but rather resembles a string-instrument, where after each stroke the vibrations still retain some sound, which gradually and insensibly decays. . . . [And so it is that] grief and joy being intermingled . . . by means of the contrary views of the imagination, produce by their union the passions of hope and fear.

6. I suggest, with some hesitation, that this accords with Hume's discussion even of the two principles of practical reason he might seem to endorse, namely:

    (i) To adopt the most effective means to our ends.
    (ii) To acquire reasonable beliefs about our ends and objectives.

For his description of these also seems as if it could be read purely psychologically. He writes (T:416f.): "The moment we perceive the falsehood of any supposition, or the insufficiency of any means our passions yield to our reason without any opposition. . . . [W]henever you convince me of my mistake, my longing ceases. . . . As soon as I discover the falsehood of that supposition, they must become indifferent to me."

On the other hand, in the case of the principle of practical reason directing us to our greater good, the case is not the same (T:416). Recall Hume's remark (T:416): " 'Tis as little contrary to reason to prefer even my own acknowledg'd lesser good to my greater, and have a more ardent affection for the former than the latter." We might take Hume to mean that the desire for our lesser good does not rest on a false belief, and yet that desire may be stronger than the desire for our greater good. The explanation, he may think, is that such a preference is a matter of character: it betrays a person's impatience and shortsightedness, impetuousness, and thought-lessness. The remedy is a change of character, not an appeal to strict reason. All this is simply a fact of human psychology; practical reason appears to have no role.

7. To conclude: in view of these passages, and the nature of Hume's account generally, I believe that if we think of practical reasoning as deliber-ation regulated by (ostensibly) correct or valid judgments and moved by principle-dependent desires associated with rational principles, then Hume does not have a conception of practical reasoning. Or at any rate, he does not have that conception of it.

What is distinctive about Hume's view of deliberation is not that it is simple and not complex: it is very complex. Nor is it that he thinks that deliberation concerns only the best means to given ends, or that it can have only a few kinds of effects on the course of action; rather, it can have many deep and profound effects. What is distinctive of his view is that it seems to be purely psychological and to lack altogether what some writers think of as the ideas of practical reason and of its authority.

HUME III

Justice as an Artificial Virtue

§1. The Capital of the Sciences

1. Today we consider Hume's account of justice as an artificial as opposed to a natural virtue. This topic is central to his fideism of nature: he wants to show that morality and our practice of it are the expression of our nature, given our place in the world and our dependence on society. Recall that in the introduction to the *Treatise*, Hume discussed the history of the sciences, how they had begun with mathematics, natural philosophy, and natural religion, and how they have very considerable dependence on the knowledge of man (*T*:xv–xvi).

This dependence must be all the greater, he says, for the sciences of logic, morals, criticism, and politics, which cover all of Hume's interests in his writings. Logic explains the workings of our reasoning faculty and the nature of our ideas. Morals and criticism consider our sentiments and tastes, whereas politics deals with people joined into society and dependent on one another. Hume wants to abandon the "lingering method" followed hitherto and, as he puts it, "to march up directly to the capital or center of those sciences, to human nature itself" (*T*:xvi).

So we have in the *Treatise* a young man's attempt to conquer what he calls "the capital" of the sciences and so to make his reputation and very considerable noise in the world. Essential to achieving this is showing that morality is a natural fact, explicable in view of our natural human interests and our need for society. This explanation is to be based on experience and

[51]

observation. Hume wants to follow Newton's maxim, "Hypotheses non fingo," and to frame no hypotheses about the essence of the soul or the body; he appeals, he says, only to principles that are manifest in the operations of nature. Explaining the basis of the virtues, both natural and artificial, and how they arise and play their different roles, is one of the moral subjects that make up the science of human nature so conceived.

2. Today I shall discuss a few basic questions connected with these matters in III:ii:1–6. Much will have to be left out. But before I go on, a caution about Hume's language, which at times is subtly different from ours. For example, one notices from the subtitle of the *Treatise*—"Being an Attempt to Introduce the Experimental Method of Reasoning into Moral Subjects"— that the meaning of "moral" is very different than it is now. Some changes of meaning are amusing, as when Adam Smith says, "Virtue, according to Aristotle, consists in the habit of mediocrity according to right reason."[1]

So we are warned that "artificial" does not mean what it means today: false, fake, not genuine, not real, and the like. The meaning of words, like water under the influence of gravity, seems to go downhill; this has happened with "artificial." This is illustrated by an anecdote (too good to be false) about Charles II. When the king went for the first time to look at St. Paul's Cathedral in London, rebuilt by Christopher Wren after the great fire of 1666, he said solemnly, after having stood some time under the dome: "It's awful and artificial," meaning that it inspired awe but was at the same time a work of reason. These were words of highest praise.

3. Hume's text plainly confirms this meaning. For example, the idea of the artificial virtues is mentioned along with three senses of "natural" (*T*:473f.).

The first sense of "natural" is as opposed to miracles, and in this sense all of the virtues, both natural and artificial, are natural.

Second, there is the sense of "natural" as opposed to the unusual, in

---

1. *The Theory of Moral Sentiments* (Oxford: Oxford University Press, 1976), p. 270. Other examples are these: "sensible" means "obvious" or "readily perceived," "experiments" means "observations of others under various conditions" (*T*:xxiii), "specious" means "plausible" (not plausible-seeming but false), "complacency" means "tranquil pleasure or satisfaction" (*E*:181), "jealous" (as in "the cautious, jealous virtue of justice") means "scrupulously vigilant" (*E*:184). And about virtue Hume says something close to Smith: "No quality . . . is absolutely blameable or praise-worthy. It is all according to its degree. A due medium, says the Peripatetic, is the characteristic of virtue. But this medium is chiefly determined by utility. . . . By such reasonings, we fix the proper . . . mediocrity in all moral and prudential disquisitions" (*E*:233).

which case virtue is unnatural, heroic virtue being as unusual and as little natural as the most brutal barbarity.

Finally, "natural" is opposed to artifice: actions themselves are artificial as performed with a certain design and intention. Our designs and projects are principles as necessary in their operation as heat and cold, moist and dry, but taking them as ours, it is usual to contrast them with the other principles of nature (ibid.). Again: Hume says the remedy for our uncultivated ideas of morality and the partiality of our affections is derived not from nature but from artifice, "or more properly speaking, nature provides a remedy in the judgment and understanding" (T:489).

The third sense of "natural"—as opposed to artifice—is clearly the relevant one. So to conclude: the artificial virtues involve, in ways that the natural virtues do not, design and intention, judgment and understanding, and are the work of reason generally, as seen in our projects and conventions, laws and institutions.

§2. The Elements of Hume's Problem

1. With these remarks as a preface, I now set out what I believe are the elements of Hume's problem: namely, to explain *all* the virtues, both natural and artificial, as part of the natural fact of morality. Now III:ii:1—titled "Justice, whether a natural or an artificial virtue?"—should do precisely this, but it does not do it as well as it might. This is in part because Hume tries to establish his main point by what he thinks is a short and convincing argument, but when this argument is stated in paragraphs 4 and 9 it is unclear. While the fallacy, or circularity, he has in mind is indeed a fallacy, citing it fails to make his point.[2] Fortunately no harm is done to Hume's aims, and so I ignore the short argument and depart from his initial exposition.

2. The same mistake is repeated in III:iii:1, paragraphs 3–5. The mistake arises because Hume fails to distinguish three basic moral concepts: the right, the good, and moral worth. These apply respectively, first, to actions (as kinds or types) and institutions—as right or wrong; next, to states of affairs, activities, or things of various kinds—as good or bad; and finally, to our character as a whole, or to various dispositions and motives from which we act, as well as to particular actions thought of as virtuous in view of the dispositions and motives from which they are done—as morally worthy or unworthy, or, in extreme cases, evil. When we call actions right, we abstract from motive and judge them as a kind of action, say, as one that advances the good of society consistent with one's duty and the rights of others. Such an action we may do from a good or a bad motive, say,

To begin: consider such natural virtues as benevolence and generosity, clemency and charity, love of life and kindness to children (*T*:417, 578). These are all quite easy for Hume to explain. This is because he ascribes to them two features.

First, they are natural dispositions (or what he sometimes calls implanted instincts) to perform certain kinds (types) of actions on certain kinds (types) of occasions—to be kind to children, say, when they need kindness.

Second, their performance gives rise to good in each case: a single act of kindness to children, in itself, always produces good (*T*:574).

As we would have expected, we learn further in paragraph 9 that only the natural virtues existed in the rude and natural condition of humankind before the civilized state. So a third feature of the natural virtues is that they constitute the natural and partial morality of our affections. This was the morality of the first stage. At that time the virtues of justice, fidelity, and honesty did not exist, and mention of them would have been greeted as unintelligible and sophistical.

2. By contrast with the first feature above, the artificial virtues of justice, fidelity, and honesty are understood as dispositions of character to comply with certain schemes of rules or conventions, dispositions that do not express an original principle of our nature, or of one or more implanted instincts. In such cases the rules and conventions are too varied and numerous, too complex and changing, to be the objects of original principles, or even of a small number of such principles. And to go beyond a small number of principles might endlessly multiply hypotheses about our nature and undercut the idea of a science of human nature (*T*:xvi–xix; 473).

As we shall see, in contrast with the second feature above, a single act of justice or fidelity, when taken by itself, is often contrary to the good of society and on balance may produce harm. Yet we still think that the just action should be done, and done from a sense of duty.

---

from a sense of duty or benevolence, or hypocritically, hoping our ostensibly morally worthy action will serve us in good stead later. Hume's mistake is not to see that we need the two concepts of moral worth of character and the concept of right applied to actions as kinds. He uses only the concept of moral worth to answer two different questions and thus falls into error because this one concept cannot give the answer to both the question whether an action (as type) in abstraction from motive is right and whether a particular action, now looking to its motive, is morally worthy. This is all there is to his short argument and the alleged circle. A fuller discussion is found in J. L. Mackie, *Hume's Moral Theory* (London: Routledge and Kegan Paul, 1980), pp. 78–82.

3. Thus Hume's problem is this: How did human beings, beginning in the rude and natural state, and possessing only the natural virtues, eventually reach the civilized stage in which they also possessed the artificial virtues, with the features just noted?

Now, this is a question about origins, and when Hume talks in this section in paragraphs 10–16 (T:480–484) about the original motive to justice, I believe that he means the original motive that might, for the first time, have led to just schemes of rules or conventions. He argues that this original motive to justice could not have been private interest or reputation, or self-love, or regard for public interest, or the love of mankind (since there is no such thing), or private benevolence, or regard for the interests of the party concerned. For none of these as original principles or implanted instincts would have led to or sustained conventions of justice as we know them.

Hume says in paragraph 7 (T:479) that he wants to maintain that "it may be establish'd as an undoubted maxim, *that no action can be virtuous, or morally good, unless there be in human nature some motive to produce it, distinct from the sense of its morality.*" The italics indicate the importance in his mind of what he is saying. Yet the statement is hard to interpret. In the following two paragraphs Hume himself says it is not true. For he grants in paragraph 9 (T:479–480) that when we are in civilized society, and educated according to its practices, then if we have made a promise to repay a sum of money, our regard to justice (our sense of its morality), and our abhorrence of villainy and knavery, are sufficient reasons for us to repay the debt.

Thus I am led to interpret the italicized statement of paragraph 7 (T:479) as in effect imposing a condition on any account of how civilized society with its conventions and rules of justice could have come about. It cannot arise directly, or indirectly, from the natural virtues alone; it will essentially rely upon understanding and judgment, design and intention. In this process it will be moved by interests that are entirely natural, present from the start, and fully part of human nature. It turns out that these interests are, importantly, our concern for ourselves, our family, and our friends.

4. Before we turn to this, two remarks. First, Hume uses the idea of virtue, I suggest, because virtues as dispositions belong to our character; they are psychological features of our person that together influence what we do and how we behave. To have and to acquire the virtues belongs to

our nature. It is not surprising that Hume should use this idea, given his aim of showing that morality is a natural fact.

The other remark is that Hume is rejecting the natural law doctrine coming down from medieval Christianity and found in Grotius, Pufendorf, and Locke. Recall that for them moral obligation rests on natural law or on divine law. This law is addressed to us by God, who has legitimate authority over us as our creator; it is a dictate of divine reason or of divine will. In either case we are directed to comply on pain of penal sanctions. And while this law commands only what is, all things considered, good for us and human society, it is not in acting from it as for our good that we fulfill our obligation, but rather in acting from it as imposed by God and seeing ourselves as obedient to God's authority.

Now, here it is obvious that God's law when supported by sanctions can give us a motive for doing many things to which we have, in Hume's sense, no natural inclination. If we fear God's sanctions, as we must, then we have a motive of fear for not doing whatever God will punish. So against this background, with which Hume is well acquainted, we might read paragraph 7 in another way as follows:

> It may be established as an undoubted maxim, that no action can be virtuous, or morally good, unless there is in human nature some motive to produce it, distinct from a motive arising from its being sanctioned as a divine command.

Thus understood, this statement becomes a maxim of inquiry that imposes a condition that we must meet in trying to account for the origin of justice and of property, the subject of III:ii:2, to which we now turn.

§3. The Origin of Justice and Property

This section contains Hume's main theoretical sketch of the origins of justice and property. It takes up two questions, which are explained as follows: *first*, the manner in which the rules of justice are established by the artifice of men (paragraph 1 [T:484]); and *second*, what reasons lead us to annex the idea of virtue to justice—that is, complying with the rules of justice (paragraph 23 [T:498]).

Note that for the most part Hume means by justice the basic conventions regulating property: its stability and possession, its transference by consent, and the performance of promises. He calls these basic conventions "laws of nature" (T:484), even "fundamental" laws (T:526); also "laws of justice" (T:532), "rules of justice" (T:484), and "rules of morality" as well (T:516). I shall often call them "conventions of justice," since "convention" is Hume's term for indicating their distinctive features that make them essential to human society. By these laws of justice he doesn't mean any laws governing property that we might imagine established, but laws with those features, which I shall discuss below.

Outline of Section 2 by Paragraphs (*Treatise*:484–501)

1: The two questions to be examined: first, how the rules of justice are established by the artifice of human beings, paragraphs 2–22; second, why we annex the idea of virtue to justice, paragraphs 23–28.

2–4: The inconveniences of our situation in nature alone remedied by society; affection between the sexes makes us aware of these benefits.

5–7: The circumstances of justice: the subjective circumstances of the limited generosity of our temper; the objective ones of the instability of external goods in view of the scarcities of nature.

8–11: The remedy, which our uncultivated ideas of morality cannot supply, is given by artifice, or better, by judgment and understanding, which promote conventions mutually recognized as in the common interest.

12–14: The work and consequences of justice: once established, little remains to be done toward harmony and concord; avidity is given the proper direction to control itself; and the rules of justice are simple and obvious.

15–17: The state of nature as a golden age is a useful fiction in showing the origin of justice in the inconveniences of our selfishness and in the scarcities in nature; abundance and benevolence would make justice unknown.

18–22: Concluding observations on how rules of justice are es-

tablished by the artifices of men, stressing points con-
firming previous observations; while a single act of justice
is often in itself prejudicial to society, the whole scheme
is essential to it and to the well-being of all its members.

23–24: The second question, why we annex the idea of virtue to
justice: the natural obligation to justice has been explained,
now to explain the moral obligation; two stages of development, with the sense of justice arising at the second.

25–27: Three supplements to the sense of justice: the artifices of
politicians (which may strengthen but not originate it);
education in the family; and our interest in our reputation, than which nothing touches us more nearly.

28: Addendum: there is no such thing as property in a state
of nature and so no such thing as justice or injustice in
that state.

§4. The Circumstances of Justice

1. Many topics in this section call for discussion, but time allows mention
of only a few. I comment on, first, Hume's idea of the circumstances of
justice; next, his idea of convention; then on his idea of the most obvious
and best scheme for specifying property; and finally, the two stages of development he distinguishes in paragraph 24 (T:499–500), ending with that of
the sense of justice.

The circumstances of justice are discussed in two places, paragraphs
5–7 (T:486–488) and paragraph 16 (T:494–495). Here we see that Hume, in
arguing that morality is a natural fact—I emphasize this always—is trying
to identify the conditions of our situation in nature that render particular
virtues useful or necessary for us and society, in this case the artificial virtues
of justice and fidelity. He fixes on how the virtues arise and what work
they do in human life: for here lies their explanation.

Paragraph 16 gives a perspicuous rendering: here Hume says that justice
arises from human conventions intended to remedy the inconveniences proceeding from our "selfishness and limited generosity," the fact that possession of external objects is easily changed from one person to another, by

theft or violence, say, and all that "join'd to the scarcity [of those objects] in comparison of the wants and desires of men." The problem of property is to make secure and stable the ownership of these external objects, for these can be taken from us intact and enjoyed by others, whereas goods of mind and body cannot.

2. A noteworthy feature of Hume's account of the circumstances of justice is that while it focuses on our interest in and avidity for property, he does not assert the false doctrine of the egoism of individuals. In fact, Hume says that while each of us cares most for ourselves, and then for our family and friends in that order, the total care we have for all these others exceeds our care for ourselves. Beyond a certain circle, which is perhaps quite large, we care very little, except insofar as our sympathy is aroused. But this limited generosity, as he calls it, does not suit us for social life: "So noble an affection [he has been recounting fathers' affection for their wives and children], instead of fitting men for large societies, is almost as contrary to them, as the most narrow selfishness" (T:487). (For the sense of "large," see paragraph 24 in T:498–499.) We might equally mention the collective self-centeredness of groups of all kinds, universities and churches along with the rest. These can be worse than individual egoisms when supported by religious and philosophical doctrines. Hume is quite realistic about this, and his view of the circumstances of justice allows for it.

§5. The Idea of Convention

1. Let's now take up the important topic of convention in the very important paragraphs 9–11 (T:489–491), where the term "convention" is used for the first time in this section. We learn here that the remedy for the inconveniences of the circumstances of justice and the partiality of our natural, uncultivated ideas of morality is derived not from nature but from artifice, "or more properly speaking, nature provides a remedy in the judgment and understanding, for what is irregular and incommodious in the affections" (T:489). Once we acquire an attachment to society, and once we observe that the main disturbance to it arises from instability in the possession of external goods, we seek a remedy by putting these goods on the same sure footing as the advantages of mind and body. "This can be done after no

other manner, than by a convention enter'd into by all the members of the society to bestow stability on the possession of those external goods, and leave every one in the peaceable enjoyment of what he may acquire by his fortune and industry" (*T*:489).

This basic convention is not contrary to our interests, or to those of our families and friends, but only contrary to their impetuous and heedless, we might say irrational, tendencies. Hume thinks that "we cannot better consult both these interests, than by such a convention; because it is by that means that we maintain society, which is so necessary to their well-being and subsistence, as well as to our own" (*T*:489).

If we take Hume literally here (and why not?), he is suggesting that the convention, or scheme of conventions, he is describing is the best scheme: "there is no better way to consult both these interests," ours and others'. He doesn't mean that it is the best scheme we can imagine, much less the best scheme allowing that human beings and our situation in nature might have been different. He means it is the practically best scheme, accepting ourselves and our situation in nature as it is, without weeping and lament. I return to the idea of the practically best scheme later, as it plays a role in explaining why Hume thinks that we should act justly even though just acts, taken alone, are not infrequently detrimental to society.

2. In paragraph 10 (*T*:490), Hume states many features of conventions. I mention these.

(a) A convention is not a promise, for promises themselves, Hume argues in section 5, arise from conventions.

(b) A convention has two aspects (so I interpret Hume). One is its content, given by the rule of the convention. Thus a convention involves a rule. The other aspect is the shared awareness of a common interest, which all members of society express to one another, and the recognition of this common interest leads all to regulate their conduct by the rule.

(c) But we follow the rule conditionally: we leave others in possession of their goods provided (as Hume emphasizes) that others conduct themselves likewise toward us. A convention expresses an idea of reciprocity.

(d) For a convention to exist (I take Hume to say), three conditions must hold: first, this shared sense of a common interest is mutually (publicly) expressed, and so the existence of this common interest is public knowledge; second, the relevant rule is available and also publicly known;

and third, as expected, all (or most) adhere to the rule, producing an appropriate regulation of conduct. The last condition means that the rule must be actually followed in society for a convention to exist (as opposed to a merely possible convention).

(e) We may properly speak of a convention or an agreement among the members of society, because although there is, and has been, no promise, it is still true that, just as in the case of a promise, each of our actions is taken with reference to the actions we expect of the others.

(f) So further, the conduct taken together is a case of actions taken in mutual interdependence and on the basis of shared expectations publicly confirmed. The convention is treated as normative in that violations of it are objected to and criticized and the offending party is expected to accept these reproofs and suitable penalties.

(g) A convention is no less a convention because it has been established gradually and perhaps at times in the past has been frequently violated. It is enough that it is finally established and acted upon in the required way now.

(h) It is desirable (though perhaps not always possible) that conventions be simple and obvious. Conventions that are obvious and simple will be thought of in the first place and easily remembered. It is desirable also that their general application be free from doubt and uncertainty (T:502; 514; 526).

As stated, this idea of convention is complicated. I'm unsure that I have done justice to Hume's view. I think that he is saying all these things and more, and that paragraphs 9–11, and indeed this whole section, are among the more wonderful parts of the text. Here his observant and subtle powers of thought are acutely and succinctly expressed. Hume gives a summary of much of the account of justice and convention later in paragraph 22 (T:497–498).

EXAMPLES AND SUPPLEMENTARY REMARKS

Consider first some examples of coordination conventions: these govern situations that involve no conflict of interest between the parties. What is important is to have a convention that coordinates what we are to do. A good example is which side of the road to drive on; another is who has the right of way, the car coming from the right or the left. In the first case, either convention—drive on the right or drive on the left—is equally good, but we must pick one or the other. The other example may give an advantage—the right of way—to either party in a particular case, as it is better to have the right of way; but the advantages are likely to even out over many occasions, removing any conflict of interest. In the longer run all are equally likely to benefit.

This consequence of repeated occasions is of first importance: when there are repeated or similar occasions (or repeated, or iterated, play, in the language of game theory), the situation is entirely different from isolated, single occasions. Hume's examples of gold and silver as money and of languages are of this kind, as are most (all?) of the conventions he is concerned with. Why do we speak our language in the same way, even pronouncing the sounds exactly alike, if not because we all want to be understood, which is better achieved the more exact the coordination of grammar and sound.

One of the points of Hume's example of the men in the boat, in which each man has one oar, is that the convention is simple and obvious and requires no thought. Simplicity and obviousness are desirable features of conventions that Hume emphasizes, and are listed as (h) above.

Another kind of convention arises once a so-called prisoners' dilemma game is indefinitely repeated. A PD-game has the following kind of matrix, given on the left below; observe the contrast with the coordination games on the right.

5,5	−3,8
8,−3	0,0

−5,−5	0,0
0,0	−5,−5

or

5,5	0,0
0,0	−5,−5

When there is but one play of the game, both players in the PD-game select the lower right and receive 0. If they could somehow enter into a binding agreement, which they cannot, that player 1 will pick the first row and player 2 the first column, they would each receive 5. But in the case of repeated play with a high probability of the game continuing, perhaps in perpetuity, practically speaking, cooperation is possible and normally takes place. Clearly this happens because players form expectations and see the possibility of greater gains into the future should both pick the first row and column indefinitely.

An obvious strategy is tit-for-tat: player 1, say, starts with the first row and does in each later play of the game what player 2 did on the previous play. If both players follow tit-for-tat, then they cooperate indefinitely. When the probability of the game's continuing is high enough, the threat in tit-for-tat will ensure cooperation, but so will many other strategies. There are numerous strategies that will stop player 2 from using the second column. Indeed, there is a theorem in game theory, known as the folk theorem, which says that in a repeated PD-game, a player has a guaranteed payoff at least as large as what that player is able to get when all the other players are opposed (here I suppose an n-person PD-game; n may be 1). This is one way of seeing how repeated play over time makes cooperation possible even between persons who are self-interested, or as Hume would say, who are moved by limited altruism and confined generosity, which is more realistic.

The cases Hume is interested in are all repeated games of some kind, if we make the comparison with game theory at all. He is concerned in fact with cases where the game continues indefinitely—in perpetuity, practically speaking. Moreover, there are a great many players. Such games are very difficult to deal with formally; problems such as the development of trust and of reputation are crucial but hard to analyze. Hume is confident that cooperation will develop; for that it does so and becomes established on the basis of limited altruism and confined generosity is precisely his first stage of development of the conventions of justice and promising. Those motives he calls the natural obligation to justice (T:498; 522f.). Hume is, I think, the first to see that in a small society natural obligation suffices to lead people to honor the conventions of justice. So we have the very important further feature of conventions: that of being self-enforcing and therefore stable. So let's add:

> In a small society the conventions of justice are self-enforcing and stable by natural obligation; and in a large society they are similarly self-enforcing and stable with the addition of the sense of justice and moral sentiment.[3]

3. For further information on this topic, see Robert Axelrod, *The Evolution of Cooperation* (New York: Basic Books, 1984); David Kreps, *A Course in Microeconomic Theory* (Princeton: Princeton University Press, 1990), chap. 14 (with statement and intuitive proof folk theorem, pp. 508f.); David Lewis, *Convention* (Cambridge, Mass.: Harvard University Press, 1969); and Robert Sugden, *The Economics of Rights, Cooperation, and Welfare* (Oxford: Basil Blackwell, 1986), who tries to follow at many points what he takes to be Hume's view.

§6. Justice as a Best Scheme of Conventions

1. Earlier I said that Hume assumes that there is a practically best scheme of conventions for specifying property, where by practically best I took him to mean not that it is the best imaginable, but the best given human beings as they are—partial and quarrelsome, prone to violence and impatience—and realistically seeing their situation with desires that far outrun the scarcities of nature.

Hume discusses a feature of this practically best system in paragraph 22 (T:497–498), namely, that a single act of justice is frequently contrary to the advantage of society. This discussion follows a contrast he has drawn in paragraph 21 (T:496–497) between how one might have thought justice could be established by "public interest [pursued] naturally" (considered in section 1, paragraphs 14–16 [T:482–483]) and how he has shown it is actually established. Here he says that if the public interest had been pursued naturally, people "wou'd never have dream'd of restraining each other by these rules; and if they pursu'd their own interest, without any precaution, they wou'd run head-long into every kind of injustice and violence. These rules, therefore, are artificial, and seek their end in an oblique and indirect manner; nor is the interest, which gives rise to them, of a kind that cou'd be pursu'd by the natural and inartificial passions of men" (T:496–497).

He notes that although the conventions of justice are established by interest, their connection with it is "somewhat singular."

> A single act of justice is frequently contrary to public interest; and were it to stand alone, without being follow'd by other acts, may, in itself, be very prejudicial to society. When a man of merit, of a beneficent disposition, restores a great fortune to a miser, or a seditious bigot, he has acted justly and laudably, but the public is a real sufferer. . . . But however single acts of justice may be contrary, either to public or private interest, 'tis certain . . . the whole plan or scheme is highly conducive, or indeed absolutely requisite, both to the support of society, and the well-being of every individual. (T:497)

2. We see, then, that what Hume considers to be just is the whole plan or scheme. But surely, we might reply, some schemes are better than others,

and surely the best scheme (assuming that there is one and that it exists) will not specify to be just acts deleterious to society. We may think that Hume is too pessimistic about the practically best scheme, and certainly we are not ready to believe that the quite conservative scheme he actually proposes cannot be improved (the value of equality is largely ignored). To see Hume's point, suppose our practically best scheme actually exists. There will still be, he thinks, single acts of justice with unhappy consequences. He says: "'Tis impossible to separate the good from the ill. Property must be stable, and must be fix'd by general rules. Tho' in one instance the public be a sufferer, this momentary ill is amply compensated by the steady prose-cution of the rule" (T:497).

Such, then, is Hume's answer: even our best practicable scheme, grant-ing that it is really feasible, will be liable to the same defect. This is because the laws of property cannot determine possession and transfer according to who is best qualified at this or that moment to use this or that piece of property, as the particular utilities of the case might decide it. This is a recipe for endless disorder and quarrels, and calls forth the partialities of the natural affections, which the rules of justice are designed to restrain. See his statement on this in paragraph 2 of section 3 (T:502).

3. But rather than pursue this matter further, I mention here a contrast between Hume and Bishop Butler, which, like the earlier contrast between Hume and Grotius, Pufendorf, and Locke, sheds light on Hume's desire to show that the virtues and morality generally are the outcome of our nature and place in the world, and are to be explained as such. To his *Analogy of Religion* (1736), Butler attached a short appendix titled "On the Nature of Virtue." In this he argued, among other things, that many of our conscien-tious moral judgments do not seem to be guided by the principle of the greatest balance of happiness. Rather, our conscience, which Butler views as authoritative and regulative of our nature, is such as to "condemn false-hood, unprovoked violence, injustice, and to approve of benevolence to some preferably to others, abstracted from all consideration, which conduct is likeliest to produce an overbalance of happiness or misery" (section 8).[4]

In such manner Butler believes God has framed our conscience and we are to act accordingly. Butler entertains the purely hypothetical possibility

4. Schneewind, *Moral Philosophy from Montaigne to Kant*, 2:543.

that God might follow the principle of the greatest happiness; but even if so, that does not change the fact that our conscience as framed by God is to be our guide. We are to follow conscience.

Hume does not question Butler's actual moral judgments: he agrees that falsehood, unprovoked violence, and injustice are wrong, and he approves of benevolence to some preferably to others. But he will have nothing to do with Butler's theological background. He wants to show how our moral judgments in fact arise and have coherence and purpose, given our nature and situation in the world. His account of the artificial virtue of justice as specifying the best practicable scheme of property is an example of his attempt to do this and a reason for paying it attention.

§7. The Two Stages of Development

1. We now come to Hume's second question (paragraphs 23–24 [T:498–500]): Why do we annex the idea of virtue to compliance with the rules of justice? He has completed his answer to the first question—how the rules of justice are established by the artifices of human beings—with a review of some main points at the end of paragraph 22. He says in paragraph 18 (T:495) that he has shown that justice originates only from our selfishness and confined generosity, along with the scanty provisions of nature for our wants. He refers to this as explaining the "natural obligation to justice, viz. interest." It remains to show the basis of the moral obligation to justice, or of the sense of right and wrong. While this cannot be done satisfactorily until Part III, he gives a brief sketch in paragraph 24.

About this sketch, two points. First, the development of the sense of justice occurs in two stages. The first stage, which has occupied Hume so far, explains the natural obligation to justice. The interests we have in ourselves, our family and friends, and our circle generally are viewed as sufficient to induce us to adopt the conventions of justice. In a small society, the mutual sense of common interest is obvious and public recognition of it immediate; coordination rules are clear, and even though there are prisoners' dilemma situations, say, viewing them one by one, they are repeated day after day. Practically speaking, social life is in perpetuity, and cooperation is sure and reliable. In a small society, before it becomes a tribe or a nation, the natural obligation suffices to support the rules of justice.

2. In a large society, however, our natural obligation often fails to move us; we may be tempted to cheat when we can get away with it, and we may lose sight of our interest in upholding existing conventions. But even so, we never fail to note the injury to ourselves done by the injustice of others; and no matter how distant from us these persons are, their injustice still displeases us. This is because we view it as injurious to society and harmful to everyone affected by actions of the guilty party. This displeasure with injustice, Hume says, arises from sympathy. He holds that whatever in human actions causes uneasiness upon the general survey is called vice, and what causes satisfaction is called virtue. He has at last found, he thinks, the reason—the explanation of—why we annex the idea of virtue to complying with the rules of justice. So he sums up his conclusion thus: *"Self-interest is the original motive to the establishment of justice, but a sympathy with public interest is the source of the* moral approbation *which attends that virtue."*

Several comments on the preceding. The general survey Hume refers to here is a survey from the point of view of the judicious spectator, which he examines in III:iii:1. We shall discuss this point of view on the last day. The important thing here is that Hume takes himself to have found an explanation of the sense of justice, and of why it comes after a long development moved not literally by self-interest, as he occasionally says, but by our confined generosities, our affections for family and friends, and other such ties. These identify the original motives he looked for in paragraphs 13–16 of section 1 (T:482–483) that lead to the first establishment of justice. When we ask how these differ from the natural and direct motives he considered there, the answer is that those motives were untutored and unguided by artifice, that is, by judgment and understanding, by design and intention. In that rude and natural stage, people lacked the background of experience in society to recognize the best scheme of conventions.

Another observation is that the uneasiness caused by sympathy working through the point of view of the judicious spectator gives rise to the moral distinction between right and wrong, just and unjust. In such fashion we learn the difference between these ideas and can identify them in particular cases. This is an *epistemological* thesis about how we recognize moral distinctions, about how we are able to use the appropriate concepts in a consistent and coherent way and in general agreement with one another. But this is getting ahead.

What needs to be seen is that this epistemological thesis is different from a thesis about moral motivation, that is, how best to account for the fact that our moral knowledge, or beliefs, may influence what we do, or what desires lead us to do the right or the just thing, or to fail in that. I interpret Hume in paragraphs 25–27 (*T*:500–501) to distinguish three different kinds of moral motives, or incentives. One is the artifice of politicians; another is our education and upbringing, and the many motives we acquired in the course of that. The last is the desire for a character, as Hume sometimes says, or for our reputation, or to be esteemed and honored by others. Nothing, he thinks, could be dearer to us than that; and in a decent society the desire for a character would firmly support our sense of duty and of justice.

HUME IV

The Critique of Rational Intuitionism

§1. Introduction

1. Today we consider Hume's arguments against the rationalist doctrine he opposes in II:iii:3 and III:i:1. As preparation for this, I will spend some time simply laying out that doctrine as found in Volume II of Samuel Clarke's *Discourse on Natural Religion* (presented as the Boyle Lectures for 1705, published in 1706).[1] Rational intuitionism is an important traditional view, and this is a good occasion for a survey of it.

In a way I shall try to explain, rational intuitionism sees moral thought as a form of *theoretical* as opposed to *practical* reason. Kant's doctrine as well as Hume's is in sharp contrast with it. All along I have interpreted Hume as wanting to show that morality, and our practice of it, is the expression of our nature, given our place in the world and our dependence on society. It is part of Hume's fideism of nature to establish that morality is a natural phenomenon fully continuous with human psychology. I have also said that Hume's view lacks a conception of practical reason and psychologizes moral deliberation by relying on laws of association and of the emotions, and invoking the strengths of desires and their influence.[2] On the

---

1. My citations from Clarke are from Schneewind, *Moral Philosophy from Montaigne to Kant.*

2. A moral doctrine that affirms the idea of practical reason may object to Hume's view for just this reason, in much the way Frege objected to psychologism in logic. This is not, of course, to deny that there is a psychology of morals but to say that it must be compatible with an appropriate role of practical reason.

other hand, Kant does have a conception of practical reason. Thus Clarke's doctrine will add to our understanding of the doctrines debated in this period and extend the significant contrasts we have ready to hand.

2. While Hume does not name his opponents in the *Treatise*, he does mention Ralph Cudworth and Samuel Clarke in the *Enquiry*. In a footnote that begins with a reference to Montesquieu's *Esprit des Lois*, Malebranche is credited with having been the first who started the abstract theory of morals founded on certain relations. Hume says: "This illustrious writer [Montesquieu], however, sets out with a different theory, and supposes all right to be founded on certain *rapports* or relations; which is a system, that, in my opinion, never will be reconciled with true philosophy. Father Malebranche . . . was the first that started this abstract theory of morals, which was afterwards adopted by Cudworth, Clarke, and others; and as it excludes all sentiment, and pretends to found everything on reason, it has not wanted followers in this philosophical age" (E:197n.).

In the rest of the footnote, Hume claims that his account of the justice of civil laws and the laws of property is a clear refutation of this rationalist view. Thus it seems safe to count Cudworth and Clarke, as well as Grotius, Pufendorf, and Locke, as typical representatives of the view Hume wants to reject.

§2. Some of Clarke's Main Claims

1. Clarke wants to say first that there are certain necessary and eternal relations between things, and consequent upon (or following from) these relations, certain actions are *fit* to be done and others not fit to be done, according to whether those actions are *more* fitting than the other actions we can do in the situation at hand. Thus:

(a) Each kind of thing is said to have a nature (an essence) that characterizes it, which nature can be known by reason; and in virtue of their nature things stand in certain relations.

(b) Consequent upon these natures as standing in various relations in different situations, certain relations of fitness obtain, so that certain actions are *more* fitting than others. As an example, Clarke says: " 'Tis a thing evidently and infinitely more fit that any one particular innocent and good being should by the supreme ruler and disposer of all things be placed and preserved in an easy and happy estate, than that, without any fault or demerit of its own, it should be made extremely, remedilessly and endlessly miserable" (Schneewind, I:296). God stands in such a relation to human beings that, given the nature of God as Creator and their nature as subordinate rational creatures, it is *more* fit, in consequence, that God situate the innocent so as to make them happy rather than unhappy.

2. Further, the following:

(c) Fitness and the relation of "more fit than" are indefinable moral relations, or else definable only in terms of each other. We should allow that they might be definable in terms of other moral concepts, such as the reasonable. They are not, however, definable in terms of nonmoral (nonnormative) concepts.

We may think of the indefinable relation of "more fit than" as specified by ordered pairs of ordered triples, with agents (characterized by certain natures) in a situation S and the various actions of those agents in that situation such that it follows that action A_1, say, is more fit than action B_1. To wit:

$$>([A_1, \text{rat}_1 \ldots {}_n, \text{sit } S][B_1, \text{rat}_1 \ldots {}_n, \text{sit } S]),$$

where A_1 and B_1 are actions available to agent$_1$.

That an action is more fit is said to be necessary and known by reason. Greater fitness is consequent upon the facts of the case. For example, it is impossible that, given the nature of God and of human beings, and given the relation of creator to created in which they stand, it should not be more fitting for God to situate the innocent so as to make them happy rather than unhappy. What kind of necessity or impossibility does Clarke have in mind? I suppose it is metaphysical necessity: the thought is that it is not possible, given the nature of God (with the essences of things in the divine reason), that there should be a world—an order of things with their essences—such that the consequent relations of fitness are compatible with its being more fit for God to make the innocent unhappy. None of this is very clear, as the concepts here call for much explanation.

Note that for Clarke the basic concept seems to be that of comparative fitness: this kind of action is more fitting than that kind of action in a certain kind of situation. For example, surely it is more fitting that God should make the innocent more happy than that he should make them miserable. I mention this because often the comparative claim seems more compelling.

3. Clarke and Cudworth were concerned to argue against the view that first principles of right and wrong are founded on the Divine Will. As a matter of theological doctrine, the essences of things lie in the divine reason; hence the relations of fitness consequent upon the essences of things and situations are directives to the Divine Will. As Clarke says: "The will of God always and necessarily does determine itself to choose to act only what is agreeable to Justice, Equity . . . [as fixed by these relations]" (Schneewind, I:295). In this connection, Cudworth (*Treatise*, Bk. I, Ch. III [Schneewind, I:282ff.]) argues against Descartes, whereas Clarke spends much of his time attacking Hobbes (Schneewind, I:297f.). With this background, the following comments:

(d) The relations between the nature of things upon which the relations of fitness derive are recognized by the reason of any sufficiently rational being, divine, angelic, or human.

Thus I shall say that the nature of things specifies an independent and prior order of relations of right and wrong, an order known by reason and authoritative with respect to divine, and of course to human, will. This order is independent in that it is not dependent on our knowledge of it, nor on our will; it is prior in that it is necessary and immutable, eternal and universal. In particular, it is independent of the distinctive constitution of human nature and of the special features of our psychology.

4. I digress for a moment to call attention to a contrast between the rational intuitionism and the moral sense school. Hutcheson realized that his doctrine of the moral sense implied the possibility that the content of right and wrong as discerned by that sense might be different from the content of right and wrong as known to divine reason. The rationalist doctrine asserting that content to be the same for all rational beings was given up.[3] God implanted the moral sense in us so that we approve and disapprove of various actions and are moved to conduct ourselves accordingly. But the ultimate reasons for our approvals and disapprovals—that is, God's reasons for arranging our moral sense so that we respond to actions and traits of

3. In Hume III, section 6, we noted that Butler said something like this in "On the Nature of Virtue."

character in certain ways—may be founded on different principles than the principles expressed in our approvals and disapprovals. Hutcheson was reluctant to pursue this possibility.

But Hume does precisely this and goes beyond it: he abandons entirely the idea of a theological basis of morality and proceeds to treat the virtues, both natural and artificial, as well as our moral sentiments as natural facts. It is of no concern to him that our moral beliefs should be peculiar to us. He treats our judgments of moral approval and disapproval as part of human psychology, and he observes the similarities between our psychology and that of animals (see I:iii:16, II:ii:12). Why we have a morality, how we acquire it, and the way it works, is one of the moral subjects to which he is applying the experimental method of reasoning. With Hume we are in another world altogether.

5. To return to the rationalists. In order to explain, or perhaps better to illustrate, how relations of fitness founded on the nature of things might be known by reason, both Cudworth and Clarke appeal to an analogy with the truths of arithmetic and geometry.

(e) First principles of more and less fitness are known by reason in the way the truths about numbers and geometrical figures are known: such truths are seen to be necessary and self-evident, at least in the case of the axioms, such as the axiom that the whole is greater than its parts.

> That there is a fitness or suitableness of certain circumstances to certain persons, and an unsuitableness of others founded in the nature of things and the qualifications of persons, antecedent to all positive appointment . . . is as manifest as that the properties which flow from the essences of different mathematical figures have different congruities or incongruities between themselves; or that in mechanics certain weights and powers have very different forces and different effects one upon another, according to their different distances or different positions and situations in respect of each other.
>
> For instance: that God is infinitely superior to men is as clear as that infinity is larger than a point, or eternity longer than a moment. And 'tis certainly as fit that men should honour and worship, obey and imitate God, rather than on the contrary in all their actions endeavor to dishonour and disobey him. (Schneewind, I:297f.)

It might be an axiom of fitness that it is more fitting to do more good rather than less. Admittedly, this is rather trivial, but Clarke talks as if there are certain basic axioms of fitness from which further principles can be derived. But he doesn't try carefully to spell out what these axioms are, and the derivations are loosely sketched.

6. It is striking that Clarke insists on the following:

(f) Acting wrongly is the same thing as deliberately asserting falsehoods.

'Tis as natural and (morally speaking) necessary that the will should be determined in every action by the reason of the thing as 'tis natural and (absolutely speaking) necessary that the understanding should submit to demonstrated truth. And 'tis as absurd and blameworthy to mistake negligently plain right and wrong . . . as it would be absurd and ridiculous for a man in arithmetic matters, ignorantly to believe that twice two is not equal to four; or wilfully and obstinately to contend, against his own clear knowledge, that the whole is not equal to all its parts. . . .

In a word, all wilful wickedness and perversion of right is the very same insolence and absurdity in moral matters as it would be in natural things for a man to pretend to alter the certain proportions of numbers, to take away the demonstrable relations and properties of mathematical figures, to make light darkness, and darkness light, or to call sweet bitter, and bitter sweet. (Schneewind, I:300)

7. Earlier I said that Clarke's doctrine sees moral thought as a form of theoretical, and not of practical, reason. Our survey indicates why one is drawn to say this. For one thing, fitness and comparative fitness are determined by the essences of things and follow from those essences. Presumably these matters are known by theoretical reason. For another, acting wrongly is said to be the same absurdity as willfully asserting a false statement, or refusing to recognize a true statement. Moral error is put on all fours with the denial, or the attempted denial, of mathematical truths.

Finally, the essences of things and the consequent fitness of actions suffice to determine obligations. For Clarke, obligations are separate from and independent of divine command; God's commands do indeed enjoin these obligations but are not needed to make them obligations. In this sense,

God's commands are secondary.[4] All this seems like regarding moral thought as a form of theoretical reason.

This means that, in Clarke's view, agreement in moral judgment is to be understood as founded in the same way as agreement in arithmetic or geometry: as the common recognition of truths characterizing an order of objects and their relations, prior to and independent of our practical reasoning and our conceptions of person and society that enter into it. I return to this last point when we come to Kant.

§3. The Content of Right and Wrong

1. Clarke sees the content of first principles concerning our relations with other human beings as given by:

(g) A principle of equity and a principle of benevolence, stated thus: "In respect of our fellow-creatures, the rule of righteousness is, that in particular we deal with every man as in like circumstances we could reasonably expect he should deal with us; and that in general we endeavor, by an universal benevolence, to promote the welfare and happiness of all men. The former branch of this rule, is equity; the latter, is love" (Schneewind, I:303). The first, the principle of equity, he states as: "Whatever I judge reasonable or unreasonable for another to do for me, that by the same judgment, I declare reasonable or unreasonable that I in like case should do for him. And to deny this either in word or action is as if a man should contend that, though two and three are equal to five, yet five are not equal to two and three" (Schneewind, I:304). This is then carefully qualified and explained in an interesting way as follows:

4. This point seems to be a new departure with Clarke and a break with the tradition of natural law (which I mentioned the first day) as it had come down from the late scholastics Suarez and Vasquez and followed by Grotius, Pufendorf, and Locke. To explain: suppose that our reason informs us of what is right and wrong. Now consider the question: Why is it obligatory to do what is right and not do what is wrong? By the beginning of the seventeenth century, the standard answer was this: right and wrong depend on the nature (the essences) of things and on what is *conveniens* (fitting) to their nature, and not on the decrees of God. Yet the motivating significance and the bindingness of a norm of right and wrong depends essentially on there being a command expressing God's will that the right be done and the wrong be avoided. On this point, see the instructive discussion in John Finnis, *Natural Law and Natural Rights* (Oxford: Oxford University Press, 1980), pp. 43ff., which I follow here.

In considering what is fit for you to do to another, you always take into the account, not only every circumstance of the action, but also every circumstance wherein the person differs from you; and in judging what you would desire that another, if your circumstances were transposed, should do to you, you always consider not what any unreasonable passion or private interest would prompt you, but what impartial reason would dictate to you to desire. For example: A magistrate, in order to deal equitably with a criminal, is not to consider what fear or self-love could cause him, in the criminal's case, to desire; but what reason and the public good would oblige him to acknowledge was fit and just for him to expect. (Schneewind, I:304)

There is a lot packed into this statement. Something resembling it appears in Leibniz's "Common Sense Idea of Justice" (1702–3),[5] and Kant's categorical imperative articulates an analogous idea with considerable elaboration, as we shall see. Note also that Clarke thinks of impartial reason as informing us what to desire, which presupposes a capacity to be moved by reason in a way that Hume rejects. "The second branch of right and wrong is Universal Benevolence, that is: Not only the doing barely what is just and right, in our dealings with every man; but also a constant endeavoring to promote in general, to the utmost of our power, the welfare and happiness of all men" (Schneewind, I:304).

2. Finally, two last points already evident as follows:

(h) The first principles binding upon us as human beings are the *same* principles, have the same *content*, as the principles binding on *all* rational beings, since the same principles are known by such beings in virtue of their powers of reason. "That the *same* reason of things, with regard to which the will of God always and necessarily does determine itself to act in constant conformity to the eternal rules of justice . . . and truth, ought also constantly to determine the wills of all subordinate rational beings, to govern all their actions by the *same* rules, is very evident" (Schneewind I: 299; my italics).

Of course, in applying these principles we must take account of the

---

5. Patrick Riley, trans. and ed., *The Political Writings of Leibniz* (Cambridge: Cambridge University Press, 1972), pp. 54ff.

different capacities and abilities of different kinds of rational beings, and consider their various stations in the world and in society. But this doesn't affect the main point. And last:

(i) Our moral conduct, when properly fitting, is an *imitatio dei*, insofar as this is appropriate to us as creatures.

To conclude: we are to act in accordance with an order of fitness that lies in the divine reason: an order that directs both God's will and our will. This order is given to our reason, and it is the same for all rational beings, although its principles in their application allow adjustments for our particular capacities and station.

§4. Rational Intuitionism's Moral Psychology

1. So far I've not said anything about the moral psychology of rational intuitionism. I now turn to this. Clarke gives two main kinds of explanation why some people do not know the correct and self-evident first principles:

(j) One is extreme weakness of intellect; the other is corruption of character or perverse customs and habits, as these may lead people to doubt or to question those principles (Schneewind, I:299).

An implicit consequent thesis is:

(k) When the faculties of rational (and created) beings reach their normal fruition, provided they have not been corrupted by willful passions and bad habits, their basic psychology is such that they have an affection to act from, and not merely in accordance with, the principles of fitness known by their reason.

I stress this point because it bears on Hume's case against the rationalists. They assert that given our nature, the intellectual apprehension of the principles of fitness—the very apprehension itself—gives rise to certain affections in us to act from those principles. This is the basis of conscience: we cannot act against those principles without being condemned in our own eyes. Variants of this idea are found repeatedly in the history of moral philosophy: Price and Sidgwick, Moore, and Ross are examples. Initially, it seems not impossible that if there are indeed such principles of fitness, recognition of them should of itself generate a desire to act from them. It may seem strange that this should be so, but why should it be impossible?

If this psychology seems difficult to explain, why couldn't we say that it is simply an axiom of the psychology of rational (and created) beings?

2. Hume contends that reason alone can never be the motive to any action, where reason here is Hume's strict reason. But do the rationalists deny this? For one thing, their conception of reason is broader than Hume's strict reason, and for another, they held the view (noted above) that knowledge of certain truths about relations of fitness generates a motive (a desire) to do the more fitting action. Earlier we saw how far-reaching the effects of deliberation on our passions can be even on Hume's view. So why should it be supposed that knowledge of the comparative fitnesses of actions cannot generate morally appropriate motivation? To be sure, this is a very thin moral psychology, but I think Hume's direct attack on it in III:i:1 is less telling than his full-dress account of morality given in II and III.

Of course, Clarke recognizes that we often act contrary to what we know to be right. His view is that there is always *some* inclination aroused by this knowledge. He compares it to the case of truth in this way: "For originally and in reality, 'tis as natural and (morally speaking) necessary, that the will should be determined in every action by the reason of the thing and the right of the case as 'tis natural and (absolutely speaking) necessary that the understanding should submit to a demonstrated truth" (Schneewind, I:300). He recognizes that the parallel is not exact, for he says that it is not in our power to withhold our assent to plain speculative truth, but to act according to what is right is within our natural liberty, and yet we may not do so. Yet should we not do so, we must, unless lacking in intellect or utterly corrupted and perverted, stand condemned before our conscience (Schneewind, I:300). So let's add:

(1) Our moral conscience as rational beings testifies to the fact that knowledge of first principles arouses of itself in rational beings motives to do what is appropriate as defined by the known relations of fitness.

§5. Hume's Critique of Rational Intuitionism

1. With this survey of rational intuitionism in front of us, we are ready to look at Hume's critique of it in III:i:1. It is here, as I have said, that Hume mounts his fullest attack. An outline of this section by paragraphs is as follows:

1:      Introduction.

2–3:   Statement of the question.

4–6:   Statement of the knockout argument, as I call it.

7–10: This argument supported by recalling II:iii:3, paragraphs 1–7.

11–12: Paragraph 6 of II:iii:3 further invoked.

13–14: Puzzling interlude.

15:     Against Wollaston.

16:     Conclusion of the knockout argument.

2. This argument is followed by another meant to show that morality cannot be demonstrated by reason:

17–20: If morality is demonstrable, it must consist in some moral relation derivable from the four philosophical relations.

21:     Such a moral relation must meet two conditions: the first is that it has relata in both the mental and physical spheres.

22:     The second is that not only must there be a connection between the moral relation and the will, but also the connection must be necessary and causal, a matter of psychological influence. No relation meets these conditions.

23:     Summary of paragraphs 18–22.

24–25: These claims supported by examples of the ungrateful oak sapling and of incestuous animals.

26:     Nor does morality consist in a matter of fact.

27:     It seems almost inconceivable that the relation of "ought" should be deducible from "is."

3. The knockout argument in paragraphs 4–6 (T:456–457), given here a bit more fully, is one that we have met before. In its barest form, it is as follows:

Reason alone cannot move us to action.

Knowledge of morality can move us to action.

Therefore: Moral distinctions are not discerned by reason.

Before commenting on how Clarke would reply, let's recall the important distinction we made in the previous lecture (at the end of §7) between
the *epistemological* question—how moral distinctions are known or ascertained, whether by reason or in some other way, say by moral sense—and
the question about *motivation*—how best to account for the fact that our
moral knowledge and beliefs influence what we do. Hume accepts this
distinction when he says, "'Tis one thing to know virtue, and another to
conform the will to it" (T:465).

The reason for stressing this distinction is that, as I said last time,
Hume's moral sense doctrine addresses the epistemological question: it is
intended to account for how we make moral distinctions. The question of
what desires and motives lead us to act on our moral beliefs is for him
another matter.

4. To return to Clarke: how he could reply to Hume's argument is clear
from our sketch of his rational moral psychology. He might grant that the
bare knowledge of morality alone does not move us, but that knowledge,
given our nature as rational beings, generates in us a principle-dependent
desire, as I called it,[6] to act accordingly. This is part of what it means to
be created in the image of God. As so created, we have a basic predisposition
to desire to do what is right once our reason reaches fruition and we come
to know what is right.

I believe Hume's attempted knockout argument is powerless against
this reply. To be sure, Clarke's reply is also unsatisfactory. While he may
be able to answer the epistemological question at this general level, he has
yet to answer the motivational question in a convincing way, and both
questions must be answered by an adequate doctrine. It is not enough to
say that, given our nature, knowledge of the principles of fitness generates
desires to act accordingly.

A convincing account will say why the principles of fitness, in view of
their content—what they specifically declare to be right and wrong, good
and bad—have the central role and significance in our life that they do.
This account should lay out how these principles connect with human beings' needs, aims, and purposes; it should say why, for example, oppression
and tyranny, murder and torture, injustice and degradation and the rest,

6. See Hume II, section 5, paragraph 3.

are wrongs, and not only wrongs but great wrongs. From what Clarke has said, it is not clear why the answers should refer to the fitnesses of things at all; he doesn't say how those relations connect with our moral psychology and the fundamental ends of human life. This is not to say that he couldn't have done this. With Hume's first argument, then, there seems to be no convincing conclusion either way.

§6. Hume's Second Argument: Morality Not Demonstrable

1. This brings us to Hume's second argument (in paragraphs 18–25 [T:463–468]), which does have some force, for it challenges the rational intuitionist to specify the relation of fitness in such a way that it both coheres with our moral convictions and is a working, and not an idle, part of a plausible account of moral motivation. To be such a working part, the relation of fitness itself must have a role. Hume thinks that the relation of fitness cannot be specified.

His argument in paragraphs 18–19 (T:463–464) is that morality cannot be demonstrated from the four philosophical relations that provide the basis of demonstrative reasoning—resemblance, contrariety, degrees in quality, and proportion in quantity and number. Once again, Hume's argument tries for too much. Clarke claims that certain principles of fitness are self-evident and serve as axioms from which other principles of fitness can be derived. He would see his doctrine as showing the incorrectness of Hume's narrow view of demonstrative reason. Hume can't simply reject Clarke's reply.

2. So in paragraphs 20–22 (T:464–466), he challenges the intuitionist to specify the relation of fitness subject to two essential conditions. The first is that it relate both acts of mind and external objects, and not acts of mind alone, or external objects alone. The relation must hold between items in both spheres. Hume thinks it unlikely that there is a suitable relation answering to this condition.

The second essential condition that Hume holds the relation of fitness cannot meet is given in paragraph 22. Here he says, on the doctrine he is rejecting: "'Tis not only suppos'd, that these relations [of fitness], being eternal and immutable, are the same, when consider'd by every rational creature, but their *effects* are also suppos'd to be necessarily the same; and 'tis concluded they have no less, or rather a greater, influence in directing the will of the deity, than in governing the rational and virtuous of our own species. These two particulars are evidently distinct. 'Tis one thing to know virtue, and another to conform the will to it." He continues by saying that if one is to show that the fitnesses of things express eternal laws "*obligatory* on every rational mind . . . we must also point out the connexion betwixt the relation and the will; and . . . prove that this connexion is so necessary, that in every well-disposed mind, it must take place and have its influence."

Hume believes that his account of causal connection earlier in the *Treatise*, I:iii, is sufficient to show that the proof of the necessity of such a connection cannot be given. The revealing point here is that Hume is talking about psychological, or motivational, influence. He thinks that it is simply a fact of human nature, which his whole account of morality supports, that there is no such general causal influence and certainly no necessary causal connection at all. But it seems clear that Clarke is not talking about causal influence, or alleging a necessary causal law. He thinks of the fitnesses of things as known by theoretical reason (in the sense earlier explained) and as providing correct normative grounds for moral judgments on actions. Hume is using different basic ideas than Clarke, and there is no meeting of minds.

3. The final paragraph, 27 (T:469–470), is subject to two interpretations. The one most common for many decades now is to take it as stating Hume's law, so-called: namely, the principle of moral (or normative) reasoning that to reach a moral (or normative) conclusion, there must be at least one moral (or normative) premise. Assuming that moral (or normative) concepts are not reducible to nonmoral (or non-normative) concepts, this law is correct. We may call it Hume's Law if we like, but it is not, I think, what Hume meant to say.

For a sound textual interpretation of what Hume meant, we should see the paragraph as the parting shot of the long argument against Clarke, and look back to what he has been arguing in the more immediately preceding paragraphs. For this purpose, paragraphs 22 (T:465–466) and 26 (T:468–469) seem particularly important, the latter especially so. In paragraph 26, Hume says that morality is not a matter of fact discovered by the understanding. He writes: "You can never find it [the vice], till you turn your reflexion into your own breast, and find a sentiment of disapprobation, which arises in you, towards this action. Here is a matter of fact; but 'tis the object of feeling, not of reason. It lies in yourself, not in the object. So that when you pronounce any action or character to be vicious, you mean nothing, but that from the constitution of your nature you have a feeling or sentiment of blame from the contemplation of it" (T:468–469).

Focusing on this and similar statements, we interpret the last paragraph thus. What Hume means is that we use "ought" and "ought not" in connection with our judgments of praise and blame, these judgments being made (when made properly) from the point of view of the judicious spectator (discussed next time). Now, these judgments express a sentiment of blame, say, from contemplating a certain matter of fact. Yet Hume has argued (in paragraph 22) that there is no demonstrative or normative law that connects the sentiment of blame, expressed by "ought not," with the matter of fact. Thus "ought" does not follow from "is." So understood, the last paragraph doesn't characterize moral or normative reasoning in general, but is rather a consequence of Hume's particular view of moral judgments and how they fit into his doctrine as a whole. His view of these judgments we come to next time.

I have presented Clarke's view with hardly any critical comment. But I note here two points of difficulty that we shall come back to later when we consider Kant's idea of practical reason. One is the idea that acting wrongly is like denying truths about numbers; surely tyranny and oppression are not at all like that! The other is its apparent inability to give a convincing account of how the fitnesses of things connect with the requirements of social life, with the final aims and purposes of human life, and with our moral psychology generally.

HUME V

The Judicious Spectator

§1. Introduction

1. I now turn to our last topic: Hume's idea of the *judicious spectator* and its role in his account of moral judgments. (I use Hume's term "judicious spectator" [*T*:581] and not "impartial spectator," since the latter is used by Adam Smith for a somewhat different idea.) In discussing this topic, I shall raise once again the question whether Hume has a conception of practical reason, and consider how the text might decide this one way or the other. Now, saying that Hume lacks such a conception is not intended as a criticism, though it may be a fault. Our purpose is to understand Hume in his own terms. I mention this question to bring out the contrast with Kant, who I think clearly does have a conception of practical reason.

2. The main parts of section 1 of III:iii by paragraphs are as follows:

1–5: Introduction and summary of relevant preceding parts.

6–13: Preliminary statement of the main idea: that sympathy is the basis of moral distinctions, and a summary of relevant earlier accounts of sympathy (see especially *T*:316–320).

14–18: The first objection from the variability of sympathy: the idea of the judicious spectator introduced.

19–22: The second objection: How is it that virtue in rags is still virtue? Special features of the imagination.

23: Summary of answers to the two objections: epistemological and motivational questions distinguished.

24–29: Classification of the virtues into four kinds; the role of
sympathy stressed.

30–31: Summary of the hypothesis about the basis of moral distinctions: the role of the judicious spectator.

In my remarks, I am guided by the view that Hume is concerned to
explain and to find a place for morals as a natural human phenomenon
within his science of human nature. The *Treatise* is an account of epistemol-
ogy naturalized (to borrow Quine's well-known phrase) and of morality
psychologized. Our being able to take up the point of view of the judicious
spectator is a central feature of human life, and it must be accounted for
by the psychological principles Hume has laid out in Books I and II. Book
III is an application and elaboration of much that has gone before.

§2. Hume's Account of Sympathy

1. Sympathy is discussed in §11 of Part II of Book III (*T*:316–320) and summarized later in paragraph 7 of III:iii.1 (*T*:575f.). The account of sympathy shows
us how serious Hume was in trying to lay the groundwork for his account
of morals in a science of human nature. A feeling so basic for the natural
fact of morality as this called for a foundation in his theory of the passions.
A bare outline is as follows:

First, we witness, say, certain signs in the conversation, countenance,
and behavior of others which, on the basis of our experience, arouse in us
the idea of the feeling or emotion that we take (or infer) them to be experiencing. The explanation for that idea's arising in us is the past association
of these ideas in our experience: previously in our lives, certain feelings and
emotions have regularly led us to behave as we see others now behaving.

Next, the idea of the feeling that we take others to have is then converted into a lively impression of that feeling in virtue of the always present
impression of our self in our consciousness. Indeed, this impression of our
self is so lively that nothing can exceed it in vivacity and vividness. Thus

other persons are conceived with a vivacity depending on the closeness of their relation to our selves, on how similar our conception of them is to our conception of our self.

Note here that we do not directly discern others' mental states. It is always a matter of inference from their behavior and external actions. Hume says: "No passion of another discovers itself immediately to the mind. We are only sensible of its causes or effects. From *these* we infer the passions: And consequently *these* give rise to our sympathy" (T:576). Finally, the degree of similarity we recognize with others increases as we recognize that their desires, passions, and propensities resemble our own and that their peculiar manners and their culture and language are similar to ours. It also increases with the degree of closeness we have with them: through, for example, family ties, bonds of acquaintance and friendship, and the like.

When these aspects all work together, our ever-present and supremely lively impression of self converts our idea of the other's passions into an impression of reflection. That lively impression of self transmits enough energy to the idea of others' passion so that it is raised to a passion in us.

2. I pass over as not needing comment the resemblance between this view of sympathy and the account of causal connection in I:iii. Instead I note two peculiarities about it. First, it is not an account of sympathy as we normally understand it, but rather of what we may call imparted feeling. It explains sympathy as a kind of contagion, or even infection, that we catch from others as a kind of resonance of our nature with theirs. This comes out in what Hume says later in paragraph 7 (T:575f.): "We may begin with considering anew the nature and force of *sympathy*. The minds of all men are similar in their feelings and operations, nor can any one be actuated by any affection, of which all the others are not, in some degree, susceptible. As in strings equally wound up, the motion of one communicates itself to the rest; so all the affections readily pass from one person to another, and beget correspondent movements in every human creature."

On Hume's view, it would seem that when by sympathy we have the idea of another's feeling, that very idea is enlivened to become the same feeling in us. But in fact, when we sympathize with people, for example, when they are sick, we do not have the same feeling they do. If someone feels humiliated by the ravages his disease has wrought on his appearance, leaving him weak and despondent, we feel for him, certainly, but we don't feel humiliated. His state may arouse in us a desire to comfort and to help, but this kind of desire is not what Hume describes. What he describes is imparted feeling: it is a view of us as passive and not as moved to do something to further the good of the other, as in the case of proper sympathy.

3. I mention briefly a second matter. How are we to interpret Hume's mention of the impression or conception of self, which he says is always intimately present at the highest level of vivacity (T:317)? It is this impression or conception—Hume uses both terms—that gives the idea of another's feeling the liveliness of an impression.

Now, this impression of self cannot be a simple impression, since Hume holds in I:vi:4 that there is no such impression. We might conjecture, as Kemp Smith does, that II is earlier than I and that Hume is just inconsistent; but let's try to avoid saying this. We suppose instead that Hume's preferred meaning may be the conception he used in II in connection with pride. There he says (T:277), "This object is self, or that succession of related ideas and impressions, of which we have an intimate memory and consciousness." And later "that connected succession of perceptions, which we call self." He says (T:340): "Ourself, independent of the perception of every other object, is in reality nothing; for which reason we must turn our view to external objects; and 'tis natural for us to consider with most attention such as lie contiguous to us, or resemble us."

Perhaps for our limited purposes here it's best to say that Hume views the self as that connected succession of perceptions of which we have an intimate memory and consciousness, the vividness of which is sustained by our directing our attention to the persons who most resemble us and to the things that belong to us.

4. Two further points about Hume's view of sympathy:

One is that his view stresses its *partiality:* we sympathize more with people as they are like us, close to us, similar to us in culture and language, and so on. Sympathy is not to be mistaken for the love of mankind as such—there is no such thing—and it extends beyond our species, since we sympathize with animals (T:481).

Another point is that the partiality of sympathy shows the crucial role of the point of view of the judicious spectator in correcting it. For this point of view to work as a basis for moral judgment, some form of reason, working in tandem with the imagination, must play a fundamental part. Indeed,

I shall press the question how far, strictly speaking, sympathy, in Hume's sense or in ours, is needed at all.

§3. The First Objection: The Idea of the Judicious Spectator

1. Let's now turn to paragraphs 14–18 (T:580–584), where Hume discusses the first of two objections to his view that sympathy is the basis of moral distinctions. It is in reply that he introduces the point of view of the judicious spectator. The objection is that our actual sympathies are not only highly variable but, as just noted, highly partial and largely influenced by our affinities to persons near to us in space and time, and similar to us in language and culture, in shared interests and family ties. Outside a small circle of family and friends, no one is likely to share the same concerns with anyone else.

But we do, nevertheless, agree more or less in our moral judgments. This general agreement he accepts as a fact: it is not to be doubted but rather to be explained by psychological principles of his science of human nature. Today we are less sure of this agreement: often it seems something to be achieved; and even so we may think it worth trying to achieve only for the more basic essentials.

2. To begin: Hume explains our agreement by saying that our moral judgments express the judgments we *would* render if we *were* to take up the point of view of the judicious spectator. This point of view is characterized in such a way that when we assume it, our moral judgments are brought into line. Our agreement in judgment is accounted for once we understand two things:

First, what features of the point of view of the judicious spectator bring our judgments into agreement, and how they do so.

Second, what motivates us to assume that point of view in the first place and to be guided by its judgments. Clearly, that point of view would serve no purpose if either we were not moved to assume it, except perhaps when we simply felt like it, or we had no inclination to be guided by the judgment rendered. It might be a curiosity, one might say: so our moral judgments would agree if we saw things as judicious spectators! But since we are *not* such spectators, why ought we to judge like them and act accordingly? That's a familiar kind of objection.

3. When introducing the features of the judicious spectator's point of

view, Hume repeats that our situation with regard to persons and things is in continual fluctuation and that we each have, given our partial affinities, a distinctive position with regard to others. It is impossible, then, to have a reasonable discussion with any hope of reaching agreement if we each insist on viewing matters only as they appear to us from our own personal point of view. He says: "In order, therefore, to prevent those continual *contradictions,* and arrive at a more *stable* judgment of things, we fix on some *steady* and *general* points of view; and always, in our thoughts, place ourselves in them, whatever may be our present situation" (*T*:581f.).

Hume compares moral judgments with those of beauty. These we must also correct. He says (*T*:582): "In like manner, external beauty is determin'd merely by pleasure; and 'tis evident, a beautiful countenance cannot give so much pleasure, when seen at the distance of twenty paces, as when it is brought nearer us. We say not, however, that it appears to us less beautiful: Because we know what effect it will have in such a position, and by that reflexion we correct its momentary appearance." In the next paragraph he adds: "Such corrections are common with regard to all the senses; and in- deed 'twere impossible we cou'd ever make use of language, or communi- cate our sentiments to one another, did we not correct the momentary appearances of things, and overlook our present situation."

By these remarks, Hume implies that the same holds for moral judg- ments: they too may be founded not only on moral sentiments we *do* have (by actually taking up the judicious spectator's point of view), but *also* on sentiments we *know* we *would* have *were* we to take up that point of view. In ordinary life, then, we can use our implicit knowledge of how a properly judicious spectator would judge.

4. Thus we must fix on some steady and general point of view that will lead us to agreement in judgment. To do so, this point of view must satisfy, of course, certain conditions, of which the following seem the most impor- tant.

First, that point of view must be specified so as to call into operation *at least one* sentiment (or passion) common to all (normal) persons; because otherwise we would be indifferent from that point of view, and we would make no moral distinctions at all, since these cannot be discovered, or made, by reason alone.

Second, that point of view must not, on the other hand, call into operation two or more passions, because these passions might conflict and people might then be led to contrary or to vacillating judgments. Nothing in our psychology guarantees harmony between different passions from that standpoint.

Third, the one sentiment called into operation must be such that *everyone* who takes up the point of view of the judicious spectator is led to make the *same* judgment concerning the qualities of character and the propriety of the actions under consideration.

Fourth, for the previous condition to be met, that one sentiment must be comprehensive in scope: that is, it must be responsive to the good and harm of all persons, wherever they are in space and time. Otherwise the point of view of the judicious spectator would not succeed in bringing everyone's judgments into agreement: our judgments today with those of the ancient Romans, or our judgments as Scots with those of the Chinese. This is needed to secure that we approve or disapprove of Caesar and Brutus for the same reasons the Romans did. As the condition requires, that sentiment must take the good and the harm of everyone into account.

Fifth and last, in order to achieve agreement in judgment, the point of view of the judicious spectator must include a directive specifying a standard by which we are to assess the actions and the qualities of character under review. This standard is to approve and disapprove of those actions and qualities according to how they affect the persons who associate in daily life and in their common affairs with the people who have these qualities and who do these actions.

> Being thus loosen'd from our first station [that of ordinary life], we cannot afterward fix ourselves so commodiously by any means as by a sympathy with those, who have any commerce with the person we consider. (T:583)

> 'Tis therefore from the influence of characters and qualities, upon those who have an intercourse with any person, that we praise or blame him. (T:582)

I take Hume to think, then, that the only psychological mechanism that can explain our agreement in moral judgment is that of sympathy, as called into operation and adjusted by the point of view of the judicious spectator. No other passion of our constitution has the features necessary to give rise to our moral sentiments and to secure general agreement among persons scattered in space and time, and in different societies with different cultures. While conceivably we might be coldly indifferent from that point of view, Hume supposes that although our direct and indirect passions are indeed quiescent, the mechanism of sympathy is always operative and comprehensive in scope. Just as the general appetite to good is responsive to our own good and harm "conceived merely in idea, and . . . considered as to exist in any future period of time" (T:438), so by our nature we sympathize with the good and harm of everyone, however distant in space or time. The general appetite to good connects the interests of our self from the present into the future; while sympathy transmuted by the point of view of the judicious spectator arouses our concern impartially for the interests of persons everywhere. So transmuted, sympathy, in union with the general appetite to good, lays down lines of judgment that can hold together the social world.

§4. The Second Objection: Virtue in Rags Is Still Virtue

1. In paragraphs 19–22 (T:584–586), summarized in paragraph 23 (T:586–587), Hume takes up the second apparent objection to his view that sympathy is the basis of moral distinctions. The problem is the following. We count persons as virtuous who have those qualities that are fit to be either immediately agreeable to themselves or others, or else useful to others or themselves. We do this even if a misfortune—being unjustly imprisoned in a dungeon—or a lack of opportunity prevents these qualities from *actually* producing the beneficial results they would produce under normal circumstances. Hume says (T:584f.): "Virtue in rags is still virtue. . . . [W]here any object, in all its parts, is fitted to attain any agreeable end, it naturally gives us pleasure, and is esteem'd beautiful, even tho' some external circumstances be wanting to render it altogether effectual. 'Tis sufficient if every thing be compleat in the object itself. . . . A man, whose limbs and shape promise strength and activity, is esteem'd handsome, tho' condemn'd to perpetual imprisonment."

This feature of our moral judgments is a problem for Hume. The mechanism of sympathy (as explained in *T*:316–320) is a mechanism of imparted feeling, a kind of diffusion or contagion, which passes from one person to another (*T*:576, 605). How, then, can the esteem of persons whose character causes no actual beneficial results be accounted for? There is no good or harm with which to sympathize.

Hume's answer is to appeal to a special feature of our imagination:

> The imagination has a set of passions belonging to it, upon which our sentiments of beauty much depend. These passions are mov'd by degrees of liveliness and strength, which are inferior to *belief,* and independent of the real existence of their objects. Where a character is, in every respect, fitted to be beneficial to society, the imagination passes easily from the cause to the effect, without considering that there are still some circumstances wanting to render the cause a compleat one. *General rules* create a species of probability, which sometimes influences the judgment, and always the imagination. (*T*:585)

The imagination, then, is moved by *lesser* degrees of liveliness, and hence still associates the qualities *fit* to produce beneficial effects with those effects, whether or not the latter have occurred. This gives rise to a sympathy which then determines our judgment.

2. Note at this point that Hume must introduce, as he explicitly recognizes, a second kind of correction into our moral judgments: we are more affected by virtuous character when it actually realizes beneficial results, but we do not *say* that it is more virtuous than another character equally fit to do so. Hume remarks (*T*:585):

> We know that an alteration of fortune may render the benevolent disposition entirely impotent; and therefore we separate, as much as possible, the fortune from the disposition. The case is the same, as when we correct the different sentiments of virtue, which proceed from its different distances from ourselves. The passions do not always follow our corrections; but these corrections serve sufficiently to regulate our abstract notions, and [these corrections] are alone regarded, when we pronounce in general concerning the degrees of vice and virtue.

Thus we separate the virtuous character from its lucky or unlucky circumstances. This separation is made in our *judgments,* and it is our judgments, not our actual sentiments, that regulate our abstract notions, which I take to be our general moral views about the virtues.

Thus Hume's account of moral judgment is *doubly hypothetical.*

First, these judgments are governed not by our actual sympathies in everyday life, which vary from person to person, but by the sympathies we would feel were we to assume the point of view of the judicious spectator. But also:

Second, our judgments of persons are governed not by the sympathies we would feel even from that point of view, but by the sympathies we would feel from that standpoint if, in fact, those persons had the good fortune to produce the good effects their characters are fit to produce under normal circumstances.

§5. The Epistemological Role of the Moral Sentiments

1. So far I have simply laid out Hume's idea of the judicious spectator by commenting on citations from the text. Having done this, we can now discuss the *epistemological* role of the spectator's point of view, namely, to explain how, by way of Hume's psychological principles, we make moral distinctions. Thus:

(a) The virtues and vices are *known* to us in virtue of the *peculiar* moral sentiments we experience when we take up that point of view, sentiments which arise as the outcome of transmuted sympathy (see below).

(b) What moves us to act in accordance with our moral sentiments is a separate question altogether; for what moves us depends, for example, on our desiring a character (as Hume puts it), that is, our wanting to be esteemed as virtuous by our friends and associates as well as our wanting to be virtuous as the outcome of our family training and education (T:500f., 620f.). The basis of these motives requires its own separate account.

2. We recognize moral distinctions from the judicious spectator's point of view by our experiencing sympathy in a *special* way: as the *peculiar* (and distinctive) sentiment of moral approbation, sometimes described as a peculiar kind of pleasure (T:471f.) or moral taste (T:581). So while the mechanism

of sympathy is in play, the pleasures of others to which we respond from that point of view are transmuted into a peculiar, distinctive moral sentiment known to us in our moral experience. This sentiment suffices to determine our judgment and hence to explain our agreement once we take up the judicious spectator's point of view.

Hume notes the *epistemological* as opposed to the *motivational* role of sympathy thus transmuted when he says (T:583f.): "This [our sympathy with others from the spectator's point of view] is far from being as lively as when our own interest is concern'd . . . nor has it such an influence on our love and hatred: But being equally conformable to our calm and general principles, 'tis said to have an equal authority over our reason, and to command our judgment and opinion." Thus in everyday life, when we compare an action of some historical figure with that of our neighbor, and blame them equally (T:584), "[t]he meaning of which is, that we know from reflexion, that the former action wou'd excite as strong sentiments of disapprobation as the latter, were it plac'd in the same position." Further, and already cited: "We know, that an alteration of fortune may render the benevolent disposition impotent, and therefore we separate . . . the fortune from the disposition. . . . [T]hese corrections . . . regulate our abstract notions, and are alone regarded, when we pronounce . . . concerning the degrees of vice and virtue" (T:585). Again: "Sentiments must touch the heart, to make them controul our passions: But they need not extend beyond the imagination, to make them influence our [moral] taste" (T:586).

Thus the sympathy transmuted into moral sentiment does its work by determining our judgments, thereby making general agreement possible. Why we are moved to take up this position and to act from the judgments we make from it is a completely different question. I return to this below in section 7.

3. I now ask whether Hume offers an analysis of moral judgments of the kind we would expect in a contemporary work, and whether that analysis supports the idea that the main role of the point of view of the judicious spectator is epistemological.

I think that it is unlikely that Hume intends to give an analysis in the contemporary sense at all. Many different analyses are suggested by his rather loose remarks, often several variations on one page, for example in paragraph 3 of III:i:2 (T:471f.), which shows, I think, that he is not doing that. If he were, he would be careful to stick with a particular analysis. Moreover, it's not clear that he knows what is meant by an analysis in our sense. The question itself is misplaced, since Hume need not answer it to do what he wants. His aim is to explain, by principles drawn from his science of human nature, how we actually make moral distinctions; he offers a psychological account of moral judgments and of their social role. This is not the same as giving an analysis of the meaning of moral judgments.

If, however, we ask which familiar analysis of moral judgments (in our sense) accords most closely with Hume's view, there seem to be two main candidates. One is some kind of ideal observer analysis. It is found in such passages as: "'Tis only when a character is considered in general, without reference to our particular interest, that it causes such a feeling or sentiment, as denominates it morally good or evil" (T:472). Or the passage we cited last time from paragraph 6 of III:i:1: "When you pronounce any action or character to be vicious, you mean nothing, but that from the constitution of your nature you have a feeling or sentiment of blame from the contemplation of it" (T:469).

We might say, then, that the assertion that a quality of character is morally virtuous means that it would be approved by any normal person (with normal faculties of reason, feeling, and judgment) when that person takes up the point of view of the judicious spectator.

4. The other candidate is a projective analysis suggested by Mackie.[1] The main idea is that Hume's view about moral judgments runs parallel with his view of our beliefs about necessary causal connections. Just as in the latter we ascribe a power or a necessary connection to objects, which we never observe in them (T:169), so also in our moral judgments we ascribe to qualities of character moral attributes of being virtuous or vicious, which we do not observe in them (T:468f.). We are led to do this by our feelings and sentiments, which we *project* onto what is being judged.

Several points support this second view. It is suggested at one place when Hume says (T:471): "We do not infer a character to be virtuous, because it pleases: But in feeling that it pleases after such a particular manner, we in effect feel that it is virtuous." If we take the "feel that" here as expressing a judgment, we have a projectivist interpretation of this sentence.

1. Mackie, *Hume's Moral Theory*, pp. 71–75.

This is little to go on. But it is suggestive that in his account of causal connection Hume says: "'Tis a common observation, that the mind has a great propensity to *spread itself* [my italics] on external objects, and to conjoin with them any internal impression, which they occasion, and which always make their appearance at the same time that these objects discover themselves to the senses" (T:167). This passage seems naturally to apply to moral judgments. Moreover, there is an explicit statement later in the *Enquiry* (294): "The distinct boundaries and offices of *reason* and *taste* are easily ascertained. The former conveys the knowledge of truth and falsehood: the latter gives the sentiment of beauty and deformity, of vice and virtue. The one discovers objects as they really stand in nature, without addition or diminution: the other has a productive faculty and *gilding or staining* [my italics] all natural objects with the colors borrowed from internal sentiment, raises in a manner a new creation."

The projectivist view explains, then, why Hume used Hutcheson's term "moral sense," and why he compares moral attributes to secondary qualities. It also accords with Hume's believing that the spectator's point of view orders our use of moral language; for given the agreement in our sentiments (as projected), we quite reasonably, although mistakenly, take the predicates "virtuous" and "vicious" to denote certain properties or qualities of character.

I incline to favor this projective view, not of course because it is Hume's, but because if we ask which contemporary view fits his aims best, this is perhaps the strongest candidate. It's less an analysis of meaning and more an explanation of how we make moral judgments and of why we mistakenly take them as attributing properties to things. So understood, it goes best with his science of human nature.

§6. Whether Hume Has a Conception of Practical Reason

Let's now consider whether Hume's account of the judicious spectator and its epistemological role includes a conception of practical reason, or whether it is instead an account of the psychological processes whereby our moral judgments are expressed. In Hume's mind, I believe, it is a psychological account. There are, however, passages that suggest how this account might become, if pressed, a conception of practical reasoning. Here are two such ways of pressing it.

First, we might use the point of view of the judicious spectator as a criterion to work out, or to construct, what our moral judgments should be. Given the account of that doubly hypothetical point of view, we can figure out analytically what the content of the approvals of the judicious spectator would be regarding various kinds of qualities of character or regarding certain actions and institutions. This content could be spelled out so as to provide a mutually recognized content for morals. Once the public use of this criterion was justified by its various features—for example, by the fact that it characterized a general and stable point of view from which everyone's interests are impartially taken into consideration (with further elaborations as required)—the grounds for accepting this criterion would have been given.

Alternatively, we might simply introduce something like Bentham's or Sidgwick's principle of utility as the fundamental principle of practical reasoning. One ground for doing this might be that, on the basis of Hume's account of our moral psychology, that principle is well adapted to our nature and would be readily accepted. On this view, moral questions are decided directly or indirectly (there are various possibilities) by an appeal to the principle of utility as the final arbiter of reasonable moral opinion. This kind of view is developed with great care and detail in Sidgwick's *Methods of Ethics* (7th ed., 1907). (For Sidgwick, a method of ethics is simply a method of practical reasoning.)

Now, it seems clear that Hume has neither of these views in mind. While *we* may find them hinted at in what he sometimes says, they are foreign to his overall aim, which is to give an account of our moral judgments in line with his psychological account of the understanding and the passions. This account rests on the psychological principles of the association of ideas, on the principles of custom and facility, and on such principles as those of the predominant passion and of the greater influence of more particular and determinate ideas, and so on. The problem that concerns Hume in the second objection to the point of view of the judicious spectator—how to explain that virtue in rags is still virtue—would never have bothered him had he been following either of the above alternatives. His supposition that the imagination has its own special passions that make it more responsive would have been unnecessary. He doesn't have, or at least he doesn't invoke, our conception of moral judgments as guided by criteria and principles justified by certain formal or material constraints on what can serve as sound or valid reasons.

§7. The Concluding Section of the *Treatise*

1. The concluding section of the *Treatise* provides a key, I think, to how to interpret Book III as a "system of ethics," as Hume refers to it. A contemporary reader is likely to say: Hume's account is purely psychological; it describes the role of morals in society and how it arises from the basic propensities of our nature. This is psychology, we say, and not moral philosophy. Hume simply fails to address the fundamental philosophical question, the question of the correct normative content of right and justice. To say this, I believe, is seriously to misunderstand Hume. In the short last section of the *Treatise*, which consists in but six paragraphs, he discusses three philosophical questions. These I sketch briefly, though not in the order he addresses them.

In paragraphs 4–5 (*T*:619–620), Hume states that although justice is artificial, the sense of its morality is natural; and he affirms once again[2] the steadfast and immutable basis of justice, or of what I called the practically best scheme of the conventions of justice (Lecture III, section 6). We might think that, like other human inventions, this one is fragile and transitory. But against this he says: "The interest, on which justice is founded, is the greatest imaginable, and extends to all times and places. It cannot possibly be serv'd by any other invention. It is obvious, and discovers itself on the very first formation of society. All these causes render the rules of justice stedfast and immutable . . . as human nature" (*T*:620). He adds that they would have no greater stability if they were founded on original instincts. One might object, with Clarke, that they would have greater stability if they were founded on principles of fittingness deriving from the essences

2. For an earlier statement, see *T*:526, where he refers to the conventions of justice specifying property as the three fundamental laws of nature.

of things—principles seen to be necessary and self-evident by theoretical reason, like the axioms of geometry. To Hume this greater stability and immutability is simply an illusion, as these ideas and principles cannot be sustained. The deeper and more secure foundations for morals alleged by other philosophical doctrines do not exist. And in any case, what can be more immutable than nature itself, of which human nature is but a part?

All very well, one might say, but Hume hasn't bothered to answer questions people often ask, for example: Why should we be moral? This question, though, is no more a live question for him than it is for Kant. Neither of them is concerned in the least with rational egoists who want to be persuaded that following virtue is to their advantage or for their good. He thinks that it is so obvious that this course is for our good that those who don't understand it are dupes. On this, see his reply to the sensible knave in section 9 of the *Enquiry Concerning the Principles of Morals* and his discussion of the fancied monster in the early paragraphs of section 7 of the same work. That he does think the answer to be obvious is indicated by his short answer to it in the first half of the last paragraph of the *Treatise* (620), where he considers the happiness and dignity of virtue. In realizing our desire for a character acquired from our life in society, we achieve new luster in the eyes of others and gain the peace and inward satisfaction of being able to bear our own survey. This is about all the answer he bothers to give.

2. In the third paragraph, Hume urges an advantage of his system of ethics over those of Clarke and Hutcheson (or so I interpret him). He remarks that "all lovers of virtue" must be pleased to see that moral distinctions are derived from so noble a source as sympathy and that they disclose the "generosity and capacity of human nature." Hume takes it to be plain from ordinary life that "a sense of morals is a principle inherent in the soul" and one that powerfully affects us. He continues in paragraph 3:

> But this sense must certainly acquire new force, when reflecting on itself, it approves of those principles, from whence it is deriv'd, and finds nothing but what is great and good in its rise and origin. Those who resolve the sense of morals into original instincts of the human mind, may defend the cause of virtue with sufficient authority; but

want the advantage, which those possess [as does the author of the *Treatise*], who account for that sense by an extensive sympathy with mankind. According to the latter system [the system of this book], not only virtue must be approv'd of, but also the sense of virtue: And not only that sense, but also the principles, from whence it is deriv'd. So that nothing is presented on any side, but what is laudable and good. (*T*:619)

This is an important statement. Hume is saying that his science of human nature also shows that our moral sense is *reflectively stable:* that is, that when we understand the basis of our moral sense—how it is connected with sympathy and the propensities of our nature, and the rest—we confirm it as derived from a noble and generous source. This self-understanding roots our moral sense more solidly and discloses to us the happiness and dignity of virtue (*T*:620). This is one advantage he claims for his system over those of Clarke and Hutcheson; for in their views the why of the fitness of things, or of the sense of morals, remains opaque: it has no intelligible connection with natural human affections and desires. Hume thinks he has laid out—as an anatomist of human nature—all the facts needed to convince us that we should accept and be happy with our moral sentiments, with our nature as it is. This is all part of what I have called his fideism of nature.

Here we should note a remarkable feature of Hume's fideism. One might suppose offhand that of course the moral sense must confirm itself and so be reflectively stable. What other criterion does that sense have but itself to set against its own judgments? This thought is soon abandoned once we recall those later anatomists of human nature and its moral psychology—Marx and Nietzsche, Freud and Pareto (to mention several)—whose views can undermine and put in doubt our common moral sentiments. Indeed, such undercutting views were not uncommon in Hume's day, as the cases of Hobbes, Mandeville, and La Rochefoucauld remind us. A unique feature of Hume among the great moralists is that he is happy and contented with what he is. He is utterly without lament or sense of loss, with no trace of romantic anguish and self-pity. He doesn't complain against the world, a world that for him is a world without the God of religion, and the better for it.

Appendix: Hume's Disowning the *Treatise*

The *Treatise* was published anonymously and never publicly acknowledged by Hume in his lifetime, although it was acknowledged posthumously both in *My Own Life* and in the Advertisement to the first posthumous edition of the *Essays and Treatises* of 1777. In that Advertisement he also disowned the *Treatise*. He said:

> Most of the principles and reasonings, contained in this volume, were published in a work of three volumes, called *A Treatise of Human Nature:* a work which the Author had projected before he left College, and which he wrote and published not long after. But not finding it successful, he was sensible of his error in going to press too early, and he cast the whole anew in the following pieces, where some negligences in his former reasoning and more in the expression, are, he hopes, corrected. Yet several writers, who have honored the Author's Philosophy with answers, have taken care to direct all their batteries against that juvenile work, which the Author never acknowledged, and have affected to triumph in any advantages, which they imagined, they had obtained over it: A practice very contrary to all the rules of candour and fair-dealing, and a strong instance of those polemical artifices, which bigotted zeal thinks itself authorized to employ. Henceforth, the Author desires that the following Pieces may alone be regarded as containing his philosophical sentiments and principles.

To what does Hume refer as "some negligences in his former reasoning"? Two are connected, I conjecture, with the view of sympathy. It is noteworthy that in the *Enquiry Concerning the Principles of Morals* the role of sympathy is assumed by what Hume calls the principle of humanity; there is an instructive footnote explaining why he does this. It reads as follows:

> It is needless to push our researches so far as to ask, why we have humanity or fellow-feeling with others. It is sufficient, that this is experienced to be a principle in human nature. We must stop somewhere in our examination of causes; and there are, in every science, some

general principles, beyond which we cannot hope to find any principle more general. No man is absolutely indifferent to the happiness and misery of others. The first has a natural tendency to give pleasure; the second pain. This every one may find in himself. It is not probable, that these principles can be resolved into principles more simple and universal. . . . But if it were possible, it belongs not to the present subject. (*E:*219–220n.)

Perhaps Hume felt that in the *Treatise* he had pushed the account of sympathy too far. He may also have realized that it explained imparted feeling, which was not what he wanted; and that, as presented, his account relied on a dubious idea of the self, which he came to think mistaken. If this was his view, he seems correct in thinking the principle of humanity to be superior. Nevertheless, it is melancholy to see that he disowned the *Treatise* with its many wonderful parts lacking improved or matching replacements anywhere else.

LEIBNIZ

LEIBNIZ I

His Metaphysical Perfectionism

[The two Leibniz lectures were delivered between the fourth and fifth Kant lectures. They may be read on their own, or in the context of the argument of the second half of the Kant lectures.—Ed.]

§1. Introduction

1. Our aims in taking up Leibniz (1646–1716) are modest. Like Kant's, his philosophical doctrine is comprehensive and extremely complex, and we can only touch upon several matters relevant to our study of Kant's moral philosophy. Leibniz was the dominant figure in Germany in philosophy in Kant's time, and Kant must have carefully studied his published works, four of which we read: the *Discourse* (1686), the *New System* (1695), *Nature and Grace* (1714), and the *Vindication* (an appendix to the *Theodicy* [1710]). Much of Leibniz's voluminous writing was not published in his lifetime (many are unfinished, or short pieces); the *New Essays,* for example, did not appear until the mid-1760s. It was Wolff who made Leibniz's system widely known in Germany, though in a rather superficial form.

Had Kant died in the mid-1760s or 1770s, he would perhaps still be known to historians of philosophy as a minor if somewhat interesting figure much influenced by Leibniz. The reason for looking at Leibniz is that, while Kant went beyond these influences and developed his own distinctive views, the fact remains that Leibniz's ideas often shape Kant's mature doctrine in striking and subtle ways. We examine some of these as time permits to deepen our understanding of Kant.

2. There are five matters I wish to emphasize, although we won't discuss all five in the two lectures devoted to Leibniz, but will consider some as we proceed later on. They are the following:

First, the idea of philosophy as apology, as the defense of faith. This idea is marked in the *Discourse, Nature and Grace,* the *Vindication,* and of course in the *Theodicy,* which we don't read. The writers we study are much concerned with the relation between modern science and Christianity, and with science and accepted moral beliefs.[1] Spinoza, Leibniz, and Kant answer these questions in different ways, but they face a common problem. In some respects, of these three, Spinoza's way is the most radical: his pantheism incorporates the new scientific and deterministic view of the world while preserving important features of a religious (but heterodox) doctrine. His view is one that neither Leibniz nor Kant can accept, and they are on guard against falling into Spinozism, so-called, something then to be avoided at all costs. (Likewise, in the late seventeenth century, falling into Hobbism was similarly to be avoided.) Leibniz was particularly worried about this, and some think that he did not succeed and that there are deep Spinozistic elements in his view.

Of the writers we study, Leibniz is the great conservative in the best sense of the term. That is, he fully accepted an orthodox Christian view, and he confronted and mastered—indeed, he contributed to—the new science of his day, making use of it in his philosophical theology. He is a great conservative in the way Aquinas was in the thirteenth century: Aquinas confronted the new Aristotelianism and used it for his own aims and purposes in his magnificent *Summa Theologica,* his restatement of Christian theology. Similarly, Leibniz incorporated modern science into traditional philosophical theology; and in this enlarged and revised scheme he tried to resolve all the outstanding problems. Thus, for example, he used the new science in his definition of truth, in his distinction between necessary and contingent truths, in his account of free will and God's foreknowledge, and in his vindication of God's justice in the *Theodicy.* Even further, Leibniz intended the *Discourse* as part of a larger plan to reunify the Protestant

1. This paragraph and the next reprise material from the Introductory Lecture, §4. [Ed.]

denominations and beyond that to reunify Catholics and Protestants. He hoped that its framework of thought would enable the leading theological disputes to be resolved.[2] From our standpoint, Leibniz's moral philosophy—his metaphysical perfectionism, as I shall call it—is less original than the others', but it nevertheless represents an important doctrine and one particularly instructive in contrast to Hume and Kant.

Another idea is that of moral philosophy as importantly a study of the ethics of creation, that is, of the principles of good and evil and of right and wrong that guide the divine will in the creation of the world. This idea of moral philosophy is evident in the *Theodicy* and the *Vindication*, but it is plain in the other things we read as well. It is also closely connected with the previous idea of philosophy as the defense of faith. Although Leibniz argues in a familiar way in the *Theodicy* that God exists and out of moral necessity creates the best of all possible worlds (Part I, paragraphs 7–10), this part of the work is brief. For the most part, he seems to take this for granted as a doctrine of faith.

Like other apologetic writers, Leibniz tries to meet objections to Christian faith and wants to show that it is fully compatible with reasonable belief. Faith is defended by maintaining that, from the point of view of faith, the objections raised against it fail to show it to be either unreasonable or incoherent. To affirm the faith, one need not prove its beliefs. Rather, it suffices to rebut objections, and for this it suffices to state certain possibilities showing that the objections may be false. This establishes that the objections are not conclusive, and so faith stands. So if Leibniz can say how God can both foresee and permit Judas' sin, say, without God's being blameworthy, then the apologetic purpose of the *Theodicy* succeeds.

A third idea is that of the most perfect state of things: this is found at the end of the *Discourse*, in *Nature and Grace,* and of course in the *Theodicy*. A brief statement of it occurs in *Nature and Grace* §15. This is a traditional idea, but Leibniz's version of it contains striking aspects found later in Kant. Here Leibniz speaks of our entering as members into the City of God by virtue of our reason; that City is the most perfect state, formed and governed by the greatest and the best of all monarchs. In it there is no crime

2. See Robert Sleigh, *Leibniz and Arnauld: A Commentary on Their Correspondence* (New Haven: Yale University Press, 1990), p. 10.

without punishment, no good actions without proportionate recompense, and, finally, as much virtue and happiness as possible. And note particularly that this most perfect state does not disturb nature or disrupt its laws; but by the very order of natural things as given by preestablished harmony, "nature itself leads to grace, and grace in making use of nature, perfects it." Recall *KP*:43, where Kant says that the moral law (when we follow it) "gives to the sensible world, as sensuous nature, the form of an intelligible world" without interfering with its laws.

An analogous idea of the highest good is prominent in the dialectic of the second *Critique* in connection with the postulates of practical faith; here its role seems quite problematic and gives rise to serious questions of interpretation. Later we'll have to consider in what ways Kant's idea of the highest good resembles Leibniz's most perfect state. Sometimes Kant takes an idea found in Leibniz and uses it in a very different way, as when in the first *Critique* he treats the idea of the highest systematic unity of nature not as a metaphysical truth but as a regulative idea to guide speculative reason in ordering the knowledge of the understanding. We shall ask: Does Kant do something similar with the idea of the highest good, and is his use of it consistent with his account of the moral law?

The two remaining ideas of Leibniz that I want to touch upon I consider in this and in the next lecture. One of these is the idea of metaphysical perfectionism, which Kant views as a form of heteronomy in both the *Groundwork* (II:81–88) and the second *Critique* (40f.). This idea I examine today.

The other idea is that of freedom and its relation to Leibniz's idea of a complete concept of an individual person. Kant criticizes this idea in the second *Critique* (97) as no better than "the freedom of a turnspit, which when once wound up also carries out its motions of itself." Leibniz's idea of freedom I take up next time, but as preparation, I survey his predicate-in-subject account of truth in section 4.

§2. Leibniz's Metaphysical Perfectionism

1. One feature of this view, as I have said, is that it is an ethics of creation: it specifies principles that lie in God's reason and guide God in selecting the best of all possible worlds, the world most fitting to create. For Leibniz,

God is the absolutely perfect being (*Discourse*:§1), and God would act imperfectly should God act less perfectly than God is capable of acting (ibid.:§3).

Therefore, since God is omnipotent (omnipotence is a perfection of God), and God knows which world is the most perfect (omniscience is another perfection of God), God creates the best, that is, the most perfect, of all possible worlds. Thus the world that exists is the best of all possible worlds. Not to believe this is unworthy of faith, for it is not to believe that God is perfect in wisdom and goodness.

2. Leibniz occasionally states principles that characterize the best of all possible worlds. For example, he says that in whatever manner God might have created the world, it would always have been regular and in a certain order. For any world must have laws: "God, however, has chosen the *most perfect* [possible world], that is to say, the one which [of those possible] is at the same time the *simplest in hypotheses* and the *richest in phenomena*," as illustrated by "the case [of] a geometric line [consider, e.g., a circle], whose construction was easy, but whose properties and effects are extremely remarkable and of great significance" (*Discourse*:§6).

Leibniz adds that the manner of the perfection of the world is conveyed only imperfectly by such comparisons, but they help us to conceive in at least some fashion what cannot be otherwise expressed. The world that exists is the best of all possible worlds, best in the sense of the most perfect that could have existed. This is so since God is absolutely perfect, and God would have acted imperfectly if God had created a world different from ours, even in the least manner.

3. Now, besides being an ethics of creation, Leibniz's metaphysical perfectionism has the following feature:

> There exists a moral order in the universe fixed and given by the divine nature (in Leibniz's case), an order prior to and independent of us that flows from the divine perfections, and this order specifies the appropriate moral ideals and conceptions for human virtues, as well as the grounds of the principles of right and justice.

Since God's perfection implies the moral perfections, God is a model for us and is to be imitated as far as this is possible and fitting for free and intelligent spirits like ourselves. The moral life is a form of the *imitatio dei* (*Discourse*:§§9, 15, 36; and *Nature and Grace:* §14).

In saying above that the moral order is prior to and independent of us, I do not mean that it is, as in Hume, rooted in our given natural psychological constitution. Nor is it, as we later discuss, an order implicit in and constructed by our pure practical reason, as I believe Kant holds.

In this respect, Leibniz's doctrine is like the rationalistic intuitionism of Clarke. Like Clarke, he maintains that the principles of perfection that specify the best of all possible worlds are eternal truths: they rest on and lie in the divine reason. These truths are superior to and prior to the divine will. Leibniz insists on this point (for example, against the Cartesians) and states it early in section 2 of the *Discourse*.

4. A third feature of Leibniz's perfectionism is this: it is pluralistic, that is, there are two or more first principles that specify certain perfectionist values—kinds of good and evil—and each principle has a role in identifying the best of all possible worlds. The best world (all things considered) is specified by the most fitting balance of all the various perfections. It is not found by seeing which one maximizes the fulfillment of any one principle (or value) taken by itself. The most fitting balance of perfections, and so the most perfect world among the possible worlds, is known to God, but Leibniz would say that we cannot state, other than formally, how that balance is determined or how that judgment is made.

To illustrate by Leibniz's remark cited a moment ago: two aspects of the world's perfection are that it is at the same time the simplest in hypotheses and the richest in phenomena. Consider the two perfections:

   (i) simplicity in hypotheses; and
   (ii) richness in phenomena

How are these two aspects to be balanced against each other? Other things being equal, both greater simplicity and greater richness (diversity) add to perfection, but since neither alone is to be maximized, the best combination, among those possible, must somehow be identified. The most perfect balance of perfections rests with God's intuitive judgment. We can't say much about it.

The same problems of balance are brought out even more clearly by this passage from *Nature and Grace* (§10):

   It follows from the supreme perfection of God that he chose the best possible plan in producing the universe; a plan in which there is the greatest variety together with the greatest order; the most carefully used plot of ground, place, time; the greatest effect by the most simplest means; the most power, knowledge, happiness and goodness in created things that the universe could allow. For, since all the possibles have a claim to existence in God's understanding in proportion to their perfections, the result of all these claims must be the most perfect actual world possible.

Here we have still further values to balance against one another, and this includes balancing goods against evils in attaining the greatest total perfection. Thus, Leibniz often appeals to an aesthetic analogy, as illustrated in "Dialogue on Human Freedom" (1695); see also "The Ultimate Origination of Things" (Ariew and Garber:153). "It's a bit like what happens in music and painting, for shadows and dissonances truly enhance the other parts, and the wise author of such works derives such a great benefit for the total perfection of the work from these particular imperfections that it is much better to make a place for them than to attempt to do without them. Thus, we must believe that God would not have allowed sin nor would he have created things he knows will sin, if he could not derive from them a good incomparably greater than the resulting evil" (Ariew and Garber:115).

None of this is intended as criticism of Leibniz. Pluralistic metaphysical perfectionism is a possible moral doctrine. No doubt a natural setting for it is the ethics of creation. To my knowledge, Leibniz never gives a careful and reasonably systematic account of the principles of perfection, or of perfectionism's basic values. The pressure of other work was always so great that he never found time for this. We have to piece together his views from scattered pieces and notes.[3]

§3. The Concept of a Perfection

1. Now we must ask: What is a perfection? One difficulty with perfectionism is that while it seems quite evident that there is an intuitive idea of perfection, it is hard to make it sufficiently clear.

3. Some of these are in Patrick Riley, ed., *The Political Writings of Leibniz* (Cambridge: Cambridge University Press, 1972).

Leibniz tries to characterize a perfection in the *Discourse* §1. He says: "One thing which can surely be said about [perfection] is that those forms or natures which are not susceptible of it to the highest degree, say the nature of numbers or of figures, do not admit of perfection."

Leibniz says that number, with respect to its size (relative to others), does not admit of perfection: there is no greatest number. The same is true for area. However, the power and knowledge of God does admit of perfection, since omnipotence and omniscience are the suitably defined upper limits. Omnipotence is being able to create any possible world, say, and omniscience is knowing all these worlds (their content and possible history) down to the last detail, and knowing which world is best and why. Thus omniscience and omnipotence are perfections of God.

The intuitive idea seems to be that the properties of a thing that render it more or less perfect must at least be properties that have a natural upper bound derived from the nature of the property and / or from the nature of the thing. A property of a thing that may increase beyond any limit (as given by the nature of that thing) cannot be a perfection. This gives a necessary condition for a perfection.

2. Let's try to get the feel of the intuitive idea by looking at some commonsense examples. First consider artifacts: a perfect watch or a perfect ruler. A perfect watch keeps accurate (exact) time, down to the least unit of time that counts for anything. As physics develops, it needs more accurate watches (such as atomic clocks). A perfect ruler has, say, a perfectly straight edge marked with perfectly accurate units of length (again *modulo* what we can distinguish in practice). There is a concept of a perfectly straight edge (line) as a limit, but there is not a concept of a perfectly long line, since length, like area, has no intrinsic upper bound.

Consider next the roles that we assume in certain activities and these activities themselves. A perfect shortstop makes no errors over a season, completes all the double plays, and much else, and all this with a certain grace and style, yet still within the limits of normal human capacity and skill. A perfect shortstop does not have superhuman quickness, speed, or throwing arm. Certain constraints and limits are given by the normal range of human abilities.

We can also form some notion of a perfect baseball game; and this is different from that of a perfect game of any kind, which is a much more difficult notion and perhaps so vague as not to be usable. (In baseball, the term "perfect game" refers to a no-hitter of a certain kind. But this is not a perfect game! It is too unbalanced in desirable qualities.) Try other notions of perfection: a perfect piece of music, a perfect sonata, a perfect classical sonata, a perfect Mozart piano sonata. Or specialize to a perfect opera, a perfect Italian opera (style), a perfect Verdi opera (individual style), and so on. Each notion is sharper than the preceding.

3. Reviewing these examples shows that the intuitive idea of perfection seems to be either of the following:

(a) An appropriate balance in how a plurality of criteria are satisfied or exemplified, which balance has a kind of internal limit that arises from the concept of the object in question together with certain natural constraints. In this case, should any of the criteria be satisfied to a greater or lesser degree, the balance would be worse. Or:

(b) In some cases, e.g., that of a straight line, one feature may have an internal limit and may suffice for the object in question to be perfect.

This explanation of the intuitive idea of perfection is vague. I think that it can be made sharper only by examples and contrasts, and by fixing on the particular use we want to make of it. Thus contrast perfectionist pluralism as a moral doctrine with the idea of maximizing happiness (as the sole first principle) as it appears in classical utilitarianism. The latter has no internal limit. Any limits are imposed from the outside as constraints: one maximizes happiness subject to the given constraints, whatever they are. And the constraints may vary from case to case.[4] This is a significant feature of it.

Hence what seems essential to perfectionism is that the concept of perfection in a given case should specify its limit or balance, at least in significant part, from within: from the nature of the perfectionist properties and/or the nature of that which is perfect or has the balance of perfections. So perfection involves the concept of completeness as internally specified: while anything less is worse, nothing more is needed. A limit or balance is reached that is not determined from the outside by constraints that may vary arbitrarily from case to case, as in the way in which maximizing happi-

---

4. F. H. Bradley in *Ethical Studies* (Indianapolis: Bobbs-Merrill, 1951), chap. 3, makes much of this point in his attack on J. S. Mill's utilitarianism.

ness is constrained by limited resources, or limited time and energy, and changing from time to time. No doubt this leaves much obscure!

4. What is metaphysical perfection? In this case, the perfections are perfections of a perfect being. God is an absolutely perfect being. So Leibniz thinks that we have the concept of such a being with the properties of omniscience and omnipotence, as well as the moral perfections: wisdom, goodness, and justice. Further, such a being not only exists, since existence is a perfection; but also it exists necessarily. God is necessarily existent. God is also simple and not consisting of parts. God, as the absolutely perfect being, is also independent of all created beings in the sense that God's existence does not depend on their existing. God is also self-sufficient.

I shall not discuss these ideas; I merely mention them here to give some sense to the concept of metaphysical perfection: the concept of God as the absolutely perfect being who creates the world as the best of all possible worlds.

Recall that, aside from his argument for God's necessary existence in *Theodicy*, paragraphs 7–8, Leibniz is not in that work trying to prove to us that the world is the best, or the most perfect, possible. The reasons sufficient to do that are far beyond our comprehension; they can be known only to God. Rather, Leibniz's aim is to provide a defense of faith: we are given a way of taking the world that presents us with grounds for believing that the world is the best possible. In discussing the question whether God caused Judas to sin, answering that God did not, Leibniz says: "It is enough to know [that God made the best choice of worlds] without understanding it" (*Discourse*:§30). Enough for what? For faith and piety.

§4. Leibniz's Predicate-in-Subject Theory of Truth

1. I now give a very brief sketch of what I shall call Leibniz's predicate-in-subject theory of truth. I do this as preparation for considering next time his account of freedom, which is intended to explain why it is, for example, that God in creating Judas does not cause Judas to sin, and how it is that although God foresees and permits Judas's sin, Judas sins freely. This account of truth must allow Leibniz to hold that:

(a) The world is freely created by God, who has attributes of reason, moral perfection, and will, and who creates the world for the best of reasons, not arbitrarily or by logical necessity.

(b) This requires that the actual world must be the best of all possible worlds; and the created things that make up the world—the complete substances—must be genuinely created things, having their own active forces and tendencies that move them to act in accordance with their own principles.

As we will discuss next time, Leibniz views created things as moved by their own active powers, while he thinks that Descartes does not; and he sees created things not as Spinoza does, as mere attributes and modes of the one complete substance, but as genuine substances.

2. One way to present Leibniz's view is to think of him as starting from an idea of what a true proposition is. His basic thought might be said to be this:

A proposition is true if and only if the concept expressed by its predicate is contained in the concept expressed by its subject.

Thus Leibniz says: "[T]he predicate is present in the subject; or else I do not know what truth is."[5]

"Necessary and Contingent Truths" (ca. 1686) has a quite full statement of Leibniz's predicate-in-subject theory of truth. In the quotations from this essay below, the first asserts that all knowledge has an a priori reason for its truth; the second defines necessary truths as about the essences of things lying in the divine reason, and the third characterizes contingent truths as about the existence of things in space and time.

> 1. An affirmative truth is one whose predicate is in the subject; and so in every true affirmative proposition, necessary or contingent, universal or particular, the notion of the predicate is in some way contained in the notion of the subject. Moreover, it is contained in the notion of the subject in such a way that if anyone were to understand perfectly each of the two notions just as God understands it, he would by that very fact per-

5. *The Leibniz-Arnauld Correspondence*, ed. and trans. H. T. Mason (Manchester: Manchester University Press, 1967), letter of July 1686, p. 63.

ceive that the predicate is in the subject. From this it follows that all knowledge of propositions that is in God, whether it is simple knowledge, concerning the essence of things, or whether it is knowledge of vision, concerning the existence of things, or mediate knowledge concerning conditioned existences, results immediately from the perfect understanding of each term which can be the subject or predicate of any proposition. That is, the a priori knowledge of complexes arises from the understanding of that which is not complex.

2. An *absolutely necessary* proposition is one which can be resolved [in a finite number of steps] into identical propositions, or whose opposite implies a contradiction.

3. In the case of a contingent truth, even though the predicate is really in the subject, yet one never arrives at a demonstration or an identity, even though the resolution of each term is continued indefinitely. In such cases it is only God, who comprehends the infinite at once, who can see how the one is in the other, and can understand a priori the perfect reason for contingency; in creatures this is supplied a posteriori, by experience.

3. To explain: take the proposition "Caesar crossed the Rubicon," in which the subject is "Caesar." The proposition is contingent, since it concerns the existence of things: it refers to an individual at a time and place, namely, the historical individual Caesar. Its subject expresses the complete individual concept (or notion) of Caesar. (Leibniz holds that a proper name of an individual substance, e.g., "Caesar," expresses a complete individual concept.) The predicate term is "crossed the Rubicon," which expresses the complex attribute of crossing the Rubicon.

The proposition expressed by the sentence "Caesar crossed the Rubicon" is true if and only if the concept expressed by the predicate term, "crossed the Rubicon," is included in the complete individual concept expressed by the subject term, the proper name "Caesar."

Here by "included in" Leibniz means included in the complete analysis of all the attributes that make up the complete individual concept of Caesar. This complete individual concept, on Leibniz's view, includes everything that characterizes Caesar. It includes the attribute of crossing the Rubicon, of being the winner of the Battle of Pharsalus, of being dictator of Rome; and also of being descended after *n* generations from Adam, of being assassinated in Rome more than a century prior to Saint Paul's martyrdom there, and so on. Each substance (or monad), from its own point of view, mirrors the whole universe, past, present, and future; and therefore it mirrors down to the last detail the infinitely many aspects of the universe to which it belongs. As Leibniz even says at one place in his correspondence with Arnauld, "[E]ach possible individual of any one world contains in the concept of him the laws of his world" (Mason:43).

4. In subsection 2 above, I said that one way to present Leibniz's account of truth was to begin with his idea of a true proposition as one in which the concept of the predicate is in the concept of the subject. But another way to begin is to start with his idea of the complete concept of an individual thing, or monad (to use his term). To this end, let's think of a monad as represented by a complete list of all its properties, not only a complete list at any moment of time, but a complete list of all its properties for every moment of time. So when we say something true about a monad, the concept of the predicate must be in the concept of the subject, that is, it must appear somewhere on the complete (infinite) list that represents the monad.

Starting with this idea of an individual thing, or monad, how may we imagine that God selects the best of all possible worlds, and why should this process involve (as we look at it and not as God does) an infinite resolution that never ends? Begin first with what we may call *bare* monads: these are possibles (like all possibles) that lie in God's reason. Their mark is that their lists of properties do not contain any properties that reflect the properties of any (one or more) other monads. In a world consisting of two bare monads, say, neither monad reflects the other.

5. Next, imagine a world consisting of *partially reflecting* monads. Recall from the *Monadology* §7 that monads are windowless: that is, complete substances that do not causally affect one another. Nevertheless, they do reflect, or represent, one another's properties. Thus a world of partially reflecting monads is one in which, say, each monad reflects the properties of at least one or more of the other monads. No monad is completely self-contained, but some at least are partial in that there are some monads whose properties they do not reflect. From here, we move to a world of *completely reflecting*

monads. From the list of properties of any one monad, we can discern all the properties of all the other monads. Now, what distinguishes one monad from another is not that their lists of properties as such are different, but that the reflecting properties of each monad are indexed by the monad's point of view on the universe. Since each monad expresses the universe from its own point of view, the monads are distinct from one another, as can be seen from how their lists of reflecting properties are indexed.

Now, take a further step to a world of *time-coordinated* completely reflecting monads. By this I mean that the reflecting properties of each monad are listed in the right time sequence, so that the monads reflect one another's state at the appropriate moment: we thus have a world in which what Leibniz calls preestablished harmony is satisfied. We imagine, then, that God looks only at those worlds which satisfy this condition, the reason being that only the class of these worlds can contain the best of all possible worlds. Leibniz says in the *Monadology* (§§56, 58): "This interconnection . . . of all created things to each other, and each to all the others, brings it about that each simple substance has relations that express all the others . . . [and] each simple substance is a perpetual, living mirror of the universe. . . . And this is a way of obtaining as much variety as possible, but with the greatest order possible, that is, it is a way of obtaining as much perfection as possible."

In this sketch, I have supposed that bare monads and partially reflecting monads and the rest are possibles lying in the divine reason. The reason why only a world of time-coordinated and completely reflecting monads exists lies in God's free selection of the best of all possible worlds guided by the principle of perfection. This sketch also lays out why God's choice of the best world involves an infinity of comparisons going far beyond the capacity of any finite intelligence. We can see why, given Leibniz's idea of a monad, bare or otherwise, the concept of the predicate of all true propositions about a monad will be contained in the concept of its subject. And given the preestablished harmony of the best world, not only will the concept of the predicate of crossing the Rubicon be in the complete concept of Caesar, but also so will the concept of the predicate of being assassinated in Rome a century before Saint Paul's martyrdom there.

6. With his theory of truth and his conception of monads as mirroring the universe each from its own point of view, Leibniz explains the principle

of sufficient reason, and the distinction between necessary and contingent truths, thus:

(a) Every proposition must be either true or false.

(b) A proposition is true or false in virtue of the relation concept-inclusion (as explained above) between the concepts expressed by its subject and predicate terms: true when the inclusion relation holds, false otherwise.

(c) Therefore, for every true proposition, of whatever kind, there exists an a priori proof of it (known to God). This proof takes the form, in general, of an analysis of the concept expressed by the subject term carried to the point where this concept is seen to include the concept expressed in the predicate term. (*Discourse*:§13; and "Necessary and Contingent Truths," paragraph 1).

(d) In those cases where the a priori proof of the proposition can be carried out in a finite number of steps, and the last step of the proof reduces the proposition to an identity (such as *A* is *A,* etc.), so that its denial would violate the Principle of Contradiction, the proposition is a necessary truth. Its contradictory is impossible. It is true in any world that God might have created: it is true in all possible worlds, so understood. We can know these finitely demonstrable truths about the essences of things, about numbers and geometrical objects, and about moral goodness and justice ("Necessary and Contingent Truths," paragraphs 1 and 2).

(e) In those cases where the a priori proof of the proposition cannot be carried out in a finite number of steps, but rather involves the infinite analysis of an infinitely complex complete individual concept, and even infinitely many comparisons of other worlds that God might have created, the proposition is contingent and its truth depends on the Principle of the Best. Carrying out the proof would require an analysis taking infinitely many steps, which can never be completed. God doesn't see the end of the analysis, for the analysis has no end. But only God sees the answer—by God's intuitive vision of the possibles all at once.

§5. Some Comments on Leibniz's Account of Truth

1. First, the statement (c) above is one form of the Principle of Sufficient Reason: it says that every true proposition has an a priori proof of its truth.

Leibniz often uses this name, "the Principle of Sufficient Reason," to refer to various less general principles. The form above is, I think, the most general form of the principle. Thus he says: "There are two first principles of all reasonings, the principle of contradiction . . . and the principle that a reason must be given, that is, that every true proposition which is known per se, has an a priori proof, or that a reason can be given for every truth, or as is commonly said, that nothing happens without a cause. Arithmetic and geometry do not need this principle, but physics and mechanics do."[6]

Another quotation brings out how contingent truths depend on God's decrees and choice of the best of all possible worlds.

The demonstration of this predicate of Caesar [that he resolved to cross the Rubicon] is not as absolute as are those of numbers or of geometry, but presupposes the series of things which God has chosen freely, and which is founded on the first decree of God, namely to do always what is most perfect, and on the decree which God has made [in consequence of the first], in regard to human nature, that man will always do (though freely) what appears best. . . . [E]very truth which is founded on decrees of this kind is contingent, although it is certain. (*Discourse:*§13 [Ariew and Garber:46])

2. A second comment on Leibniz's account of truth is that today we use the term "a priori" as an epistemological term. It says something about how a proposition can be known, namely, that it can be known independently of experience. But this is not Leibniz's idea of the a priori: when he says that true propositions have an a priori proof, he means a proof based on the ultimate reasons for their being true and not false. Clearly Leibniz does not mean that we (human beings) can know contingent propositions to be true independent of experience. The proofs he has in mind can be known only by God, because only God sees by intuitive vision of the possible existences the answer to the requisite infinite analysis.

A further comment, related to the preceding one, is that Leibniz's con-

---

6. Gerhardt, *Philosophischen Schriften,* VII:309, in *Leibniz Selections,* ed. Philip R. Weiner (New York: Scribners, 1951), p. 94.

ception of the contingent is, we might say, proof-theoretic.[7] That is, it draws the distinction between necessary and contingent true propositions according to how they can be, or are, established by someone who is omniscient. This is seen from how he uses the conception of contingency and by his saying, for example, in referring to the Principle of Sufficient Reason, that "the principle that nothing ever happens without the possibility that an omniscient mind could give some reason why it should have happened rather than not" (Bodeman's *Catalogue of Leibniz's* MSS [1895], in Wiener: 95). And he says in "Necessary and Contingent Truths" (4.2) that "existential or contingent propositions differ entirely from these [the eternal truths about essences]. Their truth is understood a priori by the infinite mind alone, and cannot be demonstrated by any resolution." These quotations show the extent to which Leibniz's distinction between necessary and contingent truths looks at the question from God's point of view.

3. A third comment: it is tempting to object that Leibniz's account of contingency in terms of proofs requiring an infinite analysis that only God can see the answer to does not give us a real, bona fide conception of contingency. The contingency that we complain is missing is perhaps that of brute fact: that is, a fact that simply has no explanation even when everything is known, as, for example, the ultimate laws of nature, should there be such. That conception of contingency, though, is precisely what Leibniz rejects: it violates his principle of sufficient reason. This principle requires that the world must be fully intelligible through and through, not to us, admittedly, but to a perfect infinite intelligence. Thus the ultimate laws of nature, even as subordinate maxims, will manifest an appropriate perfection. Leibniz believes that the laws of physics do this in the form of principles of conservation, for example, as well as of maximum and minimum principles leading to the calculus of variations (*Discourse*:§§19–22). Nothing is opaque to God. That our world satisfies this condition is part of Christian faith (no doubt of other faiths as well). It is also a thesis of idealism.

A last comment: above we reviewed two beginnings for Leibniz's account of the predicate-in-subject doctrine. One was the idea of a true proposition as one whose predicate concept is in the subject concept; the other

---

7. See R. M. Adams, "Leibniz's Theory of Contingency," in *Leibniz: Critical and Interpretative Essays*, ed. M. Hooker (Minneapolis: University of Minnesota Press, 1982), pp. 259ff.

was the idea of a monad as a windowless form of mental life specified completely by a list of all its properties over time. It is natural to ask which of these is better, and which came first in Leibniz's mind.

Concerning the last question, I have no opinion, though a study of further texts might give an answer. I think, though, the second idea, beginning with windowless monads, may be better: it goes deeper into Leibniz's overall doctrine, and together with the idea of perfection it enables us to see quite easily why the predicate-in-subject doctrine holds of all true affirmative contingent propositions. So I think it to be more instructive and in any case sufficient to render Leibniz's view intelligible. Certainly he has additional ideas in mind, as his use of the analogy to an infinite series shows;[8] note his mention of surd relations and of showing that the error is less than any assignable quantity ("Necessary and Contingent Truths," paragraph 3). But I don't think that these other things are necessary to give sense to the predicate-in-subject doctrine. The elementary intuitive idea of monads as discussed above seems sufficient to do that.

Note in conclusion that obviously Leibniz's theory of truth is framed for his philosophical theology and its apologetic aims. It is not an account of how we, human beings, learn the meaning and reference of the terms in our language and apply them in everyday life. Certainly Leibniz could not have been unaware of this. But for him, that is not the point. He is not trying to explain our use of language, how its terms get their meaning and reference. Rather, he wants to maintain certain very general considerations about all truths seen as fully accessible only from God's point of view. He thinks that our actual language hooks up suitably in some way with these truths; and this enables us to understand his theory. And that is enough for his purposes. It is not what we think of today as philosophy of language, however suggestive and valuable it might be for that.

---

8. What these ideas might be are instructively discussed by John Carriero in "Leibniz on Infinite Resolution and Intra-mundane Contingency, Part One: Infinite Resolution," *Studia Leibnitiana* 25 (1993), pp. 1–26.

Spirits as Active Substances: Their Freedom

§1. The Complete Individual Concept Includes Active Powers

1. Leibniz's predicate-in-subject account of truth, which we took up last time in sections 4–5, with its distinction between necessary and contingent truths, serves his purposes provided that it helps him to maintain two things:

(a) The world is freely created by God, who has attributes of reason, moral perfection, and will, and who creates the world for the best of reasons, not arbitrarily or by logical necessity.

(b) This requires that the actual world must be the best of all possible worlds, and that the created things that make up the world—the complete substances—must be genuinely created things, having their own active forces and tendencies that move them to act in accordance with their own principles.

Now, Leibniz believes that to speak of God's, or anyone's, free choice, there must exist alternatives: this is a necessary condition of freedom. Thus he thinks of the best of all possible worlds, and other less favored worlds, including ones with much evil, as possible and of God's choice of the best as contingent. But how are we to understand a possible world?

Following Robert Adams's suggestion, perhaps the clearest explanation is to form the basic concept of a possible world just as we form the complete concept of an individual.[1] Such a concept of an individual contains in itself

1. See R. M. Adams, "Leibniz's Theory of Contingency," in Hooker, *Leibniz: Critical and Interpretative Essays*, pp. 247f.

no contradiction: it has a consistent description. We get the basic concept of a possible world by combining into a world a plurality of individuals, or monads, and by supposing relations between the monads to be arranged by preestablished harmony. Should this be done so that the world so conceived has a consistent description and contains no contradiction, then Leibniz says it is possible in itself. So long as we specify possible worlds without bringing in God's choice of the best, we avoid any complications arising from the fact that God's choice of the best possible world is in some way necessary. It is at least morally necessary, that is, practically necessary as required by moral reasons or by God's moral perfections. But I avoid the tangles of this question, which troubled Leibniz and which he seems never to have resolved.[2] I don't know if he thought that the proposition that God creates the best world is contingent, though he did think it morally necessary.

2. To satisfy condition (b) above, Leibniz hopes his predicate-in-subject view of truth enables him to regard complete individual substances as genuinely created things, and for this they must have active powers of their own. This is essential for him in the case of spirits (minds with reason and will), for it enables them to think, deliberate, and act on their own, and to be spontaneously active, voluntarily moved, and able to follow the dictates of their reason. The succession of thoughts, feelings, and actions that they undergo must not be merely lifeless happenings—simply part of the divine picture show—as Leibniz thinks is the case, in their different ways, with Descartes and Spinoza.

To explain Leibniz's criticisms of Descartes and Spinoza, let's begin by asking what a complete individual concept, where the substance in question is a spirit, is a concept of. Suppose first that we think of the complete individual concept of Caesar as a complete story of Caesar's life. (Let's restrict ourselves to this for simplicity.) The story starts with Caesar's birth at such and such a time, his crossing the Rubicon, his assassination, and the rest. To this we add the story of Caesar's thoughts, feelings, desires, perceptions, and so on. And much else: the story recounts a complete and full sequence of events over the life of Caesar. Think of this life as the complete film of Caesar, as it were. Given this story, we suppose that when God creates

2. See ibid., pp. 266–272.

Caesar, God creates the frames in this film, each frame smoothly following the preceding ones, so that we have a continuous appearance of a life.

On this view, the concept of an individual substance is the concept of a (possible) complete story of a life. A life is regarded as a continuous sequence of frames; the frames are, so to speak, pictures, and have in themselves no active powers. This is how Leibniz sees both Cartesian occasionalism and Spinoza's view of the world as one substance with its infinitely many attributes and modes.

3. Leibniz's idea of a complete individual concept is quite different. This concept is not that of a story of a life told, say, in film, but the concept of an active substance with powers of its own, so that, from within itself and its total present state, it deliberates and acts, and moves spontaneously and voluntarily to another state in accordance with its own peculiar law. Leibniz views the complete individual concept as it lies in God's intellect as including the concepts of these powers. Thus Leibniz says of our world: "If this world were only possible, the individual concept of a body in this world, containing certain movements as possibilities, would also contain our laws of motion . . . but . . . as mere possibilities. . . . [E]ach possible individual of any world contains in the concept of him the laws of his world" (*Leibniz-Arnauld Correspondence*, p. 43).

At the initial creation of the individual substance, God actualizes but does not create these active powers that are part of the complete concept, as God's decrees do not change a concept's content but simply give it being. These active powers then cause the successive changes of state over time and act in accordance with certain principles and laws that characterize the individual in question.

In the case of physics, these laws are sufficiently simple so that we can foresee the future states and configurations of physical systems from a knowledge of their present states. (I skip Leibniz's account of this; see his sketch in the *Discourse*:§§17–22 and in the *New System*.) With spirits, however, this is impossible: while there exist principles from which the thoughts and actions of spirits can be foreseen by God, these principles are, in general, unknown to us. They may, as I understand Leibniz, be different for different individuals, although there are some common principles (for example, that we choose in accordance with the greatest apparent good). I believe, however, that Leibniz rejects the idea that natural science or social thought can establish principles and laws from which our decisions and actions can in general be predicted. In practical decisions, our task is to do the best we can to deliberate and to choose wisely (*Discourse*:§§10, 30). I come back to this below.

4. Now, as I have said, Leibniz associates the idea of a life as a picture show with Descartes and Spinoza. He thinks that this idea denies genuine creation, for according to it, spirits are not independent and freely active substances. Leibniz argues for active powers in his critique of Cartesian physics. Since Descartes defined body simply as extension and motion as merely the change of place of a body in space (relative to other bodies), Leibniz thought that Descartes could not give a correct account of the basic dynamic principles of mechanics. For in Cartesian physics, nothing in the nature of body, as extension only, can explain inertia or resistance, or account for acceleration and its relation to force. Descartes seems to have thought that the laws of inertia and of motion in a straight line (in the absence of other bodies) are consequences of God's immutability and of God's preserving the same quantity of motion.[3]

Of course, Leibniz believed with Descartes that God sustains created substances and maintains them in existence. We are always dependent on God. But he insists that God creates substances as having certain active powers and tendencies on which the first principles and laws of physics are founded; and this does not involve the continual creation and re-creation of things by God in ways that directly reflect the divine nature. For example, Leibniz says such things as the following in comments on a dissertation by John Christopher Sturm, *De Idolo Naturae*. Sturm had said that the movements of things that take place now are the result of an eternal law once decreed by God, and that there is no need of a new command of God now. Leibniz thinks this view is still ambiguous (Wiener:142): "For I ask if . . . this command . . . decreed originally, attributed to things only an *extrinsic denomination;* or if, in forming them, it created in them some permanent impression, . . . an *indwelling* law (although it is most often unknown to the creatures in whom it resides), whence proceed all actions and all pas-

<hr>

3. Leibniz's argument against Descartes can be found in two short papers in the *Journal des Savans* in 1691 and 1693, and in a letter to Father Bouvet, reprinted in Wiener, 100–105; see also the two selections in Ariew and Garber, 245–256.

sions" (*On Nature Itself; or On the Force Residing in Created Things and their Actions* [1698]).

Leibniz goes on to say that the former view seems to be that of the Cartesians (occasionalism), while the latter seems to be the most true. He adds (ibid.:142): "This past decree does not exist at present [so] it can produce nothing now unless it then left after it some perduring effect, which now still continues and operates. . . . [I]t is not sufficient . . . that in creating things . . . God willed that they should observe a certain law in their progress, if . . . no lasting effect was produced in them. And assuredly it is contrary to the notion of the divine power and will . . . that God should will and nevertheless in willing produce . . . nothing; that he is always acting and never effecting; that . . . *he leaves no work.*"

Leibniz believes we must say that (ibid.:143) "the law decreed by God left some trace of itself impressed on things; if things were so formed . . . as to render them fit to accomplish the will of the legislator, then . . . a certain . . . form or force . . . is impressed on things, whence proceeds the series of phenomena according to the prescription of the first command." Again (ibid.:144f.): "The very substance of things consists in their power of acting and suffering, whence it follows that not even durable things can be produced if a force of some permanence cannot be impressed upon them by the divine power," for otherwise (ibid.:145) "all things would be only certain passing or evanescent modifications, and . . . apparitions, of one permanent and divine substance."

This last remark suggests the idea above of a divine picture show, a "pernicious doctrine" that Leibniz attributes to Spinoza. And with it we conclude our review of Leibniz's account of the active powers of monads, and so of their genuine, internal spontaneity. As we shall see, this spontaneity is a further necessary condition of the true freedom of rational spirits.

§2. Spirits as Individual Rational Substances

1. We have seen that Leibniz wants to maintain that substances genuinely act from powers and principles present in them and that are to be counted as their own. In addition, he also holds that in the case of rational spirits

capable of deliberation, these principles and powers are not explicable by physics and social thought. Self-conscious and rational minds have various distinctive powers and principles of action of which they are at least partly, though as we shall see not fully, aware. As already noted, one such principle is that spirits act for the sake of the greatest apparent good (*Discourse:* §30:1). The upshot is that the complete concept of an individual rational substance has in it the concept of its active powers and impressed principles with its laws of development.

To this we can add that not only are these principles and laws not explicable by physics and social science, but also there is a complete concept of an individual spirit (as a possible individual) paired with any kind of free and spontaneous and reasoned self-conscious and self-determined life that we can imagine and consistently describe. And if we can so describe it, God would bring it into existence, should the individual specified by this concept belong to the best of all possible worlds. I believe that Leibniz would say that his system allows the real possibility of the most free and self-determined and reasoned life that we can imagine without contradiction. Call such a life true freedom. Then he would say his doctrine does not exclude it.

To be fair to Leibniz, it is important to stress this point. Of course, here I abstract from the foreknowledge God has of our actions, including God's foreknowledge of our thoughts and the course of our future deliberations. I shall not discuss the question whether God's foreknowledge is incompatible with our freedom. I mean to leave this aside, as Leibniz does in effect: when we are deciding what to do, these philosophical problems have no practical relevance. Of course, God foresees our thoughts and actions, but there is no possible way that our deliberations and conduct can be foreseen or predicted by natural science or social thought, however much we may know. Nor can it be foreseen by us ("Necessary and Contingent Truths," paragraph 7). Our task as spirits is always to decide by reason and deliberation as we seek to identify the greatest apparent good (*Discourse:*§§10, 30).

2. These points need further elaboration. In discussing miracles and the actions of God on the substances of individuals, Leibniz distinguishes between general order and universal laws as being above what he calls "subordinate maxims" (*Discourse:*§16). The subordinate maxims I take to be the laws of physics and of the other natural sciences. These are simple enough

to be known by us. And while miracles may be inconsistent with those laws, they are not inconsistent with the general order and universal laws of God's creation. Leibniz says (*Discourse:*§16): "I say that God's miracles and extraordinary concourses of God have the peculiarity that they cannot be foreseen by the reasoning of any created spirit, no matter how enlightened, because the distinct comprehension of the general order surpasses all of them. On the other hand, everything that we call natural depends on the less general maxims that creatures can understand." He says in *New System* §5:

> We must not be indifferent to the different grades of minds or reasonable souls, the higher orders being incomparably more perfect than those forms buried in matter, being like little Gods by contrast with the latter, and are made in the image of God. . . . That is why God governs minds as a Prince governs his subjects, and even as a father cares for his children, whereas he disposes of other substances as an engineer manipulates his machines. Thus minds have particular laws which put them above the revolutions of matter; and we may say that everything else is made only for them. (Wiener:108–109)

And in §8: "Reasonable souls follow much higher laws and are exempt from anything which might make them lose the quality of being citizens of a society of spirits. [This society I take to be the City of God]" (Wiener:110).

These and other passages suggest that Leibniz holds that for us there is no way to use the laws of nature (the subordinate maxims) to foresee the thoughts and deliberations of rational spirits. We know certain general principles, such as that we choose in accordance with the greatest apparent good, but that does not tell us anything specific about actual choices. But the question remains as to how we are to think of the higher laws that Leibniz says reasonable spirits follow.

3. Perhaps we can say something like this. In the *Discourse* §6, Leibniz distinguishes between the ordinary and extraordinary actions of God, and he maintains that God does nothing out of order. What passes for the extraordinary is so only with respect to an order already established; everything conforms to the (highest) universal order. He also says that there is nothing so irregular that we cannot find a concept, a rule, or an equation

to characterize it. Thus: "If someone drew in one stroke a line which was now straight, now circular, now of another nature, it is possible to find a concept, a rule, or an equation common to all the points on the line, in virtue of which these same changes must occur. . . . [T]here is no face . . . the outline of which does not form part of a geometrical line and cannot be traced in one stroke by a certain movement according to a rule. But when a rule is complex what conforms to it passes for irregular."

Leibniz is careful to add that he does not by these remarks claim to explain anything; he is concerned with how we may think about the world for pious and religious purposes. Still, one finds here, I think, the thought that each rational soul has its own particular principle that governs its active powers and free spiritual life (free because it shares in reason, both intellectual and deliberative).[4] Nevertheless, the world remains orderly even though those principles and powers are distinct for each spirit (person), despite certain common features.

Leibniz even says the following in "Necessary and Contingent Truths," paragraph 6: "Free or intelligent spirits . . . possess something greater and more marvellous, in a kind of imitation of God. For they are not bound by any particular subordinate laws of the universe, but act as it were by private miracle, on the sole initiative of their own power and by looking towards a final cause they interrupt . . . the course of efficient causes that act on their will . . . so that, in the case of minds, no subordinate universal laws can be established (as is possible in the case of [physical] bodies) which suffice for predicting a mind's choice."

I conclude, then, that Leibniz thought that God specified a particular, or private, law for each rational spirit. Let's say that this principle expresses a spirit's individuality: it characterizes its distinctive individuality as it expresses its particular form of life and the point of view from which it mirrors the universe. Given the principle of Fourier series for rational spirits, the range of these possible principles is wide enough to allow for any form of intellectual and moral life that we can consistently describe. This is why I said above that Leibniz believes that his system has room for all forms of

4. Call this the principle of Fourier series for free spirits. [Fourier analysis uses certain infinite series—Fourier series—to find functions that approximate periodic data.—Ed.]

free moral life. It can admit whatever criteria we think are required for such a life, provided that their application can be coherently described.

§3. True Freedom

1. To this point (in §§1–2), we have looked at two elements in Leibniz's view of the freedom of rational spirits: their spontaneity and their individuality. While Kant and others have found his view of human freedom unsatisfactory, I want to present it in the most favorable way I can so that we can see where the conflict between them really lay. As in any important case, this is never easy to do, and we may not succeed.

Now, on the question of freedom, Leibniz is a determinist and a compatibilist: he sees no incompatibility between freedom and a certain special kind of determinism. I say a special kind of determinism because it is natural to object that his view seems much like Spinoza's. But Leibniz's answer is that it is mistaken to object to determinism as such: what matters is the nature of the ultimate and active powers that do the determining. On his view, these ultimate and active powers are the wisdom and moral perfections of God, joined with God's greatness (power and omniscience). This means that true thought and sound moral judgment shape the final course of the world and determine its form and structure. Moreover, rational spirits are spontaneous and individual, expressing their own forms of life. Beyond this, the determinants of their thought and judgment can be sound reasoning and deliberation. He says, in his familiar account of freedom in *Theodicy* §288 (see §288–290, 303) that

> freedom . . . consists in intelligence, which involves a clear knowledge of the objects of deliberation, in spontaneity, whereby we determine, and in contingency, that is, in the exclusion of logical and metaphysical necessity. Intelligence is, as it were, the soul of freedom, and the rest is as its body and foundation. The free substance is self-determining and that according to the motive and good perceived by the understanding, which inclines it without compelling it; and all the conditions of freedom are comprised in these few words. It is nevertheless well to point

out that the imperfection present in our knowledge and our spontaneity, and the infallible determination that is involved in our contingency,
destroy neither freedom nor contingency.

Here Leibniz states three conditions for a free action: intelligence, spontaneity, and contingency, to which we may add individuality. Expressed
more fully, they are: intelligence, which is a clear knowledge of the object
of deliberation; spontaneity, whereby we ourselves determine the action
done (and in a manner distinctive of ourselves); and contingency, that is, the
absence of logical or metaphysical necessity. This last means the existence of
alternatives. Freedom is impossible if there is only one choice.

2. In *Theodicy* §289, Leibniz explains the meaning of intelligence as follows:

> Our knowledge is of two kinds, distinct and confused. Distinct knowl
> edge, or *intelligence*, occurs in the actual use of reason; but the senses
> supply us with confused thoughts. And we may say that we are im
> mune from bondage in so far as we act with a distinct knowledge, but
> that we are the slaves of passion in so far as our perceptions are con
> fused. . . . Yet a slave, slave as he is, nevertheless has freedom to choose
> according to state wherein he is. . . . [T]hat evil state of the slave,
> which is also our own, does not prevent us, any more than him, from
> making a free choice of that which pleases us most.

As for spontaneity, Leibniz asserts the doctrine we discussed (in §1),
namely, that each of us, as a complete substance, has within us the source
of our actions. By preestablished harmony, external things have no influence upon us. Although this is true, Leibniz is careful to say, it is true only
in a strictly philosophical sense. The point is that spontaneity is common
to us and all simple substances; in intelligent or free substances, spontaneity
is mastery over actions. Further, in §291, Leibniz writes: "Its individuality
consists in the perpetual law which brings about the sequence of perceptions
that are assigned to it, springing naturally from one another, to represent
the body that is allotted to it, and through its instrumentality the entire
universe, in accordance with the point of view proper to this simple substance."

I mention again that the individuality of a free substance (and of others as well) consists in its own distinctive principle or law that characterizes the sequences of their states (of perception, apperception, and thought) over time.

3. Finally, we come to contingency as the presence of alternatives. Leibniz had often been confronted with an objection that says: God chooses the best of necessity. The world that is the best is the best of necessity. Therefore, it is necessary that if God chooses any world, God chooses this (our) world. So God's choice is not free.

To this Leibniz made the following reply: a world that is not chosen nevertheless remains possible in its own nature. This is so even if it is not possible with respect to the divine will. Earlier we defined a world as possible in its own nature if its description does not imply a contradiction. This allows that its coexistence with God does imply a contradiction. Thus Leibniz is arguing that in creating our world, God's choice is free because there are many worlds to choose from, and each (having a consistent description) is possible in its own nature. The contingency condition is satisfied.

[Addendum: There is a good discussion of this point in Sleigh, *Leibniz and Arnauld: A Commentary on Their Correspondence*, pp. 8off. Sleigh observes that crucial to Leibniz's argument is the following. The inference from 'it is metaphysically necessary that if p then q' together with 'it is metaphysically necessary that p' to 'it is metaphysically necessary that q' is a good inference. It is a case where necessity of the consequence gives necessity of the consequent. However, the inference from 'it is metaphysically necessary that if p then q' together with 'it is necessary in its own nature that p' to 'it is necessary in its own nature that q' is not a valid inference.]

4. To conclude: we have seen that for Leibniz it is mistaken to say that being determined to seek the best is to lack freedom. Regarding this matter, he says (in the Summary added to the end of the *Theodicy*) the following:

> I deny the major of this argument [Whoever cannot fail to choose the best is not free]. Rather is it true freedom, and the most perfect, to be able to make the best use of one's free will, and always to exercise this power, without being turned aside either by outward force [freedom to act] or by inward passions [freedom to will], whereof the one enslaves our bodies and the other our souls. There is nothing less servile and

more befitting the highest degree of freedom than to be always led towards the good, and always by one's own inclination, without any constraint and without any displeasure. (Objection VIII, paragraph 1)

For Leibniz, what is important is that God's freedom so understood, and our freedom as imperfect approximations to God's, should be fundamental causes both in the world and in our life. All this is in contrast to Spinoza, who, Leibniz thought, held that there are no final causes in nature, and that while we think of things as good and evil according to how they affect us, God is indifferent to them. Moreover, in Spinoza's scheme, as Leibniz understands it, there is no such thing as divine choice: for by necessity of the divine nature and its infinity, everything possible must be actual, and so there is nothing to choose. Choice presupposes alternatives: a choice selects this over that. It has no place when everything possible must be.

Whatever we think of Leibniz's determinist and compatibilist account of human freedom, he thought that his view was very different from Spinoza's.

§4. Reason, Judgment, and Will

1. In the previous quotation from the *Theodicy* (from paragraph 1 of Objection VIII), Leibniz refers to true freedom. I have used this phrase to refer to his account, as far as we can make it out, of what he thinks of as the fullest and most complete form of freedom as it might be shown in human life. So far we have considered four main elements of it: spontaneity, individuality, intelligence, and contingency. Now I look at some further details of those elements; one way to do this is to see what he says about reasoned deliberation, judgment, and certain aspects of free will.

We saw last time (§5.1) that Leibniz says (in *Discourse*:§13) that, as a consequence of God's first decree always to do what is most perfect, God's second decree, in regard to human nature, is that we will always do (though freely) what appears to us best. Leibniz holds what he refers to as the old axioms that the will follows the greatest good and that it flies from the greatest evil that it perceives (*New Essays*, Bk. II, Ch. XXI, §31).

And in *Discourse* §30 he says that by virtue of God's decree, "[t]he will should always tend to the [greatest] apparent good, expressing or imitating the will of God in certain particular respects with regard to which this apparent good always has some truth in it." In this way, "God determines our will to the choice of that which seems the better, nevertheless without necessitating it."

The first thing we can say, then, is that our guiding principle of deliberation is to ascertain, to the best of our ability, what is the greatest apparent good. This is the object of deliberation in true freedom. How far we achieve true freedom, rather than simply the freedom we commonly have, depends on how far we succeed in attaining a distinct knowledge of the greatest apparent good and overcoming the usual imperfections in our thinking and spontaneity.

2. Before we proceed to other elements in Leibniz's idea of true freedom, this is a good place to consider the phrase he often uses, "incline without necessitating," a phrase said of the reasons for doing something. (Recall from *Theodicy* §288 above the phrase "inclines . . . without compelling.") It is here that Leibniz's predicate-in-subject theory of truth with its account of contingency may enter his moral psychology. In one place he says: "There is the same proportion between necessity and inclination that there is in the mathematicians' analysis between exact equations and limits that give an approximation" (G. Grua, ed. and comp., G. W. Leibniz, *Textes inedits d'après les manuscrits de la Bibliothèque provinciale de Hanovre* [Paris, 1948]:479).

Here I believe there are several thoughts. One is the idea of a deliberative judgment as balancing the reasons that incline us to either side, pro or con. These reasons are indefinitely many, even possibly infinitely many. Certainly this is true of God's decision in creating the best possible world. For God's antecedent will, which looks to all particular goods and evils taken separately (though infinite in number), precedes God's consequent will, which is given by the divine judgment, all things considered, as the final decree (*Vindication*:§§24–27).

That decree reflects an infinite analysis; it is in that sense contingent, although, of course, as Leibniz says, it is also certain. In our case, it seems best to say that the reasons entering our deliberations are, in principle, open, or indefinitely many, although in practice a few reasons may be sufficiently conclusive for us to act.

3. A second thought is this: Leibniz thinks of the reasons and motives

that enter into our decisions as including all kinds of inclinations and perceptions, subconscious as well as conscious. For as complete substances we have latent in us expressions of everything in the universe from our point of view. These expressions we may experience simply as perceptions (which is actually confused knowledge) and inclinations. Thus, commenting on Locke's view that what moves us is uneasiness, he says (*New Essays*:II:xxi: §39): "Various perceptions and inclinations combine to produce a complete volition; it is the result of the conflict amongst them. There are some, imperceptible in themselves, which add up to a disquiet which impels us without our seeing why. There are some that join forces to carry us towards or away from some object, in which case there is desire or fear. . . . The eventual result of all these impulses is the prevailing effort, which makes a full volition."

The crucial point here is that while we pursue the greatest apparent good, what we perceive as that good is affected by our perceptions and inclinations; but these in turn mirror the infinite complexity of the universe, which our nature expresses. So our decisions are influenced by the way the rest of the universe affects us, not by clear knowledge, but in confused perceptions and inclinations (*Discourse*:§33; *Nature and Grace*:§13). Since our minds are finite, we can never fully grasp the infinite influences that shape our conduct, even when we have reached the highest degree of perfection possible for us. In the fullest sense, true freedom is always beyond us, at least in this life.

4. Relevant here is the argument Leibniz uses to reject the possibility of the freedom of equipoise. He wants to rebut the idea that free will can involve a perfectly balanced equilibrium of reasons pro and con, which allows the will to make the decision. (This is sometimes called the freedom of indifference.) Leibniz wants to hold instead (letter to Coste, 1707, in Ariew and Garber:194) that "with respect to the will in general, . . . choice follows the greatest inclination (by which I understand both passions and reasons, true or apparent)."

But to hold this he needs to maintain that a greatest inclination always exists. This he does by saying that we can never be in a state of perfect equilibrium of reasons pro and con. That idea is chimerical, he says, as the universe cannot be divided into two equal parts each of which might impinge on us equally (ibid., Ariew and Garber:195): "The universe has no center, and its parts are infinitely varied; thus, the case never arises in which everything is perfectly equal and strikes us equally on all sides. And although we are not always capable of perceiving all the small impressions that contribute to determining us, there is always something that determines us [to choose] between contradictories, without the case being perfectly equal on all sides."

To conclude: both in God's case and in ours, reasons incline without necessitating in view of the infinity of possible reasons involved. By intuitive vision of the possible existence of things, God sees the answer, the complete analysis, and acts with full understanding. Whereas we not only cannot complete the analysis but also can never comprehend the infinite complexity of the causes of our perceptions and inclinations, and how they influence our desires and aversions, and thereby our view of the apparent good. So to say that God determines the will to the choice of that which appears best, yet without necessitating it, seems to mean that our making that choice is not necessary but contingent (in view of Leibniz's predicate-in-subject account of truth). It is on these lines, I think, that the phrase "incline without necessitating" (*Discourse:*§§13, 30) is to be understood.

5. I now shift to other aspects of Leibniz's account of rational deliberation and their connection with his view of freedom. In the *New Essays* (II: xxi), Leibniz gives one of his fullest discussions as he comments on Locke's view in his chapter on power and freedom also in II:xxi of *An Essay Concerning Human Understanding*. I review some of the more relevant points.

In section 8 he notes the ambiguity of the term "freedom." He distinguishes between freedom in law and freedom in fact. In law the slave is not free and a subject is not entirely free, yet the rich and the poor are equally free in this sense. Whereas freedom in fact consists either in the power to do what one wills or chooses to do, or in the power to do as one should.

He says to Locke that his topic is freedom to do and that there are different degrees and kinds of this. He adds: "Speaking *generally,* a man is free to do what he wills in proportion as he has the means to do so; but there is also a *special* meaning in which 'freedom' is a matter of having the use of things which are customarily in our power, and above all with the free use of our body . . . [so] that a prisoner is not free . . . and . . . a paralytic does not have the free use of his limbs."

Leibniz goes on in section 8 to distinguish freedom to do from what he calls freedom to will. This he understands in two senses. One of these we have just examined, simply the idea that our will in its deliberations is contingent in the sense that reasons incline without necessitating.[5] The other sense is that our mind in its deliberations is free from the imperfections, or the bondage, that may arise from the passions. In this sense, the Stoics held that only the wise man is free. To achieve this inner freedom, we must be able to will as we should, that is, with proper deliberation. He says (§8): "It is in that way that God alone is perfectly free, and that created minds are free only in proportion as they are above passion; and this is a kind of freedom which pertains strictly to our understanding."

6. From all this, it seems clear that, for Leibniz, what is fundamental in true freedom is freedom of the understanding. For while we can will only the apparent good (what we think good), "the more developed the faculty of understanding is the better are the choices of the will" (§19). And again (§21): "[T]he question is not whether a man can do what he wills to do but whether his will is sufficiently independent. It is not a question . . . whether his legs are free . . . but whether he has a free mind and what it consists in. On this way of looking at things, intelligences will differ in how free they are, and the supreme Intelligence will possess a perfect freedom of which created beings are not capable."

But how is freedom of the understanding to be achieved? One way, surely, is by gaining control of our passions and appetites. Much of II:xxi is taken up with Leibniz's numerous suggestions about how we can escape from their bondage and achieve greater moral perfection. He considers how by forming appropriate resolutions and habits, and by having a sound way of reasoning in practical matters, we can gradually master and control our passions and inclinations. And this we can do as the mind may use various devices to make one desire prevail over another (§40; cf. §47; Discourse:§30 [Ariew and Garber:61]; letter to Coste [Ariew and Garber:195]): "Since the

5. He says: "[T]he strongest reasons or impressions which the understanding presents to the will do not prevent the act of will from being contingent, and do not confer upon it an absolute or (so to speak) metaphysical necessity. It is in this sense that I always say that the understanding can determine the will, in accordance with the perceptions and reasons that prevail, in a manner which, although it is certain and infallible, inclines without necessitating."

final result is determined by how things weigh against one another . . . the most pressing disquiet [may] not prevail . . . it may be outweighed by all of them taken together. The mind can avail itself of the trick of 'dichoto- mies', to make first one prevail and then another; just as in a meeting one can ensure that one faction prevails by getting a majority of votes, through the order in which one puts the questions to a vote." But we have to set up these devices in advance, "for once the battle has been engaged there is no time left to make use of such artifices: everything which then impinges on us weighs in the balance and contributes to determining a *resultant direc- tion*, almost as in mechanics; so that without some prompt diversion we will be unable to stop it."

It is best if we proceed methodically in deliberation, adhering to ways of thought indicated by reason rather than by chance. It helps also to have a practice of withdrawing into oneself occasionally, and asking oneself, "Where am I going?" "How far have I come?" or reminding oneself to come to the point and set to work (§47). It is through such methods and strata- gems that we become masters of ourselves. For Leibniz, true happiness ought to be the object of our desires, but unless appetite is directed by reason, we endeavor after present rather than lasting pleasure, which is happiness (§51). This power of deliberative reason resembles Hume's strength of mind: "the prevalence of the calm passions above the violent" (*Treatise*:418). And Leibniz might give a similar account of how it develops.

§5. A Note on the Practical Point of View

1. Before moving back again to Kant, let's observe that when we deliberate and try to reach the best decision, we should never, on Leibniz's view, be concerned with trying to predicate, or foresee, what we will decide. To do that would not be to deliberate but to do something else. In any event, what we will do cannot be ascertained by the laws of nature or social thought—and I assume that these include the laws of psychology, if there are such. It is true that God knows what we will decide, but that knowledge is beyond us and has no relevance for reasoned deliberation here and now. He says (*Discourse*:§30): "Perhaps it is certain from all eternity that I shall

sin? Answer this question yourself: perhaps not; and without considering what you cannot know and what can give you no light, act according to your duty, which you can know."

I emphasize this point because it distinguishes the point of view of deliberation from that of physical science and social thought, which try to bring the phenomena under a system of laws of nature. That there is this difference both Leibniz and Kant agree, though in Kant the difference has a much larger role.

2. But if Kant and Leibniz agree on this, they disagree on a different matter of fundamental significance. Leibniz's account of deliberation from the practical point of view would appear to be the origin of Wolff's doctrine of willing as such as opposed to Kant's doctrine of the pure will. This contrast we considered in Kant 1:§3. Now Wolff says in a letter to Leibniz (May 4, 1715 [Ariew and Garber:232]):

> The sensation of perfection excites a certain pleasure and the sensation of imperfection a certain displeasure. And the emotions, by virtue of which the mind is, in the end, inclined or disinclined, are modifications of this pleasure and displeasure; I explain the origin of natural obligation in this way. As soon as the perfection toward which the action tends, and which it indicates, is represented in the intellect, pleasure arises, which causes us to cling more closely to the action we should contemplate. And so, once the circumstances overflowing with good for us or for others have been noticed, the pleasure is modified and is transformed into an emotion by virtue of which the mind is at last inclined toward appetition. . . . [F]rom this inborn disposition toward obligation, I deduce all practical morals. . . . From this also comes the general rule or law of nature that our actions ought to be directed toward the highest perfection in ourselves and others.

While it would take a far longer discussion to make the point convincingly, I suggest that if we put statements of this kind together with Leibniz's account of reasoned deliberation in weighing competing considerations as we try to identify the greatest apparent good, we see a doctrine of the kind Kant aims to reject and to replace with the idea of a pure will relying on pure practical reason alone.

KANT

KANT I

Groundwork: Preface and Part I

§1. Introductory Comments

1. I shall say very little about Kant's life, which presents a striking contrast
with Hume's. While Hume was precocious, conceiving the *Treatise* in his
teens and completing it before he was thirty, Kant's major works, the three
Critiques of the 1780s, matured slowly. Kant was born in April 1724 and died
in February 1804, a little before his eightieth birthday. When the first edition
of the *Critique of Pure Reason* was published in 1781, following the decade
of the 1770s in which he wrote very little, he was fifty-seven years old and
beginning to feel that time was short. The *Critique of Practical Reason* appeared in 1788 and the *Critique of Judgment* in 1790, with the second edition
of the first *Critique* in 1787. This was not all in those years: the *Prolegomena
to Any Future Metaphysics* was published in 1783, the *Groundwork of the Metaphysics of Morals* in 1785, and the *Metaphysical Foundations of Natural Science*
in 1786. In addition to all these, there were several essays important for his
political philosophy: "Idea for a Universal History" and "What Is Enlightenment" both in 1784, and "What Is Orientation in Thinking" in 1786, among
others. When the last *Critique* appeared, Kant was sixty-six and still going
strong. He had yet to bring out *Religion within the Limits of Reason Alone*
(1793), the *Metaphysics of Morals* (1797), and two important essays in political
philosophy, "On the Common Saying: 'That may be true in theory, but it
does not apply in practice'" and "Perpetual Peace," both in 1795. In 1798,

when his last work, *The Contest of the Faculties,* appeared, he was seventy-four.

Another contrast is that Hume was lowland Scottish gentry who had no difficulty supporting himself, often staying at the family estate at Ninewells and eventually becoming quite wealthy from his writings and legacies to the tune of £1,000 per annum, a substantial sum in those days. Kant was a poor boy. His father was a harness maker; the family lived in the working-class section of Königsberg. At the age of eight, he entered the Pietist school the Fridericianum, which he grew to hate; for the rest of his life he regarded his years there as time in prison. He had to struggle to earn a living when he went to the university in 1740 when he was sixteen; and when he left the university in 1746 he became a *Hauslehrer,* or tutor, for well-to-do families near Königsberg for nearly ten years. When he returned to the university and began lecturing as *Dozent* in the fall of 1755, to make ends meet he lectured twenty hours or more per week, which seems to us quite incredible, on all kinds of subjects: logic, metaphysics, ethics, theory of law, geography, anthropology, and more. He didn't reach a somewhat comfortable financial security until he became a professor *ordinarius* in 1770.

2. For all their differences, one of the remarkable things about Kant is his deep respect and fondness for Hume. I say it is remarkable because it's not clear whence it arises. Almost certainly, Kant could not read English. J. G. Sulzer translated Hume's *Enquiry Concerning Human Understanding* in 1755, and most likely Kant read this. He also owned a copy of some of Hume's essays (translated 1759) that included, besides the "Natural History of Religion," the essays "On the Passions," "On Tragedy," and the "Foundations of Taste."[1] Some think that it was not until 1772, when Beattie's *Essay on the Nature and Immutability of Truth* was translated into German, that Kant became aware of the depth of Hume's criticism of the concept of causality. This work included quotations from passages in the *Treatise* more radical than anything in the *Enquiry.*[2] Others surmise that Kant saw I:iv:7 of the *Treatise* as translated by his friend Hamann before 1768 and say that

1. Karl Vorländer, *Immanuel Kant: Der Mann und das Werk* (Hamburg: Felix Meiner, 1977), 1:152n.

2. These passages are discussed in R. P. Wolff, *Kant's Theory of Mental Activity* (Cambridge, Mass.: Harvard University Press, 1963), pp. 24–32.

this was enough for Kant to see the point of Hume's critique of causation.[3] Possibly it was in one of these ways that Kant was aroused from his alleged "dogmatic slumbers" (*Prolegomena* [4:260]).[4] In any case, he was pretty wide awake by normal standards.

Whatever the source of Kant's knowledge of Hume on causation, that alone cannot, I think, account for the following extraordinary letter he wrote to Herder in 1768 (*Briefwechsel* [X:74]) in which he says:

> In the early unfolding of your [Herder's] talents I foresee with great pleasure the time when your fruitful spirit, no longer driven by the warm impulse of youthful feeling, attains that serenity which is peaceful yet full of feeling, and is the contemplative life of the philosopher, just the opposite of that dreamed of by the mystics. From what I know of you, I confidently look forward to this epoch of your genius, of all states of mind the most advantageous to its possessor and to the world, one in which Montaigne occupies the lowest place, and Hume so far as I know the highest.[5]

The letter is extraordinary not only in that Kant should write this to Herder (then a young man to whom he had been close as a student) but also in that he should say this of Hume. Not because it's not true of Hume. But how could Kant have formed such depth of appreciation? How did Kant divine Hume's character and sensibility expressed by what I have called his fideism of nature—his happy acceptance, "peaceful yet full of feeling"? His respect and fondness for Hume is a wonderful tribute to them both. (See also *KR* B788–797 for Kant's discussion of Hume as a skeptic, with his feeling for Hume expressed at B792: perhaps the "most ingenious of all the skeptics"; "so acute and estimable a man.")

---

3. See Günther Gawlick and Lother Kreimendahl, *Hume in der deutchen Aufklärung* (Stuttgart: Frommann-Holzboog, 1987), p. 191. I am indebted to J. B. Schneewind for this reference.

4. Unless otherwise indicated, Kant's works will be cited by volume and page of the *Gesammelte Schriften*, usually called the *Akademieausgabe*. This edition was first published starting in 1900 by the Prussian Academy of Sciences. Citations to the *Groundwork* are by chapter and paragraph as well as *Akademie* page of volume 4; citations from the *Critique of Pure Reason* are in the customary first and second edition pagination. [Ed.]

5. The letter can be found in Ernst Cassirer, *Kant's Life and Thought* (New Haven: Yale University Press, 1981), p. 85.

§2. Some Points about the Preface: Paragraphs 11–13

1. Today we begin our study of the first of the three topics into which our survey of Kant's moral philosophy will be divided. These three topics are the moral law, the fact of reason, and a practical faith. We begin with the *Groundwork* (as I shall call it following Paton), because even though it fails to give an adequate view of Kant's moral philosophy as a whole, it does provide a reasonably full analytic account of the moral law. It does this by elucidating the concept of morality, which Kant holds to be implicit in our commonsense judgments concerning the moral worth of actions and of the character they express.

Kant tells us in the Preface (Pref:13 [392]) that the sole aim of the *Groundwork* is "to seek out and establish the supreme principle of morality." He remarks that this inquiry "constitutes a whole and is to be separated off from every other inquiry." In contrast to Hume, he holds that looking for this principle does not proceed as part of a larger science of human nature, but begins analytically by elucidating the underlying principle(s) implicit in our commonsense judgments of moral worth.

This inquiry is a separate one in the further sense that seeking and establishing the supreme principle of morality is preliminary to a critique of *pure* practical reason, which Kant says he hopes to write in some future work, and which he attempts on a small scale in regard to the objective reality of the moral law in *Gr* III.

2. Several points mentioned in Pref:11 are of great importance for Kant's view, although their full significance will not be clear until much later.

(a) One is Kant's saying that a critique of (pure) practical reason cannot be complete until we can show the unity of practical and theoretical reason in a common principle. He believes that "in the end there can be only one and the same reason" (Pref:12 [399]). Now there are, I believe, four connected themes concerning reason in Kant's moral philosophy. We can state these as:

(i)   the supremacy of reason

(ii) the unity of reason

(iii) the equality of reason with the primacy of practical reason
      in the overall constitution of reason (for this equality, see
      KP 5:141); and

(iv) philosophy as defense, including a defense of the freedom
of reason, both theoretical and practical

Here I won't try even to hint at what these themes mean, since they
are difficult and require considerable background to state. But we shall try
to understand them, and I hope their meaning and interconnections will
eventually be clear. Setting out moral law as the supreme principle of morality is, as Kant says, preparatory for everything else. That is why I shall leave
aside many questions about how to interpret the categorical imperative and
the relations among its three formulations. Provided that we get the main
essentials right, I don't believe those questions make all that much difference. I shall note as we go on what is really essential and why.

(b) A second important point is this: Kant says (again in Pref:11 [391])
that a critique of pure practical reason is less urgent in the case of practical
reason than in the case of theoretical reason. As he argues in the first *Cri-*
tique, theoretical reason tends to exceed its appropriate limits and thereby
to fall into a kind of high-blown emptiness, which is fortunately shown in
the antinomies. Were it not for those antinomies, we could easily think
that we were talking sense: here is Kant the anti-metaphysician. By contrast,
practical reason in matters of morality "is easily brought to a high degree
of accuracy and precision even in the most ordinary intelligence" (Pref:11
[391]). This is related to the following point.

(c) Kant says (still in Pref:11 [391]) that he plans to write a critique of pure
practical reason; but when this work appears, it is entitled simply *Critique of*
Practical Reason. What happened to the adjective "pure"? The full explanation of this must wait until later when we discuss the fact of reason; but
Kant's thought is that whereas pure theoretical reason tends to transgress
its proper limits, in the case of practical reason it is empirical (not pure)
practical reason, prompted by our natural inclinations and desires, that
tends to transgress its appropriate sphere, especially when the moral law
and its basis in our person is not clear to us. Kant insists on the purity of
the moral law, that is, on the fact that it is an a priori principle that originates
in our free reason. He thinks that being fully conscious of the purity of the
law and of its origin in our person as free and autonomous is the surest
protection against our violating the moral law (see *Gr* Pref:6–8 [388–389];
and II:9n. [411]; 44n. [426]).

3. The above remarks are related to what Kant says in *Gr* I:20–22 (403–405). In I:22 (405), he discusses the need for moral philosophy. It is not needed to teach us our duties and obligations—to tell us what they are—for these we already know. He writes in I:20 (403):

> We cannot observe without admiration the great advantage which the power of practical judgment has over that of the theoretical in the minds of ordinary men. In theoretical judgments, when ordinary reason . . . depart[s] from the laws of experience and perceptions of sense, it falls into unintelligibility and self-contradiction. . . . On the practical side, however, the power of judgment first begins to show its advantages . . . when the ordinary mind excludes all sensuous motives from its practical laws. . . . [O]rdinary intelligence becomes even subtle . . . and what is most important, it can . . . have as good hope of hitting the mark as any . . . philosopher, because he can have no principle different from that of ordinary intelligence, but may easily confuse his judgment with a mass of . . . irrelevant considerations.

I have cited this passage (omitting phrases here and there) to show that Kant does not mean to teach us what is right and wrong (he would think that presumptuous) but to make us aware of the moral law as rooted in our free reason. A full awareness of this, he believes, arouses a strong desire to act from that law (*Gr* II:9n. [411]; 44n. [426]). This desire is (what we called in Hume II:§5) a conception-dependent desire: it is a desire, belonging to us as reasonable persons, to act from an ideal expressible in terms of a conception of ourselves as autonomous in virtue of our free reason, both theoretical and practical. In his moral philosophy, Kant seeks self-knowledge: not a knowledge of right and wrong—that we already possess—but a knowledge of what we desire as persons with the powers of free theoretical and practical reason.

4. I should add in this connection that Kant may also seek, as part of his Pietist background, a form of moral reflection that could reasonably be used to check the purity of our motives. In a general way we know what is right and what is wrong, but we are often tempted to act for the wrong reasons in ways we may not be aware of. One use he may have seen for the categorical imperative is as expressing a reasonable form of reflection

that could help us to guard against this by checking whether the maxim we act from is legitimate as permitted by practical reason.[6] I say a reasonable form of reflection because one thing Kant found offensive in the Pietism he was exposed to at the Fridericianum was its obsession with the purity of motives and the compulsive self-examination this could engender. By contrast, the categorical imperative articulates a mode of reflection that could order and moderate the scrutiny of our motives in a reasonable way.

I don't see Kant as at all concerned with moral skepticism. It is simply not a problem for him, however much it may trouble us. His view may provide a way to deal with it, but that is another matter. He always takes for granted, as part of the fact of reason, that all persons (barring the mentally retarded and the insane) acknowledge the supreme principle of practical reason as authoritative for their will (*KP* 5:105).

§3. The Idea of a Pure Will

1. I now turn to Pref:10 (390), which is important because here Kant explains his intentions in the *Groundwork* by distinguishing his doctrine of what he calls a pure will from Wolff's account of willing as such. Wolff's account of willing as such Kant compares to general (formal) logic, while his own account of pure will he compares to transcendental logic. What are we to make of this?

Since Kant's explanation is a bit opaque, I try a conjecture. Just as general logic studies the formal principles of valid thought and reasoning regardless of its particular content and objects, so Wolff's account of willing as such studies the psychological principles that hold for all desires regardless of their objects and what in particular they are desires for. Desires are treated as homogeneous, whatever their origin in our person. In this respect, the account is like general logic in leaving aside the content and origin of thought in ascertaining the validity of inferences. The account of willing as such, if this conjecture is correct, suggests a view of our person that sees desires as psychic forces pressing for fulfillment and satisfaction proportionate to their strength and urgency. The balance of these psychic forces deter-

---

6. Here I am indebted for valuable discussion with Michael Hardimon.

mines what we do. A person of strong will (someone with Hume's strength of mind) is someone whose deliberations are persistently controlled by the same strong desires.

By contrast, Kant's account of a pure will is like transcendental logic in this way. Transcendental logic studies all the epistemic conditions that make possible synthetic a priori knowledge of objects. We find such knowledge in mathematics and in the first principles of physics; and this knowledge must be explained. Similarly, Kant thinks that pure practical reason exists and that it is sufficient of itself to determine the will independently of our inclinations and natural desires. This fact too must be explained. To do so, we need an account of a pure will, and not an account of willing as such; for just as synthetic a priori knowledge is knowledge of a special kind and requires transcendental logic to set out its principles, so pure willing is a special kind of willing and requires its own inquiry to be understood.

The difference between theoretical reason and practical reason is, briefly, this: theoretical reason deals with knowledge of given objects, and transcendental logic sets out the principles that make synthetic a priori knowledge of those objects possible; whereas practical reason concerns how we are to bring about objects in accordance with an idea (or a conception) of those objects (*KP* 5:89f.). The principles of a pure will that Kant wants to examine are the principles of practical reason that, in his view, can effectively determine our will apart from inclinations and natural desires, and direct it to its a priori object, the highest good (*KP* 5:4). As Kant presents him, Wolff, and no doubt others also, are not aware of the significance of a pure will, an idea Kant sees as fundamental. For that reason, he sees himself as breaking "entirely new ground" (Pref:10 [390]).

2. We might put Wolff's view (as Kant sees it) as follows: recall the distinctions from Hume II:§5 between object-dependent and principle-dependent (and conception-dependent) desires. Think of all the desires that affect us, and that contend within our person, as object-dependent desires. These are like Kant's inclinations and impulses generated in us by everything from our bodily wants and needs to social processes of learning and education. Such social processes are governed, let's suppose, by Hume's laws of association, the principles of custom and facility, the principle of predominant passions, and the like. Now, Wolff considers all these desires solely with respect to their strength and, like Hume, has no conception of

practical reason. Presumably the action done is often, though not always, the one promising the greatest balance of overall satisfaction.

For Kant, this means that the person has no pure will, for such a will is an elective power guided by the principles of practical reason, that is, a power to elect which of our many (often contending) object-dependent desires we are to act from, or to reject them all entirely, as moved by principle-dependent and conception-dependent desires. In the *Religion* (6: 38), Kant refers to a member of the English House of Commons who said in the heat of debate, "Every man has his price."[7] Although we think that we ought never to do certain things no matter what—never to betray family and friends, country, or church, for example—the speaker alleges that should the price be right, we can all be bought. The Wolffian psychologist would explain this (if true) by saying something like this: desires as psychic forces all stand on a par and differ only in their strength and promise of satisfaction should their aim be realized. So for every desire or combination of desires, even when it usually decides the case by guiding deliberation, there must exist a stronger desire, or a combination of desires, that can counterbalance it. Find this counterbalancing desire or combination and you know the price.

3. As we shall see, Kant has a different conception of persons as reasonable and rational, and as possessing an elective will. He wants to study the principles of a pure will and to set out how persons with a fully effective pure will would act, and to ascertain what the structure of their desires as governed by the principles of practical reason would be. It is best, I think, to regard Kant as presenting the principles from which a fully ideal reasonable and rational agent would act, even against all object-dependent desires, should this be necessary to respect the requirements of the moral law.[8] Such an ideal (human) agent, although affected by natural inclinations and needs, as we must be belonging to the natural world, never follows them when doing so would violate the principles of pure will.

Now, Kant does not deny, as I have said, that all of our desires have

7. Sir Robert Walpole. But what he said was much less general: namely, "All those men [referring to certain patriots] have their price." See Greene and Hudson, p. 34n.

8. That an ideal agent would do this, and that we know we could do likewise, is the point of the example (at *KP* 5:30) of the Sovereign who for his dishonorable ends wants us to make a false charge against another subject.

psychological strength. But he insists on the distinction between the strength of conception-dependent and principle-dependent desires and the regulative priority—Butler would say the authority—that their corresponding principles have for ideal agents. What characterizes these agents is that the psychological strength of their conception-dependent and principle-dependent desires exactly parallels the regulative priority of the corresponding principles of practical reason. Thus, as ideally reasonable persons, we have the capacity to stand above and to assess our object-dependent desires. This gives us an elective power to determine from which of those desires, if any, we shall act. Next time I consider how this election is done: i.e., by incorporating the desire into the maxim from which we propose to act (*Rel* 6:28) and then checking whether the maxim is morally permissible by using the CI-procedure, as I shall call it.

This conception of ourselves as reasonable agents with elective wills contrasts sharply with Wolff's conception. Kant's complaint against Wolff is that he simply ignores the principles appropriate to a pure will and so his view allows no place for a conception of moral obligation rooted in pure practical reason.

§4. The Main Argument of *Groundwork* I

1. Let's look briefly at the main argument in *Groundwork* I as found in I: 8–17 (397–402). It goes as follows. (The asterisks before 1, 2, and 10 indicate these as Kant's three propositions; they appear in the order in which he introduces them.)

> *1. A good will is a will the actions of which accord with duty, not from inclination but from duty (out of duty). (paragraph 11, end [399])
>
> *2. Actions done from duty have their moral worth from the principle of volition from which they are done, and not from the purposes (objectives, states of affairs, or ends) the inclination to bring about which initially prompted the agent to consider doing the action. (paragraph 14 [399–400])
>
> 3. The will must always act from some principle of volition. (paragraphs 2 [393–394], 14 [399–400])

4. There are two kinds of principles of volition, formal and material, which are mutually exclusive and exhaustive. (paragraph 14 [399–400])

5. No material principle of volition is the principle of volition of an action done from duty. (from the definition of a material principle of volition and *2 above)

6. An action done from duty is an action done from a formal principle of volition. (from *2 through 5)

7. There is only one formal principle of volition, and this principle is the moral law. (paragraph 17 [402])

8. Respect is, by definition, the recognition of a principle of volition as law for us, that is, as directly determining our will without reference to what is wanted by our inclinations. (paragraph 16n. [401])

9. The object of respect is the moral law. (paragraphs 15 [400–401], 16n. [401])

*10. Actions done from duty are actions done from respect (or out of respect) for the moral law (paragraph 15 [400–401]). (from 6 through 9)

11. A good will is a will the actions of which accord with duty, not from inclination, but from respect for the moral law. (from *1, *10 above)

2. Several comments: Lines 3 through 9 inclusive above try to fill in what seem to be the steps in Kant's reasoning as based on the premises indicated by asterisks. However, not much depends on the rendering given being exactly right. His reasoning can no doubt be put in other ways.

Further, the aim of the argument, which seems valid, is to find the supreme principle of morality (the moral law). It starts from ordinary commonsense moral knowledge and moves to philosophical knowledge by elucidating the underlying principle found in our everyday judgments about the moral worth of actions. I do not examine the argument, for if I have it more or less right, its form and purpose are reasonably clear. But I should note that Kant views Chapters I and II of the *Groundwork* as purely analytic, as showing by the development of the universally accepted concept of morality that autonomy of the will is its foundation (*Gr* II:90 [444–445]).

§5. The Absolute Value of a Good Will

1. *Gr* I:1–3 (393–394) introduces a fundamental part of Kant's moral doctrine: the idea of the absolute value of a good will and this value's being estimable beyond all comparison.

To begin: Kant opens the *Groundwork* with the celebrated statement, "It is impossible to conceive anything at all in the world, or even out of it, that can be taken as good without qualification, except a good will."

The term "good will" is not defined, and Kant leaves us to gather its meaning from the first three paragraphs by seeing the difference between it and the things he says are good only with qualification.

Among the features of our person that Kant distinguishes from a good (or bad) will are these:

- (i) talents of mind: such as intelligence, wit, and judgment
- (ii) qualities of temperament: such as courage, resolution, and constancy of purpose; and among these qualities those particularly serviceable to a good will: moderation of affections, self-control, and sober reflection

Plainly, a good will is also to be distinguished from things wanted by our inclinations:

- (i) gifts of fortune: power, honor, wealth, and health; and
- (ii) happiness, as the complete contentment with our state, the satisfaction of our natural desires in a rational manner

Now, talents of mind, qualities of temperament, and gifts of fortune can be extremely bad when the will that makes use of them is not a good will. Even the secondary virtues, as we may call them—courage and self-control, resolution and sober reflection—have value only on the condition that they assist the will in pursuing universal ends. The primary virtues, let's say, are those the secure possession of which constitutes a good will; prominent among them are wisdom, a sense of justice, and (practical) benevolence. It is persons who have these virtues who are virtuous: particular actions issuing from these virtues have moral worth.[9] Kant sees talents of

9. Note the distinction: let's say that persons are virtuous; particular actions have moral worth.

mind and qualities of temperament as gifts of nature, whereas a good will is not a gift. It is something achieved; it results from an act of establishing a character, sometimes by a kind of conversion that endures when strengthened by the cultivation of the virtues and of the ways of thought and feeling that support them (*Rel* 6:47–50).

2. Even happiness itself is not good without qualification. The prosperity and happiness of someone with no trace of a good will cannot give pleasure to an impartial spectator. The opening paragraph then concludes with a characteristic theme of Kant's moral thought:

> A good will seems to be the indispensable condition of even the worthiness to be happy.

In the first *Critique* (B834), Kant distinguishes between the practical law derived from the motive of happiness and the practical law derived from the motive of making oneself worthy of happiness. The first he calls the pragmatic law (or rule of prudence), the second the moral law. He thinks of moral philosophy not, as he believes the Greeks did, as the study of how to achieve happiness, but rather as the study of how we are to act if we are to be worthy of the happiness we do achieve. This thought characterizes Kant's moral doctrine.

3. Kant proceeds in I:3 (394) to say that a good will is not good because of what it accomplishes or because of its fitness to bring about some independently specified and already given end. Even if those with a good will altogether lack the capacity to carry out their intentions (through lack of opportunity or of natural endowment), their good will still shines like a jewel, as having full value in itself.

This statement reminds us of Hume's remark: "Virtue in rags is still virtue" (*T*:584f.). But Hume's explanation differs sharply from Kant's. For Hume, virtuous persons are those who have qualities of character immediately agreeable to, or else useful to, themselves or their associates. His explanation of why virtue in rags is still virtue is that the imagination is more easily set in motion than the understanding, and even though no good is actually produced by the virtuous man imprisoned in a dungeon, we are moved in our judgment by sympathy with those who might have benefited from the good his character is fit to produce.

Kant cannot accept this view, for he rejects the idea of judging the moral worth of character by reference to an independently given conception of goodness, such as Hume's agreeableness and usefulness to ourselves and to others. In I:1–3 (393–394), we are told what a good will is only in a formal way: we know that persons with a good will have a firm and settled character, and consistently act from the principles of (pure) practical reason. From this we know that they adjust and correct the use of their gifts of nature and of fortune to universal ends as those principles require. But we don't know the content of these principles, and so we don't know how persons with a good will actually behave or what duties they recognize.

To conclude: a good will is always good in itself, under all conditions; whereas everything else is good only under certain conditions. And this is so whether the conditional good is a good in itself or good as a means, or both. Happiness, or the rationally ordered satisfaction of our natural desires, may be good in itself (when the ends desired and realized are permissible). But even our happiness and our enjoyment of painting and music are fully good only if we are worthy of them, or have a good will.

4. Kant says in I:3 (394) that a good will is estimable beyond all comparison, far higher in value than the satisfaction of our inclinations, indeed higher than the ordered satisfaction of all our (permissible) inclinations together (or happiness). A good will has, then, two special features: it is the only thing always good in itself without qualification; and its value is incomparably superior to the value of all other things also good in themselves. These two features mark the special status of the good will to which Kant refers (Gr I:4 [394– 395]) when he speaks of the absolute value of mere will. The second of these features is that of lexical priority, as I shall say: it means that the value of a good will outranks all other values, no matter how great their measure in their own terms. The superior claims of a good will outweigh absolutely the claims of other values should their claims come into conflict.

Now, we don't yet know how to understand these two features, and it is useless to speculate at this stage. We know that Kant has both a formal conception of a good will and a formal conception of right. He begins with these two interdependent formal conceptions. The goodness of all other things—talents of mind and qualities of temperament, gifts of nature and of fortune, and happiness—is conditioned: their goodness depends on being compatible with the substantive requirements on actions and institutions imposed by these formal conceptions. This is the general meaning of the priority of right in his doctrine.

But what those substantive requirements are cannot be known until we have worked through *Gr* II. Taken alone, much that Kant says in *Gr* I is misleading and can be understood only in light of what comes later.

§6. The Special Purpose of Reason

1. *Gr* I:5–7 (395–396) are important in explaining how Kant understands a good will and its connection with reason. Kant knows that what he has said about the absolute and incomparable value of a good will in I:1–3 (393–394) may seem extreme, even though it matches our commonsense judgments. To allay this feeling, he examines the question in light of the idea that nature gives us no capacity, including that of reason, unless that capacity is best suited for achieving its purpose.

For what purpose, then, do we have reason? Certainly not for the purpose of securing our own happiness, for nature could achieve that purpose much better by endowing us with the appropriate instincts.

The purpose, Kant thinks, for which nature did give us reason must be to produce a good will. Our having the capacity to reason and to understand the principles of reason is clearly necessary if we are to have a will that can take an interest in the principles of practical reason. So in a world in which nature distributes her endowments in a purposive manner, the purpose of our having reason must be to produce a good will. Certainly, one might object that there might be other candidate purposes, yet Kant thinks that in eliminating the purpose of forwarding our happiness, he has ruled out the only live alternative.

2. An important distinction is made in paragraph 7 (396) between the highest good and the complete good. The highest good is the good will, the condition of all other goods, even of our demands for happiness. Yet the good will is not the complete good: this is specified as a good will's enjoying a happiness appropriate to it. But nature can achieve that highest purpose even if the second purpose of achieving happiness should not be successful, or, as Kant says, is less than zero.

Kant adds that in achieving the first purpose of our having a good will, we attain a kind of contentment *(Zufriedenheit):* that of fulfilling a purpose specified solely by reason. This contentment is not to be confused with the pleasure of satisfying our inclinations and needs. Rather, it is the satisfaction we find in acting from the principles of practical reason in which, as reasonable and rational agents, we take a practical interest. To make this motivation fully intelligible, I believe it is best understood in terms of a conception-dependent desire. This we come back to later.

§7. Two Roles of the Good Will

1. Finally, I comment briefly on two roles of the good will in Kant's doctrine.

The *first* role of the capacity for a good will, a capacity based on the powers of practical reason and moral sensibility, Kant views as the condition of our being members of a possible realm of ends. The powers of practical reason are essential to our humanity as reasonable and rational. Hence the capacity for a good will specifies the *scope* of the moral law, that is, its range of application: namely, to human persons as possessing the powers of practical reason and moral sensibility. It is as such persons that we are bound by the duties of justice and beneficence. At the same time, others must respect the duties of justice and beneficence in their conduct toward us, so while we are bound by the moral law, we are also protected by it.

The *second* role is distinctive of Kant's thought: it has a positive and a negative side. The negative side is that Kant believes that unless we pursue our aims within the limits of the moral law, human life is worthless, without any value. This follows from the strict way Kant views the priority of right. An illustrative saying is the following (*MdS* 6:332): "If justice perishes, then it is no longer worthwhile for men to live upon the earth."

The positive side is that we can and do give meaning to our life in the world, and indeed even to the world itself, by respecting the moral law and striving to achieve a good will. This side is found in Kant's discussion in the *Critique of Judgment* (in §§82–84) of human beings as the ultimate purpose of nature in virtue of their capacity for culture and as the final purpose of creation in virtue of their powers as moral persons. I cannot consider these difficult sections here and simply cite the text to give some sense of Kant's thought. From *KU* §84:

> [I]n this world of ours there is only one kind of being with a causality that is teleological, that is, directed to purposes, but is yet so constituted that the law in terms of which these beings must determine their purposes is presented . . . as unconditioned and independent of conditions in nature, and yet necessary in itself. That being is man . . . considered as a noumenon. Man is the only natural being in whom we . . . recognize, as part of his constitution, a supersensible ability *(freedom).*
>
> Now about man, as a moral being, . . . we cannot go on to ask: For what end . . . does he exist? His existence has itself the highest purpose within it; and to this purpose he can subject all of nature as far as he is able. . . . Now if things in the world which are dependent beings as regards their existence, require a supreme cause that acts in terms of purposes, then man is the final purpose of creation. For without man the chain of mutually subordinated purposes would not have a complete basis. Only in man, and even in him only as a moral subject, do we find unconditioned legislation regarding purposes.
>
> [in the footnote to §84]: [I]t [the principle of morality] is the only possible thing in the order of purposes that is absolutely unconditioned as concerns nature, and hence alone qualifies man, the subject of morality, to be the *final purpose* of creation. . . . This proves that happiness can only be a conditioned purpose, so that it is only as a moral being that man can be the final purpose of creation, with man's state of happiness connected with that . . . purpose only as its consequence and as dependent of the degree to which man is in harmony with that purpose, the purpose of his existence.

2. How we feel about Kant's moral philosophy as a whole depends a great deal on what we make of the two roles of the value of a good will and the significance he attaches to the moral law as shown in the above quotations from *KU* §84.

In one form or other, the first role of the capacity for a good will—

that of its being a condition of our being members of a realm of ends—is widely accepted, as it is basic to much democratic thought. Of course, it is not original with Kant, since in this he is much influenced by Rousseau, whose *Social Contract* and *Émile* he read when they were published in 1762 (his French was good). These works, Kant tells us, led to a fundamental change in his thought, and as a consequence he was moved to give deeper philosophical expression to ideas he found in Rousseau.

The second role—particularly in its negative side that the value of human life depends on our honoring the moral law—is much more disputable. Many think it an aberration to attach that kind of significance to morality, especially when it is expressed by the categorical imperative and includes the priority of right. These matters I shall not discuss here. To do so sensibly requires much more background about Kant's view than we have at present.

3. I conclude by observing that the significance Kant gives to the moral law and our acting from it has an obvious religious aspect, and that his text occasionally has a devotional character. In the second *Critique*, there are two obvious examples. One is the passage beginning: "Duty! Thou sublime and mighty name . . . what origin is worthy of thee?" (5:86f.). The other is the passage beginning: "Two things fill the mind . . . with admiration and awe . . . the starry heavens above me and the moral law within me" (5:161f.).

While it is a necessary condition for Kant's view to count as religious that he should hold that there are some things of far greater significance than the everyday values of secular life and our happiness as a whole, this is not sufficient to make it religious. One could give this significance to certain moral virtues and excellences, say, to a certain nobility and courage, and steadfastness in friendship, as Aristotle might be said to have done. This does not give his view a religious aspect, as profound as it might be.

What gives a view a religious aspect, I think, is that it has a conception of the world as a whole that presents it as in certain respects holy, or else as worthy of devotion and reverence. The everyday values of secular life must take a secondary place. If this is right, then what gives Kant's view a religious aspect is the dominant place he gives to the moral law in conceiving of the world itself. For it is in following the moral law as it applies to us, and in striving to fashion in ourselves a firm good will, and in shaping our social world accordingly that alone qualifies us to be the final purpose of creation. Without this, our life in the world, and the world itself, lose their meaning and point.

Now, perhaps, we see the significance of the mention of the world in the first sentence of *Groundwork* I: "It is impossible to conceive anything in the world, or even out of it, that can be taken as good without qualification, except a good will."

At first it seems strange that Kant should mention the world here. Why go to such an extreme? we ask. Now perhaps we see why it is there.[10] It comes as no surprise, then, that in the second *Critique* he should say that the step to religion is taken for the sake of the highest good and to preserve our devotion to the moral law.

These religious, even Pietist, aspects of Kant's moral philosophy seem obvious; any account of it that overlooks them misses much that is essential to it.

10. I owe thanks here to T. M. Scanlon, who saw this connection.

The Categorical Imperative: The First Formulation

§1. Introduction

1. Our aim is to achieve an overall view of how the more distinctive themes of Kant's moral philosophy fit together. Recall the four themes mentioned last time: the supremacy of reason; the unity of reason; the equality of reason (theoretical and practical) with the primacy of the practical in the constitution of reason; and, finally, philosophy as defense, which includes the defense of the freedom of reason. We want to know what these themes mean and how they are connected with special aspects of Kant's doctrine, such as the priority of right, and an idea of moral philosophy as concerned not with how to be happy but with how to be worthy of happiness, and of course with the moral law as a law of freedom.

As essential preparation for understanding these matters, it is best to begin with how Kant thinks of the moral law, the categorical imperative, and the procedure by which that imperative is applied to us as human beings situated in our social world. This last I call the categorical imperative procedure, or the CI-procedure. I shall not give a full account of this procedure, and many difficult points of interpretation are omitted. My reason for omitting these matters is that Kant wants to show that there *is* pure practical reason. He wants to do this by showing how practical reason is manifest in our everyday moral thought, feeling, and conduct (*KP* 5:3). For this purpose, it does not greatly matter, I think, what specific formulation of the CI-procedure we adopt, provided that it meets certain essential conditions.

2. Here I note two of these conditions (leaving two others until later).

First, the categorical imperative procedure must not be merely formal but have sufficient structure to specify requirements on moral deliberation so that suitably many maxims are shown to be fit or unfit to be made universal law. Otherwise, the categorical imperative as it applies to us would be empty and without content, and so also the moral law. Call this the content condition.

Second, the categorical imperative procedure must exhibit the categorical imperative, and similarly the moral law, as a principle of autonomy, so that from our consciousness of this law as supremely authoritative and regulative for us (as it applies to us via the categorical imperative and its procedure), we can recognize that we are free. Call this the freedom condition.[1]

Of course, the meaning of these two conditions is obscure at this point. I mention them only to indicate that we have some leeway in giving an account of the categorical imperative provided that certain essential requirements are met.

3. Now, there are two reasons for studying the CI-procedure: one is to use it as a way of generating the content—the first principles along with the essential rights, duties, permissions, and the rest—of a reasonable moral doctrine. I don't believe that the CI-procedure is adequate for this purpose. This is not to deny that it is surely highly instructive as one of the more, if not the most, illuminating formulations of the requirement to express our reasons universally when assuming a moral point of view (an idea that goes back at least to Leibniz and Clarke).

The other reason for studying the CI-procedure is to elucidate and give meaning to the themes and features that distinguish Kant's view. Provided that the account of that procedure satisfies the content and freedom conditions (and the two we add later), its main value for us, or so I think, is to bring to life and to make intelligible Kant's characteristic and

1. In Kant VII, two further conditions are added: the fact of reason condition and the motivation condition.

deeper ideas. It does this by providing a means for their expression: by referring to it we can give a more specific sense to the unity of reason, say, and to the idea of acting under the idea of freedom. But this is getting ahead.

§2. Features of Ideal Moral Agents

1. In a moment we look at a highly schematic account of Kant's categorical imperative using the law of nature formula. I assume that this imperative is applied in the normal conditions of human life by what I have called the categorical imperative procedure, or, as I have said, the CI-procedure for short. This procedure specifies the content of the moral law as it applies to us as reasonable and rational persons in the natural world, endowed with conscience and moral sensibility, and affected by, but not determined by, our natural desires and inclinations. These desires and inclinations reflect our needs as finite beings having a particular place in our social world and situated in the order of nature.

In referring above to human persons I used the phrase "reasonable and rational." My intention is to mark the fact that Kant uses *vernünftig* to express a full conception of reason that covers the terms "reasonable" and "rational" as we often use them. In English, we know what is meant when someone says, "Their proposal is rational, given their circumstances, but it is unreasonable all the same." The meaning is roughly that the people in question are pushing a hard and unfair bargain which they know to be in their own interests but which they wouldn't expect us to accept unless they knew their position is strong. "Reasonable" can also mean "judicious," "ready to listen to reason," where this has the sense of being willing to listen to and consider the reasons offered by others. *Vernünftig* can have the same meanings in German: it can have the broad sense of "reasonable" as well as the narrower (often the economist's) sense of "rational" to mean roughly furthering our interests in the most effective way. Kant's usage varies, but when applied to persons, *vernünftig* usually covers being both reasonable and rational. His use of "reason" often has the even fuller sense of the philosophical tradition. Think of what *Vernunft* means in the title *The Critique of Pure Reason*! We are worlds away from "rational" in the narrow sense. It's a deep question (which I leave aside here) whether Kant's conception of reason includes far more than reason.

It is useful, then, to use "reasonable" and "rational" as handy terms to mark the distinction that Kant makes between the two forms of practical reason, pure and empirical. Pure practical reason is expressed in the categorical imperative, empirical practical reason in the hypothetical imperative. These forms of practical reason must also be distinguished from particular categorical and hypothetical imperatives (as we shall see in a moment, the particular maxims at step [1]) that satisfy the corresponding requirements of practical reason in particular circumstances. The terms "reasonable" and "rational" remind us of the fullness of Kant's conception of practical reason and of the two forms of reason it comprehends.

2. Recall what we said last time in connection with Gr Pref:10 (390–391): that Kant is concerned with the principles of a pure will, that is, with the reasoning of fully reasonable and rational human agents. Such agents are ideal: although affected by natural desires and inclinations, they are not determined by them and always act as the principles of pure reason require. They are also, let's suppose, lucid and sincere in the sense that they know (or can formulate) the reasons from which they act, and they can state these reasons when appropriate.

Now, I take the CI-procedure to represent in procedural form all the requirements of practical reason (both pure and empirical) as those requirements apply to our maxims. (This procedural representation is important later when we discuss Kant's moral constructivism.) In assessing the maxims implicit in their actions, I suppose that ideal reasonable and rational agents, who are also lucid and sincere, use these principles intuitively in their moral thought and judgment.

Further, Kant takes for granted that the application of this procedure presupposes a certain moral sensibility and a capacity for moral judgment (MdS, Intro 6:399–402).[2] Having a moral sensibility means, among other things, knowing that wanting to make a deceitful promise raises a moral question: Is such a promise permissible? Similarly, if great suffering tempts us to want to take our life, that raises a moral question; so also do the

---

2. On this presupposition, see the instructive discussion by Barbara Herman, "The Practice of Moral Judgment," *Journal of Philosophy* (August 1985), 414–436; reprinted in *The Practice of Moral Judgment* (Cambridge, Mass.: Harvard University Press, 1993), pp. 73–93.

needs and misery of others who seek my help. By representing the requirements of practical reason, the CI-procedure articulates a mode of reflection
that Kant thinks can help us to gain clarity about such matters, given our
moral sensibility and capacity for judgment as developed, as it must be, in
growing up and living in society.

It is a serious misconception to think of the CI-procedure as an algorithm intended to yield, more or less mechanically, a correct judgment.
There is no such algorithm, and Kant knows this. It is equally a misconception to think of this procedure as a set of debating rules that can trap liars
and cheats, scoundrels and cynics, into exposing their hand. There are no
such rules.

3. To clarify the remark above about a sincere agent, let's distinguish
three kinds of reasons: explanatory reasons, agents' reasons, and grounding
reasons.

Explanatory reasons are part of an explanation of why someone acted as
he did. The explanation is partly psychological—a belief-desire explanation,
say—but it may refer to repressed or unconscious motives, and to other
psychological elements that agents are unaware of and would not count
among their reasons.

Agents' reasons are the reasons that agents count as their reasons and
that truthful and sincere agents would, when appropriate, acknowledge as
their reasons. When people are lucid before themselves, that is, when they
know what moves them and do not act under the promptings of repressed
or unconscious motives, then agents' reasons tend to coincide, or else to
overlap, with explanatory reasons. Kant's ideal reasonable and rational and
sincere agents are also lucid.

Grounding reasons are of two kinds: reasons of rationality and justifying
reasons. Reasons of rationality are those that show a decision or an action
(for an agent in certain circumstances) to be rational, or sensible, as the
case may be; while justifying reasons show a decision or an action to be
reasonable, right, or just, or whatever is appropriate.

In the case of ideal agents—those who are reasonable, rational, and
lucid as well as truthful and sincere—the three kinds of reasons tend to
coincide, or else to overlap, when the actions in question are fully inten-
tional, i.e., undertaken in the light of deliberation and judgment.

§3. The Four-Step CI-Procedure

1. It is important to recognize that the moral law, the categorical imperative, and the CI-procedure are three different things.

The moral law is an idea of reason. It specifies a principle that applies to all reasonable and rational beings (or reasonable beings for short) whether or not they are, like us, finite beings with needs. It holds for God and the angels, and for reasonable beings elsewhere in the universe (should there be such), as well as for us.

The categorical imperative, as an imperative, is directed only to those reasonable beings who, because they are finite beings with needs, experience the moral law as a constraint. As such beings, we experience the moral law in that way, and so the categorical imperative specifies how that law is to apply to us (*Gr* II:12–15 [412–414]).

For the categorical imperative to be applied to our situation, it must be adapted to our circumstances in the order of nature. This adaptation is made by the CI-procedure as it takes into account the normal conditions of human life by means of the law of nature formulation (*Gr* II:33 [421]).

2. With these remarks as a preface, I now set out the CI-procedure in four steps.[3] At the first step, we have the agent's maxim, which is, let's suppose, rational from the agent's point of view: that is, the maxim is rational given the agent's situation and the available alternatives, together with the agent's desires, abilities, and beliefs (taken to be rational in the circumstances). Kant speaks of a maxim as a subjective principle: it is a principle from which the subject acts (*Gr* II:30n. [421]). When the agent's maxim is rational from the agent's point of view, as supposed here, it may be said to be subjectively valid.

The maxim is also assumed to be sincere: that is, it reflects the agent's actual reasons for the intended action as the agent, presumed to be lucid,

3. *Modulo* a few minor variations, my account of the CI-procedure follows that of Onora (Nell) O'Neill in her *Acting on Principle* (New York: Columbia University Press, 1975). See also Paul Dietrichson, "When Is a Maxim Universalizable?" *Kantstudien* (1964); and Thomas Pogge, "The Categorical Imperative," in *Grundelgung zur Metaphysick der Sitten: Ein Kooperativer Kommentar*, ed. Ofried Höffe (Frankfurt: Vittorio Klosterman, 1989). I have followed Barbara Herman's supposition in a number of her papers that when we apply the CI-procedure, we are to assume that the agent's maxim is rational.

would truthfully describe them. The CI-procedure applies, then, to maxims that lucid and rational agents have arrived at in view of what they regard as the relevant features of their circumstances. We should add that the procedure applies equally well to maxims that rational and sincere agents might arrive at (but have not), given the normal circumstances of human life.

To conclude: the agent's maxim at the first step is both sincere and rational. It is a particular hypothetical imperative (to be distinguished from the hypothetical imperative); and since it uses the first-person pronoun, let's say that it expresses the agent's personal intention to act from the maxim. It has this standard form:

(1) I am to do X in circumstances C in order to bring about Y unless Z. (Here X is an action and Y is an end, a state of affairs.)

Note that the maxim has an "in order to" clause and so refers to an end. For Kant, *all* actions have ends (*MdS*, Intro 6:384f.). The nature of the clause is important in distinguishing between duties of justice and other kinds of duties, but I leave this aside here.

3. The second step generalizes the maxim of the first step; the result is what we may call a universal precept (not Kant's terminology) that applies to everyone. When this precept passes the test of the CI-procedure, it is a practical law, an objective principle valid for every rational being (*Gr* II: 30n. [421]). So we have:

(2) Everyone is to do X in circumstances C in order to bring about Y unless Z.

At the third step we are to transform the universal precept at (2) into a law of nature to obtain:

(3) Everyone always does X in circumstances C in order to bring about Y, as if by a law of nature (as if such a law was implanted in us by natural instinct) (II:37 [422–423]).

The fourth step is the most complicated; it raises questions which we cannot thoroughly discuss here. The intuitive idea is this:

(4) We are to adjoin the as-if law of nature at step (3) to the existing laws of nature (as these are understood by us) and then think through as best we can what the order of nature would be once the effects of the newly adjoined law of nature have had sufficient time to work themselves out.

It is assumed that a new order of nature results from the addition of the law at step (3) to the other laws of nature, and that this new order of nature has a settled equilibrium state the relevant features of which we are able to figure out. Let us call this new order of nature an "adjusted social world." Let's also think of this social world as associated with the maxim at step (1), and impute to the agent a legislative intention, an intention as it were to legislate such a world. Here the thought is that an ideal reasonable agent considering whether to act from the maxim at step (1) implicitly accepts the requirements of pure practical reason represented in the steps leading up to and including step (4).

4. Kant's categorical imperative can now be stated as follows: We are permitted to act from our rational and sincere maxim at step (1) only if two conditions are satisfied:

First, we must be able to intend, as sincere, reasonable, and rational agents, to act from that maxim when we regard ourselves as a member of the adjusted social world associated with it, and thus as acting within that world and subject to its conditions; and

Second, we must be able to will this adjusted social world itself and affirm it should we belong to it.

Hence, if we cannot at the same time both will this adjusted social world and intend to act from that maxim as a member of it, we cannot now act from the maxim, even though it is, by assumption, fully rational in our present circumstances. The categorical imperative, as represented by the CI-procedure, applies to us no matter what the consequences of our compliance with it may be for our natural desires and needs. This reflects the priority of pure practical reason over empirical practical reason.

Finally, it should be kept in mind that this rendering of the CI-procedure draws on the law of nature formulation, which reads (II:33 [421]):

Act as if the maxim of your action were to become through your will a universal law of nature.

We have interpreted this formulation as an imputed legislative intention: it's as if we had the power of legislative reason and must exercise it as a condition of acting on our maxim. We must check whether we can do what we now intend in the adjusted social world as well as will that world.

§4. Kant's Second Example: The Deceitful Promise

1. The second and fourth of Kant's four examples are, at first sight at least, more plausible than the other two. So I illustrate briefly how the four steps of the CI-procedure apply in these cases. I begin with the second, that of the deceitful promise (*Gr* II:36 [422]).

Step (1): I am to make a deceitful promise in circumstances *C* (that is, when I am in embarrassing straits and need money, even though I know that I cannot repay the debt, and have no intention of doing so) in order to further my own personal advantage.

Step (2): Everyone is to make a deceitful promise in circumstances *C*, etc., as above.

Step (3): Everyone makes (or tries to make) a deceitful promise in circumstances *C*, etc. (as if by a law of nature).

Step (4): Adjoin the law of nature at step (3) to other laws of nature (as known by us) and figure out the equilibrium state that would result. This adjusted social world is one in which no one can make a deceitful promise in circumstances *C*, as much as they would like to do so.

Now, the law of nature at (3) is psychological: we try to make a deceitful promise, as if by a law of nature. But since other laws in certain circumstances may inhibit this law's operation, we don't say flatly that everyone does make a deceitful promise. The readiness of everyone to try in those circumstances may hold as a psychological law, even though it may be that other laws entail that deceitful promises cannot actually be made.

The contradiction in conception test rejects the deceitful promise maxim because a rational agent cannot intend to act from that maxim in the social world of the legislative intention. This follows from the fact that if rational agents intend to do something, they must believe with reason that they can do it and that, in their circumstances, it is within their power. An intention is a plan of some kind: it is not rational to plan to do what we know we cannot do.

2. The point of introducing the two intentions that may prove incompatible is to find a place for Kant's speaking of the agent's maxim as contradicting itself, of its not being self-consistent. But why does Kant think that in the adjusted social world no one can make a false promise? His remarks are brief: he says that the universality of the law at (3) "would make promising, and the very purpose of promising, itself impossible; since no one would believe they were being promised anything, but would laugh at utterances of this kind as empty shams" (Gr II:36 [422]).

Now, plainly Kant assumes as a law of nature that people learn from experience and remember the past; hence once it becomes, as it were, a law of nature that everyone tries to make a false promise (in certain circumstances), the existence of the law becomes public knowledge. Everyone knows of it, and knows that others know of it, and so on. We need not suppose that all laws of nature are public knowledge; obviously they are not. But as a way of interpreting the requirements of the CI-procedure in terms of the law of nature formulation, it is not inappropriate to assume the public recognition of the as-it-were laws of nature generated by people acting from certain maxims.

We make this explicit by saying that in the equilibrium state of the adjusted social world, the as-it-were laws of nature at step (3) are publicly recognized as laws of nature, and we are to apply the CI-procedure accordingly. Let's refer to this public recognition of the as-it-were laws of nature issuing from maxims at step (1) as the publicity condition on universal moral precepts. Kant views acceptable precepts of this kind as belonging to the public moral legislation, so to speak, of a moral community.

3. A further condition is this: we are to think of the adjusted social world as if it has long since reached its conjectured equilibrium state. It is as if it always has existed, exists now, and always will exist. Call this the perpetuity condition.

It is not as if the agent working through the CI-procedure says, "I will that my maxim be a law of nature from now on." This would allow time for the equilibrium state to be reached, in which interval the agent might gain a considerable fortune by deceit. But clearly Kant asks us to regard this state as existing now: people laugh right away at attempts to make deceitful promises. There is no lapse of time. This reading is also required by the important paragraph I:19 (403), but I shall not pursue this here.

§5. Kant's Fourth Example: The Maxim of Indifference

1. To examine the other more plausible example of the use of the four-step procedure, I turn to the fourth example (*Gr* II:38 [423]). The maxim to be tested is one expressing indifference to the needs and happiness of others who request our help and assistance.

In this case the personal and the legislative intentions are perfectly compatible: we can indeed intend to follow our maxim at step (1) in the world of the legislative intention. Rather, we have to decide, as a member of the adjusted social world associated with the maxim at step (1), whether we can will that world as members of it. This is the contradiction in the will test (which Kant illustrates by the second pair of examples) in contrast to the contradiction in conception test (which he illustrates by the first pair of examples). At step (1) the agent's maxim is:

I am not to do anything in order to help others when they are in need, or to assist them in distress, unless at the time it is rational for me to do so, in view of my own interests.

Now, the adjusted social world associated with this maxim is a social world in which no one ever does anything to help others when they need it or to assist others in distress. And this is true of everyone, past, present, and future. This is the relevant equilibrium state; we must suppose this state to obtain, as it were, like any other order of nature, in perpetuity, backwards and forwards in time. Moreover, as before, Kant takes it for granted that everyone in the adjusted social world knows the laws of human conduct that arise from generalized maxims. Thus the publicity and the perpetuity conditions hold.

2. Now, there is a difficulty in understanding the contradiction in the will test. To explain: Kant says that we cannot will the adjusted social world

associated with the maxim of indifference because presumably many situations may arise in that world in which we need the love and sympathy of others. In those situations, by a law originating from our own will, we would have robbed ourselves of what we need and require. It would be irrational, he suggests, for us to will a social world in which everyone, as it were by a law of nature, is deaf to our appeals for help and assistance, unless of course their self-interest moves them otherwise.

The difficulty in question becomes evident once we note that the test Kant applies to the maxim of indifference seems too strong, for it rejects all maxims leading to any form of the precept of mutual aid. The reason is that any such precept will sometimes enjoin us to help others when they are in need. But situations may arise in any associated adjusted social world in which we very much want not to help others, unless the precept involved is quite trivial. Our circumstances may be such that doing so is extremely inconvenient, given our current plans. Once again, by a law originating from our own will, we would have prevented ourselves from doing what we very much want.

The general difficulty is this: in any adjusted social world, all moral precepts will oppose our settled intentions and plans and natural desires on at least some occasions; in those cases they will be contrary to our will. Indeed, one role of moral norms is to provide precisely such opposition as the situation requires. Thus the test of the CI-procedure, as Kant states it, seems to call for some revision.

3. The difficulty is not easily disposed of, but two things may preserve Kant's main thought.

First, we must give more content to the will of ideal agents in deciding whether they can will an adjusted social world. What do such agents will? What priorities if any do they have?

Second, we must specify further the point of view from which these decisions about social worlds are made: What kind of information do ideal agents have and what can they assume about their position and role in an adjusted social world?

Consider the content of the will of an ideal agent: one way out, I think (I don't say the only one), is to develop an appropriate conception of what we may call "true human needs," a phrase Kant uses several times in the

Metaphysics of Morals (6:393, 432f.; 453ff.).[4] I understand Kant to say that we have certain true human needs, certain requisite conditions, the fulfillment of which is necessary if human beings are to enjoy their lives. It is a duty to ourselves to try to secure these needs, and one form of avarice tempts us to violate this duty (*MdS* 6:432). Thus, we must will (so far as circumstances allow) a social world in which that guarantee obtains. Kant suggests what he calls a "maxim of common interest," which may be understood as follows:

> I am to help others in order that their true needs be met when I am in a position to do so, but not to the extent that I become needy myself.

Thus Kant thinks that we have this universal duty, for we are to be considered fellow human beings (*MdS* 6:453): "rational beings with needs, united by nature in one dwelling place for the purpose of helping one another."

In view of the foregoing, it is clear that as between the adjusted social world associated with the precept of indifference and the one associated with the precept of mutual assistance, as ideal agents we can will only the latter: only that world *guarantees* the fulfillment of our true human needs, to the securing of which a rational, prudent being gives priority. As part of the CI-procedure, let's suppose that we have such needs and that they are more or less the same for everyone.

In applying the CI-procedure as revised, we understand that any general precept will restrict our actions as moved by our desires on some and perhaps many occasions. We must compare alternative social worlds and estimate the overall consequences of willing one of these worlds rather than another. In order to do this, we may have to take into account the rough balance of likely effects over time on our true human needs. For this idea to work, even in the kind of case discussed here, we require some account of these needs. Kant holds, I think, that we have "true human needs" (or basic needs) not only for food, drink, and rest, but also for education and

---

4. In adopting this way out, we are amending, or adding to, Kant's account. It is, I think, Kantian in spirit, provided that, as I believe, it doesn't compromise the essential elements of his doctrine.

culture, as well as for various conditions essential for the development and exercise of our moral sensibility and conscience, and for the powers of reason, thought, and judgment. I shall not pursue this suggestion here.

§6. Two Limits on Information

1. Consider now the point of view from which ideal agents decide whether they can will a social world. I believe that Kant may have assumed that the decision at step (4) is subject to at least two kinds of limits on information. That some limits are necessary seems evident from the kind of objection raised by Sidgwick.[5]

The first limit is that we are to ignore the more particular features of persons, including ourselves, as well as the specific content of their and our final ends and desires. Some support for this suggestion appears where Kant is characterizing the realm of ends; he says (Gr II:62 [433]):

> I understand by a "realm" a systematic union of different rational beings under common laws. Now since laws determine ends as regards their universal validity, we shall be able—if we abstract from the personal differences between rational beings, and also from all the content of their private ends—to conceive a whole of ends in systematic conjunction (a whole both of rational beings as ends in themselves and also of their own ends which each may set before himself); that is, we shall be able to conceive of a realm of ends which is possible in accordance with the above principles.[6]

The second limit is that when we ask ourselves whether we can will the adjusted social world associated with our maxim, we are to reason as

---

5. "We can . . . conceive of a man, he says, in whom the spirit of independence and the distaste for incurring obligations would be so strong that he would choose to endure any privations rather than receive the aid of others. But even granting that every one, in the actual moment of distress, must necessarily wish for the assistance of others; still a strong man, after balancing the chances of life, may easily think that he and such as he have more to gain, on the whole, by the general adoption of the egoistic maxim; benevolence being likely to bring them more trouble than profit." See Henry Sidgwick, *The Methods of Ethics*, 7th ed. (London: Macmillan, 1907), pp. 389n.

6. Rawls prefers "realm" to Paton's "kingdom" in "kingdom of ends." [Ed.]

if we do not know what place we may have in that world. I find it hard to read, say, Kant's discussion of the Typic (*KP* 5:69f.) without feeling that some such idea is implicit. He says: "Ask yourself whether, if the action which you propose should take place by a law of a system of nature of which you were a part, you could regard it as possible through your will. Everyone does, in fact, decide by this rule whether actions are morally good or bad. Thus people ask: if one belonged to such an order of things in which . . . everyone looked with complete indifference on the needs of others, would they assent of their own will to being a member of such an order?"

Here what suggests some limit on our knowledge of our place in the adjusted social world is Kant's speaking of our being "a part" of that system of nature, and the suggestion at the end of the passage that we are to consider whether we would "assent of [our] own will," that is, freely assent, to being a member of such a world. That surely depends on what we know about our place in that world. If I know that the fulfillment of my true needs is assured (as socially practicable) by the generalized precepts at step (2), presumably yes; otherwise, probably not.

2. If these two suggestions are correct, the CI-procedure is misapplied when we project into the adjusted social world either the specific content of our final ends or the particular features of our present or likely future political or social circumstances. No one can know, for example, that he is one of Sidgwick's strong men. And in a society where everyone is either a noble or a serf, the nobles cannot reason from a maxim of mutual assistance that limits it to members of their class. Such a maxim relies on illicit information. Rather, they must first guarantee the fulfillment of their own and others' true human needs.

To sum up: we must reason at step (4) not only on the basis of a conception of true human needs but also from a suitably general point of view that satisfies these two limits on particular (as opposed to general) information. This is because the requirements of pure and empirical practical reason represented in the CI-procedure force us to view ourselves as proposing public moral practice for an ongoing social world enduring over time. Any such public law for a realm of ends the members of which are free and equal and reasonable persons must answer to these conditions.

§7. The Structure of Motives

1. With the CI-procedure before us, we can now consider the structure of motives in a person with a firm good will.[7] In the main argument of *Groundwork* I, Kant distinguishes between actions that both accord with duty and are done from duty, and actions that merely accord with duty but arise from inclination. The latter have legality but not morality. The moral worth of actions depends on the principles of volition from which they are done, and not on the purposes—the aims, states of affairs, or ends—the desires for which move us to do the actions.

The distinction Kant has in mind here is explained in the footnote to *Gr* II:14 (413), where he sets out the contrast between our taking an interest in something and our acting from interest. He says:

> The first expression ["take an interest"] signifies practical interest in the action; the second ["acting from interest"] pathological interest in the object of the action. The first indicates the dependence of the will on the principles of reason itself; the second its dependence on the principles of reason at the service of inclination—that is to say, where reason merely supplies a practical rule for meeting the need of inclination. In the first case what interests me is the action; in the second case what interests me is the object of the action (so far as it is pleasant to me).

The distinction Kant makes here is basic. An action done for the sake of duty is one done from an interest taken in the action itself as correctly answering, or so we think, the principles of practical reason. This taking an interest in the action itself in virtue of its meeting those principles is what gives the action its morality as opposed to its mere legality.

2. There are several important consequences of this distinction. I mention two: first, on Kant's view, every action is moved by some interest.

7. For instructive discussions, see Barbara Herman, "On the Value of Acting from the Motive of Duty," *Philosophical Review* (July 1981), 359–382; reprinted in *The Practice of Moral Judgment*, pp. 1–22; and Henry Allison, *Kant's Theory of Freedom* (Cambridge: Cambridge University Press, 1990), chap. 6.

Contrary to what is occasionally said, there is no such thing in Kant as an action from reason alone, if that means an action without a moving interest. Moreover, for Kant every action has an object, or aim—sometimes an aim wanted by inclinations, but sometimes an aim falling under an obligatory end determined by the principles of practical reason.

A second point is that actions of a person with a fully good will—someone whose character is marked by the primary virtues of wisdom, justice, and benevolence and supported by the secondary virtues—often involves both kinds of interests: a practical interest taken in the principles of practical reason and interests in the objects of needs and inclinations. This is so, for example, whenever persons with a good will act within their rights to secure their interests; for here what they do is shaped by those interests, but only after they have confirmed that their interests are compatible with the rights of others. This means that the interests moving our actions are of different kinds and arranged in a certain structure, with the practical interest we take in the moral law itself, so far as we have a good will, always having an effective regulative priority. The nature of that structure is best seen in how we work through the categorical imperative procedure.

Suppose that we were the person tempted to make the deceitful promise of Kant's second example, reviewed above in §4. What tempted us to do that was our inclinations as arising from our needs in a difficult situation. What led us to check our maxim by the CI-procedure—I assume we did this—was not our inclinations but our moral sensibility and the practical interest we take in the moral law. Without this sensibility and practical interest, we would not bother to check, by an exercise of elective will, whether we could incorporate that inclination into a permissible maxim, one that is acceptable to the CI-procedure.[8]

The deliberation of working through the CI-procedure, like every other activity, including reasoning and thought of all kinds, is moved by some interest. This is as true in Kant as it is in Hume. The contrast with Hume lies in the nature of the moving interests and a structure that gives practical interests regulative priority.

---

8. This accords with what Kant says in the *Religion* (6:24): "[F]reedom of the will is of a wholly unique nature in that an incentive can determine the will to action only insofar as the individual has incorporated it into his maxim (has made it into the general rule in accordance with which he will conduct himself)."

3. In *Gr* I:10–12 (397–399), Kant reviews three examples of actions done from duty and showing full moral worth in contrast with actions that, while according with duty, show little or no moral worth. In each case, there is an immediate inclination to do one's duty: the duties to preserve one's life, to help others in need, and to assure one's own happiness. This immediate inclination is so generally present that the moral worth of these actions, if such there is, is not manifest. Kant is concerned with the cases in which moral worth is clearly manifest, for it is in such cases that the principles implicit in our everyday moral judgments are most easily seen.

Kant's second example of the sympathetic friend of man has aroused the greatest consternation. It led Schiller to pen these often quoted lines:

> Gladly I serve my friends, but alas I do so with pleasure.
> Hence I am plagued with doubt that I am not a virtuous person.
> To this the answer is given:
> Surely your only resource is to try to despise them entirely,
> And then with aversion do what your duty enjoins you.

These lines are amusing but rest on the failure to see the difference between Wolff's account of willing as such and Kant's doctrine of a pure will with its idea of an elective will. They overlook the distinction between the practical interest from which we act—an interest having regulative priority in determining what is permissible for us to do—and the other inclinations and affections that we have while we act. These affections may show in our manner of action and in our countenance and expression: we do our duty cheerfully and gladly. But our doing our duty is not dependent on these affections. In persons with a good will, they are not needed as assisting or cooperating psychic forces for them to do their duty.

4. Questions of duty are to be settled solely by considerations of practical reason, and we are to act from inclinations only when we see that the maxims that they suggest are permissible by the CI-procedure. Only in this case are they adopted by the elective will of persons of a fully virtuous character. This does not mean that we are to be without feelings and affections, or that we are not to do our duty cheerfully and gladly. Nor does it mean that the virtuous character of persons of good will is always manifest and plain for all to see. It does mean that in hard times, when like the friend of man they are afflicted with a deadly insensibility, they can still do

as duty requires. Only then perhaps is their virtuous character clearly evident, but this is not at all to say that it was not there before.

It must be admitted that Kant's exposition in I:10–12 (397–399) is not consistent. His aim is to set out an argument giving the nature of the moral law as it can be seen in our commonsense judgments of the moral worth of actions. This he wants to do by focusing on actions that we agree accord with duty but are not supported by the person's inclinations. All along the person may have been of fully virtuous character, yet only now, for the first time, is this fact clear for us to see. The essential contrast is between being virtuous all along and this virtue's being made openly manifest in difficult and trying circumstances.

Yet Kant wavers from this presentation, especially in the second example of the friend of man, by making the contrast that between someone moved by natural inclination alone—who enjoys making others happy as his own work—and who never even appears to consider the moral law at all, and someone who under great stress does manage to act from duty alone. If, as it seems, the friend of man is the same person throughout I:11 (398–399), he must have undergone some kind of conversion of character. This wavering in Kant's exposition should not be allowed to obscure his main doctrine of a pure will with its regulative priority of pure practical interest. I haven't said that Kant's doctrine is fully defensible, but it is perfectly compatible with doing our duty cheerfully and gladly, with all the affections that grace human life. On this, see Kant's reply to Schiller (*Rel* 6:23f., n.).

The Categorical Imperative: The Second Formulation

§1. The Relation between the Formulations

1. One problem in understanding the categorical imperative is to decide how the three formulations are related. Since Kant states each formulation in different ways, there are actually three families of formulations. Last time I set out the categorical imperative in terms of the law of nature formula, which we called the CI-procedure. Our question today is how the two later formulations are related to it.

At the end of the central argument of *Groundwork* (II:12–71 [412–436]), Kant gives a review of the formulas and a summary of the main conclusions (II:72–79 [436–440]). He starts this review by saying that the three ways of representing the principle of morality are actually three different formulations of precisely the same law. Each of them contains a combination of the other two (72). Moreover, when Kant introduces the first formulation (in 31 [421]), he says that there is only a single categorical imperative.

I assume, then, that there is only one categorical imperative with three formulations that are in some way equivalent. The problem is that those formulations are not the same. In particular, the second formulation introduces new and quite different concepts. It reads (II:49 [428–429]):

> Act in such a way that you always treat humanity, whether in your own person or in the person of any other, never simply as a means, but always at the same time as an end.

We need an explanation, surely, of how this formulation, with its three concepts of a person, of humanity, and of treating humanity as an end (an end-in-itself), can be equivalent to the first and third formulations.

There is also the further difficulty that, taken by itself, the discussion in II:46–49 (427–429) preceding the second formulation is quite obscure. I believe that it is best understood in light of what Kant says elsewhere: in the *Groundwork* I:1–7 (393–396) on the absolute value of a good will and the role of reason, as well as what comes later in II:70–71 (435–436); 76–77 (437–438). Very important also is the *Doctrine of Virtue*, as we shall see.

2. Let's begin our account of the relations among the three formulations by looking at what Kant says in his review at II:72–75 (436–437). There, besides saying that these formulations represent the same law, he makes two significant remarks.

First, Kant says that there is a difference between the formulations that is subjectively rather than objectively practical. This suggests that there is not an objective difference between them. The purpose of having several formulations (and these formulations in particular) is to bring the idea of reason—that is, the moral law—nearer to intuition (in accordance with a certain analogy) and so nearer to feeling. At the end of this review (II:75 [436–437]), Kant says that if we wish to gain access, or entry, for the moral law, it is useful to bring one and the same action under all three formulations, and in this way, so far as we can, to bring "it [the action] nearer to intuition."

The second significant remark Kant makes in this passage is that it is better when making a moral judgment to proceed always in accordance with the strict method and take as our basis the universal formula of the categorical imperative: "Act on the maxim that can at the same time be made a universal law." I read this to say that the basis of the strict method is the categorical imperative itself. Yet since we are finite beings with needs, we cannot apply that imperative to our actions directly but can do so only after we have interpreted it in terms of the law of nature formula by setting out the CI-procedure. While this procedure is not the categorical imperative itself, it does provide us with the most usable expression of the strict method based on it.

Thus, whenever we try to check what the categorical imperative requires of us by testing maxims, we are always to apply the CI-procedure. The other formulations cannot add to the content of that imperative ascertained in that way. We are not to read them so that they yield any requirements not already given by our most usable expression of the strict method: the four-step procedure.

3. The point of the other formulations, then, is to look at the CI-procedure from different points of view. My conjecture is this: in the first formulation (using the law of nature formula) we look at a moral situation from the agent's point of view. As reasonable and conscientious persons, we are to submit our rational maxims (which are prompted, say, by our inclinations in some actual or possible context of daily life) to the test of the CI-procedure. Viewing ourselves as subject to moral requirements, we want to check whether acting on our maxim is permissible.

In the second formulation, however, the categorical imperative directs us to view ourselves and other persons as affected by our proposed action. That is, we and others are viewed as passive; or, as Kant puts it, we are to treat humanity, both in ourselves and others, always as an end. In the third formulation (that of autonomy) we come back again to the agent's point of view, but this time not as someone subject to moral requirements, but as someone who is, as it were, legislating universal law: here the CI-procedure is seen as that procedure the adherence to which with a full grasp of its meaning enables us to regard ourselves as making universal law for a possible realm of ends (not kingdom of ends).

This reading departs from Kant's text in one respect (although I don't think it distorts his main point). He says that the various formulations are equivalent in that each includes the other two. But if we take the law of nature formulation as the most usable procedure for us to work out what the categorical imperative asks of us, the second and third formulations are not alternative ways of specifying the same content, nor can they add to its content. Rather, they depend on the CI-procedure and its content—the maxims it accepts—as already laid out. Our task today is to see whether this suggestion is true to Kant's account of the second formulation.

§2. Statements of the Second Formulation

1. There are four statements of the second formulation that it is useful to have in front of us. We have *first* the main statement (II:49 [428–429]):

Act in such a way that you always treat humanity, whether in your own person or in the person of any other, never simply as a means, but always at the same time as an end.

In the review of formulations (II:74 [436]), Kant says, *second:*

A reasonable and rational being in virtue of its nature is an end and consequently an end in itself, and must serve for every maxim as a condition limiting all merely relative and arbitrary ends.

In II:77 (437–438), in the review of the whole argument, we have, *third:*

So act in relation to every reasonable and rational being (both yourself and others) that that being may at the same time count in your maxim as an end in itself.

This formulation, Kant says, is basically the same as a *fourth* (II:77 [437–438]):

Act on a maxim which at the same time contains in itself its own universal validity for every reasonable and rational being.

2. These principles are not the same, although the first three we can recognize as variants of the second formulation. But it is offhand surprising that Kant counts the fourth as a form of the second formulation, since it lacks the special vocabulary of the other three statements. It says nothing about treating humanity as an end in itself. He does so, I think, because, as we shall see, it seems to fit the second formulation as I shall interpret it, especially in its negative interpretation.

Despite the differences in their formulations, two points are important in the first three, leaving aside the fourth.

All three variants stress that we are to treat humanity in our person and in the persons of others in a certain way: never simply as a means but always as an end-in-itself. The second variant adds the thought that since the nature of a reasonable and rational being marks it as an end in itself, that nature must serve as a condition limiting all maxims in the pursuit of merely relative and arbitrary ends, that is, ends of inclinations and pathological interests (*Gr* II:14n. [413]). This thought is also implicit in the other variants.

§3. Duties of Justice and Duties of Virtue

1. I want to explain what I shall call the negative and positive interpretations of the second formulation. The terms "negative" and "positive" are taken from what Kant says in commenting on the fourth example (II:54 [430]) and his saying in II:77 (437–438) that in conceiving of an end not as something to be produced but as self-standing, or independent, we are to think of it only negatively, that is, as an end against which we should never act, and so as something that must never be counted merely as a means.

For reasons already discussed, I assume that the CI-procedure is our best way of following the strict method and so we should take as our basis the universal formula of the categorical imperative. If this is correct, this procedure accepts only those maxims action from which respects the conditions stated in the preceding variants of the second formulation. The question is: How are we to understand this?

2. As background to presenting the negative and positive interpretations, we need first to consider the contrast between the duties of justice and the duties of virtue. There are two principles that Kant treats much like special cases of the moral law. These are the principles of justice and of virtue. The principle of justice says (*MdS* 6:231):

> Every action is right [*recht*] which by itself or by its maxim enables the freedom of each individual will to co-exist with the freedom of everyone else in accordance with universal law.

The first principle of the doctrine of virtue says (*MdS* 6:395):

> Act according to a maxim of ends which it can be a universal law for everyone to have.

Duties of narrow obligation	Duties of wide obligation	
Duties of justice	Duties of virtue	
Apply to outer acts: deeds and not ends	Duties to do or not to do	Duties of commission
	Outer acts	Inner acts	
Duties of narrow requirement		Duties of wide requirement
Necessary and sufficient	Necessary but not sufficient	

One way to see the difference between these principles is that in the principle of justice, the "in order to" clause in the agent's maxim is simply "in order to advance my interests." The clause plays no essential role, and the principle regulates (outer) actions whatever our ends and interests may be. The focus of duties of justice is on what we do: on our deeds, not our ends. But in the principle of virtue, the "in order clause" is essential; recall that in the maxim of mutual help, it took the form: "in order that others' true needs be met."

3. Some contrasts between duties of justice and duties of virtue:

(a) Kant thinks of duties of justice (those specified by a system of just law) as those that can be externally legislated and enforced, or imposed on us by others—for example, by being sanctioned by rewards and punishments. These duties require only specific acts of various kinds, which may be done from any motive, including (as noted above) self-interested motives of all kinds. See the figure on this page.

By contrast, ethical duties cannot be externally imposed on us; we must impose them on ourselves (by internal legislation, as it were). These are duties to pursue certain ends by certain plans and to give those ends a certain weight in our deliberations and conduct. They are, then, duties to act from a certain motive. For Kant, to act from a certain motive (*Bewegungsgrund*) is simply to view a certain end, or state of affairs, as that for the sake of which certain plans are to be followed, and to deliberate and act accordingly (II:46 [427–428]).

(b) Duties of justice are said to be of narrow obligation, whereas duties of virtue are said to be of wide obligation (*MdS*, Intro 6:390). This difference refers to how the duties are established and justified in Kant's scheme. Thus the duties of justice are justified by the principle of justice, and so are, by definition, of narrow obligation; while the duties of virtue are justified by the principle of virtue, and so are, likewise by definition, of wide obligation.

(c) Kant also distinguishes between duties of narrow and wide requirement. This difference refers to how the duties are fulfilled. To fulfill duties of narrow requirement, we must do or not do certain specific acts. On the other hand, duties of wide requirement are fulfilled by adopting and carrying out plans of conduct that give weight to achieving certain ends, which Kant calls "obligatory ends." The basic duties of virtue are of wide requirement: for example, the duty to cultivate our moral and natural perfection. No specifc rules can be given for doing this; it calls for overall plans the carrying out of which is a matter of judgment and good sense.

Now, all duties of justice are duties of narrow requirement: they are fulfilled simply by not doing those specific acts that just law forbids, and doing what it specifically requires. Our motives (ends in view) do not matter, and the doing of specific acts is sufficient. But duties of virtue may also be of narrow requirement, although in a weaker sense. Take the duty not to take our own life: as long as I do not kill myself, I may appear to fulfill this duty. But while necessary, this is not sufficient. Beyond this, I must not kill myself for the right reason (as odd as that sounds): namely, I am not to kill myself as an act to be avoided as a condition, say, of cultivating my moral and natural perfection. If I do not take my life because the law punishes suicides, perhaps by expunging their names from all public records, and if I were a suicide my glorious name would be stricken from all public buildings, then I only appear to fulfill that duty. Similar considerations apply to other duties of virtue that require the avoidance of certain acts: those requiring us not to lie or to fall into self-deception, not to engage in mockery, and so on. These are all cases where certain actions must be done or not done, if the ends specified by the duties of virtue are to be attained.

§4. What Is Humanity?

1. We must now ask what humanity is and what it means to treat it, both in ourselves and in others, as an end-in-itself. If our conjecture is correct,

this meaning is explicable in terms of the maxims accepted by the CI-procedure, once we look at that procedure from the point of view of ourselves and others as affected by the proposed action, and so as passive.

Now, Kant means by humanity those of our powers and capacities that characterize us as reasonable and rational persons who belong to the natural world. Our having humanity is our being both *vernünftig* and animating a human body: reasonable and rational persons, situated in nature with other animals. These powers include, first, those of moral personality, which make it possible for us to have a good will and a good moral character; and second, those capacities and skills to be developed by culture: by the arts and sciences and so forth.

2. To confirm this, let's look at three places in the *Doctrine of Virtue*. The term "humanity" *(Menschheit)* occurs in many passages in this work (I count twenty [there may be more] where it [or a variant] occurs one or more times.)[1] I believe that all of them confirm the above characterization of humanity. Two examples:

(a) At *MdS* 6:387f., Kant explains the concept of qualitative perfection that is used in stating the various duties we have to perfect ourselves. He says that we have the duty to take as one of our ends the perfection of man as such, or "humanity really." These perfections are found in what we can realize by our own actions, not in the gifts we receive from nature. The duty of perfection has two main headings:

(i) the duty to cultivate our natural powers, the highest of which is understanding, including the power to have and apply concepts, among which are the concepts that belong with the concept of duty. We have, then, a duty to raise ourselves from a rough state of animality and to realize ever more fully that humanity in virtue of which we are capable of setting ends.

(ii) the duty of cultivating our will to the purest attitude of virtue, in which acting from a pure practical interest taken in the moral law is the motive, and that law the rule, of our actions.

Thus to realize our humanity is to realize both our moral powers and our natural capacities as expressed in human culture.

---

1. In addition to those in Gregor's index, add these: 87f. (423), 112 (445), 125 (455), 128 (458), 133 (462), 136 (465), 143 (470).

(b) In section XII of the Preface to the *Doctrine of Virtue*, Kant considers the psychological basis of our receptiveness to the thought of duty as such. He believes that there are certain moral dispositions—moral feeling and conscience, love of one's neighbor and respect for oneself—that are natural dispositions of the mind to be affected by concepts of duty. No one has a duty to acquire these natural dispositions, as they are antecedent dispositions on the side of feeling. Our awareness of these dispositions is not of empirical origin, but is known to us only from a knowledge of the moral law and of its effect on our sensibility. Kant goes on to say (*MdS* 6: 400): "No man is entirely without moral feeling, for were he completely lacking in the capacity for it, he would be morally dead. And if . . . the moral life-force could no longer excite this feeling, then humanity would dissolve (by chemical laws, as it were) into mere animality." Thus we might say that humanity is animated pure practical reason. Kant goes on to say that we no more have a special sense for moral good and evil than we do for truth and falsehood; rather, our power of choice *(Willkür)* has a susceptibility to be moved by pure practical reason and its principles, and this is moral feeling.

(c) In §34, Kant says that nature has implanted in man susceptibility to the feelings of sympathetic joy and sorrow, and that to use these feelings as a means of promoting active and rational benevolence is a particular, though only conditioned, duty. He goes on to say (*MdS* 6:457): "It is called the duty of humanity *(humanitas)* because it regards man not merely as a rational being but also as an animal endowed with reason."

He proceeds to distinguish between humanity as located in the power and will to share in others' feelings, which is free because based on practical reason, and mere susceptibility to the joy and sadness of others, which is unfree, merely imparted feeling (as in Hume's *Treatise*) (*MdS* 6:458). Kant thinks that we have an indirect duty to cultivate the sympathetic natural feelings as feelings appropriate to our moral duties and to find in them means to participate in the fate of others, as those duties require. This active "benevolence is required for its own sake in order to present the world in its full perfection as a beautiful moral whole" (*MdS* 6:459; see 457–459). From these typical passages we can read the second formulation as follows: We are always to act so as to treat the powers that constitute our humanity, both in our own person and in the persons of others, never solely as a means, but at the same time as an end: that is, as powers the realization and exercise of which is good in itself, and in case of the moral powers of a good will, the one thing absolutely good in itself in all the world. A check of the other uses of the term "humanity" (II:51 [429], 53 [430], 55 [430–431], 70 [435], 78 [438–439]) all fit this interpretation.

§5. The Negative Interpretation

1. We are now in a position to explain the positive and negative interpretations, which can be paired respectively with the first and second pair of examples. The positive interpretation is quite easy to understand, so I begin with the more difficult negative interpretation. This says, if our conjecture is correct, that the CI-procedure accepts only maxims action on which respects the limits set by reasonable and rational persons who are to be treated as ends-in-themselves (II:77 [437–438]). What are we to make of this suggestion?

Consider once again the example of promising (discussed in Kant II), only this time as illustrating the second formulation (II:52 [429–430]). If we assume that the knowledge and working beliefs of people, and also their circumstances, are sufficiently similar so that they would all assess any proposed (rational) maxim in the same way, then we obtain a plausible interpretation as follows.

Kant is saying that, in the case of a deceitful promise, the promisee (the person to whom the deceitful promise is made) cannot possibly endorse the promisor's way of acting. When I am the promisee, I cannot, as a reasonable being, hold or contain in my person the promisor's end. Kant's text is: "ohne daß dieser [the promisee] zugleich den Zweck in sich enthalte."

Now, the phrase "in sich enthalte" sounds as stilted in German as the parallel phrase does in English: it is not natural in either language to speak of containing in our person other people's ends. We are tempted to render Kant's text into English more idiomatically, for example, by saying that the promisee "shares" the end of the promisor's action, but this has misleading connotations of agreeing or consenting. We must guess what Kant has in mind, recalling that in the fourth formulation above, Kant uses the same phrase, "in sich enthalten."

2. I interpret the text as follows: if the promisee were to apply the CI-procedure to the maxim from which the deceitful promisor acts, the promisee would reject it, just as the promisor would also reject it were the promisor to follow that procedure. When Kant speaks of lack of agreement (in the second sentence of II:52 [429–430]), he means that the promisor's maxim cannot be endorsed by the promisee. Thus if promisor and promisee both act from maxims that pass the CI-procedure, they would accept and reject the same maxims, and both would contain in their persons (and in this sense endorse) each other's (permissible) ends.

If this reading is correct, we can see why in II:77 (437–438) Kant says that:

> So act in relation to every reasonable and rational being (both yourself and others) that that being may at the same time count in your maxim as an end in itself

is fundamentally the same as:

> Act on a maxim which at the same time contains in itself its own universal validity for every reasonable and rational being.

Here it is the maxim that contains in itself *(in sich enhält)* its own validity, which must mean that every reasonable and rational person who applies the CI-procedure correctly will see that the maxim passes, and therefore that all can endorse it.

3. This interpretation may seem a bit thin, even disappointing. Surely Kant means more than this! Indeed he does in the positive interpretation for the duties of virtue. But the negative interpretation fits the important case of the duties of justice. That Kant has these duties in mind in the promising example is shown by his saying that the requirement that others must be able to contain in their person the end of our action is even more plainly violated in attempts on the freedom and property of others (the rights of man). For in these cases, it is clear that we intend to treat others merely as means: we know perfectly well that they cannot endorse our end; we clearly fail to treat them as ends against which we should never act.

Of course, the duties of virtue also satisfy this interpretation, since others can endorse the maxims of ends from which we act when we fulfill our duties of virtue. The difference is that with those duties we also promote the ends enjoined by those maxims: stated in a summary way, we cultivate our own moral and natural perfection and further the happiness of others. Whereas the duties of justice can be met simply by acting within the limits established by a just system of law, and even though we pursue only our own interests and are indifferent to those of others. The duties of justice require no more than the mutual endorsability of the maxims governing our outer actions.

To conclude: humanity in us is simply our powers of reason and thought, and of moral judgment and sensibility. To treat persons as ends in matters of justice—to treat humanity in them as an end—and never as means only is to conduct ourselves in ways that are publicly justifiable to their and our common human reason, and of offering such justifications as the occasion demands. If, further, we care for justice (we count respecting the right of persons as our end and widen our concept of duty beyond what is due [MdS 6:390f.]), then we act from what Kant calls the obligation of virtue (MdS 6:410). We take a pure practical interest in associating with others in ways that they can publicly endorse. That is a very important idea.[2]

4. We have yet to consider the first example of suicide (II:51 [429]). Does the negative interpretation apply to it? Let's look at the fuller statement Kant gives in MdS 6:422f. There he writes:

> Man cannot renounce his personality as long as he is a subject of duty, and hence so long as he lives. It is a contradiction that he should have the moral title to withdraw from all obligation, that is freely to act as if he needed no moral title for this action. To destroy the subject of morality in one's own person is to root out the existence of morality

---

2. The motivation of our desiring to associate with others in ways that they can publicly endorse, or in ways that can be mutually justified, both to them and to us, is taken as a basic assumption of T. M. Scanlon's contractualism. See his "Contractualism and Utilitarianism," in *Utilitarianism and Beyond*, ed. A. Sen and B. Williams (Cambridge: Cambridge University Press, 1982), pp. 103–128.

itself from the world, so far as this is in one's power; and yet morality is an end-in-itself. Thus to dispose of oneself as a mere means to an arbitrary end [an end of natural inclination] is to abase humanity in one's own person *(homo noumenon)*, which was yet entrusted to man as being in the world of nature *(homo phenomenon)* for its preservation.

I don't read this passage as saying that suicide is always wrong. Rather, it says that a moral title for it is always needed, which cannot be given by the ends wanted by natural inclination. The casuistical questions Kant lists in this section imply that such a title can be given by conflicting grounds of obligation *(MdS* 6:224); for these may be at times stronger than the ground not to take our life. Otherwise, the questions listed are not questions! Kant asks, for example, whether it is wrong of a commanding general to carry poison so that if captured he can avoid being ransomed on conditions prejudicial to his country (a reference to Frederick the Great). While Kant's doctrine excludes suicide for reasons based solely on our natural inclinations, it is not always forbidden whatever the reasons. What is required are very strong reasons based on obligatory ends, which may conflict in particular circumstances.

The difficult passage in *Gr* II:77 (437–438) may also apply to suicide. Kant says that a subject (person) that is capable of a good will cannot without contradiction be subordinated to any other object. He is, I think, invoking the priority of the value of a good will found at *Gr* I:3 (394). When we take our life for reasons based on natural inclinations, we subordinate our moral powers to something of merely relative value; this, Kant may think, is a contradiction in the order of values. This fits what Kant says about suicide above in the *Doctrine of Virtue*.

There is, however, an important gap. We still lack an argument of the appropriate kind relying solely on the CI-procedure for the prohibition against suicide. What we can say, though, is that given such an argument, it would then be true that suicide fits under the negative interpretation. It would mean that humanity in us—our moral sensibility and powers of pure practical reason—could not endorse our suicidal action if prompted by our natural inclinations.

§6. The Positive Interpretation

1. The meaning of the positive interpretation is now clear. We treat humanity in our own person and in the person of others as an end-in-itself in a positive way by conscientiously promoting the obligatory ends specified by the duties of virtue. Described summarily, we do this by striving to advance our own perfection (moral and natural) and the happiness of others, where this is specified by their permissible ends (*MdS* 6:8; 450). Assuming that the duties of virtue are given by maxims of ends enjoined by the CI-procedure, the second formulation does not add to the content of the moral law as specified by the strict method (II:74 [436]). It gives another way to look at the content of that law—its matter, as it were (II:73 [436]).

Read this way, the positive interpretation emphasizes that there are objective ends: those valid for all reasonable and rational persons in the sense that every such person must count these ends as ends they are to advance. Thus the moral law not only imposes limits on the means we may adopt in the pursuit of ends as permitted by the duties of justice, but also directs us to hold certain ends as obligatory. In a phrase: the moral law determines elements of the matter, as well as determining the form, of pure will (*MdS* 6:384f.). This is important in connection with Kant's account of freedom: for us to be fully free, pure practical reason must specify at least some of our final ends as well as setting limits on the means we can use for achieving them. Whether it must specify *all* our final ends is a difficult question of interpretation we'll discuss later.

2. The term "humanity" is appropriate in both the positive and negative interpretations: in the negative because it is reasonable and rational beings as possessing humanity that constitute the limits against which we must not act; in the positive because the obligatory ends are intimately connected with the good of human persons: more specifically, with cultivation of their moral and natural perfection and the fulfillment of their proper happiness (as given by their permissible ends). Once obligatory ends are seen as certain values associated with human persons, we see the way in which the good of a (perfected) reasonable and rational person who is happy is an end-in-itself. In this connection, recall from *Gr* I:1–3 (393–394) that moral perfection (a secure good will) is the supreme form of intrinsic value.

Further, the idea of a positive and a negative interpretation of the second formulation is suggested by the fact that there is a natural contrast between the first and the second pair of examples. In the first pair, the point stressed is that we are not to treat humanity in ourselves, or in the person of others, as a mere means to the ends wanted by our natural desires. Whereas in the second pair of examples, Kant stresses that we must go beyond this and make our conduct cohere with humanity in our person, that is, we must promote our greater perfection (moral and natural) and further the happiness of others. Kant draws an intuitively natural contrast between the two pairs of examples and uses the words "negative" and "positive" to express the difference. Hence our terminology.

Often Kant states a basic idea of the *Groundwork* more clearly in a later work. This comes from the second *Critique* 5:87:

> The moral law is *holy* (inviolable). Man is indeed unholy enough; but he must regard *humanity* in his own person as holy. In all creation everything he chooses, and over which he has any power, may be used *merely as a means;* man alone, and with him every rational creature, is an *end in himself.* By virtue of the autonomy of his freedom he is subject to the moral law, which is holy. Just for this reason every will, even every person's own individual will, in relation to itself, is restricted to the condition of agreement with the *autonomy* of a reasonable being, that is to say, that it is not to be subject to any purpose that cannot accord with a law which might arise from the will of the *passive* [*leiden-den*] subject itself; the latter is therefore never to be used merely as a means but itself also at the same time as an end [emphasis on "passive" (for *leidenden*) is mine].

This fits the interpretation proposed, since whether a precept of justice or of virtue might arise from the will of the passive subject is settled by the CI-procedure.

§7. Conclusion: Remarks on *Groundwork* II:46–49 (427–429)

1. There is a difficulty with the suggested reading of the second formulation that must be faced. It concerns the fact that the passages II:46–49 (427–429),

which precede the formulation, have not been mentioned. But, then, how does Kant see their point?

They are, I believe, a preliminary commentary that prepares the way for the idea of humanity. This is borne out by their content. Thus II:46 (427–428) gives a definition of the will of a reasonable being and reviews various distinctions required in giving an account of actions, such as: objective ends versus subjective ends; subjective grounds of desires, or impulsions *(Triebfeder)* versus objective grounds of volition, or motives *(Bewegungsgründe)*; subjective ends based on impulsions versus objective ends based on motives valid for all reasonable beings. After distinguishing formal and material practical principles, Kant states the main point, namely, that material ends have only relative value and can ground only hypothetical imperatives. Whereas, II:47 (428) goes on to say, something whose existence has in itself an absolute value can be the ground of a categorical imperative and so of universal practical laws.

Next, II:48 (428) explains the idea that reasonable beings are persons because their moral powers of reason and moral sensibility already mark them out as ends in themselves—that is, as things that ought not to be used merely as means—and consequently to that extent imposes a limit on how they may be treated. Persons, then, do not have merely relative value for us; they are also objective ends, that is, things the existence of which is an end in itself. In this paragraph, Kant wants to distinguish between our moral powers on the one hand and our inclinations as sources of needs on the other, even going so far (indeed, too far!) as to say that it is the universal wish of a reasonable being to be without inclinations altogether. His point is that we are ends in ourselves, not as subjects of inclinations—of needs and desires—but in virtue of our moral powers of reason and moral sensibility, and thus of our capability to have a good will. This refers us back to I:1–7 (393–396), to the special role of reason and the idea of a good will as the only thing absolutely good in itself.

2. With this in mind, how are we to understand the apparent argument in II:49 (428–429) preceding the statement of the second formulation and grounded on the principle that reasonable nature exists as an end-in-itself? The argument is tedious, but let's persevere. It aims to establish that reasonable nature is an end-in-itself, and therefore that it is an objective principle— valid for all reasonable beings—that reasonable nature, whether that nature

belongs to the agent or to another, is to be regarded as an end-in-itself. Kant's reasoning seems to go as follows (asterisks denote Kant's premises):

(1) Let A be any (arbitrarily chosen) reasonable (human) being.

*(2) Then A necessarily conceives of A's reasonable nature as an end-in-itself.

(3) Thus A's reasonable nature is a subjective end for A. (Definition of subjective end, II:46 [427–428].)

(4) But since A is any reasonable being (from [1]), all reasonable beings necessarily conceive of their own nature as an end-in-itself. (Generalization of [3].)

*(5) Furthermore, A conceives of A's reasonable nature as an end-in-itself for reasons equally valid for all reasonable beings likewise to conceive of A's nature as an end-in-itself.

(6) Now, let B be any reasonable being different from A. Then (from [5]) the reasons for which A regards A's reasonable nature as an end-in-itself are equally valid for B to regard A's nature as an end-in-itself; and vice versa.

(7) Therefore (from [6]) all reasonable beings necessarily conceive of one another's reasonable nature as an end-in-itself. (Generalization of [6].)

(8) Thus reasonable nature is necessarily viewed as an end-in-itself by all reasonable beings, and so it is an objective principle that all reasonable beings are so to conceive of it. (Definition of objective principle, II:46 [427–428].)

3. Several comments on this argument. Contained in the two premises (2) and (5) is a basic point:

The reasons on the basis of which A conceives of, or regards, A's reasonable nature as an end-in-itself are not facts about this nature that include an essential reference to A. It is not that it is A's reasonable nature rather than B's that makes it an end-in-itself for A, but that it is the reasonable nature of some reasonable being. To illustrate: the fact that A is hungry yields a reason for A to get something to eat, but not because it is A that is hungry, but because some reasonable being is hungry, and A is in a good position to secure food for that reasonable being, namely, A.

This point just explained may suggest an argument Kant cannot have intended. Consider the following reasoning (I shorten the presentation a bit):

(1) Each reasonable being necessarily conceives its own reasonable nature as an end-in-itself in the sense that it necessarily regards itself as a subject of inclinations and desires, the satisfaction of which is good, and so as providing reasons why it should act in one way rather than another.

(2) The satisfaction of its own inclinations is good because they are the inclinations of some reasonable being as an end-in-itself.

(3) But since this consideration holds for any reasonable being, it holds for all; so the inclinations of all reasonable beings specify reasons equally valid for any other reasonable being.

(4) Therefore, the fulfillment of inclinations and desires is, in general, good; and to treat reasonable nature as an end-in-itself is to consider everyone's inclinations and desires, one's own included, as defining *pro tanto* reasons equally valid for all.

Now, utilitarians maintain that the principle of utility, by taking everyone's desires and inclinations into account on an impartial basis, treats everyone as ends-in-themselves and never as means only. To treat persons as means only, they say, is to disregard their desires and inclinations, or not to give them an appropriate weight. I mention this misreading of Kant's argument to indicate what we must avoid. For by viewing people as subjects of desires and inclinations and assigning value to their satisfaction as such, (classical) utilitarianism is at odds with Kant's doctrine at a fundamental level. He cannot have meant the argument of II:49 (428–429) in this way; for him, only permissible desires and inclinations—ones that suggest to us maxims acceptable to the CI-procedure—can specify good reasons.

I add as an addendum: the footnote to II:52 (429–430) deserves notice. Here Kant repudiates the suggestion that the second formulation comes to the same thing as the precept "Quod tibi non vis fieri" (don't do unto others what you do not want done to yourself). That he thinks of the negative statement of the Golden Rule in this connection is perhaps significant. More relevant is his protest that this precept is not acceptable as it stands, as shown by his last remark: it seems he imagines the convicted criminal to say to the judge, "If you were me you would not want to be sentenced, therefore etc."

What Kant must mean is that, to be reasonable, the criminal must assess the judge's action by reasoning in accordance with the CI-procedure and not in terms of the criminal's own situation and desire not to be punished. What is wrong with the Golden Rule (in both its positive and negative versions) is that as stated it allows our natural inclinations and the special circumstances to play an improper role in our deliberations. But in saying this Kant implies that the CI-procedure specifies their proper role.

KANT IV

The Categorical Imperative: The Third Formulation

§1. Gaining Entry for the Moral Law

1. Recall our conjecture about how the three formulations of the categorical imperative are related. The first formulation specifies the CI-procedure in terms of the law of nature formula. This procedure is neither the moral law nor the categorical imperative, but it is, I have suggested, the most usable way for us, beginning from the universal formula of the categorical imperative as the strict method, to work out what the categorical imperative requires of us. The second and third formulations do not add to the content of the moral requirements specified by the CI-procedure; rather, they lay out two further points of view that complement it.

Thus, in the first formulation, we look at the moral situation from the agent's point of view, and regard ourselves as subject to the moral law. In the second, we are directed to view ourselves and other persons as affected by our action, and so as passive. The question is how we are treating humanity both in ourselves and in others. In the third formulation, that of autonomy, which we discuss today, we come back again to the agent's point of view, this time regarding the agent not as someone subject to the categorical imperative, but as someone who is, as it were, legislating moral requirements. Here the CI-procedure is seen as that procedure adherence to which with a full grasp of its meaning enables us to regard ourselves as making universal law for a possible realm of ends.

2. Recall also that Kant says in his review (at II:72–75 [436–437]) that

there is a difference between the formulations that is subjectively rather than objectively practical. The reason for having several formulations is to bring an idea of reason nearer to intuition (in accordance with a certain analogy) and so nearer to feeling. At the end of the review, Kant says that if we wish to gain access, or entry, for the moral law, it is useful to bring one and the same action under all three formulations, and in this way, as far as we can, to bring "it [the action] nearer to intuition."

Here Kant's text may not convey his full meaning. For while there is no doubt that the pronoun *sie* would normally be taken to refer to the action, earlier in II:72 (436) he says that the moral law is an idea of reason which it is the purpose of the different formulations to bring nearer to intuition. So "an idea of reason" may be the best reference for the pronoun (Paton's "universal formula" is incorrect). In any case, since the moral law is an idea of reason (II:3 [407–408]; 72 [436]), Kant's point is that the three formulations of the categorical imperative are more effective than any one in bringing that law as an idea of reason nearer to intuition, thus gaining access, or entry, for it.

3. Let's consider what Kant may mean by gaining entry for the moral law. Last time, we saw that it is a feature of our humanity that we have certain moral dispositions, such as moral feeling and conscience, love of neighbors, and self-respect. It is basic to Kant's moral psychology that the more clearly the moral law is presented to us as an idea of reason, and the more clearly we understand its origins in our person as free, the more forcefully it arouses our moral sensibility (lacking which we are morally dead [*MdS* 6:400]).

Further, Kant thinks that the moral law can move us so strongly as to outweigh all of our natural inclinations, even the love of life itself (*KP* 5: 30). So his thought is that the three formulations, when viewed in tandem, present the moral law more clearly and disclose to us its origins in our person, all in such a way that we may be strongly moved to act from it. Somehow they work together to bring an idea of reason nearer to intuition by a certain analogy. Our task is to look at the third formulation in this light, to try to understand how an idea of reason (here the moral law) is brought nearer to intuition, and to identify the analogy Kant has in mind.

4. I mention two passages relevant to the preceding. In II:9 (410–411), Kant says that a metaphysics of morals (an account of the laws of freedom

and the principles of a pure will: the principles of practical reason [*Gr* Pref: 2–4 (387–388); 8–10 (389–391)]) not only is the necessary theoretical basis for a clear knowledge of our duties, but also is of first importance for the actual fulfillment of the moral law. He adds: "The pure thought of duty, and in general the moral law, has by way of reason alone . . . an influence on the human heart so much more powerful than all further incentives capable of being called up from the field of experience that, in consciousness of its own dignity, reason despises these incentives and is able gradually to become their master."[1]

In Kant's reply to Sulzer in II:9n. (411), he says that popular moral instruction fails because it doesn't present the principles of morals as principles of *pure* practical reason. Popular instruction relies on a great variety of considerations appealing to many kinds of motives. Whereas Kant thinks that ordinary observation shows that "[w]hen a righteous act is represented as being done with a steadfast mind in a complete disregard of any advantage in this or in another world . . . it leaves far behind any similar action affected even in the slightest degree by an external incentive and casts it into the shade. . . . It uplifts the soul and arouses a wish that we too could act in this way."

Kant's thought is this: when we are presented with a clear conception of the moral law, and see it exemplified in someone's life, we are made fully aware for the first time of the dignity of our nature as free, reasonable, and rational persons. Were it not for this clear conception of the moral law as a law of freedom and the awareness of its powerful effect on us as such a law, Kant thinks we would not know what we are: our nature as free persons would remain hidden to us. A clear understanding and awareness of the moral law is the way to this self-knowledge.

We have yet to discuss why Kant thinks that the moral law is a law of freedom. But that the CI-procedure be able to exhibit it as such is the second condition we imposed on an acceptable rendering of the categorical imperative (the first was that of significant content). We return to this when we discuss the fact of reason.

1. Here we see a feature of what I shall call Kant's "Manichean" moral psychology as opposed to his "Augustinian" moral psychology. These psychologies we take up later in connection with the *Religion*.

§2. The Formulation of Autonomy and Its Interpretation

1. I begin by stating three variants of this formulation from the ten or so found in II:55–80 (430–440). The first expresses autonomy as an idea of reason (end of II:55 [430–431]; 57 [431–432]):

(a) [T]he supreme condition of the will's conformity with universal practical reason . . . [is] the idea of the will of every reasonable and rational being as a will that makes universal law.

In II:75 (436–437), we have an important formulation of the principle, that of complete determination (using Kant's terminology). I count it as one of autonomy, given its order in the review of formulas:

(b) All maxims as proceeding from our making of law ought to cohere into a possible realm of ends as a realm of nature.

This translates Kant's words "zuzammenstimmen . . . zu einem möglichen Reiche der Zwecke" not as "harmonize with" (Paton) but as "cohere into." I think that it is closer to Kant's thought, which is not that there is a realm of ends, already there, so to speak, with which our making of law must somehow harmonize. Rather, our making of law as we intelligently and conscientiously follow the principles of practical reason (as procedurally represented by the CI-procedure) constitutes, or constructs, the public moral law for a realm of ends. This thought will be important later when we come to Kant's moral constructivism.

In II:78 (438–439), in the part of the review of the argument that covers the third formulation, we have an additional imperative formulation:

(c) Act as if your maxims had to serve at the same time as a universal law (for all reasonable and rational persons).

These three different formulations illustrate the very different ways in which Kant may state a basic thought or principle. A contemporary writer would not normally write so loosely or use such a diversity of expressions. No matter: it's possible to get the sense if you listen to the music.

2. The problem in interpreting the second formulation is in seeing how

it can be equivalent to the other formulations, given the new concepts it introduces. The problem with the third formulation is seeing how it differs importantly from the first. For if it doesn't, what is the point of it? What does it add?

The answer is provided by noticing, first, that all the variants stress the idea that we are to act in such a way that we can regard ourselves as legislating universally through our maxims; and second, that some of the formulations make it explicit that, in legislating universally, we are to view ourselves as members of a possible realm of ends (a moral commonwealth). With the autonomy formulation, there is a shift of point of view that fits our conjecture: we now come back to viewing ourselves not as subjects of the moral law, but as legislators, as it were, of the public moral law of a possible realm of ends. This connects with Kant's reasons for using the term "autonomy" as he explains them in II:60 (432–433).

3. We should ask: Why does Kant in his discussion of the contrast between autonomy and heteronomy (II:80 [440]) refer to the principle of autonomy as the sole principle of morality? Perhaps the explanation is that the third formulation is the last in order of presentation. The two preceding formulations presupposed the final point of view of ourselves as legislative members of a possible realm of ends. There is a natural progression from one formulation to the next, with the second depending on the first and the third depending on the preceding two and uniting them in the idea of autonomy, in the idea of the moral law as a law we give to ourselves as free and equal persons. This is Kant's rendering of Rousseau's statement in the *Social Contract*, Book I, Chapter 8, paragraph 3: "car l'impulsion du seul appétit est esclavage, et l'obéissance à la loi qu'on s'est prescrite est liberté."

Thus in order to regard ourselves as free and equal legislative members of a realm of ends, we must be sure that the maxims from which we act answer to the requirements of practical reason represented in the CI-procedure, and hence that our maxims do not subject others to purposes that do not accord with a law they can endorse as consistent with their humanity.

Of course, the thought of our legislating for a possible realm of ends is purely hypothetical. We are to view our maxims as authorized by precepts that could serve as the publicly recognized moral law of such a commonwealth. We do this as individuals, and not as one corporate body, all of us acting collectively through an institutional procedure.

4. Now, what we legislate, viewed as a moral law for a possible realm of ends, is the whole family of general precepts appearing at step (2) that are accepted by the CI-procedure. Put another way: we legislate the adjusted social world at step (4) when we take that world to be the one paired with the totality of maxims from which we are to act. It's as if this totality of maxims is transformed at the same time into laws of nature. Here I rely on the variant of the third formulation ([b] above) that occurs in the review of formulations in II:75 (436–437). I state it more fully thus:

> Always act so that the totality of the maxims from which you act is such that you can regard yourself as enacting through those maxims a unified scheme of public moral precepts the endorsing of which by all reasonable and rational persons is consistent with their humanity and would bring about (under favorable conditions) a realm of ends.

Stated in this more complete way, it is obvious that this formulation introduces a problem that Kant has not so far discussed explicitly, namely, that of conflicting grounds of obligation (MdS 6:224). I shall not consider this problem here. Let's just assume that the CI-procedure can be formulated so as to yield precepts, or guidelines, by reference to which it is possible to decide, often at least, which of several moral precepts is supported by the strongest grounds of obligation, should those precepts conflict in particular cases. I doubt that Kant has an adequate account of this problem; and to pursue it would detract from more basic questions.

§3. The Supremacy of Reason

1. Kant's discussion of autonomy in II:55–60 (430–433) contains two important claims that we should try to understand. The first claim may be stated as follows (see II:56 [431]): it is just because we can, as reasonable and rational, regard ourselves as legislating the content of the categorical imperative (as it applies to us) that we are legitimately subject to its requirements.

From II:60 (432–433), this can be stated thus: we are subject only to laws that we might have made as reasonable and rational; and we are bound only to act in conformity with a will that is our own, and which has, as nature's purpose for it, the role of making universal law. Kant explains here why he uses the term "autonomy."

Finally, drawing on II:78 (438–439): all persons, as ends in themselves, must be able to regard themselves as makers of universal law with respect to any law whatever to which they may be legitimately subjected.

2. Now, why should Kant claim that we are bound only by a law that we can give to ourselves? Is this a further idea not already contained in viewing ourselves as subject to the moral law as a law of our reason (as indirectly represented by the CI-procedure)? Or can we explain Kant's claim by drawing out what is already implicit in what we have said about how the formulations are related? His claim follows once we recall two points we have assumed.

One is that the CI-procedure specifies the entire content of the categorical imperative as it applies to us, so the totality of precepts (the generalized maxims at step [2]) that pass that procedure define all the norms to which we are legitimately subject.

The other point is that it is through the CI-procedure that we can view ourselves as making universal law for a realm of ends, and so as making law for ourselves as a member thereof.

Thus all the moral norms to which we are legitimately subject are norms we can view ourselves as legislating as reasonable and rational persons. Kant's claim is the upshot of how we have supposed the first and third formulations to be related.

3. The second important claim Kant puts forward is this (II:58 [432]): that a supremely legislative will (that is, one subject to no higher or more authoritative will) cannot itself be dependent on any interest. Kant means that such a will cannot be dependent on interests derived from natural desires, but depends solely on interests taken in the principles of practical reason (Gr II:14n. [413]).

In II:60 (432–433), we get some idea of what Kant means: he says that heretofore writers have regarded people as if they were subject to the moral law in much the same way that they are subject to the law of the state.

They have asked what natural interests, or what inclinations, prompt us to comply with the moral law, or with the law of nature viewed as the law of God known by reason, which we have an obligation to obey in virtue of God's commands. On their view, the moral law is like the sovereign's law enforced by sanctions. Kant's objection is that these sanctions lead us (indeed, compel us [*KP* 5:146ff.]) to comply with the moral law not for its own sake, but for the sake of something else: our lives, or properties, or whatever we might lose from the sanctions that uphold the law. Whereas when the moral law is properly exhibited to us without allurements of pleasure or threats of pain, we take a pure practical interest in it. It needs no such sanctions.

4. What is involved here is a very fundamental point, difficult to state clearly: namely, the supremacy of reason, in this case pure practical reason. In Kant I, we noted this as one of the main themes of Kant's moral philosophy. It is not surprising that it should come up here in connection with the autonomy formulation.

Now, as rationalists, Cudworth and Clarke, and Leibniz too (as we shall see), also accept the supremacy of reason. But with them this is expressed by saying that God's reason is prior to and governs the divine will. As we saw, for Clarke the content of God's reason, as far as it concerns right and wrong, is known to us by rational intuition. We grasp that content as given by a prior and independent moral order determining the fitnesses of things. While God's legislative reason may be autonomous (if we use Kant's language here), Clarke would find it unthinkable to say that we are autonomous, that is, that we can be bound only by a law we can give to ourselves as reasonable and rational, or as free and equal legislative members of a possible realm of ends. He would think this to be a radical and alarming doctrine.

For Kant, however, God's reason is intuitive reason and quite different from our own (*KU* §77). We comprehend only our human reason, with its various powers and concepts, principles and ideas, discerned by reflecting on our thought and capacity for judgment. It is our practical human reason that must have supremacy on moral questions; we have no access to a higher, more supreme, reason. What is radical is the place Kant gives to human reason and the constructivist role he sees it as having. Later we shall come back to these matters.

§4. The Realm of Ends

1. Now that we have the three formulations in front of us, we are almost ready to discuss our question, namely, how the moral law as an idea of reason is brought nearer to intuition by means of an analogy, and what the analogy is that Kant has in mind. We must, however, first discuss what Kant says about the very important concept of the realm of ends, particularly in II:61–71 (433–436); 76–78 (437–439).

Kant introduces this concept by taking every reasonable and rational person to be autonomous and to belong to one moral world, *mundus intelligibilis* (II:78 [438–439]), in virtue of their practical reason. The realm of ends turns out to be an ideal (as Kant says in II:63 [433]); this is relevant, as I explain later. He says (II:61 [433]): "The concept of every reasonable and rational being as one who must regard himself as making universal law by all the maxims of his will and must seek to judge himself and his actions from this point of view, leads to the closely connected and very fruitful concept, that of a realm of ends."

2. Now, Kant understands a realm of ends as a systematic conjunction of reasonable and rational persons under common (moral) laws; and I think we may suppose, although this is not made explicit, that these laws are public and mutually recognized. This follows from the publicity condition of the CI-procedure (II:4 [408]) together with the shared knowledge of one another's reasonable nature. Kant's description of systematic conjunction is not easy to interpret. He says (II:62 [433]): "Since laws determine ends as regards their universal validity, we shall be able—if we abstract from the personal differences between reasonable and rational persons, and also from all the content of their private ends—to conceive a whole of all ends in systematic conjunction (a whole both of such persons as ends in themselves and also of the ends which each sets for himself)."

To understand what Kant means by a whole of ends in systematic conjunction, we should also take into account the next paragraph. Thus, as he says there (II:63 [433]), the systematic conjunction characteristic of a realm of ends arises when all reasonable and rational persons treat themselves as well as others as such persons and therefore as ends in themselves. From the second formulation, this means that everyone not only pursues their personal (permissible) ends within the limits of the duties of justice (the rights of man) but also gives significant and appropriate weight to the oblig-atory ends enjoined by the duties of virtue. These duties, to state them summarily, are to promote one's moral and natural perfection and the hap-piness of others. In addition, everyone has the end of respecting the rights of justice, for this too is meritorious (*MdS* 6:390) and an obligation (not a duty) of virtue, as Kant explains (*MdS* 6:410).

From the third formulation, Kant must suppose that in a realm of ends everyone recognizes everyone else as not only honoring their obligation of justice and duties of virtue, but also, as it were, legislating law for their moral commonwealth. For all know of themselves and of the rest that they are reasonable and rational, and this fact is mutually recognized. While this mutual recognition is clear from what Kant says, and I assume that it is a feature of a realm of ends, he does not explicitly state it. If he thought it too obvious to be worth stating, he was mistaken: what is neglected is explicitly drawing attention to the mutual recognition of the moral law in the public role of a society's moral culture. Hegel will stress just this point.

What is unclear is the role of abstracting from the personal differences between persons and from the content of their private ends in conceiving a whole of all ends in systematic conjunction. In Kant II, I suggested that this might be interpreted as imposing certain limits on information at step (4) of the CI-procedure when the agent has to decide between adjusted social worlds. Certainly Kant needs to introduce some such limits. But that conjecture, even if correct, doesn't address the question here, unless he means that clearing away the clutter of those differences makes it easier to grasp what the structure of a realm of ends involves. This seems unsatisfac-tory: it must mean more than this! But what?

3. An essential feature of the realm of ends is the condition of member-ship, as discussed in II:68–71 (434–436). This condition is simply moral per-sonality, or the powers of practical reason. Kant distinguishes between things that have a market price (those that answer to human inclinations and needs) and those that have a fancy price (those that give satisfaction to the purposeless play of our mental powers). He then introduces the con-cept of dignity. Moral personality alone has dignity (II:70 [435]): "Morality is the only condition under which reasonable persons can be ends in them-selves; for only through this is it possible to be a law-making member in a realm of ends."

Alternatively, it is moral personality as the capacity for a good will that makes us ends-in-ourselves and specifies the condition of our membership in the realm of ends. Kant says in II:67 (434) that unless a reasonable person's will can be regarded as under the practical necessity of making universal law, this person cannot be viewed as an end-in-itself. He repeats this in II: 77 (437–438), 78 (438–439).

In II:71 (435–436), Kant asserts that what explains the supreme status of the value of a good will, or as he says here "a morally good character or virtue," is just its enabling us to take part in the making of universal law: it is this that fits us to be a member of a possible realm of ends. At the end of II:71 (435–436) he says, "Autonomy is therefore the ground of the dignity of human and of every other reasonable and rational nature."

Thus the ground of dignity is the capacity to make universal law and to act from the principle of autonomy. This autonomy reflects the autonomy (or the supremacy) of pure practical reason.

4. Thus it is in virtue of the capacity for a good will that each person has dignity. This is not to say that all persons have equal value, and therefore that they are in this sense equal, for there is no measure of dignity at all. Rather, they all have dignity, and this has the force of including all persons as members in a possible realm of ends. It also removes the worth of persons from any comparison with the relative and subordinate values of things (II:48 [428]).

Nor need we give a meaning to comparisons of the dignity of different persons: with everyone included as reasonable and rational in a possible realm of ends, all questions that arise as to how to act toward persons are settled by the moral law (the content of which is specified for us by the CI-procedure). Now, in the working through of that procedure, the weight to be given to the absolute value of a good will has no special place. Weight is given to it by the wide duty to further our moral perfection, and by the duty not to put obstacles in the way of others in furthering their moral perfection. Our aim in deliberation is to meet the requirements that the categorical imperative imposes on us. The absolute value of a good will is not to be taken, as in a teleological conception, as the supreme value to be maximized.

This in no way lessens the fundamental role of the absolute value of good will. It means only that we have to understand its significance in a special way. It is not a supreme value to be pursued above all else. It lies in the background, rather, and has two roles: first, it expresses Kant's view of the dignity of persons as capable of a good will, and it identifies those to whom the moral law applies and who we must regard as members of a realm of ends. The capacity for a good will defines the aristocracy of all. The second role, as we discussed in Kant I, is that it is central to his idea of the meaning of human life and even of creation itself. It marks one of the religious aspects of his moral doctrine.

§5. Bringing the Moral Law Nearer to Intuition

1. At the end of our discussion of Hume's criticism of Clarke's rational intuitionism, I commented on the apparent inability of Clarke's view to give a convincing account of how the fitnesses of things connect with the final aims and purposes of human life, and with our moral psychology generally. Put another way, in view of the central place of moral values in our life, how do these fitnesses explain their importance? We didn't say that Clarke cannot give an answer, only that he didn't seem to do so.

By contrast, when we concluded our discussion of Hume, we noted that he did try to answer the analogous question as it arose concerning his moral sense doctrine. He did this by maintaining that this doctrine is reflectively stable: that is, when we understand the basis of our moral sense—how it is connected with sympathy and the propensities of our nature, and the content of our moral judgments—we confirm it as derived from a noble and generous source. This self-understanding, Hume thinks, renders our moral character more solid and discloses to us the happiness and dignity of virtue. He claims this as an advantage of his view over those of Clarke and Hutcheson, for in their doctrines the fitnesses of things, or the moral sense, remains opaque and has no intelligible connection with what is of central importance in human life.

Now, we may suppose that a similar difficulty arises for Kant. Why, after all, should we take any more interest in the principles of pure practical reason, as Kant thinks of them, than we should take in Clarke's fitnesses of things? Our topic then is whether Kant has an intelligible and plausible answer to this question. He thinks he does, and I indicate how it seems to go.

2. I begin with some preliminary points. Earlier we discussed Kant's saying that the purpose of having different formulations of the categorical imperative is to bring an idea of reason nearer to intuition.[2] But we left unsettled what this might mean. I now try to clarify this matter, drawing on what we have said about the three formulations.

The idea of reason to which Kant refers in II:72 (436) is surely the moral law (or, as he says, the principle of morality). Now, for Kant an ideal (as opposed to an idea of reason) is the conception of an individual thing (a particular), determinable and even determined by an idea of reason (KR B596). Humanity is an idea of reason, and a conception of a perfect human being, one determined by this idea, is an ideal, although this ideal human being exists, of course, only in thought.

Thus Kant says that the wise man of the Stoics is an ideal of a man in complete conformity with the idea of wisdom (KR B597). In II:63 (433), he indicates that the realm of ends is also an ideal of reason, and as such it is of a particular. This particular is the moral commonwealth consisting of all reasonable persons. Its members have a settled good will and fulfill all of their duties of justice and of virtue.

One further point before we can begin to pull the threads together: an intuition for Kant is the awareness, or the experience, of a particular, of an individual thing. This thing may be rather abstract, as in the case of the pure intuition of (the one) space and of (the one) time in which is ordered our experience of objects and of ourselves in our social world.

3. With this background, let's say that we may bring the idea of reason (the moral law) nearer to intuition by using all three formulations of the categorical imperative to elucidate the ideal of a realm of ends, that is, to elucidate the conception of a moral commonwealth ordered into a systematic conjunction of ends by the actions of its members as they honor the requirements of the categorical imperative. (As always, we suppose that they follow the CI-procedure as the most usable expression of that imperative.) This does not, of course, bring the idea of reason to intuition: that

2. Keep in mind that we have stated these formulations in terms of the law of nature formula; and we distinguish between the moral law, the categorical imperative, and the CI-procedure as three different things. Taking the universal law formula of the categorical imperative as the basis of the strict method (II:75 [436–437]), the CI-procedure, we say, expresses this imperative in the way most usable for us.

is impossible. An idea of reason can at best be approximated to, in thought as well as in any existing thing. All the same, the idea is brought nearer to intuition in that the realm of ends, as an ideal, is the conception of a particular. The conception of it becomes far more determinate once we comprehend the procedures of moral deliberation that inform the thought of the members of such a realm and the various duties and obligations they recognize as binding.

We still must ask why doing this might bring an action required by the moral law nearer to feeling. Moreover, what kind of feeling does Kant have in mind? The answer is similar to what he says in II:9 (410–411), which we have considered already. Just as the representation, or an exemplar, of a morally worthy action done from a steadfast regard for the requirements of the moral law apart from all advantage to oneself uplifts the soul and arouses in us the wish that we could act in the same way, so, likewise, the ideal of a realm of ends (as the conception of a particular moral world) arouses in us the wish that we could be a member of that world. We have a conception of what being a member of that commonwealth would be like and how its members conduct themselves toward one another. For example, one thing that strikes us is that they desire to act, and do act, only in ways that they can justify to one another. (As we saw last time, this is a consequence of the second formulation.)

4. On this interpretation, then, Kant's thought is this: the three formulations work in tandem to provide the concepts and principles for elaborating the conception of a realm of ends. This conception now begins to be full enough for us to form a conception of ourselves as members of such a world, and this more determinate conception of a possible society stirs our moral sensibility far more deeply than did the categorical imperative in its first formulation alone. The principles of practical reason have now been connected together to fit into a conception of a realm of ends, including a conception of ourselves as a member thereof. Understanding these conceptions makes possible the conception-dependent desire to be such a person. For we then have a conception of our relations with others, as well as of ourselves as autonomous, and of all having an equal status rooted in their pure practical reason and moral sensibility. This status is expressed by the idea of the aristocracy of all. To further this self-knowledge as the basis for such a conception-dependent desire is one aim of moral philosophy (I:20–22 [403–405]).

There are three ways, then, that we can use to bring the moral law as an idea of reason nearer to intuition. We can give three formulations of the CI-procedure; we can use these formulations and the requirements they impose to spell out how members of a realm of ends (as a particular moral commonwealth) conduct themselves toward one another; and finally, we can present moral exemplars, that is, persons who in their life and actions exhibit to a high, or to the highest, degree actions done for the sake of duty alone without the allurements of pleasure and glory and in the face of great danger and death.

Kant believes that doing these things arouses in us (given our powers of reason and moral sensibility) a pure practical interest in the moral law and its requirements. As he says in the Methodology of the second *Critique*, it is a way in which "we can give the laws of pure practical reason *access* [*Eingang*] to the human mind, and *influence* [*Einfluss*] on its maxims, that is, by which we can make the objectively practical reason subjectively practical also" (Kant's italics) (*KP* 5:151). This is accomplished because we now see what following pure practical reason means for human life: we are made aware of the content of its practically necessary object—the realm of ends—and the ideal of human life it expresses. A conception-dependent desire to be a member of such a realm is the outcome. That this is so is a fact about persons as reasonable and rational and animating a human body.

§6. What Is the Analogy?

1. Finally, what analogy does Kant have in mind in II:72 (436) when he speaks of bringing an idea of reason nearer to intuition in accordance with a certain analogy? One analogy is surely that of regarding a moral precept as a law of nature in the first formulation of the CI-procedure. But he refers to a more extensive analogy in several places (II:57 [431–432]; 72 [436]; 76 [437]; 78 [438–439]) and also in other works. A particularly full statement occurs in the second *Critique*.

We saw that in the CI-procedure at steps (3) and (4) it is supposed that all persons in the adjusted social world act from the general precept at step (2) as if by a law of nature. Now, once we view the moral law as a totality of such precepts (in line with the variant of the third formulation that we called that of complete determination), we see why Kant says at *KP* 5:43:

> This law (the moral law) gives to the sensible world, as sensuous nature (as concerns reasonable and rational persons), the form of an intelligible world . . . without interfering with the mechanism of the [sensible world]. Nature, in the widest sense, is the existence of things under laws. The sensuous nature of [reasonable beings in nature] . . . is their existence under empirically conditioned laws. . . . The supersensuous nature of the same persons . . . is their existence according to laws which are independent of all empirical conditions and which therefore belong to the autonomy of pure reason.

2. Perhaps the analogy is this. In science we pursue the ideal of unifying the knowledge of the understanding by the regulative idea of systematic unity. In doing this, we assume that nature is ordered as if it is the work of pure reason realizing in the world the highest systematic unity (*KR* B670–696). Similarly, we order our social world by acting from valid moral precepts as if they were laws of nature. In this case, it is our pure practical reason that orders the social world as it introduces systematic conjunction into a whole of ends. By giving our social world the form of an intelligible world, the principles of pure practical reason are brought closer to feeling and gain access to our moral sensibility. We now take a pure practical interest in those principles, which gives them an influence over our maxims.

Finally, note a basic contrast between an order of nature according to natural laws and an order of nature with the form of an intelligible world Kant draws some paragraphs later as follows (*KP* 5:44):

> The difference, therefore, between the laws of a system of nature to which *the will is subject* and a system of *nature which is subject to a will* (as far as the relation of the will to its free actions is concerned) rests on this: in the former, the objects must be the causes of the conceptions which determine the will, and in the latter, the will is the cause of the objects. Hence, in the latter the causality of the objects has its determin-

ing ground solely in the pure faculty of reason, which therefore may
be called pure practical reason.

We shall come back to these matters later, as the contrast Kant draws
here is related to a fundamental difference between theoretical reason as
concerned with the knowledge of given objects, and pure practical reason
as concerned with the production of objects according to a conception of
those objects (*KP* 5:15, 16, 63–65, 89f.).

[Before proceeding, readers should take note of the two Leibniz lectures.—
Ed.]

KANT V

The Priority of Right and the Object of the Moral Law

[Before proceeding, readers should take note of the two Leibniz lectures. The discussion that follows assumes familiarity with them.—Ed.]

§1. Introduction

1. Today, after our brief look at Leibniz in the two preceding lectures, we return to Kant. In discussing Leibniz, I focused on two main points: first, his metaphysical perfectionism, and second, his conception of freedom as it is set within his predicate-in-subject account of truth. On both these matters, Kant has quite different views, as we shall see. Kant's differences with respect to metaphysical perfectionism will become evident today and next time as we consider the priority of right and what I shall call Kant's moral constructivism. These terms are not standard in describing Kant's doctrine, but I hope that they will become clear as we proceed.

I recall several points about how to understand the CI-procedure. We may regard it as Kant's attempt to formulate a procedural representation of all the criteria that are relevant in guiding our moral reasoning if our reasoning is to be valid and sound. That procedure represents, in procedural form, all the requirements of practical, as opposed to theoretical, reason. Very briefly, practical reason concerns the production of objects in accordance with a conception of those objects, whereas theoretical reason concerns the knowledge of given objects (*KP* 5:14f., 65f., 89f.). Practical reason presupposes theoretical reason in the sense that the CI-procedure takes for granted an already established background of commonsense beliefs and knowledge about the world. Thus, at step (1) in deciding whether a maxim is rational, and in assessing adjusted social worlds at step (4), agents are supposed to have considerable knowledge, which is public and mutually shared. Or so I have assumed.

2. Now, the CI-procedure should not be viewed as an account of an alleged process of reasoning that we are said to be consciously and explicitly going through whenever moral questions arise. I take Kant to hold (see *Gr* I:20–22 [403–405], for example) that our moral reasoning (when it is valid and sound) satisfies the requirements of the procedure without being consciously or explicitly guided by it. People in everyday life have no explicit knowledge of these requirements; nor to reason correctly do they need to know of them. Kant's aim is not to teach us what is right and wrong: that we already know. Rather, he sees the value of the philosophical understanding of the moral law as securing more firmly our acceptance of it by revealing to us how it is rooted in our personality as autonomous and as having the moral powers that make us free and equal legislating members of a possible realm of ends. I surmised in the first lecture on Kant (§2.4) that he also wanted to find a form of moral reflection that could reasonably be used to check the purity of our motives, and I assume that he sees the CI-procedure as one way to do that. This aim, I suggested, was connected with his Pietism. One virtue of the CI-procedure presumably is that it would not encourage the obsessive concern with purity that Kant found offensive in the Pietism of the Fridericianum.

So understood, then, the CI-procedure is no more meant to teach us what is right and wrong than Frege's *Begriffsschrift* is meant to teach us how to reason with the concepts expressed by "if-then," "and," and "not," or by "some" and "all." Again, we already know how to do that. Rather, quantification theory together with higher-order logic and set theory (including proof and model theory) enable us to discover things about mathematics and about the nature of mathematical knowledge. Those subjects open doors to a deeper understanding of mathematics. Gödel's theorem is an obvious example. In Frege's case he wanted to show that, while Kant was right to think that geometry is synthetic a priori, he was wrong to think the same of arithmetic. Frege wanted to show that the truths of arithmetic are not dependent on the form of sensible intuition but are derivable from logic and definitions alone and in that sense analytic.

Similarly, as I have said, I believe that Kant saw the value of having a procedural representation of the moral law to be what it discloses about that law and about ourselves—in particular, what it shows about our persons, our freedom, and our status in the world. It prepares the way for a kind of self-knowledge that only philosophical reflection about the moral law and its roots in our persons can bring to light. At any rate, I am guided by this thought from now on. Thus the topics of the priority of right and moral constructivism, of the fact of reason and the moral law as a law of freedom, and others as well, are considered with some reference to the features of the CI-procedure as earlier set out. Those features will help us to explain how Kant understands these larger matters.

§2. The First Three of Six Conceptions of the Good

1. In order to explain the priority of right and the realm of ends as the a priori object of the moral law, I shall first distinguish six conceptions of the good in Kant's doctrine. These conceptions are built up in a sequence, one after the other, each from the one preceding it. This sequence can be presented by referring to the CI-procedure, since each conception has a role in connection with one of its four steps. Specifying these roles is an instructive way of ordering these conceptions and clarifies the relations between them.

It also allows us to say what is meant by calling the realm of ends the necessary object of a will determined by the moral law, as well as what is meant by saying of this realm that it is an object given a priori to such a pure will. Kant says (KP 5:4): "The ideas of God and immortality are . . . not conditions of the moral law, but only conditions of the necessary object of a will which is determined by this law. . . . Hence we cannot say that we know or understand either the reality or even the possibility of these ideas. Nevertheless, they are the conditions of applying the morally determined will to the object which is given to it a priori (the highest good)."

Here Kant calls this a priori object the highest good. At this point there is a complication that, for the time being, I shall resolve somewhat arbitrarily. For our purposes here, I view this a priori object as the realm of ends as it appears in the *Groundwork,* so that the conception of this realm and that of its (partial) realization are among the conceptions of the good to be surveyed. What Kant in the cited passage refers to as the highest good I put aside until we come to the postulates of practical faith as these appear in the dialectic of the second *Critique* (and elsewhere). I believe that the realm of ends as the a priori object of the moral law and the highest good are quite distinct conceptions with different roles in Kant's view. But the differences between them raise difficult questions of interpretation; later on I shall explain why I treat them as I do.

2. The first of the first three conceptions of the good is given by what we may call "unrestricted empirical practical reason." This name indicates the fact that there are no restrictions on the information available to sincere and rational agents either in framing their conceptions of happiness or in formulating their particular maxims: all the relevant particulars about their desires, abilities, and situations, as well as the available alternatives, are assumed to be known.

Now this first conception of the good is a conception of happiness as organized by the (as opposed to a particular) hypothetical imperative. This conception may be connected with step (1) of the CI-procedure, since the maxim at this step we have assumed to be the maxim of rational and sincere agents; and we further suppose a rational agent to have at any moment a rational conception of happiness. Thus the maxim satisfies the various principles of rational deliberation that characterize the hypothetical imperative. Let's refer to these principles as "the rational."

I emphasize the distinction between the hypothetical imperative, viewed as a family of principles of rational deliberation, and particular hypothetical imperatives, which are rational when they satisfy those principles given the agent's circumstances and interests. Among the principles of rational deliberation are: to take the most effective means to one's ends; to adopt the alternative most likely to achieve success; to pursue the most inclusive end (assuming each principle to have a suitable *ceteris paribus* clause). This distinction parallels the one made earlier between the categorical imperative as including all the relevant criteria of pure practical reason and the totality of particular categorical imperatives (generalized precepts at step [2]) that pass the test of the CI-procedure.

3. The second conception of the good is of the fulfillment of what I have called "true human needs." I believe (as I said in Kant II) that at the fourth step of the CI-procedure, we require some such idea to give content to the will of the agent viewed as reasonable and rational. Otherwise the agent going through the procedure cannot compare the adjusted social worlds paired with different maxims. It should be said that some other conception than that of true human needs may serve as well, or indeed better. The point is that some amendment to Kant's view seems to be required.

At first we might think that the comparison of adjusted social worlds can be made on the basis of the agent's conception of happiness. But even if the agent knows what this conception is, there is still a serious difficulty, since Kant supposes different agents to have different conceptions of their happiness. On his view, happiness is an ideal not of reason but of the imagination (Gr II:25 [417–419]), and so our conception of happiness depends on the contingencies of our life and on the particular modes of thought and feeling we have developed as we come of age. Thus, if conceptions of happiness are used in judging social worlds at step (4), then whether a maxim passes the CI-procedure would depend on the particular person who applies it.

Now, such dependence is likely to threaten Kant's view. For if our following the CI-procedure doesn't lead to at least a rough agreement as to which maxims pass when we apply the procedure intelligently and conscientiously against the background of the same information, then the moral law lacks objective content, where objective content is to be understood as follows. Recall that a maxim that is rational for a single agent is valid for that subject (agent), and so subjectively valid; whereas a moral precept (at step [2]) that passes the CI-procedure is valid for all reasonable and rational agents, and so is objectively valid. Thus to say that the moral law has objective content is simply to say that it has a content specified by moral precepts that are roughly the same for all reasonable and rational (and sincere) agents, and publicly recognizable (though perhaps not now recognized) as founded on sufficient reasons.

Observe that this second conception of the good based on true human needs is a special conception designed expressly to be used at step (4) of the CI-procedure. It is formulated to meet a need of reason,[1] namely, the need for the moral law to have sufficient objective content. Note that this conception, as opposed to the first, is restricted: that is, it is framed in view of the restrictions on information to which agents are subject at step (4).

4. The third conception of the good is the good as the fulfillment in everyday life of (what Kant calls) permissible ends (*MdS* 6:389), that is, ends that respect the limits of the moral law. As we saw in Kant III, it is these ends alone that specify the happiness of others that we are to further by the duties of virtue. Thus we are to revise, abandon, or repress desires and inclinations that prompt us to rational and sincere maxims at step (1) that are rejected by the CI-procedure. We must not balance the strength and importance to us of our natural desires against the strength and importance to us of the pure practical interest we take in acting from the moral law (for this interest, see *Gr* II:14n. [413]). The priority of right excludes such balancing entirely, as we discuss further below.

Whenever our maxim is rejected, then, we must reconsider our intended course of action, for in this case the claim to satisfy the desires in question is rejected. At this point, the contrast with a teleological moral doctrine such as utilitarianism is clear, since for Kant the conception of permissible ends presupposes that the moral law and the principles of pure practical reason are already in place. On the other hand, classical utilitarianism starts with a conception of the good—as pleasure, or as happiness, or as the satisfaction of desire, preferences, or interests; and it may also impose the condition that these desires, preferences, or interests be rational. (Desires, preferences, and interests are not the same, but I won't go into this.) The point is that in a teleological doctrine, a conception of the good is given prior to and independently of the right (or the moral law); thus, for example, utilitarianism defines the right as maximizing the good (say, as happiness or the satisfaction of rational preferences), and moral worth of

---

1. Kant refers to the idea of a need of reason at *KP* 5:4f., 125f., 141–146, and at 142n. and 143n. See also "Orientation in Thought," 8:136–142, in *Political Writings*, trans. H. B. Nisbet (Cambridge: Cambridge University Press, 1991), pp. 240–245. We come back to this idea later.

character as having, say, a character that can be relied on to lead us to do what is right.[2]

By contrast, in Kant's view, unrestricted rationality, or the rational, is framed by, and absolutely subordinated to, a procedure that incorporates the constraints of the CI-procedure, or what I shall call "the reasonable." It is by this procedure that admissible conceptions of the good and their permissible ends are specified.

§3. The Second Three Conceptions of the Good

1. The first of the three remaining conceptions of the good is the conception of the good will. This is Kant's conception of moral worth: a fully good will is the supreme (although not the complete) good of persons and of their characters as reasonable and rational. This good consists in a firm and settled highest-order desire, or to use Kant's term, pure practical interest, which leads us to take an interest in acting from duty (*Gr* II:14n. [413]).

Here we can make a distinction: we have true purity of will when we can always act as duty requires from pure practical interest, however strongly doing our duty may be opposed by our natural desires and inclinations (*KP* 5:155f., 159f.). In this case, pure practical interest is always strong enough by itself to ensure that we act from (not merely in accordance with) the demands of duty even in extreme situations—for example, when we are threatened with death by the sovereign if we do not make false charges against an honest man. We have a good will when we strive to the best of our ability to become someone with a pure will, that is, someone who can always act, whenever it is a matter of duty, from pure practical interest. We may have a good will, so defined, although we have not yet attained a pure will.[3]

Kant holds, then, that other interests and inclinations, when they also

2. Here there are many possibilities, such as Sidgwick's account (*Methods of Ethics*, Bk. III, Ch. 12) of moral worth as specified by the marginal utility of the practice of praising and blaming certain traits of character.

3. See also "Theory and Practice, Pt. I," 8:284f. (Nisbet:69f.).

move us to do what duty requires, do not detract from the moral worth of our action or from the purity of our character as long as two conditions are met. They are:

(i) that when a question of duty is involved, we decide the case entirely by considerations of duty, leaving aside all reasons of interest and inclination;

(ii) that our pure practical interest in acting from the considerations of duty is strong enough by itself to ensure that we do as we ought. It is only when our pure practical interest is not strong enough to ensure this, and those other motives are needed for us to act properly, that our will, or moral character, is less than fully good.

In this connection, Kant notes that we may need the support of what he calls free sympathy in acting from moral principles (*MdS* 6:457). While having this free sympathy is of course not a defect—it is rather to be cultivated by us—our needing it to act rightly shows a lack of purity in our character, which is a defect. One reason is that the feeling of free sympathy cannot always be counted on to support our doing as we should; so whether we conduct ourselves as we ought depends at least to some degree on happenstance. This shows that we have not yet fully achieved the freedom that is possible for us.

From Kant I:§7, recall the two roles of the concept of a good will in Kant's doctrine: first, as an absolute and incomparable value the realization of which gives meaning to human life and makes humankind the final end of creation (*KU* §84 and the footnote); and second, as a value such that our having the powers of reason and moral sensibility to realize a good will is the condition of being a member of a possible realm of ends and marks the range of application of the moral law.

2. The next conception of the good is the good as the object of the moral law, which I take to be given by the ideal of a realm of ends, as this ideal was discussed in Kant IV. This ideal object is simply the conception of the social world that would come about (at least under reasonably favorable conditions) if everyone were to follow the totality of precepts that result from the correct application of the CI-procedure.

As noted previously, Kant sometimes refers to the realm of ends as the necessary object of a will that is determined by the moral law, or alternatively, as an object that is given a priori to a will determined by that law

(*KP* 5:4). By this I take him to mean that the realm of ends is an (ideal) object—a social world—the moral constitution and regulation of which is specified by the totality of precepts that meet the test of the CI-procedure (when these precepts are adjusted and coordinated by the requirement of complete determination; *Gr* II:75 [436–437]).

Put another way, the ideal of a realm of ends is not a social world that can be described prior to and independently of the concepts and principles of pure practical reason and the procedure by which they are applied. That realm is not an already given describable (ideal) object—a social world—the nature of which determines the content of the moral law. This would be the case, for example, if this law were understood as stating what must be done in order to bring about a good society the nature and institutions of which are already specified prior to and independently of the moral law.

3. Finally, there is Kant's conception of the complete good. This is the good attained when the ideal of a realm of ends is realized and each member both has a good will and has achieved happiness, so far as the conditions of human life allow. We must add this qualification, since the ideal of a realm of ends is an ideal of reason, and as such cannot be fully realized. Also, happiness must be specified by the fulfillment of ends that respect the requirements of the moral law and so are permissible ends. I assume that it is reasonable to try to approach this complete good (so understood) in the natural world, at least under reasonably favorable conditions. In doing this, we are not being visionaries who lack a sense of realism, of what is in fact possible. A realm of ends is in that sense a natural good, one that can be reasonably striven for (although never fully achieved) in the order of nature.

Kant holds (as indicated above) that in the complete good, the good will is the supreme good, that is, we must have a good will if the other goods we enjoy are to be truly good and our enjoyment of them fully appropriate. This applies in particular to the good of happiness, since he thinks that only our having a good will can make us fully worthy of happiness. This is a recurrent theme in his doctrine. Kant also believes that two goods so different in their nature, and in their foundations in our persons, as a good will and happiness are incommensurable. In deciding what to do, we are not to balance them against each other; they can be combined into one unified and complete good only by the relation of the strict priority of one over the other. We shall come back to this idea later.

§4. Autonomy and Heteronomy

1. Following this survey of the six conceptions of the good, let's consider what Kant says about the autonomy and heteronomy of moral conceptions as a whole (*Gr* II:81–88 [441–444]; *KP* 5:41). He thinks that only his own doctrine presents morality as autonomous and not heteronomous. He says (*Gr* II:81 [441]):

> If the will seeks the law that is to determine it anywhere else than in the fitness of its maxims for its own making of universal law—if therefore in going beyond itself it seeks this law in the character of any of its objects—the result is always heteronomy. In that case the will does not give itself the law, but the object does so in virtue of its relation to the will. This relation, whether based on inclination or on rational ideas [*Vorstellungen der Vernunft*], can give rise only to hypothetical imperatives: "I ought to do something *because I will something else*." (Kant's italics)

What Kant thinks is at stake here is the supremacy of reason. Pure practical reason cannot take its directives from any object, not even from a rational idea presented as an object to reason. Think of the rational ideas of right and goodness lying in the divine reason as presented to our reason as objects. I believe that Kant wants rather to say: "I ought to do something because I will—from pure practical interest—the principles of pure practical reason; and not because I will something else, even should this something else be based on rational ideas." (It goes without saying that it must not be based on inclination.)

Put another way: pure practical reason must construct out of itself its own object. Advancing that object from pure practical interest will not involve a hypothetical imperative. So he adds, after the lines just cited, that a categorical imperative "must abstract from all objects to this extent—

that they (objects) should be without any *influence* at all on the will so that practical reason (the will) may not merely administer an alien interest but may simply manifest its own sovereign authority as the supreme maker of law" (Kant's italics).

2. Perhaps the matter can be put this way: rather than starting from a conception of the good given independently of the right, we start from a conception of the right—of the moral law—given by pure (as opposed to empirical) practical reason. We then specify in the light of this conception (by using the CI-procedure) what ends are permissible and what moral precepts specify our duties of justice and of virtue. From these, we work out what social arrangements are right and just.

We might say that a moral conception is not to revolve around the good as an independent object, but around a (formal) conception of the right (together with a [formal] conception of a good will), as constructed by our pure practical reason, into which any permissible good must fit. Or as Kant puts it when he explains what he calls "the paradox of method" in critically examining practical reason (*KP* 5:62f.): "*The paradox is that the concept of good and evil is not defined prior to the moral law, to which, it would seem, the former would have to serve as a foundation; rather the concept of good and evil must be defined after and by means of the law.*" (Kant puts this entire sentence in italics.)

Kant believes that once we start from the good as a prior and independently given object, the moral conception must be heteronomous. This is because in this case pure practical reason is not, as it should be, its own sovereign authority as the supreme maker of law (the phrase Kant uses in *Gr* II:81 [441]). Heteronomy means precisely this lack of sovereign authority.

Now, in the italicized sentence above, the concept of good and evil should be understood broadly to include both the morally good and the right. This is clear from Kant's account in Analytic II of the second *Critique*. Thus heteronomy will be as true of Leibniz's metaphysical perfectionism (with its conception of a prior moral order given to and known by our reason) as it is of the psychological naturalism that underlies Hume's doctrine of sympathy as the basis of morals. In these views, what determines our will is the conception of a given object, not an object (e.g., the realm of ends) developed from principles originating in our practical reason.

3. Let's consider in more detail why Kant thinks that perfectionism is a form of heteronomy (*Gr* II:85 [443]). Since his view is more fully presented in the second *Critique* (5:41), I summarize his argument there. He begins by saying that perfectionism is based on reason because perfection, as a character of things, can be thought, or known, only by reason. Concepts of perfection he distinguishes into the theoretical and the practical: theoretical perfection is simply the perfection of anything as a thing of its kind (transcendental perfection), or else the perfection of a thing generally (metaphysical perfection). These forms of perfection, Kant thinks, are irrelevant to pure practical reason, so he turns to practical perfection.

Now, for Kant, the concept of perfection in its practical meaning is simply the fitness or the adequacy of a thing to all kinds of ends. Thus the perfection characteristic of human beings is the development of disciplined skills and talents that enable us to realize our (appropriate) ends. The supreme perfection in substance (that is, in God), when regarded from a practical standpoint, is the sufficiency of God (in view of God's omniscience and omnipotence) to all ends in general. For Kant, the difficulty with perfectionism as a moral doctrine is evident: it is only if ends are already given that the concept of perfection can help to determine the will. In the absence of an antecedent criterion for appropriate ends, perfectionism is indeterminate, or as Kant says (in *Gr* II:85 [443]), empty and indefinite. Since ends must be found to complete perfectionism, it becomes a variant of the happiness principle after all, and so falls into heteronomy.

4. There are two reasons why this critique of perfectionism fails to exhibit the full force of Kant's doctrine of autonomy. The first is that it makes it appear that the fault of perfectionism is that it is empty or indeterminate, that is, it presupposes certain ends as given. This suggests that if the required ends were given by an object specified by a rational idea of a prior moral order, then Kant would have no objection. But this is not so. Whenever the object is prior to practical reason itself, and specifies its content or an end to be furthered by its principles, Kant holds that heteronomy results.

This point must be understood broadly. It says that there neither exists nor subsists *any* such object, whether the Supreme Being, or a given moral order of values (as exemplified, say, by the relations between Platonic Ideas, or by ideas lying in the divine reason), or an order of nature, or the constitution of human nature, or the psychic economy of our natural feelings and the laws of harmony of our inclinations and needs. Kant's radical sense of autonomy is that any such allegedly independent object must first stand trial, so to speak, at the bar of the supremely authoritative principles of pure practical reason before we can grant its reasonableness. Otherwise, our pure practical reason loses its sovereign authority as the supreme maker of law.

5. I think that a second defect in Kant's account of why perfectionism is heteronomous can be seen from his remarks in *Gr* II:88 (444). He says:

> However the object determines the will [when an object is made the basis of prescribing a rule to determine the will]—whether by means of inclination, as in the principle of personal happiness, or by means of reason directed to objects of our possible volitions generally, as in the principle of perfection—the will never determines itself immediately by the thought of an action, but only by the impulsion which the anticipated effect of the action exercises on the will: "I ought to do something because I will something else" . . . and consequently, speaking strictly, it is nature which would make law.

Why does Kant think it is nature that would make law in the case of metaphysical perfectionism once this doctrine is seen as a form of rational intuitionism? Why can't we know the given order of moral values and then be moved by the thought of a certain action as expressing that order? The text reads as if Kant thinks that there are only two alternatives: either pure practical reason as itself the supreme maker of law determines the object for the will, or else, if the will has an object, even an object specified by rational ideas given to our reason, the will is determined by an impulsion arising from the expected effect of doing the action, in which case nature would make law. Yet this is incorrect, for there is a third alternative. If we were to act from the principles of a moral order lying in divine reason, affirming those principles as such as the supreme law, then not nature but our acceptance of the rational ideas lying in God's reason would make law. This is just Leibniz's view: we should act on these ideas as far as we can know them.

Besides holding that we cannot discern these ideas, Kant's point must be that even if we could, our pure practical reason must be the supreme maker of its own principles, and this supremacy requires that, at the highest level, we must always judge by those principles. We cannot simply accept at that level even rational ideas allegedly lying in the divine reason, should it be possible to discern them (*Gr* II:5 [408–409]): "Even the Holy One of the Gospel must be compared with our idea of moral perfection before he can be recognized as such."

It is essential in understanding Kant's moral philosophy to see it opposed just as much to the rational intuitionism of Leibniz and Clarke as it is to the moral sense doctrine of Hutcheson and Hume. This fact has not, I think, been sufficiently appreciated, and it needs emphasis. To conclude: for Kant, then, practical reason constructs for the will its own object out of itself and does not rely on a prior and antecedent order of values. Of course, this phrase "constructs for the will its own object out of itself" is a metaphor of sorts. It is also obscure. We will try to get it under control next time when we discuss Kant's constructivism. I think that it can be given a reasonably clear sense, and I will try to do so.

§5. The Priority of Right

1. The preceding sketch of the six conceptions of the good in Kant's view indicates how they are built up, or constructed, in an ordered sequence one after the other, each conception (except the first) depending on the preceding ones. If we count the second (that of true human needs) as part of the CI-procedure itself, we can say that beginning with the third (that of permissible ends), the remaining conceptions presuppose an already given conception of right. This conception is represented by the CI-procedure as formulating in a procedural way the requirements of the moral law as applied (via that procedure) to the conditions of human life. Only the first conception of the good is entirely independent of the moral law, since it is the rational without restriction.

The sequence of conceptions beginning with the second exemplifies the priority of pure practical reason over empirical practical reason and displays the distinctive deontological and constructivist structure of Kant's view. It has two forms of practical reason, the reasonable and the rational. One form of the unity of practical reason is shown in how the reasonable frames the rational and limits it absolutely. Then we proceed step by step to generate different conceptions of the good, and obtain the conceptions of the good will and ideal of a complete good as a (partially) achieved realm of ends. The contrast between the deontological and constructivist structure of Kant's doctrine and the linear structure of a teleological view starting from an independent conception of the good is clear.

2. The meaning of the priority of right needs to be carefully understood. It does not mean that Kant's moral doctrine includes no conceptions of the good, nor does it mean that the conceptions used are somehow deduced from a previously specified concept of right. How the six conceptions are arrived at can best be understood by looking at the CI-procedure and seeing how the six conceptions are connected to the way in which it is applied.

An important point about the priority of right is this: the right and the good are complementary; the priority of right does not deny this. No moral doctrine can do without one or more conceptions of the good, and an acceptable conception of right must leave adequate space for such conceptions. Various conceptions of the good fully worthy of the devotion of those who affirm them must fit within the limits drawn by the conception of right itself—by the space it allows for the pursuit of permissible ends. We might say: the right draws the limit; the good shows the point.

Thus a (partially) realized realm of ends must allow sufficient space for ways of life that its members find worthy of their devotion; and Kant certainly thinks his view allows this. What the priority of right insists upon is that conceptions of the good must answer to certain prior constraints springing from pure practical reason.

3. In the preceding explanation of the priority of right, I assume that happiness (specified as the fulfillment of permissible ends) is indeed a good for Kant, one of the two main kinds of value he recognizes. The other is the absolute value of a good will and the cultivation of virtue. In saying this, I have in mind many aspects of his view: thus for him it is part of our humanity as reasonable and rational persons in the order of nature that we have a propensity to seek our happiness, and so (failing special circumstances) there is no duty to do so.

Asceticism is not part of his doctrine: in fact, we have a duty to put enough aside for ourselves so that we can enjoy life (MdS 6:452). Again, he regularly connects happiness with the rational, and so with the reasoning falling under the hypothetical imperative. He distinguishes (*KP* 5:58–62) between good and evil on the one hand, and our weal and woe on the other, never doubting the value of the latter (when it respects the limits of the moral law).[4]

Moreover, he counts, as two kinds of value, the value of persons (their moral worth) and the value of their (psychological) states (see his comments on the plight of the Stoic [*KP* 5:60]); his examples of different values include goods of both kinds (*KP* 5:60f.). So while happiness (as involving the fulfillment of an ordered plan of permissible ends) is not, let's say, a moral value, it is a value. Under reasonably favorable conditions, a (partially) realized realm of ends will be a happy commonwealth (as human societies go), since its members recognize the duty to further one another's (permissible) ends. Happiness (in due proportion to virtue) is an essential element in the highest good (the conception of which has a central role in Kant's doctrine of practical faith).

Finally, I note Kant's important statement (*KP* 5:61) that since we are persons with needs belonging to the order of nature, our reason has a commission *(Auftrag)*, or assignment, which it cannot decline, to attend to the interest of our sensible nature and to work out practical maxims with a view to our happiness in this life, and if possible the next. I believe, then, that the interpretation we have followed is true to the main lines of Kant's thought.

But there are remarks belonging to what we may call Kant's Manichean strain that question the value of happiness; for example, the remark in *Gr* II:48 (428) that it must be the universal wish of every rational being to be wholly free of inclinations (see also *KP* 5:118). I put aside this deeply troubling aspect of Kant's thought for now. We shall return to it when we discuss the moral psychology of the *Religion*.

§6. A Note on True Human Needs

1. Of the six conceptions of the good we have surveyed, all but that of true human needs are quite straightforward and clearly found if not expressly asserted in Kant's text. The difficulty with the conception of true human

---

4. See also Kant's reply to Garve on this point in "Theory and Practice, Pt. I," 8:278–284 (Nisbet: 64–68).

needs is that, while the phrase occurs in the text, the problem that this conception addresses—the problem of how the agent at step (4) is to assess
alternative adjusted social worlds—is not. Kant does not discuss it in the
form in which we have considered it, so we seem to have little to guide us.

If this were not bad enough, there is also the fact that the meaning of
the phrase "true human needs" is not very exact and cannot be gathered
from the few places that Kant uses it. In view of all this, I offer the conception of true human needs with some hesitation and recognize that other
ways of dealing with the problem may be preferable.

2. What clues have we to guide us in specifying this problematic conception? One clue is clearly the following: in Kant II:§2, we assumed that Kant
is concerned in the first instance with ideally reasonable and rational human
agents. He wants first to work out what practical reason requires of agents
who are, as we are, finite beings in the order of nature. Human beings also
animate pure and empirical practical reason; it is in reference to their powers of practical reason that their humanity is defined. Keep in mind that to
commit suicide is, as far as any one person can do it, to root out the basis
of morality in the world, and so is permissible only for the strongest of
reasons and never for reasons relating solely to our happiness.

Another clue seems equally clear. This is that Kant thinks of the agent
who is working through the CI-procedure as primarily concerned with that
agent's own interests. We should emphatically not say that those working
through the procedure are selfish, that is, have interests only in themselves—in their own wealth and power, in their own prestige and well-
being—and consider other people only as they affect their own interests.
Of course, all their interests belonging to them as agents are interests of a
self, as it were. But this last is a truism. Interests in a self and interests of
a self are two very different kinds of things and should never be confused.

So let's say that in working through the CI-procedure, agents are own-
interested. That is, they are concerned with their own interests, which may
be of all kinds as long as those interests are compatible with their being
reasonable, rational, and sincere.

3. We can take a further step and say that certain needs are particularly
basic. For example, Kant thinks that the state of nature is a state of injustice.
There is no security and order of law for anyone, and this makes it a state
of war even if there are no actual hostilities (MdS 6:350). We have a primary

duty to leave a state of nature and to join with others in a civil society regulated by law. Of course, we can't make this duty a presupposition of the CI-procedure, as any such duty must come later, but it does indicate that Kant thinks that we always need security and order in our relations with others, and thus need the basic social conditions that ensure this. Call these needs for certain basic social conditions required for a viable society.

Another kind of basic needs are those necessary to develop and exercise our capacity for rationality: that is, to form, revise, and rationally advance a scheme of ordered ends, which specifies what Kant considers as our happiness. Here I am not, for the moment, counting those ends themselves as basic; rather, what is basic is the need to develop and exercise the capacity of rationality itself as it forms and orders those ends. Whatever an agent's idea of happiness may be, it is essential in all normal cases to develop and preserve the capacity of rationality.

4. Thus we obtain two basic needs: the need for security and order in society, required to remove the state of war, and the need for those conditions necessary to develop and exercise our capacity for rationality in order to advance our happiness. These two needs suffice, I assume, to reject any maxim of indifference and to endorse an acceptable maxim of mutual aid. Note that we have not relied on anyone's particular idea of happiness (for reasons discussed in §2.3 above), nor have we mentioned our capacity to be reasonable or our moral sensibility. Whether they, and other things as well, can also be relied on, I leave aside here. My aim is simply to illustrate how the idea of true human needs can be filled out relying only on truly basic—even universal—needs of human beings conceived as finite rational agents in the order of nature. Here a certain idea of rational agents and their needs plays a guiding role.

How much, if anything, Kant's view requires beyond this I leave here as an open question. I have only tried to show that given the structure of his view, and what he says at various places, we have a number of clues as to how to proceed.[5]

---

5. Two instructive discussions of this general question are found in Paul Dietrichson, "Kant's Criteria of Universalizability," in *Kant: Foundations of the Metaphysics of Morals*, ed. R. P. Wolff (Indianapolis: Bobbs-Merrill, 1969), esp. pp. 189–199; and in Barbara Herman, "Mutual Aid and Respect for Persons," *Ethics* (1984), pp. 577–602 (reprinted in *The Practice of Moral Judgment*, pp. 45–72), who has a valuable discussion of true human needs (see esp. pp. 55ff.). My very brief account is closest to hers.

KANT VI

Moral Constructivism

§1. Rational Intuitionism: A Final Look

1. In several of the preceding lectures, we have contrasted Kant's moral doctrine with the metaphysical perfectionism of Leibniz construed as a variant of rational intuitionism. I begin today by mentioning this contrast one last time. I do this because, as I noted previously, it is not sufficiently appreciated that Kant would reject rational intuitionism as a form of heteronomy just as firmly (or so I think) as he would reject Hume's psychological naturalism.

Last time, I said that part of the explanation for the failure to appreciate this fact about Kant's view may lie in Kant's own exposition: he nowhere clearly describes rational intuitionism and then shows why he thinks that it is heteronomous. Possibly he lacks a clear conception of it. Whether or not this is so, the fullest discussions are those against perfectionism (*Gr* II: 81–88 [441–444]; and *KP* 5:41), and as we have seen, these discussions do not state the deeper grounds of his rejection of intuitionism.

One main weakness is that Kant supposes there to be only two possibilities: either the moral law is founded on an object given to it, in which case it depends on our susceptibility and the pleasure we anticipate from realizing that object, or the moral law as pure practical reason determines (constructs) its own object out of itself. That these are the only alternatives Kant envisages is seen in this passage, which is one of several (*KP* 5:62):

> Either: a principle of reason is thought of as already the determining ground of the will without reference to possible objects of the faculty of desire . . . [and] then that principle is a practical law a priori, and pure reason is assumed to be in itself practical; . . . [o]r a determining ground of the faculty of desire precedes the maxim of the will, and this determining ground presupposes an object of pleasure or displeasure and consequently something that pleases or displeases . . . [and so] determines actions which are good only with reference to our inclinations.

What is missing here is the recognition that intuitionism says that knowledge of the order of values can arouse moral feelings and the desire to act accordingly. Here the relation of the object of thought to feeling seems quite similar to the way in which Kant says knowledge of the moral law gives rise to the feelings of moral shame and self-reproach in Analytic III (*KP* 5:72–81). Of course, the difference is that the principles of practical reason are principles of our own reason, principles we give to ourselves as reasonable and rational. But the full force of the contrast with intuitionism is not made.

2. Yet one is tempted to ask: even though Kant fails to present his deeper objections to intuitionism, why isn't it just obvious anyway that for him it is a form of heteronomy?

One reason may be that in the rational intuitionism of Clarke and Leibniz, basic moral concepts are unanalyzable, and so are conceptually independent of natural concepts. Some might think that this gives a certain autonomy to practical reason. Another reason is that first principles as grasped by rational intuition are viewed as synthetic a priori and thus as independent of any particular order of nature. It is tempting to think that such principles could not be heteronomous. After all, they are synthetic a priori, they are known by reason alone, and they are independent of and prior to any order of nature. Doesn't all this sound rather like Kant?

Yet in Kant's moral constructivism, it suffices for heteronomy that first principles are founded on relations among objects the nature of which is not affected or determined by our conception of ourselves as reasonable and rational persons (possessing the powers of practical reason) and by our conception of the public role of moral principles in a possible realm of ends. Kant's idea of autonomy requires that there exists no moral order prior to

and independent of those conceptions that determine the form of the procedure that specifies the content of the duties of justice and of virtue. Heteronomy obtains not only when these first principles are fixed by our special
psychological constitution, a psychology which distinguishes us from other
rational persons, as in Hume, but also when first principles are fixed by an
order of moral values grasped by rational intuition, as with Clarke's fitnesses
of things or in Leibniz's hierarchy of perfections.

§2. Kant's Moral Constructivism

1. I begin with a general statement, which I shall then try to elucidate.
An essential feature of Kant's moral constructivism is that the particular
categorical imperatives that give the content of the duties of justice and
of virtue are viewed as specified by a procedure of construction (the CI-
procedure), the form and structure of which mirror both of our two powers
of practical reason as well as our status as free and equal moral persons.
As we shall see, this conception of the person as both reasonable and rational, and as free and equal, Kant regards as implicit in our everyday moral
consciousness, the fact of reason.

A Kantian doctrine may hold (as Kant did) that the procedure by which
first principles are specified, or constructed, is synthetic a priori. This
thought, however, must be properly understood, and I return to it in §4. For
the present, it simply means that the form and structure of the constructivist
procedure are seen as a procedural representation of all the requirements
of practical reason, both pure and empirical. I believe that it is Kant's intention that the CI-procedure represent all such requirements, as far as this
can be done. In characterizing his constructivism, I suppose that it does so,
but whether it actually does is of course another matter.

2. It is characteristic of Kant's doctrine that a relatively complex conception of the person plays a central role in specifying the content of his moral
view. By contrast, rational intuitionism requires but a sparse conception of
the person, based on the idea of the person as knower. This is because the
content of first principles is already given, and thus persons need only to
be able to know what these principles are and to be moved by this knowledge. A basic psychological assumption of rational intuitionism is that peo-

ple can recognize first principles and that the recognition of those principles as true of a prior order of moral values gives rise to a desire to act from them for their own sake. Moral motivation is defined by reference to desires that have a special kind of causal origin, namely, the reasoned grasp of first principles.

This sparse conception of the person together with this psychological assumption characterizes the moral psychology of Sidgwick, Moore, and Ross. Of course, intuitionism is not forced to so sparse a conception. The point is rather that, since the content of first principles is already given, it is simply unnecessary to have a more elaborate moral psychology, or a fuller conception of the person, of a kind required to specify the form, structure, and content of a constructivist moral view.

§3. The Constructivist Procedure

1. So much for explaining Kant's moral constructivism by the contrast with rational intuitionism. Let's turn to a more specific account of the constructivist features of his view. While Kant's constructivism belongs within moral philosophy, it also has some affinity with his constructivist ideas in the philosophy of mathematics. Indeed, his account of the synthetic a priori nature of arithmetic and geometry is, of course, one of the historical origins of those views.[1]

One similarity is basic: in both cases, the idea is to formulate a procedural representation in which, as far as possible, all the relevant criteria of correct reasoning—moral or mathematical—are exhibited and open to view.[2] The idea is that judgments are valid and sound if they result from

1. Especially valuable are Charles Parsons, "Kant's Philosophy of Arithmetic" (1969), reprinted in *Mathematics in Philosophy* (Ithaca: Cornell University Press, 1983), and his article "Mathematics, Foundations of," in *The Encyclopedia of Philosophy*, ed. Paul Edwards, 8 vols. (New York: Academic Press, 1977); and Michael Friedman, "Kant's Theory of Geometry," *Philosophical Review* 94, no. 4 (October 1985), 455–506.

2. Because the procedure is thought as embedding, as far as possible, all the relevant criteria, it is said to specify an ideal, say, of the ideal mathematician, or the ideal of a rational and reasonable person who understands and applies the categorical imperative procedure correctly, or the ideal of a realm of ends, a community of such ideal persons. We must say "*as far as possible* all the relevant criteria," because no specification of these criteria can be final; any rendering of them is always to be checked by critical reflection.

going through the correct procedure correctly and rely only on true premises. In Kant's account of moral reasoning, the procedural representation
is given by the categorical imperative procedure, which incorporates the
requirements that pure practical reason imposes on our rational maxims.
In arithmetic, the procedure expresses how the natural numbers are generated from the basic concept of a unit, each number from the preceding.
Different numbers are distinguished by their place in the series thus generated. The procedure exhibits the basic properties that ground facts about
numbers, so propositions about numbers that are correctly derived from
it are correct.

There are also important constructivist elements in Kant's account of
the basis of Newtonian mechanics.[3] The roots of constructivism lie deep
in Kant's transcendental idealism, but these parallels I shall not consider
further.

2. Our aim is to see the way in which Kant's moral doctrine has features
that quite naturally lead us to think of it as constructivist, and how this
connects with the themes of the supremacy and the unity of reason and
with the moral law as a law of freedom. To this end, let's consider three
questions.

First, in moral constructivism, what is it that is constructed? The answer
is: the content of the doctrine.[4] In Kant's view, this means that the totality of
particular categorical imperatives (general precepts at step [2]) that pass the
test of the CI-procedure are seen as constructed by a procedure of construction
worked through by rational agents subject to various reasonable constraints.
These agents are rational in that, subject to the reasonable constraints of the
procedure, they are guided by empirical practical reason or the principles of
rational deliberation that fall under the hypothetical imperative.

A second question is this: Is the CI-procedure itself constructed? No, it
is not. Rather, it is simply laid out. Kant believes that our everyday human
understanding is implicitly aware of the requirements of practical reason,
both pure and empirical; as we shall see, this is part of his doctrine of the

---

3. For this, see Michael Friedman, "The Metaphysical Foundations of Newtonian Science," in
Kant's Philosophy of Physical Science, ed. R. E. Butts (Dordrecht: Reidel, 1986), pp. 25–60.

4. It should be noted that this content can never be specified completely. The moral law is
an idea of reason, and since an idea of reason can never be fully realized, neither can the content
of such an idea. It is always a matter of approximation, and always subject to error and correction.

fact of reason. So we look at how Kant seems to reason when he presents his various examples, and we try to lay out in procedural form all the conditions he seems to rely on. Our aim in doing this is to incorporate into that procedure all the relevant criteria of practical reason, so that the judgments that result from a correct use of the procedure are themselves correct (given the requisite true beliefs about the social world). These judgments are correct because they meet all the requirements of practical reason, both pure and empirical.

Third, what more exactly does it mean to say, as I said a while back, that the form and structure of the CI-procedure mirrors our free moral personality as both reasonable and rational? The idea here is that not everything can be constructed. Every construction has a basis, certain materials, as it were, from which it begins. While the CI-procedure is not, as noted above, constructed but laid out, it does have a basis: the conception of free and equal persons as reasonable and rational, a conception that is mirrored in the procedure.

We discern how persons are mirrored in the procedure by noting what powers and abilities, what kinds of beliefs and wants, and the like, they must have as agents who are viewed as implicitly guided by the procedure and as being moved to conform to the particular categorical imperatives it authenticates. We look at the procedure as laid out and we consider the use Kant makes of it, and from that we elaborate what his conception of persons must be. This conception, along with the conception of a society of such persons, each of whom can be a legislative member of a realm of ends, constitutes the basis of Kant's constructivism.

Thus we don't say that the conceptions of person and society are constructed. It is unclear what that could mean. Nor do we say they are laid out. Rather, these conceptions are elicited from our moral experience and reflection and from what is involved in our being able to work through the CI-procedure and to act from the moral law as it applies to us.

3. To illustrate: that we are both reasonable and rational is mirrored in the fact that the CI-procedure involves both forms of reasoning. We are said to be rational at step (1), and indeed at all steps, since the deliberations of agents within the constraints of the procedure always fall under the rational. We are also said to be reasonable, since if we weren't moved by the reasonable, we would not take what Kant calls a pure practical interest in

checking our maxims against the procedure's requirements, nor when a maxim is rejected would we have such an interest in revising our intentions and checking whether our revised maxim is acceptable. The deliberations of agents within the steps of the procedure and subject to its reasonable constraints mirror our rationality; our motivation as persons in caring about those constraints and taking an interest in acting in ways that meet the procedure's requirements mirrors our being reasonable.

The conception of free and equal persons as reasonable and rational is the basis of the construction: unless this conception and the powers of moral personality it includes—our humanity—are animated, as it were, in human beings, the moral law would have no basis in the world. Recall here Kant's thought that to commit suicide is to root out the existence of morality from the world (*MdS* 6:422f.).

Note here—what is perhaps obvious—that not only does the CI-procedure exhibit the principles of practical reason, both reasonable and rational, but also its form and structure are drawn from the conceptions of person and of the public role of moral precepts within what Kant calls the systematic whole of ends of a realm of ends. It is the union of the principles of practical reason with those conceptions that shapes the procedure's form and structure. The principles of practical reason, both the reasonable, as exhibited in the conditions imposed on the agents going through the CI-procedure, and the rational, as exhibited in their ways of reasoning, select the precepts of morality.

§4. An Observation and an Objection

1. The observation about constructivism concerns the relation of priority between the order of moral values and the conceptions implicit in our practical reason. By contrast with rational intuitionism, constructivism sees the substantive principles that express the order of moral values as constructed by a procedure the form and structure of which are taken from the conceptions and principles implicit in our practical reasoning. As already stated, the union of practical reason with conceptions of society and person is complete and independent. For moral purposes, this union needs no grounding, and the principles of practical reason rely on nothing prior to it.

Another way to state the relation of priority is to say that it concerns the order of explanation.[5] Rational intuitionism says: the procedure is correct because following it correctly usually gives the correct (independently given) result. Constructivism says: the result is correct because it issues from the correct reasonable and rational procedure correctly followed.[6] Both views use as the fundamental criterion what we think on due reflection. Our judgment as to the correct view of moral or political reasoning depends on which seems soundest after full consideration and judgment.[7] Both ways of stating the contrast between moral constructivism and intuitionism are right and come to the same thing: the first, we might say, is more vivid; the second is clearer and more rigorous.

2. The objection to constructivism is this: what we think on due reflection is itself something prior to and independent of practical reason and the conceptions of person and society.[8] After all, we revise our formulation of a constructivist procedure according to whether its ideas, procedures, and principles yield judgments that fit with our convictions after full consideration. But surely, the objection continues, these convictions, whether general or more particular, are intuitions! So why isn't constructivism simply a form of intuitionism?

In reply, both constructivism and intuitionism must rely on due reflection. Otherwise, constructivism cannot check its formulation of the correct procedure. The contrast with intuitionism lies in the order of explanation: in whether we say the judgment is correct because it followed a procedure that usually gives the correct result determined independently, or whether we say, as in constructivism, that the judgment is correct because it issues

5. This way of putting it was suggested to me by Thomas Nagel.

6. To illustrate the contrast thus stated, the following statement of Christine Korsgaard: "The point I want to emphasize here is that the Kantian approach frees us from assessing the rationality of choice by means of the apparently ontological task of assessing the thing chosen: we do not need to identify especially rational ends. Instead, it is the reasoning that goes into the choice itself—the procedures of full justification—that determines the rationality of the choice and so certifies the goodness of the object. Thus, the goodness of rationally chosen ends is a matter of the demands of practical reason rather than of ontology." From "Two Distinctions of Goodness," *Philosophical Review* (April 1983), 183; reprinted in *Creating the Kingdom of Ends* (Cambridge: Cambridge University Press, 1996).

7. This means that, as reasonable and rational, the best criterion we have at any given moment of whether a conception of right and justice applies to us is whether it is the one most acceptable to us on due reflection.

8. I am indebted to Gregory Kavka and David Estlund for discussion on this point.

from what we think on reflection is the correct procedure of practical reason correctly followed and using only true premises.

As to how we find the correct procedure, constructivism says: by reflection, using our power of reason. It also says that neither theoretical nor practical reason is transparent to itself. We can misdescribe our reason as we can misdescribe anything else. This may lead us to think that there is some moral order prior to and independent of reason that we are trying to describe. Constructivism does not deny that it may seem so, but it says that we are really using our reason to describe itself. This is a struggle, for the task of coming to understand what to think on full consideration continues indefinitely.

Moreover, the principles of practical reason and our conceptions of person and society (that is, of the realm of ends) are united in practical reason. These conceptions do not stand alone and as such constitute the basic moral truths. In various ways, the formulation of our conceptions of practical reason and of person and society depends on beliefs of all kinds. Constructivism says that when, if ever, due reflection is achieved, and our principles and ideals along with our other beliefs about society, person, and world are in line, then our moral conception will have a certain structure in which the requirements of the principles of practical reason (as represented in an appropriate procedure) have a certain role in determining its content.

As to whether our general and high-level convictions about practical reason are intuitions, as some say, they may of course be called that. However, as I have said, constructivism views these so-called intuitions not as convictions about an independent order of moral values, but as convictions about practical reason itself, about its principles and its ideas of reason.

§5. Two Conceptions of Objectivity

1. It is important to see that the contrast between rational intuitionism and Kant's moral constructivism is not a contrast between objectivism and subjectivism. Both views have a conception of objectivity, but each understands objectivity in a different way.

In rational intuitionism, a correct moral judgment, or principle, is one that is true of a prior and independent order of moral values. This order is prior to the criteria of reasonableness and rationality as well as prior to the appropriate conception of persons as autonomous and responsible and as free and equal members of a moral community. Indeed, it is that order that settles what those reasonable and rational criteria are, and how autonomy and responsibility are to be conceived.

By contrast, in Kant's doctrine, as we have interpreted it, a correct moral judgment is one that conforms to all the relevant criteria of reasonableness and rationality the total force of which is expressed by the way they are combined into the CI-procedure. Kant thinks of this procedure as suitably combining all the requirements of our practical reason, both pure and empirical, into one unified scheme of practical reasoning. This is an aspect of the unity of reason. That procedure's form is a priori, rooted in our pure practical reason, and thus for us practically necessary. A judgment supported by those principles and precepts will, then, be acknowledged as correct by any fully reasonable and rational (and informed) person. This is what Kant means when he says that these judgments are universally communicable.

2. Now, a conception of objectivity includes an account of our agreement in judgments and of how it comes about. Kant accounts for this agreement by our sharing in a common practical reason. For this idea to succeed, we must suppose, as Kant does, that no matter who applies the CI-procedure, roughly the same judgments are reached, provided that the procedure is applied intelligently and conscientiously and against the background of roughly the same beliefs and information. Reasonable and rational persons must recognize more or less the same reasons and give them more or less the same weight. Indeed, for the idea of judgment, as opposed to the idea of simply giving voice to our psychological state, even to apply, we must be able to reach agreement in judgment, not of course always, but much of the time, and in the light of what are viewed as publicly recognized criteria of practical reason.

Moreover—and this is essential—when we can't reach agreement, we must be able to explain our failure. We must be able to refer to such things as the difficulties of the question at hand: for example, the difficulties of surveying and assessing all the evidence available, or the delicate balance of competing reasons on opposite sides of the question. In such cases, we expect that reasonable persons may differ. Disagreement may also arise from a lack of reasonableness or rationality or conscientiousness on the part of one or more persons involved. But if we say this, we must be careful that the test of this lack of reasonableness or conscientiousness is not simply the fact of disagreement itself, much less the fact that other persons disagree with us. We must have independent grounds identifiable in the particular circumstances for thinking that such causes of the failure to agree are at work.

3. I believe that Kant's conception of objectivity falls under the following general characterization of objectivity: namely, moral convictions are objective if reasonable and rational persons who are sufficiently intelligent and conscientious in exercising their powers of practical reason would eventually endorse those convictions, when all concerned know the relevant facts and have sufficiently surveyed the relevant considerations. To say that a moral conviction is objective, then, is to say that there are reasons sufficient to convince all reasonable persons that it is valid or correct. To assert a moral judgment is to imply that there are such reasons and that the judgment can be justified to a community of such persons.

Moreover, this is normally sufficient: it is not required that the correctness of the conviction enter into an empirical explanation of how we know it is correct. In general, this explanation is trivial: we know that it is correct because we have correctly applied the principles of practical reason.[9] Of course, Kant's constructivism distinguishes his account of objectivity from other such accounts. But his view is no less objective for that.

4. Finally, to prevent misunderstanding, a further point about constructivism. No such view, including Kant's, says that the facts relevant for moral reasoning are constructed, any more than it says that ideas of reason such as those of person and society are constructed.

To explain: we can distinguish two kinds of facts relevant to moral reasoning. One is appealed to in giving reasons as to why an action or institution is, say, right or wrong, or just or unjust; the other is the kind of facts about what is unjust, or the nature of the virtues, or of the moral doctrine

---

9. As noted in the text, we may, however, seek an empirical explanation for the failure to reach agreement, and this explanation may refer to psychological elements such as prejudice and bias, or to various situational elements. Usually explanations of failure refer to things that interfere with our ability to make reasoned and impartial judgments.

itself. To illustrate the first kind: to argue that slavery is unjust, we appeal to the fact that it allows some persons cruelly to demean and abuse others. To illustrate the second: we may appeal straightaway to the fact that deceitful promises are unjust, or to the fact that indifference to the needs of others is lacking in virtue. Finally, a fact about Kant's moral doctrine itself is that it distinguishes between duties of justice and duties of virtue.

With regard to the first kind of relevant facts, a constructivist procedure is framed to yield the principles and criteria that specify which facts about actions, institutions, persons, and the social world generally are relevant in moral deliberation. For the claim that slavery is unjust, relevant facts about it are not when it arose historically, or whether it is economically efficient, but that it allows some persons cruelly to demean and abuse others. That is a fact about slavery.

Moreover, the idea of constructing facts seems incoherent, while the idea of a constructivist procedure yielding principles and precepts identifying which facts count as reasons is quite clear. Recall how the categorical imperative procedure accepts some maxims and rejects others. The idea of constructivism is that, apart from a reasonable constructivist conception, facts are simply facts. What is wanted is a framework of reasoning within which to identify which facts are relevant from the appropriate point of view and to determine their weight as reasons. So understood, a constructivist moral doctrine is not at odds with our commonsense ideas of truth and matters of fact.

With regard to the second kind of relevant facts—those about the moral doctrine itself—we say that these are not constructed but rather are facts about the possibilities of construction.[10] When Kant elaborates his doctrine from the fundamental ideas of reason expressed in the CI-procedure, it is a possibility of construction, implicit in the family of conceptions and principles of practical reasoning that are the basis of the construction, that slavery is unjust and that there is a basic distinction between the duties of justice and the duties of virtue. We may think of these as analogous to the way in which the infinity of primes is viewed (in constructivist arithmetic) as a

10. The possibilities referred to here are those characterizing the moral or political conception that meets the tests of objectivity discussed earlier in this section. It is such a conception that concerns us.

possibility of construction.[11] This analogy does not commit us to a constructivist view of mathematics: instead we use it to clarify the meaning of moral and political constructivism. For this it suffices to understand the analogy; the truth of constructivism in mathematics is a separate matter.

§6. The Categorical Imperative: In What Way Synthetic A Priori?

1. To complete the account of constructivism, I consider what Kant means in describing the categorical imperative as a synthetic a priori practical proposition (*Gr* II:28 [420]). Doing this will clarify the sense in which the moral law constructs out of itself its own a priori object. In §1 we saw that rational intuitionism also views the first principles of morals as synthetic a priori propositions. Of course, Kant means something quite different, but what? You may ask: Why haven't we done this sooner? After all, this is central to Kant's doctrine. The answer is that it's best to have the constructivist background already in place.

To begin with, the categorical imperative is a priori in Kant's most general sense, that is, it is knowledge grounded on principles of (pure) reason. But might someone discover that there is no a priori knowledge? He says not (*KP* 5:12): "There is no danger of this. It would be like proving by reason that there is no such thing as reason. . . . [K]nowledge through reason and a priori knowledge are the same thing."

The CI-procedure is, then, a priori, assuming that it correctly formulates the requirements of the categorical imperative through which the moral law (an idea of reason) applies to us as finite persons with needs in the order of nature.

I remark here that the idea of the a priori is much simpler in the case of practical reason than it is in the case of theoretical reason. In the first

---

11. For the idea of possibilities of construction, see Parsons's account of constructivism in his article "Mathematics, Foundations of," pp. 204f. He says, "Constructivist mathematics would proceed as if the last arbiter of mathematical existence and mathematical truth were the possibilities of construction," where the possibilities in question are those of an appropriately idealized procedure. The remark in the text about the infinity of primes rests on the fact that a constructivist proof of their infinity can be given.

Critique, we have to distinguish between the a priori in connection with the understanding and its categories as well as in connection with reason and the ideas of reason. Understanding and reason (*Verstand* and *Vernunft*) have different roles in the overall structure of knowledge, and the categories and the ideas of reason have their own distinctive roles. All of this must be kept track of. And there are also the a priori intuitions of space and time. By contrast, in the second *Critique,* there is only the a priori of practical reason itself.

2. Now, for Kant, there are two marks of a priori knowledge: necessity and universality; and these marks apply to practical as well as to theoretical knowledge.

(a) Necessity here means practical necessity: that is, what is required by the principles of pure practical reason. So whatever is required by the categorical imperative (via the CI-procedure) is practically necessary for us.

(b) As for universality, this means that the requirements in question hold for all reasonable and rational persons in virtue of their nature as such persons, independently of any particular conditions of inclination and circumstances that mark off one reasonable and rational person from another. Kant insists in the preface of the *Groundwork* (Pref:7–9 [389–390]) that "'Thou shalt lie' could not hold merely for men, other rational beings having no obligation to abide by it—and similarly with all other genuinely moral laws; that here consequently the ground of obligation must be looked for, not in the nature of man nor in the circumstances of the world in which he is placed, but solely a priori in the concepts of pure reason."

So far, all this is quite straightforward. The categorical imperative is a priori as grounded on pure practical reason; it is both practically necessary and holds universally for all reasonable and rational persons; and the same is true of particular categorical imperatives when the persons in question are, like us, finite persons with needs and hence subject to that imperative.

We must be careful to distinguish, as we have done before, the categorical imperative from the hypothetical. Two differences are these:

First, the hypothetical imperative Kant regards as analytic and not synthetic, and it holds in virtue of empirical rather than pure practical reason. For Kant, it is simply part of being rational that if we desire the end, we also desire the (most effective) means. For him, there is no difficulty in understanding how hypothetical imperatives can determine our will (*Gr* II: 24 [417]). He doesn't see it as a problem.

The second difference is that particular hypothetical imperatives are conditional: they apply to us or not depending on our specific wants and inclinations.

3. As we might expect from these two differences, the difficulty with understanding how the categorical imperative determines the will concerns how we are to understand it as a synthetic a priori and practical proposition. The problem is that in contrast with hypothetical imperatives, they are unconditional, both in regard to the means they forbid us to adopt in pursuing our ends (these means are restricted by the duties of justice) and in the obligatory ends they require us to give at least some weight to (these ends are specified by the duties of virtue). Recall that to say that particular categorical imperatives are unconditional is to say that they apply to us whatever may be the ends sought by our interests and inclinations. But if that is so, how is it possible that they can determine our will? What possible foothold can they have in our person?

There is a parallel here, as Kant indicates in passing, with the problem of synthetic a priori propositions in the first *Critique*. For in that work Kant sees no difficulty in understanding how empirical concepts apply to objects. They are abstracted from instances of those concepts met with in experience, and so we are assured of their objective reality: that is, we are assured that those concepts can apply to objects of experience. After all, the basic ones have been abstracted from instances to which those concepts already did apply. But the categories of the understanding, such as the concept of cause, are a priori and have not been abstracted from objects in experience, so how can we be assured that they can apply to objects? Thus arises the problem of the transcendental deduction.

4. How are we, then, to understand the categorical imperative as synthetic a priori? We have already noted the general sense in which this imperative is a priori as arising from practical reason. But there is also a special sense in which it is a priori: it formulates the requirements of pure practical reason and so it is a priori with respect to empirical practical reason.

The thought is that just as the categories of the understanding specify a priori conditions for the possibility of the experience of objects, the categorical imperative and particular categorical imperatives to which it leads impose a priori constraints on the permissible exercise of empirical practical reason (for our maxims must be acceptable to the CI-procedure). These constraints are synthetic a priori because:

(i) they are imposed unconditionally on reasonable and rational persons, and

(ii) they are imposed on such persons without being derived from the concept of a person as reasonable and rational.

Hence they are both synthetic (as in [i]) and not analytic (as in [ii]).

This in fact is just what Kant says in *Gr* II:28n. (420): "Without presupposing a condition taken from some inclination I connect an action with the will a priori and therefore necessarily. . . . Here we have a practical proposition in which the willing of an action is not derived analytically from some other willing already presupposed . . . but is on the contrary connected immediately with the concept of the will of a reasonable being as something which is not contained in this concept."

I have simplified the footnote by omitting the parentheses. We can elaborate the footnote as simplified as follows: Without presupposing any particular ends wanted by natural desires, the CI-procedure connects an action with what a reasonable and rational person ought to do. Here we have a practical proposition in which what ought to be done is not derived analytically from other specific ends already presupposed, as in the case of hypothetical imperatives. Nor, on the other hand, is the action derived analytically from the concept of a reasonable and rational person, again as in the case of hypothetical imperatives. Rather what such a person ought to do in a particular case is worked out directly by the CI-procedure without the intermediary of an end of specific natural desires.

5. While this elaboration accurately describes how the CI-procedure works, several questions remain to be settled.

(a) First, are particular categorical imperatives (particular duties of justice and duties of virtue) a priori? No, they are not: in arriving at them by means of the CI-procedure, we rely on certain laws of nature and use various kinds of empirical knowledge about our social world. Of course, they are unconditional in contrast with hypothetical imperatives. Thus it is no objection to Kant's view (as Mill mistakenly thinks it is; see *Utilitarianism,*

Ch. V, paragraph 22) that particular categorical imperatives are not a priori. What is synthetic a priori is the moral law and the CI-procedure as its procedural representation as it applies to us.

(b) Second, suppose it is objected that particular categorical imperatives are really hypothetical and conditional, since the CI-procedure in arriving at them relies on a conception of true human needs (or another like conception) at step (4).

In reply, it suffices to remark (as we said in Kant V) that a conception of these needs is a special conception of the good introduced to ensure content for the moral law; introducing it meets a need of pure practical reason. These considerations distinguish true human needs from particular inclinations and wants as they arise in everyday life and prompt us to formulate (rational) maxims (hypothetical imperatives) at step (1). This reply can be strengthened by connecting these true human needs with our needs as rational persons in the order of nature who need society, and so with the conditions required for a viable social order and necessary for realizing our rationality. This answer is suggested in section 6 at the end of the preceding lecture.

(c) Third, does the CI-procedure take account of the consequences of everyone's acting from particular categorical imperatives? Yes, of course: we see this from the comparison of adjusted social worlds at step (4). A moral conception that took no account of consequences at all (as it is sometimes said of Kant's view) would be simply mad. The question is always how to do so.

6. To conclude: earlier we said that pure practical reason constructs out of itself its a priori object, that is, the realm of ends as a commonwealth of reasonable and rational persons that would exist in the order of nature when all its members act from the moral law. We can now see that the phrase "out of itself" is an exaggeration; the metaphor is a bit out of control. To correct this, we say instead that pure practical reason, as represented by the three formulations of the categorical imperative, constructs its object from the materials (the matter) presented to it by rational maxims at step (1).

Alternatively, we can say that the procedure is a selection device: it accepts some maxims (as generalized precepts) and rejects others according to whether they meet the criteria of practical reason it incorporates. Like a mathematical function, the CI-procedure is applied to something (as a function is applied to a number) to give something else (a corresponding number), and can't, to speak accurately, produce its object out of itself.

Finally, at the end of Kant IV, we referred to the important passage in the second *Critique* (*KP* 5:43) where Kant says that the moral law gives to the sensible world the form of an intelligible world by specifying through the totality of the precepts it counts as valid the public order of a possible realm of ends. This public order of a possible realm of ends is the a priori necessary object of a will determined by the moral law. At *KP* 5:44 there is another important passage cited already in Kant IV:

> Through reason we are conscious of a law to which all our maxims are subject as though through our will a natural order must arise. Therefore, this law must be the idea of a supersensuous nature, a nature not empirically given yet possible through freedom; to this nature we give objective reality, at least in a practical context, because we regard it as the object of our will as pure rational beings.
>
> The difference, therefore, between the laws of a system of nature to which *the will is subject* and a system of *nature which is subject to a will* (as far as the relation of the will to its free actions is concerned) rests on this: in the former, the objects must be the causes of the conceptions which determine the will, and in the latter, the will is the cause of the objects. Hence, in the latter the causality of the objects has its determining ground solely in the pure faculty of reason, which therefore may be called pure practical reason.

Rather than simply say, as Kant does here, that "the will is the cause of the objects," we may elaborate: our will as pure practical reason constructs its own a priori object through the CI-procedure, which object is the public moral order of a possible realm of ends. So for the members of a realm of ends, their society as an object in the order of nature is not the cause of the conception of their society that determines their will. Rather, in constructing its own a priori object, their pure practical reason is free as reason is free. It has the freedom of reason.

KANT VII

The Fact of Reason

§1. Introduction

1. Today I discuss the fact of reason, one of the central ideas of Kant's moral philosophy. This idea appears for the first time in the *Critique of Practical Reason*, and focusing upon it is one way to approach that work.

I begin by stating the question that the doctrine of the fact of reason addresses. Recall that the first two chapters of the *Groundwork* are said by Kant to be merely analytic: the first develops an argument to the moral law (sketched in Kant I) from our commonsense concept of moral worth of character, and the second chapter presents the three formulations of the categorical imperative. But at the end of chapter II (*Gr* II:90 [444–445]), Kant says:

> Any one . . . who takes morality to be something, and not merely a
> chimerical idea without truth, must admit the principle we have put
> forward. This chapter . . . like the first, has been merely analytic. In
> order to prove that morality is not simply a phantom of the brain—
> a conclusion which follows if the categorical imperative, and with it
> the autonomy of the will, is true and is absolutely necessary as an *a
> priori* principle—we require a *possible synthetic use of pure practical rea-
> son.* On such a use we cannot venture without prefacing it by a *critique*
> of this power of reason itself—a critique whose main features, so far
> as sufficient for our purpose, we must outline in our final chapter.

What is involved here is Kant's view that for a concept to have objective reality—that is, for it to be applicable to something and in that sense true—it is not sufficient that it have an analysis that shows it to be consistent and intelligible. For all he has done in the first two chapters of the *Groundwork*, the moral law may still be only a "chimerical idea." What Kant wants to show is that the moral law does apply to something, and in particular, that it applies to us; for if it does, then we can act from that law and not merely in accordance with it.

2. I recall from Kant II two of the essential conditions that we said any account of the categorical imperative must satisfy.

First, the content condition: the categorical imperative must not be merely formal but must have suffcent structure to specify requirements on moral deliberation so that suitably many maxims are shown to be fit or unfit to be made universal law. Otherwise the moral law would be empty and without content.

Second, the freedom condition: the categorical imperative must represent the moral law as a principle of autonomy, so that from our consciousness of this law as supremely authoritative for us (as reasonable persons), we can recognize that we can act from the principle of autonomy as a principle of reason.

The explanation of these two conditions is as follows. The aim of the second *Critique* is to show that there is pure practical reason and that it actually shows its existence in our thought, feeling, and conduct, or in what Kant calls "the fact of reason." Put another way, the aim of the second *Critique* is to show that pure reason can be practical and can directly determine our will (*KP* 5:15). But pure reason cannot do this if it is merely formal and lacking in content. It would be empty; anything we did would satisfy it. Hence the first (content) condition.

The reason for the second condition is this: only if the moral law is a principle of autonomy in Kant's sense can this law and our capacity to act from it disclose our freedom to us, that is, disclose both our independence of the natural order (negative freedom) and our capacity to act from principles of pure practical reason with a definite content (positive freedom). Hence the second (freedom) condition.

3. But plainly, since the moral law is simply an idea of reason, the first two conditions do not alone suffice for the objective reality of pure practical

reason. It is further essential that we be conscious of the moral law as authoritative for us, and that it is possible for us to act from that law, not merely in accordance with it. Thus there are two further conditions as follows:

Third, the fact of reason condition: our consciousness of the moral law as supremely authoritative for us as reasonable and rational persons must be found in our everyday moral thought, feeling, and judgment; and the moral law must be at least implicitly recognized as such by ordinary human reason.

Fourth, the motivation condition: our consciousness of the moral law as supremely authoritative for us must be so deeply rooted in our person as reasonable and rational that this law by itself, when fully known and understood, can be a sufficient motive for us to act from it, whatever our natural desires.

Kant holds that if these four conditions are satisfied, then there is pure practical reason. These conditions are both necessary and sufficient. In the second *Critique,* he maintains that they are indeed satisfied and hence that pure practical reason exists and that we are free from a practical point of view.

§2. The First Fact of Reason Passage

1. There are altogether six fact of reason passages, as I shall call them. For expository purposes, let's think of them as extending over a number of paragraphs, even though a reference to the fact of reason may occur only once. The fact of reason is mentioned one or more times at eight places (*KP* 5:6, 31, 42, 43, 47, 55, 91, 105), but some of these belong to the same passage. Either the whole phrase "das Faktum der Vernunft" or simply "ein Faktum" occurs; in the latter case, the context makes it clear that the fact of reason, or a fact related to this fact, is meant. The six fact of reason passages are these:

   (a) The Preface 3–6: the first eight paragraphs with the phrase "ein Faktum" occurring only in paragraph 6.
   (b) In Analytic I 28–33: starting with the statement of Problems I and II in §§5–6 and continuing to the end of the statement

of Theorem IV but not including the remarks. There are three explicit references to the fact of reason, all in §7.

(c) In the first Appendix to Analytic I 41–48: the whole appendix except for the last paragraph. It may be divided into three parts: paragraphs 1–3, paragraphs 4–7, and paragraphs 8–15.

(d) In the second Appendix to Analytic I 55f.

(e) In the *Elucidation* 91–93: paragraphs 4–6.

(f) In the appendix to the *Elucidation* 103–106: paragraph 1.

2. I begin with the first passage, which opens the Preface, and, as I shall do in each case, I note only the more important points, as time permits. This passage introduces the main themes of the work. To appreciate the significance of the first sentence, recall that in the *Groundwork*, Kant had said that the only foundation of a metaphysic of morals is a critique of pure practical reason, just as a critique of pure speculative reason is the only foundation for a metaphysic of nature.

> Why this critique is not called a *Critique of Pure Practical Reason* but rather simply *Critique of Practical Reason*, though the parallelism between it and the critique of speculative reason seems to demand the latter title, will be sufficiently shown in the treatise itself. Its task is merely to show that *there is a pure practical reason,* and, in order to do this, it critically examines reason's entire *practical faculty.* If it succeeds in this task, there is no need to examine the *pure faculty itself* to see whether it, like speculative reason, presumptuously *overreaches* itself. For if pure reason is actually practical, it will show its reality and that of its concepts in action [*in der Tat*], and all disputations which aim to prove its impossibility will be vain. (*KP* 5:3) (Kant's italics)

To see what Kant means by the title without the word "pure," distinguish two senses of critique implicit in his remarks in the Preface to the first *Critique* (2nd. ed., Bxxxii–xxxvii). In one sense, a critique involves giving an overall account of the concepts and principles of reason as one unified system of concepts and principles. The aim is to set out the whole constitution of reason.

In the other sense, critique means the criticism of reason, for although it is part of Kant's conception of the unity of reason that all of the concepts of reason and their associated principles have a correct and valid use, and therefore a proper place in the constitution of reason as an organic whole (KR B670f.), there is also a natural dialectic by which our human reason is misled and its concepts and principles are fallaciously employed.

With pure speculative reason, this dialectic is profoundly deceptive, as Kant tries to show in the Transcendental Dialectic of the first Critique. Thus it is part of the sense of the title of the book to inform us that it seeks to expose the deceptive power of the natural dialectic of pure speculative reason and of the improper use of its concepts and principles in speculative metaphysics.

3. The opening paragraph of the Preface of the second Critique hints at Kant's view that there is no need for a critique of pure practical reason in the sense of a criticism of reason. Rather, the task is to show that there is pure practical reason, which exhibits its reality in our moral thought, feeling, and conduct. From the introduction (KP 5:15) we know that for Kant, whether there is pure practical reason depends on whether pure reason is sufficient of itself to determine our will and so on whether our will is free. The significance of the fact of reason is that pure practical reason exhibits its reality in this fact and in what this fact discloses, namely, our freedom. Once we recognize the fact of reason and its significance, all disputations that question the possibility of pure practical reason are vain. No metaphysical doctrines or scientific theories can put it in jeopardy. We may not be able to comprehend how we can be free, but that we are free from the point of view of practical reason, there is no doubt. Kant says (KP 5:6): "Practical reason itself, without any collusion with the speculative, provides reality to a supersensible object of the category of causality, i.e., to freedom. This [freedom] is a practical concept and as such is subject only to practical use; but what in the speculative critique could only be thought [as possible] is now confirmed by fact [durch ein Faktum bestätigt]."

4. Since the word "pure" is not used in the title of the second Critique,

the word "critique" does not have its critical sense as applied to pure practical reason. It means instead a consideration of the constitution of practical reason as a whole, both pure and empirical, and the way pure and empirical practical reason are combined in one unified scheme of practical reason. Thus Kant says in the introduction (*KP* 5:16): "Pure [practical] reason, where it is once demonstrated to exist, is in no need of a critical examination: it is pure reason itself which contains the standard for a critical investigation of its entire use." Now, if pure practical reason is in no need of critique, it can only be empirical practical reason that needs critique. This reason proceeds from our natural inclinations and desires, and attempts to organize them into an ordered system of wants so as to achieve by a rational plan our greatest happiness. Kant says as much:

> The critique of practical reason . . . has the obligation to prevent the empirically conditioned reason from presuming to be the only ground of determination of the will. The use of pure [practical] reason, if it is shown that there is such a reason, is alone immanent; the empirically conditioned use of reason, which presumes to be sovereign, is, on the contrary, transcendent, expressing itself in demands and precepts which go far beyond its own sphere. This is precisely the opposite situation from that of pure reason in its speculative use.

Had Kant wanted to stress the meaning of critique as criticism, he could have titled the work *The Critique of Empirical Practical Reason*. Yet the title as it stands is appropriate: it tells us that the work considers reason's practical faculty as a whole.

§3. The Second Passage: §§5–8 of Chapter I of the Analytic

1. I use this passage to answer the important question: What fact is the fact of reason? This question poses some difficulty since Kant is not consistent in how he specifies it. He says of the fact of reason all of the following:

(1) it is our consciousness of the moral law (*KP* 5:31);

(2) it is the moral law itself (*KP* 5:31, 47, 91);

(3) it is the consciousness of freedom of the will (*KP* 5:42);

(4) it is autonomy in the principle of morality (*KP* 5:42);

(5) it is an inevitable determination of the will by the moral law itself (*KP* 5:55);

(6) it is actual cases of actions presupposing unconditional causality (*KP* 5:104).

The fifth characterization is, I think, of no importance for our question, and so I ignore it here; the sixth, the phrasing of which seems quite different, is actually just like (1) when the whole passage is read, and so I put it under (1). This leaves (1)–(4).

2. Now, (1)–(4) are not as different as they look; in fact, they are closely related. In order to give a consistent reading of Kant's view, I shall use (1). To explain why, consider §7, *KP* 31:

> The consciousness of this fundamental law may be called a fact of reason, since one cannot by subtle arguments derive it from already given data of reason, for example, the consciousness of freedom (for this is not already given) and because it forces itself upon us as a synthetic a priori proposition based on no pure or empirical intuition, although it would be analytic if the freedom of the will were presupposed, but for this a positive concept, an intellectual intuition, would be required, and here we cannot assume it. Yet in order to avoid any misunderstanding in regarding this law as given, we must note well that: it [the Moral Law] is not an empirical fact but the sole fact of pure reason, which announces itself [through that fact] as originating law (*Sic volvo, sic iubeo*).[1]

This crucial passage begins with the first specification of the fact of reason and ends with the second. Despite this ambiguity, I follow the first characterization. Let's say:

---

1. The Latin means "Thus I will, thus I command."

The fact of reason is the fact that, as reasonable beings, we are conscious of the moral law as the supremely authoritative and regulative law for us and in our ordinary moral thought and judgment we recognize it as such.

I believe that we can give a coherent account of the fact of reason by using this formulation. To see this, consider the following points.

First, the moral law as an idea of reason is only an idea, and as such may lack, as the ideas of immortality and of God may, objective reality, and so not apply to anything. Thus the moral law cannot itself be the fact of reason. This excludes (2).

Second, the fact of reason cannot be the (direct) consciousness of freedom, since it is a feature of Kant's transcendental idealism that we have no intellectual intuition of freedom. This excludes (3).

Third, the fact of reason cannot be autonomy in the principle of morality because whether autonomy is meant as the principle of morality itself (the moral law) (2), or as freedom (3), (4) is excluded once we exclude (2) and (3).

I conclude that the fact of reason is (1): our consciousness of the moral law as supremely authoritative and regulative for us.

3. A few observations. First, the doctrine of the fact of reason settles a question that long bothered Kant: namely, whether our knowledge of the moral law is rooted in our moral consciousness of this law or in our consciousness of our freedom as reasonable beings. Kant holds that our knowledge of the moral law cannot be based on our consciousness of our freedom. For this would imply that we have an intellectual intuition of freedom, whereas our intuitions (our experiences of particular objects and processes) are always subject to the conditions of sensibility. The order of knowledge is the other way around: the fact of reason, our shared consciousness of the moral law as supremely authoritative, is the basic fact from which our moral knowledge and conception of ourselves as free must begin (*KP* 5:4n.).

Further, Kant says that our consciousness of the moral law as supremely authoritative for us is not an empirical fact but "the sole fact of pure reason." To see the significance of this, and the central role it gives to the fact of reason, consider what he says about the concept of freedom in the Preface (*KP* 5:3f.):

> The concept of freedom, insofar as its reality is shown by an apodictic law of practical reason [the fact of reason], is the keystone of the whole architecture of the system of pure [practical] reason and even of speculative reason. All other concepts (those of God and immortality) which, as mere ideas, are unsupported by anything in speculative reason, now attach themselves to the concept of freedom and gain, with it and through it, existence as objective reality. That is, their possibility is shown by the fact that there really is freedom, for this [that there really is freedom] is shown through the moral law.

Plainly, the doctrine of the fact of reason is central, not only to Kant's moral philosophy, but to his transcendental idealism as a whole. That the concept of freedom has objective reality, which is the keystone of the system of speculative as well as of practical reason, depends on the fact of reason.

§4. The Third Passage: Appendix I to Analytic I, Paragraphs 8–15

1. In this passage Kant says that the moral law can be given no deduction, that is, no justification of its objective and universal validity; instead, it rests on the fact of reason. He says further that the moral law needs no justifying grounds; rather, that law proves not only the possibility but also the actuality of freedom in those who recognize and acknowledge that law as supremely authoritative (that is, those of whom the fact of reason holds). The moral law thus gives objective, although only practical, reality to the idea of freedom, and thereby answers a need of pure speculative reason, which had to assume the possibility of freedom to be consistent with itself. That the moral law does this is sufficient authentication, or credential, as Kant says, for that law. This credential takes the place of all of those vain attempts to justify it by theoretical reason, whether speculative or empirical (*KP* 5:46ff.).

As we have seen, this is a fundamental change from the *Groundwork*. Now, what is the significance of this change?[2] It signals, I believe, Kant's recognition that each of the four forms of reason in his critical philosophy has a different place and role in what he calls the unity of reason. He thinks of reason as a self-subsistent unity of principles in which every member exists for every other, and all for the sake of each (*KR* Bxxiii; *KP* 5:119ff.). In the most general sense, the authentication of a form of reason consists in explaining its place and role within what I shall call the constitution of reason as a whole. For Kant, there can be no question of justifying reason itself. Reason must answer all questions about itself from its own resources (*KR* B504–512), and it must contain the standard for any critical examination of every use of reason (*KP* 5:16): the constitution of reason must be self-authenticating.

Once we regard the authentication[3] of a form of reason as explaining its role within the constitution of reason, then, since the forms of reason have different roles, we should expect their authentications also to be different. Each fits into the constitution of reason in a different way, and the more specific considerations that explain their role in that constitution will likewise be different. The moral law will not have the same kind of authentication that the categories do, namely, the special kind of argument Kant gives for them in the Transcendental Deduction of the first *Critique*. This deduction tries to show the categories to be presupposed in our experience of objects in space and time, in contrast to their being regulative of the use of a faculty, in the way that the ideas of reason regulate the use of the understanding.

2. On the importance of this change, I agree with much of Karl Ameriks's valuable discussion in his *Kant's Theory of Mind* (Oxford: Oxford University Press, 1982), chap. 6. He discusses the views of Beck, Paton, and Henrich, who have tried to preserve the continuity of Kant's doctrine and have questioned the fundamental nature of the change.

3. It is important to keep in mind the ambiguity in Kant's use of the term "deduction." He sometimes uses it, as in the third fact of reason passage, to mean the special kind of argument given to establish the universal validity of the categories in the Transcendental Deduction; at other times it means simply considerations that suffice to justify, or defend against challenge, our use of something already in our possession. This broad meaning Kant adopted from the legal terminology of his day, for which I have used the term "authenticate" instead. On this, see Dieter Henrich, "Kant's Notion of a Deduction," in *Kant's Transcendental Deductions*, ed. Eckart Förster (Stanford: Stanford University Press, 1989), pp. 29–46.

2. Pure speculative reason also has what Kant calls a deduction (*KR* B698), that is, a justification (or authentication) of the objective validity of its ideas and principles as transcendental principles (B679). But the moral law as an idea of pure practical reason has a different authentication than pure speculative reason's. For Kant, pure reason, as opposed both to the understanding and to empirical practical reason, is the faculty of orientation.[4] While reason's work in both spheres is similar, it performs its work of orientation differently in the theoretical and practical spheres.

In each sphere, reason provides orientation by being normative: it sets ends and organizes them into a whole so as to guide, or direct, the use of a faculty: the understanding in the theoretical sphere; the power of choice in the practical. In the theoretical sphere, pure reason is regulative rather than constitutive; the role of its ideas and principles is to specify an idea of highest possible systematic unity, and to guide us in introducing this necessary unity into our knowledge of objects and our view of the world as a whole. In this way, the work of reason yields a sufficient criterion of empirical truth (B679). Without pure reason, general conceptions of the world of all kinds—religion and myth, science and cosmology—would not be possible. The ideas and principles of reason that articulate them would not exist, for their source is reason. The role of speculative reason in regulating the understanding and unifying empirical knowledge authenticates its ideas and principles.

By contrast, in the practical sphere, pure reason is neither constitutive nor regulative but directive: that is, it immediately directs the will (as the power of choice). In this sphere, it is empirical practical reason that is regulative; for by the principle of the hypothetical imperative, empirical practical reason organizes into a rational idea of happiness the various desires and inclinations belonging to the lower faculty of desire (*KP* 5:120). In contrast, the power of choice is directed immediately by pure reason's idea of the moral law, a law through which reason constructs for that power its a priori object, the ideal of a realm of ends (a whole of all ends in systematic

---

4. For this view, and in my account of Kant's conception of the role of reason generally, I have been much indebted for some years to Susan Neiman. See her book *The Unity of Reason: Rereading Kant* (New York: Oxford University Press, 1994).

conjunction; of persons as ends in themselves and of the (permissible) ends each person pursues) (*Gr* II:62 [433]).

§5. Why Kant Might Have Abandoned a Deduction for the Moral Law

1. I now consider why Kant might have abandoned the attempt to give an argument from theoretical reason for the moral law by examining several forms such an argument might take.

During the 1770s, Kant made a number of efforts in this direction. Henrich divides them into two groups.[5] In the first, Kant tries to show how the theoretical use of reason, when applied to the totality of our desires and ends of action, necessarily gives rise in a rational agent not only to the characteristic approval of moral judgment but also to incentives to act from that judgment. In the second group, Kant tries to derive the essential elements of moral judgment from what he takes to be a necessary presupposition of moral philosophy, a presupposition which can be seen to be necessary by the use of theoretical reason alone, namely, the concept of freedom.

For each group, Henrich describes a few examples. I leave aside these details. The relevant point is that Kant tries to ground the moral law solely in theoretical reason and the concept of rationality. He tries to derive the reasonable from the rational. He starts from a conception of a self-conscious rational (versus reasonable) agent with all the powers of theoretical reason and moved only by natural needs and desires. These arguments bear witness to Kant's effort over a number of years to find a derivation of the moral law from theoretical reason.

2. Another kind of argument for the moral law, one resembling the kind of argument Kant gives for the categories, might be this: we try to show the moral law to be presupposed in our moral consciousness in much the same way that the categories are presupposed in our sensible experience

---

5. Henrich has made a study of these arguments in the *Nachlass*. He suggests that when Kant speaks of "this vainly sought deduction" of the moral law, he has his own failures in mind. See "Der Begriff der sittlichen Einsicht und Kant's Lehre vom Faktum der Vernunft," in *Die Gegenwart der Griechen im neueren Denken*, ed. Dieter Henrich et al. (Tübingen: Mohr-Siebeck, 1960), pp. 239–247. I am much indebted to this essay.

of objects in space and time. Thus we might argue that no other moral conception can specify the concepts of duty and obligation, or the concepts needed to have the peculiarly moral feelings of guilt and shame, remorse and indignation, and the like. Now, that a moral conception includes the necessary background for these concepts is certainly a reasonable requirement. But the argument tries for too much: it is implausible to deny that other moral conceptions besides Kant's also suffice for this background. The moral conceptions of two societies may differ greatly even though people in both societies are capable of moral consciousness and the moral feelings.

A basic fault in this kind of argument is that it assumes the distinction between concept and intuition, whereas in moral consciousness there is no such distinction. Theoretical reason concerns the knowledge of objects, and sensory experience provides its material basis. Practical knowledge concerns the reasonable and rational grounds for the production of objects. The complete good is the realization of a constructed object: the realm of ends as the necessary object of a will immediately determined by the moral law. Moral consciousness is not sensible experience of an object at all. In Kant's constructivism, this kind of argument has no foothold.

3. Consider a further argument. One might say: since the deduction of the categories shows that their objective validity and universal applicability are presupposed in our unified public experience of objects, a parallel argument for the moral law might show it to constitute the only possible basis for a unified public order of conduct for a plurality of persons who have conflicting aims and interests. The claim is that without the moral law, we are left with the struggle of all against all, as exemplified by the pledge of Francis I (KP 5:28). This would allow us to say that the moral law is constitutive of any unified public order of a social world.

This approach, I think, is likewise bound to fail. The requirement that a moral conception specify a unified and shared public order of conduct is again entirely reasonable. The obvious difficulty is that utilitarianism, perfectionism, and intuitionism, as well as other moral doctrines, can also specify such an order. The moral law is, as we have seen, a priori with respect to empirical practical reason. It is also a priori as an idea of reason, but it is not a priori in the further sense that any unified public order of conduct must rest on it.

Kant does not, I believe, argue that the moral law is a priori in this further sense. What in effect he does hold is that the moral law is the only way for us to construct a unified public order of conduct without falling into heteronomy. He uses the idea of autonomy implicit in a constructivist conception of pure practical reason to reject other moral views. This is why he regards perfectionism and intuitionism as heteronomous, and would think the same of utilitarianism (had he discussed it as we know it today). His appeal is always to the moral law as a principle of free constructive reason.

§6. What Kind of Authentication Does the Moral Law Have?

1. Finally, let's return to the part of the third fact of reason passage (*KP* 5: 46ff.), where Kant explains why the moral law has no deduction. Here he stresses the differences between theoretical and practical reason. Theoretical reason is concerned with the knowledge of objects given to us in our sensible experience, whereas practical reason is concerned with our capacity to produce objects in accordance with a conception of those objects. An object is understood as the end of action; for Kant, all actions have an object in this sense. Acting from pure practical reason involves, first, bringing about an object the conception of which is framed in the light of the ideas and principles of pure practical reason, and, second, being moved (in the appropriate way) by a pure practical interest in realizing that conception. Since it is in virtue of our reason that we can be fully free, only those actions meeting these two conditions are fully free. I come back to this next time.

Now, from what we have said, the authentication of the moral law can seem highly problematic. This sets the stage for Kant's introducing the doctrine of the fact of reason in the second *Critique*. For he thinks the moral law cannot be derived from the concepts of theoretical reason together with the concept of a rational agent; nor is it presupposed in our moral experience, or necessary to specify a unified order of public conduct. It also cannot be derived from the idea of freedom, since no intellectual intuition of freedom is available. Moreover, the moral law is not to be regulative of a faculty that has its own material. This kind of authentication holds for speculative reason and, within the practical sphere, for empirical practical reason, which regulates the lower faculty of desire. Yet there is still a way, Kant now asserts, in which the moral law is authenticated: "The moral law is given, as an apodictically certain fact, as it were, of pure reason, a fact of which we are a priori conscious, even if it be granted that no example could be given in which it has been followed exactly, [while] the objective reality of the moral law can be proved through . . . no exertion of the theoretical reason, whether speculative or empirically supported. Nevertheless, it is firmly established of itself." He adds: "Instead of this vainly sought deduction of the moral principle, however, something entirely different and unexpected appears: the moral principle itself serves as a principle of the deduction of an inscrutable faculty which no experience can prove but which speculative reason had to assume as at least possible (in order not to contradict itself . . .). This is the faculty of freedom, which the moral law, itself needing no justifying grounds, shows to be not only possible but actual in beings that acknowledge the law as binding upon them."

2. To conclude: Kant holds that each form of reason has its own distinctive authentication. The categories and principles of the understanding are shown (by the Transcendental Deduction) to be presupposed in our experience of objects in space and time, and pure speculative reason is authenticated by its role in organizing into a systematic unity the empirical knowledge of the understanding, thereby providing a sufficient criterion of empirical truth. Empirical practical reason has a similar role with respect to our lower faculty of desire's organizing its inclinations and wants into a rational conception of happiness. It is pure practical reason the authentication of which seems the most elusive: we long to derive its law, as Kant did for many years, from some firm foundation, either in theoretical reason or in experience, or in the necessary conditions of a unified public order of conduct, or failing all of these, from the idea of freedom itself, as Kant still hopes to do in Part III of the *Groundwork*.

But none of these ways of authenticating the moral law is available within Kant's critical philosophy. In the second *Critique*, Kant recognizes this and accepts the view that pure practical reason, with the moral law (via the categorical imperative) as its first principle, is authenticated by the fact of reason and in turn by that fact's authenticating, in those who acknowledge the moral law as binding, the objective reality of freedom, though always (and this needs emphasis) only from a practical point of view. In the same way, the moral law authenticates the ideas of God and immortality. Thus, as we have seen, along with freedom, the moral law is the keystone of the whole system of pure reason (*KP* 5:3). Pure practical reason is authenticated finally by assuming primacy over speculative reason and by cohering into, and what is more, by completing the constitution of reason as one unified body of principles: this makes reason self-authenticating as a whole (*KP* 5:119ff.).

Thus I believe that by the time of the second *Critique*, Kant has developed not only a constructivist conception of practical reason but a coherentist account of how it can be authenticated. This is the significance of his doctrine of the fact of reason and of his abandoning his hitherto vain search for a so-called deduction of the moral law. As indicated above (see footnote 3), Kant's view in the second *Critique* (as I have rendered it) has looked to some like a step backward to some kind of intuitionism or else to dogmatism. But I think that a constructivist and coherentist doctrine of practical reason is not without strengths, and I believe it is part of the legacy Kant left to the tradition of moral philosophy. However, you should know that this interpretation of his thought is not generally shared. You must regard it with caution.

§7. The Fifth and Sixth Fact of Reason Passages

1. We have seen that Kant's aim in the second *Critique* is to show that there is pure practical reason and that it is manifest in our moral thought, feeling, and conduct: in the fact of reason. We stated the four conditions that he thinks suffice to establish that pure practical reason exists, and we considered the first three fact of reason passages. Now consider the fifth and sixth fact of reason passages, both in the *Elucidation*. These passages also say that the third condition is satisfied: namely, that our consciousness of the moral law as supremely authoritative is found in our everyday moral experience and is implicitly recognized by ordinary human reason.

In the fifth passage (*KP* 5:91), Kant writes:

> With reference to the theoretical [sphere], the faculty of pure rational a priori knowledge could easily and obviously be proved from exam-

ples from the sciences. . . . But that pure reason is of itself alone practical, without any admixture of any kind of empirical grounds of determination—one had to show this from the commonest practical use of
reason by producing evidence that the highest practical principle is a
principle recognized by every natural human reason as the supreme
law of its will, as a law completely a priori and independent of any
sensuous data.

The passage continues: "It was necessary first to establish and justify it [the
moral law], by proof of the purity of its origin, in the judgment of this
common reason, before science could take it in hand to make use of it, as
it were, as a fact, which precedes all disputation about its possibility and
all consequences which may be drawn from it."[6]

It is clear that although the fact of reason is said here to be the moral
law, Kant speaks loosely (as the first part of the quotation shows). His point
is that science, that is, the metaphysics of morals, can take up the moral
law as a fact, as it were, because it is the principle acknowledged in the
fact of reason. To continue: "This circumstance is easily explained from
what has . . . been said: it is because pure practical reason necessarily must
begin with fundamental principles, which thus, as original data, must be
made the basis of the whole science and not regarded as originating from
it. On this account, the justification of moral principles as principles of pure
reason could be made with sufficient certainty through merely appealing
to the judgment of common sense."

2. In the sixth and last fact of reason passage, Kant refers to this fact in
an indirect way that he does not use elsewhere. However, I think that his
meaning is compatible with the proposed interpretation. Kant is concerned
here with the transition from our possible freedom to our actual freedom,
with whether the "can be" of the first *Critique* (that is, the possibility of
freedom introduced to resolve the third antinomy) can be made into an

6. Kant adds a bit later that "if to a man who is otherwise honest . . . we present the moral
law by which he recognizes the worthlessness of the liar, his practical reason at once forsakes the
advantage, combines with that which maintains in him respect for his own person . . . , and the
advantage after it has been separated and washed from every particle of reason . . . is easily weighed
by everyone" (*KP* 5:92f.). The whole passage is instructive in how it connects our moral feelings
with the recognition of the moral law in ordinary moral experience.

"is." He decides that it can, since (*KP* 5:104) "it was a question of whether in an actual case and, as it were, by a fact, one could prove that certain actions presupposed . . . an intellectual, sensuously unconditioned causality, regardless of whether they are actual or only commanded, i.e., objectively and practically necessary." Kant goes on later to say that there is a principle which characterizes this causality and that (*KP* 5:105) "[t]his principle . . . needs no search and no invention, having long been in the reason of all men and embodied in their being. It is the principle of morality."

3. So for Kant, the moral law is found in our everyday moral judgment and feeling, and even in our being, our character. But how do we experience the moral law in our thought? Earlier, in the second fact of reason passage, Kant asks the question "[H]ow is consciousness of the moral law possible?" and answers (*KP* 5:30): "We can come to know pure practical laws in the same way we know pure theoretical principles, by attending to the necessity with which reason prescribes them to us and to the elimination from them of all empirical conditions, which reason directs. The consciousness of pure will arises from the former as the consciousness of pure understanding [arises] from the latter."

Later in the same paragraph, Kant says that we would not have dared to introduce freedom into science had not the moral law and with it "practical reason . . . forced this concept upon us." Recall here that at (*KP* 5:31), Kant speaks of how in the consciousness of the moral law it "forces itself upon us as a synthetic a priori proposition based on no pure or empirical intuition." The moral law springs from our pure practical reason almost involuntarily. Earlier Kant had said (*KP* 5:27): "What form makes a maxim suitable for universal law giving and what form does not do so can be distinguished without instruction by the most common understanding."

At *KP* 5:29, after discussing whether our knowledge of the moral law precedes our knowledge of freedom or vice versa, Kant says: "It is . . . the moral law, of which we become immediately conscious as soon as we construct maxims for the will, which first presents itself to us."

At (*KP* 5:27), he illustrates the point by the example of the deceitful deposit. In such a case, we immediately realize that our maxim would destroy itself when taken as a universal law. To be sure, as he says (*Gr* I: 20 [403–404]), ordinary human reason does not conceive of the moral law abstractly in its universal form; rather, our reason has this law "actually before its eyes and does use it as a norm of judgment." We spontaneously acquire a facility in making moral judgments according to the requirements of pure practical reason.

4. What does Kant mean in the citation above from *KP* 5:30 where he says that we come to know pure practical laws "by attending to the necessity with which reason prescribes them to us"? We cannot explain this necessity (here practical as opposed to theoretical necessity) by appealing to pure reason itself. For this form of reason specifies that necessity; it cannot explain itself. As Kant says, "[H]uman insight comes to an end as soon as we arrive at fundamental powers or faculties" (*KP* 5:46f.).

We misunderstand Kant, I think, if we take him to be offering an explanation of practical necessity. Rather, as we have discussed, he is simply laying out the constitution of practical reason as a whole and giving an account of the role of the fundamental powers of reason as met with in our moral experience. This is the only kind of deduction—in the broad sense of authentication (see §4 above)—that the moral law admits of. An explanation of the constitution of reason is not possible, not because it lies beyond us in the unknown, but because reason cannot be judged or explained by anything else. Although certainly much reflection is required to lay out an accurate view of its constitution, and reflection itself is continual and must never cease, this constitution must, in the end, be seen as self-authenticating.

§8. Conclusion

Since we have surveyed a variety of points today, I should stress that the main ones are essentially two.

The first is that the fact of reason establishes the third condition (one of four) for pure practical reason to exist, to manifest itself in fact and deed. This is the condition that our consciousness of the moral law (via the categorical imperative) is found in our everyday moral thought, feeling, and judgment; and that that law is recognized as authoritative, at least implicitly by ordinary human reason (§§2–3, 7).

The second point is that the doctrine of the fact of reason marks a fundamental change in Kant's view and in how he understands the basis of pure practical reason. In §§4–6, we examined his idea that the authentication of each kind of reason differs from the others and that the appropriate authentication of each form of reason consists in showing its role and place within the constitution of reason as a whole. This constitution is self-authenticating, as reason is neither opaque nor transparent to itself, and can answer all questions about itself on due reflection.

The Moral Law as the Law of Freedom

§1. Concluding Remarks on Constructivism and Due Reflection

1. I pause a moment to note where we are. In the first four lectures, we examined the moral law, or rather how that law applies to us, first through the categorical imperative and then by the CI-procedure, which is the most usable formulation of the law's requirements in our case. Lectures V–VII attempted to bring out the deeper philosophical questions that Kant hoped to understand by his account of the categorical imperative and its several formulations.

We considered the sequence of six conceptions of the good and how the development of the sequence clarifies the role of the priority of right in his doctrine. Next we surveyed Kant's doctrine as a form of moral constructivism, a view that can be said undeniably to be owing to him, since the history of doctrine shows no predecessors. Last time, I suggested that his constructivist doctrine is also coherentist, in that it gives an account of how the four kinds of reason cohere together into one unified and self-authenticating constitution of reason. I also suggested that Kant's view is coherentist in the further sense that he maintains, for example in the fifth and sixth fact of reason passages, that our recognition of the moral law as supremely authoritative for us is manifest in our thought, feeling, and conduct.

2. Many questions arise regarding Kant's constructivism as I have characterized it. I mention one for clarification. It is this: how to reconcile the

idea that any construction must be checked by critical reflection with the view Kant expresses in the passage about the paradox of method: that the concept of good and evil must be determined not before the moral law but only after and by means of it (*KP* 5:62f.). The difficulty is that Kant appears to know in advance of critical reflection how a constructivist doctrine must look, but this seems to make it impossible to undertake such reflection in good faith.

In reply to this quite proper worry, we interpret constructivism as a view about how the structure and content of the soundest moral doctrine will look once it is laid out after due critical reflection. We say that it will contain, in the manner explained, a constructivist procedure incorporating all the requirements of practical reason such that the content of the doctrine—its main principles, virtues, and ideals—is constructed. Here by full reflection is not meant perfect reflection at the end of time, but such increasing critical reflection as might be achieved by a tradition of thought from one generation to the next, so that it looks more and more as if upon fuller reflection the moral view would be constructivist. There should be increasing success in formulating the doctrine as a whole.

3. Here one should distinguish between the doctrine as formulated at any particular time and the process of arriving at a formulation of it by thought and reflection over time. As the formulated doctrine is checked against our considered moral judgments, we expect there to be serious conflicts in which one or the other must give way. At this point, constructivism is committed to making only the kinds of changes consistent with it. For example, it must urge that an idea of reason used in the construction has been interpreted in a wrong way: not all the appropriate true human needs have been included and described correctly, the publicity requirements for moral precepts are misstated, or certain aspects of the ideas of reciprocity and impartiality in the idea of reasonableness have been omitted.

Of course, constructivism may urge that the apparent considered judgments are mistaken; but if so, it must show what the mistakes are and where they lie. It can't throw out a considered judgment simply because the weight of the construction is greater: errors must first be identified. As with any other view, constructivism may be false. It must prove itself by showing, as Kant says, that there is pure practical reason. Doing that involves, as we saw last time, showing that the moral law is manifest in our moral thought, feeling, and conduct—the third condition—and to do this calls for critical reflection as we have just described it.

I conclude these remarks by saying that in presenting Kant's moral philosophy, I have played down the role of the a priori and the formal, and I have given what some may think a flat reading of the categorical imperative as a synthetic a priori practical proposition. These things I have done because I believe that the downplayed elements are not at the heart of his doctrine. Emphasizing them easily leads to empty and arid formalities, which no one can accept and which we then erroneously associate with his name. Rather, the heart of his doctrine lies in his view of free constructive reason and the idea of coherence that goes with it, as examined last time. It lies also in his further ideas, such as the idea of the moral law as a law of freedom and the idea of philosophy as the defense of reasonable faith. Now it is time to turn to these matters, although too briefly. They will occupy us in this and the next two lectures.

§2. The Two Points of View

1. Kant is concerned throughout with human reason as a form of human self-consciousness. So we may think of the two points of view of theoretical and practical reason as articulating the form and structure of two different forms of self-consciousness: in one case, our self-consciousness as a subject inquiring about and investigating the natural and social world (our self-consciousness as possessing theoretical reason); in the other, our self-consciousness as a deliberating and acting subject (our self-consciousness as possessing practical reason). The first *Critique* examines the form and structure of the theoretical point of view, the second *Critique* does the same for the practical point of view.

These two points of view are in some ways similar and in some ways different. They are similar, since each is a form of one and the same reason, as the unity of reason requires. In both points of view, reason is guided by its idea of the greatest systematic unity, in one case by the idea of the greatest unity in our knowledge of objects, in the other by the idea of the greatest unity in our system of ends, both collective and individual. The two points of view must be in some ways different, since one point of view is that of theoretical reason concerned with knowledge of given objects, while the other point of view is that of practical reason concerned with the production of objects.

But while these points of view are different, the practical point of view depends on the theoretical, since it takes for granted the knowledge already established by theoretical reason. In this way, practical reason presupposes theoretical reason: the latter provides the needed background for reasonable deliberation. This is shown in the information relied on at the various steps of the CI-procedure.

2. These general remarks can be made more specific by noting that in each point of view we can distinguish five elements. One element is the kind of questions we ask from the point of view; another is the kind of interest that moves us to ask those questions. From the practical point of view, we ask what we ought to do in a particular case, or more generally, we ask what our duties are. Or still more generally, we ask what objects we ought to produce in accordance with a conception of those objects so as to lead to a whole of ends with the greatest possible systematic unity. Our interest in these questions is our pure practical interest in doing what we ought and in fulfilling our duties of justice and of virtue. Theoretical reason also has its interests, not only a positive interest in the greatest possible systematic unity of our knowledge but also a negative interest in preventing speculative folly and fanaticism from corrupting the work of reason (*KP* 5:121).

A third element is obvious and need only be mentioned, namely, that in trying to settle these questions we use, in each case, a certain family of ideas, principles, and precepts of reason, as set out in the first and second *Critiques*.

Finally, a point of view involves a fourth and fifth element: one is certain specific attitudes we must take toward ourselves and the world as we assume the point of view, while the other is certain beliefs needed to support and sustain these attitudes. Thus in the case of the practical point of view, we are to act under the idea of freedom (§5). In doing this, we are not to try to foresee our behavior, as if from the theoretical point of view, but instead we must view our reason as absolutely spontaneous and dependent on nothing outside itself. And we must firmly believe that we can act in accordance with the best reasons as established in the course of deliberation.

Connected with these matters (as we consider in Kant X) is the complex of attitudes and postulates that Kant refers to as reasonable faith.

3. Finally, there are significant relations between the two points of view that I shall not try to characterize here. But it bears repeating that while the practical point of view presupposes the knowledge established by the theoretical, the practical is primary in the constitution of reason. Both forms of reason are moved by their interests, and the interests of the practical as those of humanity itself are primary.

Again, as applied to persons and their actions, both points of view refer to one and the same thing: the very same person and action seen from two different points of view (*KP* 5:97). These are not points of view on different worlds, nor are they points of view from different worlds: they are points of view for asking different questions about one and the same world. One kind includes (roughly) questions of fact; the other includes questions about what we ought to do. These questions arise from different interests and are answered by different principles of reason originating in the two forms of reason. Their different answers are not straightforwardly contradictory, but I leave aside these complexities here.

Thus I want to consider Kant's doctrine not as a two-worlds view—a world of phenomena and an intelligible world—but instead as a doctrine with two points of view corresponding to different questions moved by different interests and answered by different ideas and principles. How these points of view are related we can best see by examining their structure and content and by seeing how we avail ourselves of them in ordinary life and in science. There is no secret about it: we have to look.

§3. Kant's Opposition to Leibniz on Freedom

1. We are not yet ready to discuss the last condition for the existence of pure practical reason—the condition stating that our consciousness of the moral law is so deeply rooted in our person that this law can be a sufficient motive, whatever our natural desires. Before discussing this condition, we first review Kant's conception of freedom and get a firmer grasp of his moral psychology as presented in *Religion* I. The moral psychology as stated there is the most adequate he ever gave; any account of his view must

include it. So we begin a rather long detour: today I start with his conception of freedom; next time we survey his moral psychology.[1]

This is an extremely difficult topic, and much that I say will be unclear.
But to begin, let's ask: Who is Kant opposing in his view of freedom? It
often helps to consider whose account is being rejected and why; doing
this clarifies the problem and may indicate the conditions of a worthwhile
solution. Following this thought, I assume that Kant is opposing Leibniz's
account, and the determinism of empiricism generally; and so he would
reject Hume's account of freedom in the *Treatise* II:iii:1–2. In his early years,
when he was much influenced by Leibniz, Kant had also thought that free
will and determinism were compatible (*Nova Dilucidatio* [1755] I:400–410).

2. Now, what is there about Leibniz's view that Kant objects to? I believe
that Kant has four objections to Leibniz's conception of freedom.

The first and most basic objection derives from Leibniz's metaphysical
perfectionism. As we have seen, for Kant, this is a form of heteronomy and
incompatible with the idea of free constructive practical reason. Kant's idea
of the moral law as a law of autonomy should not be thought of as true
of a prior and antecedent order of moral values. Rather, the supremacy of
reason means that the moral law itself must be a law of freedom, in a sense
we must further try to explain.

Kant would next object to Leibniz's view as involving predeterminism.
Kant stresses this point in the *Elucidation* (*KP* 5:94f.). By predeterminism
Kant means the following. Causal laws govern the generation of a sequence
of states of a system over time, each state at time t_n being the causal consequent of the state at t_{n-1}. Given the total state of a system, causal laws
uniquely determine its next state. So the state t_p, at the present time, must
be predetermined by some state at time t_0 in the past, and the next state
t_{p+1} must be similarly predetermined. But since we have no control over
the past, we cannot be free now: our future is already settled. Thus for
Kant, predeterminism means that the truly effective determining causes are

---

1. Kant's more sustained discussions of freedom are the following, although significant statements about freedom occur throughout: the first *Critique* (B560–586) in connection with the third
antinomy, and later in the *Canon* (B828–832); the second *Critique* in the *Elucidation* (*KP* 5:93–103);
Groundwork III; *Metaphysics of Morals*, the introduction (*MdS* 6:213–214; 221; 225–227); *Religion*, Book
I. *Prolegomena* §53 also deserves mention. For the most part I shall focus on the *Groundwork* III:4
(447–448) (where Kant states the crucial idea of acting under the idea of freedom), the *Elucidation*,
and *Religion*, Book I.

only the initial state (if there is one) and the causal laws governing the system. If there is no initial state, all states are equally predetermined, and there is no free determination at any time.

3. As we saw, Leibniz is a compatibilist: he holds that free will and determinism go together. He would reply to Kant, as he replied to Spinoza, that what really matters is what kinds of causes do the determining. Freedom does not require the absence of determining grounds but depends on whether our actions are guided by judgments of value made in light of the greatest apparent good, when these judgments themselves express our free deliberative reason in Leibniz's sense (Leibniz II:§4). Given all that, he thinks we are indeed free, and our actions fully voluntary and spontaneous, although our freedom becomes greater as we grow in knowledge and wisdom, and as our freedom less imperfectly mirrors the freedom of God.

Kant thinks that this reply to predeterminism fails to meet his objection. This is plain from what he says about comparative and psychological freedom in the *Elucidation* (*KP* 5:96f.). It is "a wretched subterfuge," he says, to think that the kinds of causes make any difference so long as predeterminism holds. His reference to an *automaton spirituale*, with the mention of Leibniz, as "at bottom . . . nothing better than the freedom of a turnspit," and on a par with an *automaton materiale*, makes his point: the spontaneity of free spirits (of spiritual substances), as Leibniz understood it, is not sufficient. Recall that the principles and laws that determine the sequence of their psychological states are part of their complete concept (viewed as possible individuals)[2] and predetermine that sequence. Kant grants that Leibniz's free spirits have spontaneity in the sense that their psychological states are determined by the active powers that constitute them as free spirits, and hence they are not determined by outside influences. However, they lack what Kant insists on and refers to as absolute spontaneity.

For this spontaneity, see the footnote to *Religion* 6:49n. (45n.).[3] Here

2. The point here is that the concepts of these principles and laws, and the active powers they direct, are already included in the complete individual concept of a possible individual as it lies in the divine intellect. These principles and powers are simply made actual at the creation. Thus Leibniz says: "[I]f this world were only possible, the individual concept of body in this world, containing certain movements as possibilities, would also contain our laws of motion . . . but also as mere possibilities. . . . [E]ach possible individual of any one world contains in the concept of him the laws of his world." *Leibniz-Arnauld Correspondence*, p. 43.

3. The references in parentheses are to Greene and Hudson.

Kant says that there is no difficulty in reconciling freedom with inner self-sufficient grounds. The problem, he says,

> is to understand how *predeterminism,* according to which voluntary actions, as events, have their determining grounds *in antecedent time* . . . can be consistent with freedom, according to which the act as well as its opposite must be within the power of the subject at the moment of its taking place.
>
>   . . . [F]reedom consists not in the contingency of the act (that it is determined by no grounds whatever), that is, not in indeterminism . . . but rather in absolute spontaneity. Such spontaneity is endangered only by predeterminism, where the determining ground is in *antecedent time,* [and hence] . . . the act [is] now no longer in *my* power but in the hands of nature. (Kant's italics)

Here Kant affirms that freedom is compatible with, and even requires, determining grounds, those that he refers to as "inner self-sufficient grounds." Freedom is not contingency or lack of determinism. The problem is to avoid predeterminism; that can only be done, it seems, by absolute spontaneity. But what is absolute spontaneity? What conception of it can we form? This brings us to the heart of Kant's view.

§4. Absolute Spontaneity

1. I suggest that we think of absolute spontaneity as the spontaneity of pure reason, so in the case of freedom in the moral sphere, it is the absolute spontaneity of our pure practical reason. Since absolute spontaneity excludes predeterminism but has its own inner sufficient grounds (*Rel* 6:49n. [45n.]), it is the spontaneity of pure reason as it weighs and evaluates reasons, always in view of its own principles, and in the course of its own exercise.

Kant thinks of this spontaneity as not bound, or causally affected, by its own previous decisions—as such—as to the weight or proper evaluation of reasons. Pure reason is the highest court of appeal concerning its own constitution and its principles and guidelines for directing its own activities.

THE MORAL LAW AS THE LAW OF FREEDOM

As such, it is always free to reconsider its prior decisions: no case is ever shut for good. In its freedom, reason makes its own judgments as it proceeds, always founding them on the merits of the case: on the evidence and grounds at hand as assessed by the principles of reason and reason's view of its own constitution and principles at that moment.

2. No doubt this suggestion as to how to conceive of absolute spontaneity is in various ways obscure. But it is not, I think, hopelessly obscure. In any case, this idea is what moves Kant, or so I think. Thus if we ask what conception of absolute spontaneity is available to us—what conception of it we can form—I suggest that we look to the freedom of pure reason, as Kant would describe it. So we look at pure reason both in the theoretical sphere, as reason organizes into the highest possible systematic unity of scientific theory the (low-level) empirical knowledge provided by the understanding, and we look at the practical sphere as pure reason constructs for itself the a priori object of the moral law, the ideal of a possible realm of ends.

For Kant, there is no separate problem of the freedom of the will, as if something called "the will" posed a special problem. For him, there is only the problem of the freedom of reason, both theoretical and practical. The practical is what is possible through freedom, through the absolute spontaneity of pure reason; even pure reason is practical. To understand him, we must try to frame a conception of this spontaneity of pure reason, however inadequate it may be. He had such a conception and we must try to think our way into it. High science (which for Kant is physics and astronomy [Newtonian mechanics]) and the moral ideal of a possible realm of ends are each equally the work of the absolute spontaneity of reason. We should look at how he thinks reason actually proceeds.

3. Leibniz would, no doubt, reply to this that he also allows for absolute spontaneity. To make his case, he might say that free spirits, as he describes them, decide by full deliberative reason in accordance with the principle of the greatest apparent good (Leibniz II:§4). Why isn't this also a conception of absolute spontaneity? By now, we know Kant's two points in reply.

First, as we saw (in Leibniz II:§4:2–4), while as spirits we pursue the greatest apparent good, what we perceive as that good is affected by our perceptions and inclinations as these are reflected in our desires and aversions; but our desires and aversions reflect the infinite complexity of the universe which our nature expresses. Hence our decisions are influenced by the way the rest of the universe affects us, i.e., not in clear knowledge but in confused perceptions and in inclinations the causes of which, because of the infinite complexity of the world, we do not, and can never, understand.

Kant might say that our practical reasoning therefore can never be lucid: that is, we cannot, as the freedom of pure reason requires, grasp the full and accurate basis of our reasoning. He agrees that it is difficult to know our real motives, and that, for purposes of self-examination, we should inquire into them (*Gr* II:1–3 [406–408]); but this is different from its being impossible to grasp the full basis of our reasoning, the principles and powers that actually determine the course of our thought in view of the infinite complexity of the world. For Kant, the freedom—the absolute spontaneity—of pure reason requires that reason can at least be lucid before itself at least in due course. While not transparent to itself, it is not opaque to itself either; through due reflection, it alone is competent to specify the ideas and principles of its own constitution.

Second, Kant would say to Leibniz that the principle to decide in accordance with the greatest apparent good is not, as we have seen, a principle of pure practical (of free constructive) reason. Nor does Leibniz have a conception of the principles of a pure will (Kant I:§3), which the freedom of reason requires. Except when he is discussing various devices that the mind can use to make one desire prevail over another (Leibniz II:§4), he can write that once deliberation begins, "everything which then impinges on us weighs in the balance and contributes to determining a resultant direction, almost as in mechanics" (*New Essays* II:xxi).

For these two reasons at least, Kant thinks that Leibniz lacks a conception of the absolute spontaneity of pure reason.

§5. The Moral Law as a Law of Freedom

1. So much for how Kant opposes Leibniz's conception of freedom and for his introducing the idea of freedom as absolute spontaneity. I turn now to examine how this idea of spontaneity enters into understanding the moral law as a law of freedom. But before doing this, I mention again the distinctive way in which Kant treats the question of free will. This question is

often seen as one for metaphysics and the philosophy of mind alone: it asks whether free will is compatible with causal determinism without reference to any particular moral view, and if not, what the consequences are for moral responsibility. But from what we have just seen, Kant's approach is quite different. Three basic points:

First, for Kant, the question of freedom depends on the specific nature of the moral conception accepted as valid, and so the question cannot be settled within metaphysics and the philosophy of mind alone.

Second, the moral law as it applies to us (however indirectly) is a principle of pure practical reason and as such a principle of autonomy; given the unity of reason, pure practical reason also fully possesses absolute spontaneity and is fully as free as pure theoretical reason.

Third, as a consequence, there is no separate question about freedom of the will, but only one question: the freedom of reason. The freedom of theoretical and that of practical reason stand or fall together.

This last point deserves comment. Two features of a Kantian account, as opposed to Kant's account, of freedom of the will so-called are that, first, it denies that there is any special problem about the will's freedom, viewing the question as simply part of the one main question of the freedom of reason as such. Second, it holds that pure practical reason is fully as free as theoretical reason; there is no need to claim that it is more free—what would that mean?—and being as free is certainly all that is needed for holding people responsible and accountable. As for the freedom of reason itself, the place to approach it is in the philosophy of mind generally. It is no longer, on a Kantian view, a problem in moral philosophy, even though very much one for it.

2. The third point above is an aspect of the equality of reason: neither theoretical nor practical reason is superior to the other. Kant refers to this equality at the end of the important §VII of the Dialectic, where he remarks that the constitution of reason as seen in the two *Critiques* puts them on a footing of equality (*KP* 5:141). Pure speculative reason is restricted to seeking the highest systematic unity in the understanding's knowledge of the objects of experience; pure practical reason is extended by the fact of reason to the ideas of freedom, God, and immortality, though always from a practical point of view. Both forms of reason have an essential and complementary role in one constitution of reason.

I won't comment further here on the distinctive features of Kant's approach. We have more urgent business: namely, to clarify the idea of the absolute spontaneity of pure reason and to try to locate where it shows itself in our everyday thought and judgment. We must also remind ourselves of various features of the moral law that lead Kant to think of it as a law of freedom and how they connect with the idea of absolute spontaneity.

3. One essential feature of reason's absolute spontaneity is its capacity to set ends for itself. Pure reason is the faculty of orientation (Kant VII:§4), and reason provides orientation by being normative: it sets ends and organizes them into a whole so as to guide the use of a faculty, the understanding in the theoretical sphere and the power of choice in the practical. Of theoretical reason Kant says that it has "as its sole object the understanding and its effective application. Just as the understanding unifies the manifold in the object by means of concepts, so reason unifies the manifold of concepts by means of ideas, positing a certain collective unity as the goal of the activities of the understanding" (KR B672).

By contrast the understanding is not free. While its operations are not governed by natural laws, and so not by the laws of association, as Hume supposed, and while it applies its own concepts (the categories) to sensible experience, its operations are guided not by ends it gives to itself but by ends given to it by speculative reason. In this sense, the understanding indeed is spontaneous but semiautomatic and unthinking. Lacking the capacity to set ends for itself, it is merely spontaneous.[4]

4. Consider now pure practical reason. Kant remarks of it in the first *Critique* (KR B576), in a passage in which he is discussing the "ought" as expressing a possible action the ground of which must be a concept of practical reason, that "[r]eason does not . . . follow the order of things as they present themselves in appearance, but frames for itself with perfect spontaneity an order of its own according to ideas [of pure reason], to which it adapts empirical conditions, and according to which it declares actions to be [practically] necessary."

We already know what Kant has in mind, namely, that pure practical reason constructs (as its a priori object) the ideal of a possible realm of ends

---

4. This contrast between reason as free and the understanding as merely spontaneous is stressed by Neiman.

as an order of its own according to ideas of reason. The particular elements of a realm of ends are to be adapted to empirical, that is, to historical and social, conditions.

By contrast with pure practical reason, empirical practical reason is not free. While it includes principles of rational deliberation, these principles take the totality of inclinations as given and seek to schedule our activities so as to satisfy our wants and needs in an orderly way. This arrangement specifies a conception of happiness. Some inclinations may be repressed or eradicated entirely; but if so, this is for the sake of a greater net balance of well-being over the course of life. Empirical practical reason has no independent standpoint from which to judge particular inclinations. It administers the fulfillment of the inclinations guided by the principles of the hypothetical imperative and subject to the constraints of pure practical reason.

The capacity of each form of pure reason to set ends for itself in virtue of its own ideas of reason is, then, an essential feature of the absolute (or perfect) spontaneity of pure reason. Lack of this spontaneity distinguishes the understanding from theoretical reason and empirical practical reason from pure practical reason.

§6. The Ideas of Freedom

1. I now try to locate where the idea of absolute spontaneity is connected with the ideas of freedom and how through them it shows itself in our thought and conduct. To this end, I review three ideas of freedom Kant uses: the idea of acting under the idea of freedom, the idea of practical freedom, and the idea of transcendental freedom. I then try to connect them with the idea of absolute spontaneity.

But first I should say that Kant's views on freedom are a tangled and complicated subject, and I do not attempt to survey them.[5] Given the time we can allow, I select three ideas of freedom found in his work and then

5. A very helpful and scholarly discussion is that of Henry Allison, *Kant's Theory of Freedom* (Cambridge: Cambridge University Press, 1990). The paper by Allen Wood, "Kant's Compatibilism," in a collection he edited, *Self and Nature in Kant's Philosophy* (Ithaca, N.Y.: Cornell University Press, 1984), pp. 73–101, illustrates some of the grave difficulties, if not unsolvable probiems, usually associated with Kant's view.

review how they might be seen to fit together and to complement one another. The result is only one possible view that I think makes reasonable sense of his doctrine. My discussion is no more than a sketch and leaves aside many questions.

2. The first and most basic idea is that of acting under the idea of freedom. Kant holds that when we engage in pure practical reasoning, we must do so under the idea of freedom (*Gr* III:4 [447–448]).

> Now I assert that every being who cannot act except under the idea of freedom is by this alone—from a practical point of view—really free: that is to say, for him all the laws inseparably bound up with freedom are valid just as much as if his will could be pronounced free on grounds valid for theoretical philosophy. . . . [W]e cannot possibly conceive of a reason as being consciously directed from the outside in regard to its judgments; for in that case the subject would attribute the determinations of his power of judgment not to his reason, but to an impulsion. Reason must look upon itself as the author of its own principles independently of alien influence. Thus, as practical reason, or as the will of a rational being, it must regard itself as free.

Here I take Kant to mean several things. One is that we must conduct our deliberations under the firm conviction that our thoughts and judgments, and the conclusions we reach, are (or at least can be) arrived at solely in the light of the evidence and reasons we review and put before ourselves for assessment.

He means also that we must believe that we can properly assess those reasons under the guidance of the moral law, or whatever norms of practical reason are appropriate, and that we can accept and act from whatever conclusions we decide are supported by the best reasons. As we deliberate, we must not believe that our powers of reason are determined by anything external to our reason, or allow anything to influence us except the reasons and evidence that are relevant for our consideration. Otherwise we abandon reason.

Thus I interpret Kant to say that when we deliberate from the practical point of view, we must, and normally do, regard our reason as having absolute spontaneity as he understands it. Acting under the idea of freedom, then, characterizes the practical point of view. This point of view, I want to say, is where the idea of absolute spontaneity, as it was described earlier (in §4), is manifest.

3. To sum up: to act under this idea means to deliberate in good faith. It is not only to deliberate reasonably and rationally as the norms of practical reason specify, but also to do so with the firm belief that our powers of reason, both theoretical and practical, are fully self-determining and point the way to what we ought to do and shall do, once known or confirmed by deliberation. We believe that the reasoning we are now engaged in, and the conclusions we shall reach, whatever they may be, and not something else, can and do determine our conduct.

Note well Kant's remark that "every being who cannot act except under the idea of freedom is by this alone—from a practical point of view—really free." Kant makes a similar statement at KP 5:47: "The moral law, which itself does not require a justification, proves not merely the possibility of freedom, but that it really belongs to beings who recognize this law as binding on themselves."

Then, some lines below (at KP 5:48), he makes it clear, as he does in the first statement, that what he says holds only from a practical point of view. The meaning of this rider we examine later in Kant X. But one thing we do know is that from a practical point of view, the laws of freedom of pure reason are just as valid for us as if our will could be said to be free for reasons valid for theoretical reason. Theoretical reason cannot provide arguments that increase their validity for us; nor, on the other hand, can it take those laws from us. To maintain this last claim belongs to philosophy as defense.

4. As for practical freedom, it is an empirical fact that we can and often do deliberate in accordance with and act from pure practical principles, and hence act under the idea of freedom; moreover, the conclusions we reach do indeed determine what we do. Everyday experience shows that practical reason is, as Kant puts it, one of the operative causes in nature (KR B374, 829–831).

By contrast, our belief in transcendental freedom is the firm conviction that our decisions as operating causes are not in fact "nature again" (KR 831). I take this to mean that we believe that our decisions issue from the absolute spontaneity of pure practical reason and are not determined by remote and unknown natural causes external to reason. Another part of this belief is the firm conviction that our decisions as informed by pure practical reason initiate a new series of appearances, a new beginning in the order of nature.

This belief, along with the postulates of God and immortality, is a postulate of reasonable faith, though distinct from them. Those postulates are necessary to guarantee the real possibility of the object of the moral law, the highest good; they are affirmed for the sake of the moral law. The postulate of freedom is more fundamental: it is the presupposition of the independence of our reason from the order of nature and thus of the spontaneity of pure reason (*KP* 5:132). As such, it is the basis of our being held responsible and accountable for our deeds.[6]

Thus the three ideas of freedom are related in this way. The basic idea is that of acting under the idea of freedom. It covers the family of basic attitudes that Kant thinks we must take toward ourselves and our powers of reason when, as reasonable and rational persons, we engage in deliberation. Practical freedom and transcendental freedom cohere into that basic idea in that they are further ideas supporting it. For example, the belief in practical freedom assures us that our deliberation is not pointless and settles what we shall do. Our belief in transcendental freedom, which Kant says is a transcendent thought (*KP* 5:135), sustains the attitude we assume toward ourselves in viewing our reason as having absolute spontaneity. Acting under the idea of freedom is the setting for the two other ideas of freedom.

5. Now, it might be objected to Kant's view that we might profess a belief in the external determination of our reason, at least in an abstract way: that is, we could say that all our thoughts are somehow determined by the principles of neurobiology, or of quantum chemistry, or that our deliberations are dictated by a master computer program. But so long as we just say this and don't act on it in a way that changes our practical reasoning, this view lacks practical effect. It might color our attitude to the world as a whole; we express a certain pessimism by referring to people

6. We shall see in Kant X that the postulate of freedom so understood belongs to both forms of reasonable faith, that is, to both the reasonable faith associated with the realm of ends as the secular object of the moral law and the reasonable faith associated with the highest good in religion. Hence reasonable faith takes two forms: the first is found in the political writings, the second in the philosophical writings, especially the three *Critiques*.

as merely deluded conglomerates of bonded chemicals, or occasionally as user-friendly configurations of fleshy computer parts. But as Leibniz maintained about believing in the foreknowledge of God, none of this will alter how we are to reason, or what we do in everyday life when practical questions arise.[7]

Kant does not discuss this objection. He might well say that even this kind of abstract and (for practical purposes) innocuous view would, in the long run, undermine our devotion to the moral law, as we later discuss (in Kant X) in regard to reasonable faith. He views our belief in transcendent(al) freedom as essential for us to sustain our devotion to the moral law over the course of a complete life. This belief rests on our moral disposition and is needed to maintain it. One role of philosophy as defense, and of the reasonable faith it supports, is to strengthen this devotion and the conviction of ourselves as free underlying it.

§7. Conclusion

Let's recall five features of the moral law that show it to be a law of freedom.

1. It is the supreme principle that governs deliberative reason from the practical point of view when we act, as reasonable and rational persons, under the idea of freedom.
2. In relation to negative freedom, it shows our independence from the order of nature, which empirical practical reason cannot do.
3. In relation to positive freedom, it exhibits the capacity of pure practical reason of being absolutely spontaneous, and so its capacity to set ends for itself and to provide its own orientation in the world. To be fully free, pure reason must do more than simply restrict means to the ends of natural desires, as specified by the duties of justice. It can also set ends for itself: the obligatory ends of the duties of virtue.

7. Recall what he wrote in the *Discourse* §30.2 (Ariew and Garber:61).

4. It is the principle of free constructive reason framing for itself, with perfect spontaneity and according to its own ideas, its own a priori object—the ideal of a possible realm of ends.

5. As the principle of pure practical reason, it has primacy in the whole constitution of reason (the primacy of the practical, an aspect of the practical point of view, to be discussed in Kant X), and in so doing, it reflects the absolute spontaneity of pure reason in determining, in the course of its exercise, its own constitution.

This is only a bare summary statement intended to remind us of what we have already discussed. All of the things referred to in 1–5 above were considered at some point. We need to see them all as doing their part in giving sense to the idea of the absolute spontaneity of pure reason. Next time we turn to the fourth condition of there being pure practical reason. After that, we take up our last topic, the unity of reason.

The Moral Psychology of the *Religion*, Book I

§1. The Three Predispositions

1. We are now ready to consider the fourth and last condition that must be satisfied if there is to be pure practical reason. Recall that this condition requires that our consciousness of the moral law must be so deeply rooted in our person that this law by itself can be for us a sufficient motive to determine our action, whatever our natural desires.

I shall proceed as follows. I begin with a survey of Kant's moral psychology as found in Book I of the *Religion*. This moral psychology I think of as Augustinian: it is more expressly set out than the moral psychology of the *Groundwork* and the second *Critique*, which betrays on occasion certain Manichean features, as discussed in §4. I focus on the *Religion* because its Augustinian view meets the requirements of the doctrine of the fact of reason, while the Manichean features do not. Once these matters are reviewed, I consider in §5 why Kant thinks the moral law by itself can be a sufficient motive.

2. My account of the main points of moral psychology of the *Religion* covers but a fragment of that marvelous work. We must be brief; my remarks are intended only for our limited aims and are hardly adequate even so. I begin straightaway with Kant's description of the three original predispositions to good (§1 of Book I), which, along with our free power of choice, constitute human nature. These predispositions are as follows (*Rel* I 6:26ff. [21ff.]).[1]

---

1. Numbers in brackets refer to the Greene and Hudson edition.

(a) The predisposition to animality in us, when we are regarded as living beings. This predisposition, Kant says, may be characterized as physical and "purely mechanical" self-love, by which he means that it does not require the exercise of reason and is generally guided by instinct and by acquired tendencies and habits. Under this predisposition fall the instincts for self-preservation, for the propagation of the species, and for the care of children; and the instinct for community with other human beings, the social impulse.

(b) The predisposition to humanity in us, when we are regarded not only as living but also as rational beings. (Observe that Kant does not use "humanity" here as he does elsewhere to refer to the powers of moral personality as animated in us [Kant III:§4]). This predisposition falls under the general heading of self-love, which is physical but which at the same time compares and judges our own happiness in relation to the happiness of others.

From this self-love comes our desire to be held of value *(Wert)* in the opinion of others, and from this in turn comes the desire for equality, which expresses itself in our wanting no one to establish superiority over us and in our anxiety that they may do so. This process works itself out so that eventually it gives rise to competition for status and position, to hypocrisy and rivalry, and to the other vices of culture, such as jealousy and envy, ingratitude and spitefulness. These vices Kant views as grafted onto this predisposition to good by the historical development of culture. By this I think he means that, given the social milieu brought about by the self-love that compares and judges, those vices are the inevitable outcome. Here we see the influence of Rousseau's *Second Discourse* and *Émile*.

(c) The predisposition to personality in us, when we are seen not only as rational beings but also as accountable, or responsible, beings. This predisposition we can think of as having two aspects.

First, there is the capacity to understand and intelligently to apply the moral law (via the CI-procedure) as an idea of pure practical reason.

Second, there is the capacity to respect this law as in itself a sufficient motive for our free power of choice.

This second aspect Kant here calls "moral feeling," and he is careful to stress that moral feeling (sensibility) is essential. (On this question, see also the *Metaphysics of Morals*, the Introduction, §§XII–XVI [*MdS* 6:398–411]). This capacity for moral feeling does not by itself determine our power of choice; rather, without it there is no possibility of this power's ranking the moral law as supremely regulative and in itself a sufficient motive. In its absence, the moral law would be for us just an intellectual object, like a mathematical equation, which could interest us only by way of the two other predispositions. Of moral feeling Kant says that it is absolutely impossible to graft anything evil upon it, by which I take him to mean that the vices arise from distortions of the other predispositions, and that moral feeling itself is incorruptible and present in everyone so long as humanity (in Kant's usual sense) is not dead in us (*MdS* 6:400).

3. I have used "rational" rather than "reasonable" to translate *vernünftig* in Kant's description of the second predisposition, and this is supported by the important footnote to *Religion* I 6:26 (21).[2] It says that the predisposition to humanity, as Kant uses the term here, includes only the rational and not the reasonable. The incentives that fall under it originate in the objects of desire and exclude moral feeling. He means, I think, that the idea of the moral law would not occur to such individuals; if it were presented to them, they would regard it with indifference or as a curiosity. There is no logical route, as we saw in discussing the fact of reason, from the rational to the reasonable. We have a susceptibility to be moved by pure practical reason, and this susceptibility is moral feeling, but as such it is sui generis.

This reading is supported by Kant's saying of these predispositions that "the first requires no reason, the second is based on practical reason, but a reason thereby subservient to the other incentives, while the third alone is rooted in reason which is practical of itself" (*Rel* I 6:28 [23]). He goes on to

2. The footnote is as follows: "We cannot regard this [predisposition] as included in the concept of the preceding [predisposition], but must necessarily treat it as a special predisposition. For from the fact that a being has reason it by no means follows that this reason, by the mere representing of the fitness of its maxims to be . . . universal laws, is thereby capable of determining the power of choice unconditionally, so as to be 'practical' of itself. . . . The most rational mortal being in the world might still stand in need of certain incentives, originating in the objects of desire, to determine his choice. He might indeed bestow the most rational reflection on all that concerns not only the greatest sum of these incentives [originating in the objects of desire] in him but also the means of attaining the end thereby determined, without ever suspecting the possibility of such a thing as the absolutely imperative moral law which proclaims that it is itself an incentive and, indeed, the highest. Were it not given us from within, we should never by any ratiocination subtilize it into existence or win over our will to it. Yet this law is the only law which informs us of the independence of our power of choice from determination by all other incentives (of our freedom) and at the same time of the accountability of all our actions."

emphasize, in a clear statement of the Augustinian moral psychology, that not only are all these dispositions good in the sense of not contradicting the moral law, but also they are predispositions toward good. Moreover, they are original, as they involve the possibility of human nature, and we cannot rid ourselves of them, nor can we exist as human beings without them.

§2. The Free Power of Choice

1. Next let's turn to the free power of choice *(freie Willkür)* and its relation to the three predispositions. Kant introduces this as the power to act from the moral law; it can exist even when we fail to exercise it. Negative freedom is our will's not being necessitated to act by any sensuous determining ground *(MdS* 6:226), which implies (as we already know) that we may elect a determining ground to act from without being necessitated. Freedom in the positive sense, Kant says, is "the power [*Vermögen*] of pure reason to be of itself practical" *(MdS* 6:213f.). Thus we are practically free and are properly held morally responsible for our actions whenever we have the power to follow the moral law, whether we do so or not. His view is that except in early childhood, or when insane, or in great sadness (itself a species of insanity), we always possess the power of autonomous action.[3]

Now, an essential feature of the Augustinian moral psychology of the *Religion* is that moral failures of all kinds, from the lesser ones of fragility and impurity to the worst extremes of wickedness and perversity of which we are capable, must all arise, not from the desires of our physical and social nature, but solely from our exercise of our free power of choice *(Rel* I 6:29–32 [23–27]). And for this exercise we are held fully accountable. He holds the view of the origin of moral evil given by Saint Augustine in the *Civitate Dei* (Bk. XIV, Chs. 3, 11–14). He says *(Rel* I 6:23f. [19f.]): "Freedom of the will is of a wholly unique nature in that an incentive can determine the will to an action *only so far as the individual has incorporated it into his maxim* (has made it the general rule in accordance with which he will conduct himself); only thus can an incentive, whatever it may be, co-exist with the absolute sponta-

3. *Lectures on Metaphysics* XXVIII:182. Cited by Allen Wood in "Kant's Compatibilism," in *Self and Nature in Kant's Philosophy* (Ithaca, N.Y.: Cornell University Press, 1984), p. 79.

neity of the will (i.e., freedom). But the moral law, in the judgment of reason, is itself an incentive, and whoever makes it his maxim is morally good."

The three predispositions, however they may affect us, cannot determine our will unless they are incorporated into our maxims by our free
power of choice. This is Kant's principle of elective will,[4] a basic principle
of his moral psychology. It means that while we must take each of the
three predispositions as given (we cannot alter or eradicate them), we can
and must order them: that is, we must decide through our power of choice
the priority and weight these predispositions are to have in our supremely
regulative principles as shown in our deliberations and conduct. Whether
we have a morally good or bad will depends on that ordering.

2. Now, our free power of choice has but certain alternatives available
to it. The number of predispositions, and the ways in which they can be
ordered, limit the scope of our free power of choice in adopting a fundamental character. If our human nature had but one predisposition, there would
be no choice at all; and in the absence of all predispositions, our nature
would be empty and the power of choice would have nothing on which
to operate (*Rel* I 6:35 [30]).[5] There is, however, a special limit on our power
of choice, namely, that we cannot repudiate the predisposition to personality. This has the consequence that we cannot exempt ourselves from the
moral law, as Satan is said to have done (*Rel* I 6:36 [31]). Kant says: "The
[Moral] Law . . . forces itself upon [us] irresistibly in virtue of [our] moral
predisposition; and were no other incentive working in opposition, [we]
would adopt the law into [our] supreme maxim as the sufficient determining ground of [our] will [free power of choice]." This is an important remark. Kant is saying that if all the predispositions were to line up on the
same side, then the predisposition to personality would always be adopted
by us as supreme and as having unconditional priority. This outcome is
determined by our nature as persons.

One might think that since we know that the predispositions conflict,
this feature of our nature is not significant. It brings out, however, the
uniqueness of the predisposition to personality, namely, that it is the *only*

---

4. The idea of elective will we noted earlier in connection with Kant's idea of a pure will in
Kant I:§3 and II:§3–4.

5. This is how I understand Kant's saying that in the absence of all incentives the power of
choice (*Willkür*) cannot be determined.

predisposition fit to serve in a supremely regulative role. Moreover, since we cannot repudiate the moral law, we cannot choose to be devils and to act against that law for its own sake (*Rel* I 6:35 [30]). We cannot reverse, so to speak, the predisposition to personality by adopting evil as our good. The limit of human perversity lies in changing the moral order among the predispositions; when we do this, we give inappropriate weight in our deliberations to reasons grounded on the predispositions of humanity and animality. We neglect the moral law and ignore the voice of conscience. But conscience can never be silenced so long as the powers of moral personality are alive in us. They are a fixed basis in our persons for a principle of identification: we cannot help but identify with the predisposition to personality and its moral law.

3. We have still to consider an essential feature of the moral psychology of the *Religion*. I refer to Kant's view that the basic features of the original predispositions establish a moral order of priority *(sittliche Ordnung)*. This order ranks the predisposition to personality as unconditionally prior and the others as unconditionally subordinate. As we saw above, our free power of choice may not follow that moral order, but its freedom, as Kant defines it, consists in its power to do so.

Let's review the features of the predispositions that Kant seems to think specify the appropriate ordering for persons with the power of free choice. Two features we have already noted.

The first is that the predisposition to personality is unconditionally good and incorruptible, by which I take Kant to mean that no vices can be grafted onto it (as can be done with the predispositions to animality and humanity) and our free power of choice cannot reverse it.

The second is that by including the moral law as an aspect, the predisposition to personality is the only one suited to be ranked as unconditionally prior. It contains the only practical principle that can be supremely regulative.

Note that in each case the comparison is between the predisposition to personality and the other two predispositions. Kant is not saying, for example, that only the moral law, and not some other moral principle—for example, a principle of perfection—is suited to be supremely regulative. To say this would go against what we said earlier (in Kant VII:§5.3), that it is a mistake to hold that only the moral law can specify a unified and shared public order.

4. There is a third important feature of the predisposition to personality. It is mentioned when Kant excludes certain explanations of human wickedness and perversity. He says (*Rel* I 6:35 [30]):

> Neither can the ground of this evil . . . be placed in a *corruption* of the morally legislative reason [the predisposition to personality]—as if reason could destroy the authority of the very law which is its own or deny the obligation arising therefrom; this is absolutely impossible. To conceive of oneself as a freely acting being and yet as exempt from the law which is appropriate to such a being (the moral law) would be tantamount to conceiving a cause operating without any laws whatsoever. . . . [T]his is a self-contradiction.

The first sentence of this passage connects with the two features noted above. To understand the second sentence, recall that Kant thinks:

(a) That when we engage in, and act from, pure practical reasoning, we must always act under the idea of freedom and think of ourselves as free, although, of course, only from a practical point of view (*Gr* III:4 [447–448]; *KP* 5:47). In so doing, we do not think of ourselves as exempt from the principles of reason appropriate to us as free.

(b) That the moral law is the only law that discloses to us not only our independence of the natural order but also of a prior and given order of values.

In virtue of our capacity to incorporate it into our maxims and to act from it, the moral law is, therefore, the only principle that fully discloses to us our freedom and autonomy. We may take Kant to say that the ordering of our predispositions ranking the predisposition to personality unconditionally prior is the only ranking that is appropriate to us as persons with a free power of choice. It is the principle that fully expresses our nature as autonomous.

5. The fourth, and last, feature of our moral psychology relevant to the ordering of predispositions is that this psychology provides a permanent basis of identification with the ideal conception of the person founded on that ordering. This psychology Kant regards as belonging to us as reasonable and rational; it characterizes our nature and we cannot change it. We can never altogether repress the pure practical interest we take in being the

kind of person who lives up to the conception of our person expressed by the appropriate ordering of predispositions.

Our identification with that ideal is disclosed in our moral feelings when we are at fault; these are described by Kant not primarily as feelings of obligation and guilt but as feelings of (moral) shame and self-reproach. His doctrine is not one of a legitimate authority that enacts principles for us to obey, but one of mutuality and self-respect in a moral community of equal persons ordered by public principles of practical reason.

Finally, the moral order of our predispositions does not reflect an antecedent order of values known to us by rational intuition, an order given apart from our conception of ourselves as persons endowed with the powers of pure practical reason, moral feeling, and the power of free choice. Rather, this moral order is rooted in the predispositions of our persons and their characteristic features and the possibilities of their combination into an appropriate ranking. Kant's moral psychology in Book I of the *Religion* goes with his constructivist moral conception and answers to its essential requirements.

§3. The Rational Representation of the Origin of Evil

1. We have seen that the ordering of predispositions we adopt is, in effect, the adoption of a moral character. But we must be careful how this is to be understood. Kant sometimes views this adoption as how we must represent to ourselves the way our character has arisen: we are to see it as something we have made and within our free power of choice (*Rel* I 6:39–44 [34–38]). This means that we are not to regard our fundamental character as determined in time: that is, we are not to regard it as a social artifact, or as determined by psychological laws, or as the product of happenstance, and the like. As reasonable and rational, we are to view our character, the ordering of our predispositions, as a matter up to us, given our free power of choice and the absolute spontaneity of reason.

How can we understand the thought that we are not to view our character as determined by causal conditions in the course of time? I suggest that it is simply a part of the beliefs and attitudes toward ourselves as we act under the idea of freedom. For in our deliberating under the idea of freedom, the order of our predispositions is shown in what we count as reasons, in the weight we give them. Our fundamental character (what Kant calls our intelligible character) is mirrored in our moral thought. Now, as we have seen, in acting under the idea of freedom, we must regard our reason as free and guided by its own principles. The same must hold for what we count as reasons and their relative weight.

Kant's thought is that if we regard our fundamental character as a social artifact, or as the result of psychological laws and accidental contingencies, we would also not regard our reason as free; and this we cannot do. Two people who so regarded themselves and whose systems of reasons were at odds could only observe to one another: "Subjected as we were to different circumstances, our fundamental characters were formed in different ways. There's nothing more to say." It is this thought that Kant rejects. Our scheme of reasons may be different from others', but we must regard ourselves, not forces for which we are not accountable, as having made them so. It is an evasion of our responsibility to say that we are constituted this way or that by nature or society or by anything external to our reason and will.[6] He says (*Rel* I 6:41 [36]):

> In the search for the rational origin of evil actions, every such action must be regarded as though the individual had fallen into it directly from a state of innocence. . . . He should have refrained from that action whatever the temporal circumstances and entanglements; for through no cause in the world can he cease to be a freely acting being. . . . But this merely amounts to saying that man need not involve himself in the evasion of seeking to establish whether or not the consequences [of his free actions] are free, since there exists in the free . . . action, which was their cause, sufficient ground for holding him accountable.

2. Kant distinguishes between our intelligible (fundamental) character and our empirical character. The latter he thinks of as manifesting in experience the causality of reason, so that our choice of an intelligible character

---

6. See also what Kant says against a preformation system of pure reason in the first *Critique* (*KR* B167f.).

is disclosed *in part*[7] in the weight we give to different kinds of reasons and in what we do. That our choice of a fundamental character should thus manifest itself follows from practical freedom (*KR* B829–831): namely, that the free decisions of our practical reason are operative causes in nature.

Now, from the point of view of practical reason, there is no physical explanation of our intelligible character (*KP* 5:99); that this is so follows from our belief in transcendental freedom. Moreover, we know about our intelligible character only by way of our actual moral thought and conduct (*KR* B578f.). From this we can discern, in rough outline anyway, the empirical character of ourselves and others. Armed with this knowledge, we can in general foresee, or estimate, what others will do in particular circumstances. (Kant says that could we know that character perfectly, which we cannot, we could accurately predict our actions in any given conditions.) As thus foreseen, Kant speaks of our conduct not as free but as necessary and subject to the laws of nature.

But all this means is that, given the knowledge of people's beliefs, interests, and circumstances, together with the knowledge of the weight they give to different kinds of reasons (their empirical character), we can tell what they will decide and do. But from a practical point of view, when we are making mutual decisions or asking others for advice, we regard those empirical characters as expressing the outcome of the deliberations of pure reason. These deliberations are the upshot of the absolute spontaneity of reason; expressing our intelligible character, they are taken as not having a physical or other explanation.

3. When in *Religion* I 6:39f. (43f.) Kant speaks of seeking the origin of evil not in time but merely in rational representation, I think he means roughly the following. Insofar as our fundamental (intelligible) character arises from our power of free choice, we are to regard it as our responsibility alone. Doing this is part of our view of ourselves in acting under the idea of freedom when complemented, as it should be, by the belief in transcen-

---

7. I say in part because our empirical characters are not the work of practical reason alone. Kant says: "The real morality of actions, their merit or guilt, even that of our own conduct, thus remains entirely hidden from us. Our imputations can only refer to the empirical character. How much of this character is ascribable to the pure effect of freedom, how much to mere nature, that is, to faults of temperament for which there is no responsibility, or to its happy constitution . . . , can never be determined; and upon it therefore no perfectly just judgments can be passed" (*KR* B58on.).

dental freedom. How our character can be evil—violate the moral order of the predispositions—is indeed inscrutable (*Rel* I 6:43f. [38f.]): since our nature is good, not evil but good should have arisen from it, yet long historical experience convinces us to the contrary. But that the choice of that character has no physical or other causal explanation we must believe from a practical point of view so as to affirm the absolute spontaneity of our reason. So to look for such an explanation, when that point of view is appropriate, contradicts, indeed is an invitation to evade, regarding ourselves as free and responsible.

As far as possible, then, I want to understand Kant's speaking of reason as not subject to the form of time (*KR* B579f.), or not subject to the conditions of time (*KP* 5:97–100), and of not looking for a first origin of character in time (*Rel* I 6:43f. [39f.]), and similarly, as describing how we are to view ourselves when we act under the idea of freedom, all the while affirming our transcendental freedom. I believe that he is describing beliefs and attitudes that we are to adopt and cultivate so as to act from the practical point of view. Alternatively, he is characterizing the form of our self-consciousness as possessing pure practical reason.

Yet I should say that this interpretation is not generally accepted: the idea of the intelligible character as permanent and timeless is more often given a metaphysical interpretation. I believe that doing this is not required by the text and goes against the conclusions of the Dialectic of the first *Critique,* as well as Kant's constantly repeating that what he says about freedom is to be understood from a practical point of view. (On this see the important Sections VII–VIII of the Dialectic of the second *Critique.*) Thus, to interpret as a metaphysical doctrine Kant's speaking of reason as not subject to the form of time, yet affecting the course of events in the world, is not allowed by his text. Or so I think. It also leads to hopeless difficulties for Kant's view.[8]

8. For metaphysical interpretations, see Norman Kemp Smith, *A Commentary to Kant's Critique of Pure Reason* (London: Macmillan, 1930), pp. 514–518, and Wood, "Kant's Compatibilism," pp. 89–101. To illustrate more fully: suppose one were to try to reconcile transcendental freedom with strict causal (physical) determinism from the first state of the world in the following way. Imagine that there are *n* noumenal selves, where *n* is the number of persons who exist at any time in the order of nature (past, present, and future). Imagine these *n* selves to make *n* transcendentally free choices of an intelligible character. The choice is alleged to be atemporal once and for all, and orders the three predispositions as the highest principles from which we act. Suppose these *n* choices

4. To continue: in a (largely) realized realm of ends, all persons view themselves and others as free, that is, as acting under the idea of freedom. They also suppose that their own and others' empirical characters as shown in their public thought and conduct reflect, more or less, their intelligible character for which each accepts responsibility. If we suppose further that the members of such a realm of ends are lucid before themselves and speak truthfully, so that they know the reasons from which they act and inform one another of them as appropriate, then from within the practical point of view they have no grounds for going behind the reasons they state to one another when acting under the idea of freedom: those reasons everyone accepts as the real reasons why they do what they do. Those reasons are not, for example, viewed as simply rationalizations. There is cause for doing that only when there is a failure of lucidity or of truthfulness, or another such failure to act under the idea of freedom (excluded by hypothesis). In a (largely) realized realm of ends, free public reasons—the reasons people freely present in good faith to one another—are viewed as real reasons and are accepted as such.

---

having been thus made, the divine intelligence then computes the size of the initial mass of the universe, its shape and the distribution of particles within it, and the appropriate first principles of physics and chemistry, and whatnot, so that beginning with the first state of the world, natural events unfold in accordance with causal laws in such a way that the n intelligible characters (which were freely selected) are reflected in n corresponding empirical characters of persons in various societies in history.

Now, this fantasy might appear to reconcile transcendental freedom and causal determinism. It allows us to say that all persons have an equal freedom to determine their intelligible character and thus to determine their course of life in the world. Moreover, we are set above the order of nature, and we have a hand in making the whole course of history, since our choice of an intelligible character imposes a further constraint on the possibilities open to the divine intelligence in creating the world.

One might think this fantasy has a certain usefulness, say in contrasting Kant's view with Leibniz's. For in Leibniz's conception, all the complete individual concepts lie from eternity in the divine reason; Judas' life as a possible is present and known to God in every detail before Judas was created as part of the best of all possible worlds. Judas never makes a choice of his intelligible character and the laws that determine his development as a spiritual substance over time—laws that, while individually distinctive and not reducible to natural laws of science, are laws all the same. Further, Judas doesn't know what his own law is, as it must cohere so as to yield preestablished harmony and the mutual reflections of all substances in the most perfect universe, each from its own point of view.

Whatever illumination we imagine we gain from this comparison, Kant would regard it as intellectually frivolous. In affirming the convictions of reasonable faith we are not to apply them theoretically in this way.

This conception of a realm of ends in which everyone is publicly recognized as acting under the idea of freedom is part of the conception of the person that specifies the conception-dependent desires in Kant's doctrine. I come back to this in §5.

§4. The Manichean Moral Psychology

1. In discussing what I shall call the Manichean moral psychology,[9] I do not suppose that Kant ever held such a view or ever clearly formulated it for himself. I think of it as his tendency to say certain things and to express them in a manner and tone that, once we fix on them, suggest a certain moral psychology. The reason for discussing it is that it brings out a development of Kant's thought in the *Religion*, or at least a sharper articulation of his view, once he undertook to consider religion at some length. Once he did this, then, with his Pietist background, his moral psychology had to be Augustinian and not Manichean. The manner and tone of the Manichean tendency are often present, but the explicit doctrine is Augustinian.

The basic idea of the Manichean moral psychology is that we have two selves: one is the good self we have as intelligences belonging to the intelligible world; and the other is the bad self we have as natural beings belonging to the sensible world. In speaking of the hardened criminal, Kant says (*Gr* III:19 [454–455]):

> This better person he believes himself to be when he transfers himself
> to the standpoint of the intelligible world. He is involuntarily con-
> strained to do so by the idea of freedom—that is, of not being depen-
> dent on determination by causes in the sensible world; and from this
> standpoint he is conscious of possessing a good will which, by his own
> admission, constitutes the law for the bad will belonging to him as a
> member of the sensible world—a law of whose authority he is aware
> even in transgressing it. The moral "I ought" is thus an "I will" for
> man as a member of the intelligible world.

9. I take the names of the two psychologies from Saint Augustine's *Confessions*. For a time before his conversion to Christianity he was a Manichee, and his many writings include an account of the sect's tenets. His own view is representative of Christian orthodoxy; Kant's Augustinian moral psychology is his more orthodox doctrine. I don't say Kant's view is orthodox.

The good self has just one predisposition, to use the language of the *Religion*, namely, the predisposition to act from the moral law. That is why for the good self the "I ought" is an "I will." The only reason we fail to act from that law as the principle of autonomy is that we are burdened with natural desires and inclinations, and hence, as Kant says, it must be the wish of every reasonable person to be wholly free from them (*Gr* II: 48 [428]). They are despised by our reason, which, in the consciousness of its own dignity, is able to achieve mastery over them (*Gr* II:9 [410– 411]). Indeed, as members of the intelligible world, we do not impute our natural desires to our proper self at all, since they are, as it were, mere incitements and solicitations aroused in us by our needs as finite beings situated in the order of nature (*Gr* III:26 [457–458]).

The bad or natural self likewise has just one predisposition, at least insofar as it is fully rational: the predisposition to happiness, or rational self-love. This predisposition in some ways parallels the two predispositions to animality and to humanity of the *Religion*, though the account of these predispositions is not the same. As moved by our natural desires and the principle of happiness, we must always experience injunctions of the moral law as a frustration, as a foreign element that blocks the way to what we want. Hence the bad or natural self lacks moral feeling; what might be mistaken for such is simply fear and hostility, or suppressed rage aimed at the self for safety's sake (*KP* 5:72–76). Finally, the bad self is also a driven self, since the satisfactions of natural desires are transitory and leave behind them a greater void than before: the inclinations, even when they are good-natured like sympathy, are blind and slavish (*KP* 5:117f.).

2. The Manichean moral psychology presents grave difficulties for Kant's moral doctrine: not only does it commit him to a serious heretical doctrine at odds with the tenor of his religious thought, but also it would seem to defeat any satisfactory account of responsibility that is acceptable to us when we act under the idea of freedom as we assume the practical point of view. Lacking the idea of the free power of choice, the Manichean psychology cannot provide such an account. For as members of the intelligible world, we are to see ourselves as all equally having no choice but to act from the moral law (we have no other predisposition), while as members of the natural world, we are to see ourselves as all equally having no choice but to pursue our own happiness. If we viewed ourselves that way from

the practical point of view, it would seem to be impossible to think of ourselves as all equally responsible while some behave far better than others. We would lack suitable reasons for holding responsible those who failed.

Of course, we could say that while our predisposition to act from the moral law as members of the intelligible world is constant and pure, our natural desires and inclinations can be of many different strengths and directions in view of our situation in the natural world. Our actual conduct, we might say, is settled by the balance of forces generated by those desires, the strength and direction of which depend on circumstances. People who do what is right are people whose predisposition to act from the moral law is not overridden by the direction and force of their natural desires; people who act badly suffer the opposite fate. We get the familiar moral fatalism of the Manichean view, which surely Kant must avoid.

3. The Augustinian moral psychology overcomes these defects by attributing to the self a free power of choice and enough complexity for a satisfactory account of responsibility. There is no longer a dualism between a good self and a bad self—two selves each with only a single predisposition, with the predisposition of one being liable to clash with that of the other—but one self with three predispositions, all of which are dispositions to good. Moreover, these predispositions have an appropriate moral order suitable for free persons capable of acting from pure practical reason. The origin of moral evil, then, lies not in a bad self with its natural desires but solely in the free power of choice, which may change the moral order of the dispositions and determine what we count as appropriate reasons in deciding what to do.

As for how to understand these moral psychologies, I believe that we should see them as ways of conceiving of our moral nature from the practical point of view, and so how to think of ourselves when we are acting under the idea of freedom. They are not, as such, empirical accounts of human psychology, nor subject to the usual criteria of empirical truth. Rather, they belong to different ways of characterizing the reflective self-consciousness of pure practical reason; as such they embody different ideal conceptions of the person.

Thus, as we have said, when acting under the idea of freedom on the Augustinian view, we cannot regard our fundamental character (the ordering that determines the weight of reasons) as a social artifact or as the upshot of merely psychological laws and happenstance. Our scheme of reasons may be different from others', but we are to regard ourselves, not forces for which we are not accountable, as having made them so. Otherwise we would abandon free reason. Here clearly a certain ideal of the person is involved, not a psychological theory.

This doesn't mean that the reasonableness of this ideal is not subject to criteria and cannot be checked. For it may be incompatible with our considered judgments on due reflection and therefore rejected. It may prove foolish and hopelessly impracticable, given the way we really are. However, this is to be decided not by prior argument, but by whether we can actually accept the ideal of the person on due consideration and whether we can affirm living in accordance with it. Kant thinks that we can, since for him the ideal of pure reason can show itself in deed.

§5. The Roots of Moral Motivation in Our Person

1. Now we can consider the fourth condition of there being pure practical reason. So, at last, we are almost home. I believe that Kant's idea is the following: it is only if we arrange our predispositions according to the moral order that we act from the sole principle appropriate for us in view of our special status in the world. Kant's basic moral conception is that of an aristocracy including each as a free and equal person. It is not an aristocracy of nature or of social class, or an aristocracy of intellect or beauty or of unusual achievement. Nor is it, as one might carelessly think, an aristocracy of moral character and moral worth.

Rather, it is an aristocracy of all. It comprises all reasonable and rational persons, whose powers of reason define our standing and are counted as belonging to persons in all walks of life, the privileges of none. Indeed, these powers characterize us as a natural kind—that of humanity—as intelligences with moral sensibility animating human bodies belonging to the natural order, but who are not merely of it.

At the end of the *Canon* (*KR* B879), Kant replies to the objection that the two articles of practical faith (the belief in God and immortality) are not much to establish after the great labor of giving a critique of reason.

Surely the common understanding could have achieved this much without help from philosophy! In reply, he says:

> Do you really require that a mode of knowledge which concerns all men should transcend the common understanding, and should only be revealed to you by philosophers? Precisely what you find fault with is the best confirmation of the correctness of [what I have said]. For we have thereby revealed to us, what could not at the start have been foreseen, namely, that in matters that concern all men without distinction nature is not guilty of any partial distribution of her gifts, and that in regard to the essential ends of human nature the highest philosophy cannot advance further than is possible under the guidance which nature has bestowed even upon the most ordinary understanding.

2. Now, our special status in the world does not mean that we also inhabit a different realm, conceived as ontologically separate from the order of nature. It means rather that we are capable of thought, feeling, and conduct grounded in and governed by the powers of theoretical and practical reason. It also means that we can live in a moral world, and to do so, we need only live by the principles of pure practical reason and thus in accordance with the moral order rooted in our predispositions and appropriate to our nature. Persons in a realm of ends display before themselves and one another their glorious status as free persons situated, as it were, above the order of nature, in the sense that they can act independently of that order in the pursuit of personal and social ideals as authorized and required by the moral law of their reason.

On the other hand, the law from which we act does not imply the rejection of the natural world. To the contrary, it is a law that, when acted upon by everyone, gives to the world of nature the form of an intelligible world (*KP* 5:43f.), a world that allows ample scope for our natural desires and affections (permissible ends), so that a realized realm of ends is not only a moral world but also, under reasonably favorable conditions, a happy world (*KR* B373).

Kant's underlying conviction is that once we fully understand this moral conception and dwell upon it in our thought, once we fully understand ourselves as members of a possible realm of ends and have this conception of ourselves, we cannot help but be deeply moved to identify with that ideal and to act in accordance with that conception. This is a fact about us rooted in our nature as depicted in the *Religion,* a fact which philosophy enables us to understand. Kant's most lyrical and elevated passages are those in which he describes the profound effects on us of a clear grasp of the moral law and how it shows our independence of nature.

Once philosophy shows that understanding the moral ideal leads to identifying with it and acting according to it, we see that the last condition (d) for the existence of pure practical reason is met: the moral law can be a sufficient motive for us, whatever our natural desires. This is the point of the two examples Kant describes in the second *Critique* (*KP* 5:30): the first brings out that natural desires cannot override the love of life, the second that the conception-dependent desire to act from the moral law can do so. Kant believes that he has shown that all four conditions are satisfied, and so there is indeed pure practical reason. The view of the second *Critique* is strengthened once he works out in the *Religion* a more adequate moral psychology. Thus our account of the doctrine of the fact of reason is now complete.

KANT X

The Unity of Reason

§1. The Practical Point of View

1. In this final lecture on Kant, I consider the unity of reason and the idea of reasonable faith in two forms (to be explained in a moment) and their relation to the idea of philosophy as defense. I note first that there are three unities of reason: the first, in the theoretical sphere, is the greatest possible systematic unity of knowledge of objects needed for a sufficient criterion of empirical truth (*KR* B679); the second, in the practical sphere, is the greatest possible systematic unity of ends in a realm of ends (*Gr* II:62ff. [433ff.]). The third is that of both theoretical and practical reason in one unified constitution of reason in which practical reason has primacy, as every interest of reason is ultimately practical (*KP* 5:119ff.).

One way to approach the unity of reason is to examine Kant's idea of reasonable faith and the postulates (as he calls them) that express it. What Kant says about these postulates raises some of the hardest questions about the unity of reason: first, how exactly is practical reason (and the practical point of view) related to theoretical reason (and the theoretical point of view) in the constitution of reason; and second, in what way in that constitution does practical reason have primacy? These are dark subjects, and I can only indicate the outlines of a possible approach.

2. Before proceeding, I stress a point mentioned last time. Recall that Kant often says that our knowledge is extended by the postulates of reasonable faith (freedom, God, and immortality), but, he always adds, it is ex-

tended only from a practical point of view. The following at *KP* 5:133f. is an example:

> Is our knowledge . . . actually extended . . . and is that *immanent* in practical reason which for speculative reason was only *transcendent?* Certainly, but *only from a practical point of view.* For we do not thereby know the nature of our souls, nor of the intelligible world, nor of the Supreme Being with respect to what they are in themselves. We have merely combined the conceptions of them in the *practical* concept of the *highest good* as the object of our will and only by means of the moral law. . . . But how freedom is possible and how we are to conceive of this kind of causality theoretically and positively is not thereby discovered. All that is comprehended is that such a causality is postulated by way of the moral law and for its own sake. . . . It is the same with the other ideas.

He means that when, say, we believe in our transcendental freedom (that our reason is absolutely spontaneous and free decisions begin a new series of events), and when we believe in God and immortality, we are not to take these convictions as expressing knowledge. They are not to be regarded by us as in the least extending our theoretical understanding of the world, as it is studied in science (*KP* 5:133; 134ff.; 137). So, for example, the reasonable belief in God has no role in physics, and the God of physics, the God of the physico-teleological proof (*KP* 5:138–141; *KU:*§85), has no role in practical faith. Yet no arguments can take from us the conviction that the ideas of freedom, God, and immortality are true concepts *(wahre Begriffe).*

What is required for this extension of our knowledge from a practical point of view is an a priori purpose, that is, an object given by moral law as its a priori object (*KP* 5:134). I shall distinguish two such objects: one is the realm of ends, as found in the *Groundwork* and the political essays; the other is the highest good, as found in the three *Critiques.* I believe that the nature and the plausibility of Kant's view in these two cases are quite different, and I shall give them different names: reasonable faith for the beliefs supporting our working for a realm of ends and *Vernunftglaube* for the beliefs supporting our striving for the highest good. I begin with the first.

§2. The Realm of Ends as Object of the Moral Law

1. In Kant V, I said that the idea of the realm of ends (as found in the *Groundwork*) and the idea of the highest good (as found in the second *Critique*) are distinct conceptions with different implications for Kant's view. At that time I didn't consider how they are distinct, but to discuss the practical point of view and the postulates of reasonable faith we must now do so.

In our account of Kant's moral constructivism, the ideal of a possible realm of ends is presented as the a priori constructed object of the moral law. An essential feature of this ideal is that it is reasonable to try to realize such a realm in the natural world, at least under reasonably favorable conditions. In so acting, we are not being deluded visionaries unmindful of what is actually possible. In that sense, a realm of ends is a natural good, one that is possible (though never fully achievable) in the order of nature.

2. The following passages support this interpretation. First, from the first *Critique* (*KR* B836): "I entitle the world a *moral world,* insofar as it may be in accordance with all moral laws . . . leaving out of account . . . the special difficulties to which morality is exposed (weakness or depravity of human nature), this world is so far thought of as an intelligible world only. To this extent . . . it is a mere idea, though at the same time a practical idea, which really can have, as it ought to have, an influence upon the sensible world, to bring that world, so far as it may be possible, in conformity with that idea."

And again (*KR* B837f.): "In an intelligible world, that is, a moral world, in the concept of which we leave out of account all the hindrances to morality (the desires), such a system . . . would itself be the cause of general happiness, since rational beings under the guidance of such principles [moral laws] would themselves be the authors both of their own enduring well-being and that of others. But such a system of self-rewarding morality is only an idea, the carrying out of which rests on the condition that everyone does what he ought."

In *Groundwork* II:78 (438–439): "A world of rational beings *(mundus intelligibilis)* is a possible realm of ends—possible, that is, through the making of their own laws by all persons as its members. . . . [A] realm of ends would actually come into existence through maxims which the categorical imperative prescribes as a rule for all rational beings, if these maxims were universally followed."

Note that a moral world is one realizable (in good part) in the natural social world, in this world. It is a society in which people attain their own mutual happiness by acting from their duties of justice and of virtue. Such is the upshot of firm adherence by all to the moral law under reasonably favorable conditions in our world. This is the idea of a self-rewarding morality.

3. Finally, recall the two passages from the second *Critique* cited at the end of Kant IV and VI. At *KP* 5:43, Kant says that the moral law gives to the order of nature (the sensible world) the form of an intelligible world without interference with the mechanism of nature. The sensuous nature of rational beings is their existence under natural laws; the supersensuous nature of the same persons is their existence under moral laws that are independent of nature and belong to the autonomy of pure reason. And at *KP* 5:44, Kant distinguishes between the laws of a system of nature to which a will is subject and a system of nature subject to a will. The latter is a system of nature in which persons have in good part realized a realm of ends: in such a realm, the objects of nature are not the cause of the moral law in the light of which persons construct the ideal of a realm of ends as the common and first object of their public will. Their actions are free as directed by reason, and they give to nature the form of an intelligible world.

I review these passages in order to support the interpretation of the ideal of a realm of ends as the constructed object of the moral law. The main point is that a realm of ends can be in good part realized in the order of nature when all act, as they can and ought to act, from the totality of precepts that meet the conditions of the CI-procedure. A moral world, an intelligible world, a *mundus intelligibilis,* is a world that consists of reasonable and rational persons acting as they ought under the idea of freedom within the world as we know it. What makes an intelligible world is not our being in another world ontologically distinct from this world, one not in space and time, but all of us, here and now, acting from the moral law under the idea of freedom. The realm of ends is a secular ideal.

In the political essays, Kant's idea of a realm of ends gains more specific content. At least it does so if we can assume, as I shall, that his hope for

a world of constitutional and representative democratic states bound together in a confederation of peoples to maintain permanent peace among
themselves can be taken as an account of the larger institutional structure
of such a realm. I come back to this below, but before I do that, let's consider the other a priori object, the highest good.

§3. The Highest Good as Object of the Moral Law

1. Now, whether in a realm of ends moral worth and happiness would be
in some manner connected depends on what the moral law enjoins. A realm
of ends would be a happy world, as social worlds go; as Kant says, it is a
world of self-rewarding morality. This follows since our duties can be arranged under two headings: first, the duty to strengthen our moral character
and to develop and make good use of our natural gifts (duties of moral
and natural perfection); and second, the duty to promote the happiness of
others.

I do not believe, however, that the content of the moral law (as specified
by the CI-procedure) enjoins that in a realm of ends people are to act so
as to make happiness strictly proportional to virtue. It is striking that Kant
never tries to show this; in the Dialectic of the second *Critique*, he simply
takes it for granted. Why he does this and apparently abandons what I have
called his moral constructivism I put aside for a moment. We should look
first at Kant's idea of the highest good in the Dialectic.

2. This idea seems to be arrived at by our focusing first on the two
basic values in Kant's doctrine: a completely good will and happiness as
the fulfillment of permissible desires organized into a rational system. The
highest good is, then, that world in which each person both has a completely good will and is fully happy. Each possesses the two basic values
to the fullest extent possible. The proportionality between moral worth and
happiness is an immediate consequence, since it follows once each person's
capacity for the two basic values is specified. Now, Kant surely thought the
capacity for moral worth to be equal. This equality is a central theme of
his moral view, and it must be an element of the highest good, whatever
holds of the capacity for happiness. Let's refer to this conception of the
highest good as the full highest good. The need for this designation is that

Kant also uses a variant of this conception of the highest good, and the two are distinct.

This variation may be seen as the highest good of a particular social world. Consider in sequence the members of a social world and assign to each an appropriate measure of achieved moral worth. Then the highest good for this particular world is given by a sequence of degrees of happiness, each degree of which is paired with the assigned measure of moral worth of the corresponding member. In this conception, the principle of proportionality is still not specified, for we haven't yet said how the measure of happiness is determined. In addition, any such principle must be justified within Kant's framework.

Leaving aside how this can be done, we see that with this variation there are as many different highest goods as there are possible sequences of degrees of moral worth in particular social worlds. Since as reasonable persons we have the power of free choice, the particular highest good of our world is still to be determined, unless we believe with Origen that God will somehow, in ways unknown to us but compatible with our freedom, see to it that in due time everyone achieves a completely good will. Otherwise, the highest good of a world depends on what free persons actually do and on the degree of moral worth they actually achieve.

3. The relevance of these remarks is that both conceptions of the highest good just noted—the full highest good and the highest good of a particular social world—are, I think, inconsistent with Kant's account of the moral law. Kant doesn't even try to show how these conceptions of the highest good result from the moral law, and thus how either can be the a priori object of a pure will. This omission is particularly noticeable in the case of the highest good of a particular world, for here the principle of proportionality seems analogous to the idea of divine rewards and punishments, bringing us into the realm of his Pietist theology.

This suggests that Kant has in mind an altogether different conception of the basis of the highest good. I believe that section V of the *Dialectic* tells us what it is, for it is here that he explains the grounds of the proportionality between virtue and happiness. Kant says (*KP* 5:130f.):

If we inquire into *God's final end* in creating the world, we must not name the *happiness* of rational beings in the world but *the highest good,* which adds a further condition to the wish of rational beings to be happy, that is, the condition of being worthy of happiness, that is, the *morality* of these beings; for this alone contains the standard by which they can hope to participate in happiness at the hand of a *wise* creator. For since *wisdom . . .* means the *knowledge of the highest good,* and practically, *the suitability of the will to the highest good,* one cannot ascribe to a supreme independent wisdom an end based merely on *benevolence.* For we cannot conceive the action of this [supreme] benevolence (with respect to the happiness of rational beings) except as conformable to the restrictive conditions of harmony with the *holiness* of His will as the highest original good.

This passage tells us two things: first, that the highest good is God's final purpose in creating the world; and second, that the requirement that happiness be proportional to virtue is necessary to make that highest good fully harmonious with the holiness of God's will as the highest source of good.

4. Earlier in this section, Kant says the following (*KP* 5:128): "The worth of character completely in accordance with the moral law is infinite, because all possible happiness in the judgment of a wise and omnipotent dispenser [*Austeiler*] of happiness has no other limit than the lack of fitness of rational beings to their duty." This passage introduces a third idea: that God dispenses the greatest happiness to creatures as limited only by their virtue. And this idea connects with a fourth idea met with before: namely, that an impartial reason recommends that virtue be accompanied by happiness. He says (*KP* 5:110) that for the highest good "happiness is also required, and indeed not merely in the partial eyes of a person who makes himself his end but even in the judgment of an impartial reason, which impartially regards persons in the world as ends in themselves. For to be in need of happiness and also worthy of it and yet not to partake of it could not be in accordance with the complete volition of an omnipotent being."

Now we understand why happiness is to be proportioned to virtue in the highest good. Since this good is the final end of God in creating the world, it must contain as much happiness as the virtue of persons permits, since God is good; yet it must not contain more, since God is holy and any greater happiness would not be in harmony with the holiness of God's will. We could say that, subject to virtue as a constraint, God as dispenser maximizes happiness.[1] So understood, the highest good is to the greatest glory of God, for (KP 5:131) "nothing glorifies God more than . . . the most estimable thing in the world, namely, respect for His command, the observance of sacred duty which His law imposes on us, when there is added to that [respect and observance] His glorious plan of crowning such an excellent order with corresponding happiness."

5. The problem with this idea of the highest good is that the idea of impartial reason is foreign to Kant's constructivism. Further, the highest good is incompatible with the idea of the realm of ends as the constructed object of the moral law: it cannot be that constructed object, for there is nothing in the CI-procedure that can generate precepts requiring us to proportion happiness to virtue. Here I simply state this without argument. Certainly that procedure, if at all adequate, will authorize penalties and punishments of various kinds, as these are necessary, let's assume, for a stable social world. But it is another matter entirely for us to try to dispense happiness in proportion to virtue.

For one thing, as Kant recognizes, it is simply not our business to judge the overall moral character of others or to try to estimate their worthiness. Moreover, given the great obscurity of our motives, which he also recognizes (Gr II:1–3 [406–408]), a maxim at step (1) that presupposed such knowledge, and led to the generalized precept to match happiness with virtue, would not be rational (and so could not even start through the CI-procedure, much less be accepted): its rationality requires more knowledge than we could ever expect to have. Only God can know these things, as Kant implies in his argument for God's existence as a necessary condition of the possibility of the highest good (KP 5:124f.). Recall also his saying there that we cannot make perfectly just judgments of merit or guilt, since we cannot know how much of a person's empirical character is the effect of freedom (KR B579n.). Matching happiness with virtue cannot, then, be part

1. I do not say that Kant consciously derived the idea of the highest good in this way, even though it seems explicit in the cited passages. Had he done so, he would have seen that it is incompatible with the fact that the moral law is given first and the postulate of God is needed rather to guarantee the possibility of its a priori object, which is already given prior to and independent of the idea of God and cannot be derived from this idea.

of the moral law as it applies to us by way of the categorical imperative and the CI-procedure that interprets it for us.

It is for these reasons that, in my presentation of Kant's doctrine, I use the secular ideal of a possible realm of ends that can be (in good part) realized in the natural world. I view the idea of the highest good as a Leibnizian element in Kant's philosophical theology (as he recognizes [KR B840]) which he never reworked so as to make it consistent with his moral philosophy. I call it Leibnizian since it rests on the idea that God would be acting imperfectly if God's object in creating the world was not the most perfect, or the highest good as Kant defines it. Any other object would be incompatible with God's goodness or with God's holiness. The highest good is the perfect maximum object identified by those two moral perfections.

§4. The Postulates of *Vernunftglaube*

1. I have reviewed the two conceptions of the a priori object of the moral law since Kant does not expressly comment on the difference between them. But which conception we use is of first importance because the postulates (the content) of *Vernunftglaube* depend on what that object is.[2] In the Dialectic, there are three such postulates: the beliefs in freedom, in God, and in immortality. Kant thinks of them as theoretical positions inseparably connected with the principles of pure practical reason (*KP* 5:120). The inseparable connection arises because the postulates simply assert that the object of the moral law is possible in the world. These beliefs we must affirm when we act from the practical point of view; for unless we do, Kant thinks, we cannot sensibly engage in practical reasoning or sustain over the course of a complete life our devotion to the moral law. The reason is that doing so presupposes that we believe that its a priori object can be realized, that the conditions of its possibility actually obtain in the world. In his lectures on religion, Kant says (*Gesammelte Schriften* 28:1072), "Without God I must be either a scoundrel or a visionary." What he means is that unless I believe

---

2. The main discussions of practical faith are these: first *Critique*, the Canon of Pure Reason, B824–856; second *Critique*, the Dialectic, §§3–9; third *Critique*, §§75–78, 84–91; "Was Heisst: Sich im Denken Orientieren?" (1786); *The Conflict of the Faculties* (1798), Part I and the Appendix. See also two letters to Lavater of April 1775, in Zweig, *Philosophical Correspondence*, pp. 79–83.

in God (whose existence is a necessary condition of the highest good), either I must abandon the moral law as hopelessly impracticable, in which case I am a scoundrel, or else I persist in following the law anyway, in which case I am a utopian visionary. Since reason excludes *both,* I must believe in God. We affirm the beliefs necessary to hold law's object before *us* as a possible object of our devoted endeavor. Thus *KR* B856: "Since the moral precept is . . . my maxim (reason prescribing that it should be so), I inevitably believe in the existence of God and in a future life, and I am certain that nothing can shake this belief, since my moral principles would thereby be themselves overthrown, and I cannot disclaim them without becoming abhorrent in my own eyes."

2. Now, if the object of the moral law is indeed the highest good, then the postulate of God's existence has a certain plausibility, whatever other difficulties it may raise. (The postulate of immortality is more problematic and I leave it aside here.) Kant's view is that our human reason can conceive of no other way by which the proportionality between virtue and happiness can come about except as the work of an omniscient and omnipotent, and morally perfect, author of the world. For it is God alone who can fully discern our hearts and minds to the bottom and who can adjust our happiness accordingly.

Kant doesn't claim that there is no other way in which this proportionality is possible; there well may be. But to sustain our devotion to the moral law, we need to form a conception that we can understand of how the highest good is possible. At this point, the need of our human reason can decide the case, provided, as always, that theoretical reason has nothing to say against it (*KP* 5:125f., 144f.).

When the object of the moral law is the secular ideal of a possible realm of ends, the basis for the postulates of God and immortality is far weaker. However, the grounds for the postulate of transcendental freedom are the same as before. We saw earlier (in Kant VIII §6.4) that this postulate has a special place. For it is different from the beliefs in God and immortality, as these beliefs guarantee the possibility of the object of the moral law when that object is the highest good and ensure that we can fulfill that law's requirements.

But the belief in freedom is more fundamental: it is a belief in the freedom, in the absolute spontaneity, of reason itself. It is the belief that reason proceeds in accordance with its own principles that only it can identify and validate, and that reason does this independently of all psychological laws such as Hume's laws of association, and indeed of external natural causes of all kinds. It is the belief in reason's absolute spontaneity, in its right and power to give a critique itself, and to specify its own constitution, as testified to in the three *Critiques*.

§5. The Content of Reasonable Faith

1. Despite the difficulties with Kant's postulates of *Vernunftglaube*, I think that the significance of the idea of reasonable faith itself remains. We have seen that he believes that we cannot sustain our devotion to the moral law, or commit ourselves to the advancement of its a priori object, the realm of ends or the highest good, as the case may be, unless we firmly believe that its object is in fact possible. What Kant says regarding the postulate of immortality holds generally (*KP* 5:122f.): "In default of it, either the moral law is quite degraded from its holiness, being made out to be indulgent . . . or men strain their notions of their vocation and their expectation to an unattainable goal, hoping to acquire complete holiness of will, and so they lose themselves in theosophic dreams. . . . In both cases the unceasing effort to obey punctually . . . a strict and inflexible command of reason, which is not ideal but real, is only hindered."

But what is the content of practical faith once we take a realm of ends as the object of the moral law? Certainly it includes the belief in our transcendental freedom, but what does it require beyond this?

2. I suggest that while it does not require the postulates of God and immortality, it does require certain beliefs about our nature and the social world. It is not enough to affirm our freedom and to recognize the freedom of all persons in virtue of their powers of reason. For we can believe that a realm of ends is possible in the world only if the order of nature and social necessities are not unfriendly to that ideal. For this to be so, it must contain forces and tendencies that in the longer run tend to bring out, or at least to support, such a realm and to educate mankind so as to further this end.

We must believe, for example, that the course of human history is progressively improving, and not becoming steadily worse, or that it does not fluctuate in perpetuity from bad to good and from good to bad. For in this case we will view the spectacle of human history as a farce that arouses loathing of our species.[3] In our social unsociability that drives us to competition and rivalry, and even to seemingly endless wars and conquests, we may not unreasonably hope to discern a plan of nature to force mankind, if it is to save itself from such destruction, to form a confederation of constitutional democratic states, which will then ensure perpetual peace and encourage the free development of culture and the arts. By this long path we may reasonably believe a realm of ends will come about in the world. Indeed, this faith itself may further this happy end.[4] Or as Kant says in his reply to Mendelssohn in "Theory and Practice" (Reiss 88f.):

> I may thus be permitted to assume that, since the human race is constantly progressing in cultural matters (in keeping with its natural purpose), it is also engaged in progressive improvement in relation to the moral end of its existence. This progress may at times be *interrupted* but it is never *broken off.* I do not need to prove this assumption; it is up to the adversary to make his case. . . . I base my argument upon my inborn duty of influencing posterity in such a way that it will make constant progress (I must thus assume that progress is possible). . . . History may well give rise to endless doubts about my hopes, and if these doubts could be proved, they might persuade me to desist from an apparently futile task. But so long as they do not have the force of certainty, I cannot exchange my duty . . . for a rule of expediency which says I ought not to attempt the impracticable. . . . [T]his uncertainty cannot detract from the maxim I have adopted, or from the necessity of assuming for practical purposes that human progress is possible.

3. "Theory and Practice," in *Kant's Political Writings*, ed. Hans Reiss, trans. H. B. Nisbet, 2nd ed. (Cambridge: Cambridge University Press, 1990), p. 88.

4. In this paragraph, I describe in the briefest fashion the idea of reasonable faith as it occurs in Kant's political essays: "The Idea of a Universal History" (1784), "Theory and Practice" (1793), and "Perpetual Peace" (1795). See Reiss, *Kant's Political Writings*.

3. The content of practical faith has now greatly changed. It fixes on nature's being (as we reasonably believe) not unfriendly to a realm of ends but instead conducive to it. Yet the idea of reasonable faith, and its connection with philosophy as defense, is still preserved. We can now say, as Kant did, that the political organization of a realm of ends will be a peaceful international society (or confederation) of peoples, each people organized as a state with some kind of a constitutional representative regime. We assume these regimes to be either liberal constitutional states or social democracies; for our purposes it does not matter which.⁵ So when the realm of ends is the object of the moral law, reasonable political faith, let's say, is the faith that such a peaceful international society of peoples is possible and favored by forces in nature. To abandon this faith is to give up on peace and democracy, and that we can never do as long as we affirm both the moral law and human freedom. Kant says (*KR* B373f.):

> This perfect state may never come into being; none the less this does not affect the rightfulness of the idea,⁶ which, in order to bring the legal organization of mankind ever nearer to its greatest possible perfection, advances this maximum as an archetype. For what the highest degree may be at which mankind may have come to a stand, and how great a gulf may still have to be left between the idea and its realization, are questions which no one can, or ought to, answer. For the issue depends on freedom; and it is in the power of freedom to pass beyond any and every specified limit.

Now, Kant emphasizes that the postulates of reasonable faith are affirmed for the sake of the moral law, that is, to sustain and to render secure and enduring our capacity to act from that law (*KP* 5:133, 137, 138). But suppose it is said that when the realm of ends is the a priori object, we may

---

5. Kant rejected the idea of a unified world state, thinking it would lead either to global tyranny or else to civil war as parts of the world with distinct cultures struggled to gain political autonomy. See Reiss, *Kant's Political Writings*, pp. 90, 113, 170.

6. This idea is that of a constitution allowing the greatest possible human freedom in accordance with laws by which the freedom of each is made to be consistent with that of all the others. Kant adds here that he does not speak of the greatest happiness "for this will follow of itself" (*KR* B373).

still need to believe in God and immortality to sustain our devotion to the moral law. Without those religious beliefs, we might lose all hope that those who are just and good won't be pushed to the wall and come to think that the wicked and evil will dominate the world in the end. We lapse into cynicism and despair, and abandon the values of peace and democracy, since it is a need of reason, it might be said, to believe that there will be a certain matching, if not exact proportionality, between moral worth and happiness.

Indeed, some may think this, and let's suppose that it is often true. And let's grant that it would be better to maintain our religious faith, for then we could preserve our allegiance to justice and virtue. But in this case, our religious beliefs would not be postulates in Kant's sense, since for him, postulates specify conditions necessary for us to conceive how the a priori object of the moral law is possible; religious beliefs are not needed for this when that object is the realm of ends. Kant's reasonable faith is more than simply belief necessary for us to uphold our moral integrity.

§6. The Unity of Reason

1. Finally, let's turn to the unity of reason. Here the main question is: What is the relation between the theoretical and the practical points of view, and how are the claims of theoretical and practical reason adjudicated within the constitution of reason? Several brief comments.

First, as noted earlier, the distinction between the phenomenal and the intelligible worlds is not an ontological distinction between worlds and different kinds of things belonging to those worlds. It is rather a distinction between points of view, their different form and structure, and how their common elements (for example, the concepts of object and representation) are related, as well as the particular interests of reason that are expressed in and specify the aims of these points of view. Epistemological and ontological distinctions are explained by reference to the elements of these points of view and the role they assume therein.

2. A further observation is that, while Kant says that the two points of view are of one and the same world, we have to be careful about what this means. For here a point of view is not a perspective. It is not, as it

were, a view of an object from a position in its surrounding space, taking into account the laws of perspective for that space, and such that the information contained in different perspectives from different positions in the same space can be pieced together to work out the properties of the object.

But precisely what we cannot do is to piece together the two points of view into one unified theoretical account of the world. At this point, Kant breaks with the long tradition of Western metaphysics and theology. When Kant says that the postulate of freedom, say, is affirmed from the practical point of view, he means that it has no role in the unifying theories of high science. None of the postulates extends in the least our theoretical understanding (*KP* 5:133, 134ff., 137). The reasonable belief in God has no role in physics, and the God of physics, the God of the physico-teleological proof (*KP* 5:138–141; *KU* §85), has no role in practical faith.

3. But if the two points of view are not related as perspectives of one and the same world, how are they related? The answer, I think, lies in how Kant understands the unity of reason: he holds that the points of view of both forms of reason articulate the point of view of an interest of pure reason, and that the unity of reason is established by a constitution that in effect orders these interests and secures for each all of its legitimate claims. The key idea is that no legitimate interest of one form of reason is sacrificed to an interest of the other; all the interests of reason, properly identified, can be and are fully guaranteed. He writes (*KP* 5:119f.): "To every power of mind an interest can be ascribed, that is, a principle that contains the conditions under which alone its exercise is advanced. Reason, as the faculty of principles, determines the interest of all the powers of mind including its own. The interest of its speculative use consists in the knowledge of objects up to the highest a priori principles; that of its practical use lies in the determination of the will with respect to the final and perfect end."

Thus, while theoretical and practical reason have different interests, the unity of reason fully validates their proper claims so that they are met without balancing or compromise or loss within the one constitution of reason. The space, as it were, that practical reason occupies by the postulates, theoretical reason denies to itself once the antinomies are revealed.

4. To illustrate: it is illegitimate, on Kant's view, for theoretical reason to claim the right to reject all beliefs that cannot be established by manifest examples in experience, even though they should be necessary for the integ-

rity of the practical use of reason and not in the least contradictory to the interests of theoretical reason (*KP* 5:A120f.). Theoretical reason has two legitimate interests: one is the positive interest in regulating the understanding and unifying into the highest possible systematic unity the low-level empirical knowledge it provides; the other is the negative interest in restricting speculative folly. So long as the postulates of practical faith do not trespass on these interests, theoretical reason has no grounds to object.

On the other hand, it is also illegitimate for empirical practical reason, which merely serves the inclinations, to be the basis of postulates. For in that case Mohammed's paradise and the fantasies of theosophists would press their monstrosities on reason to reason's destruction (*KP* 5:120f.). But the postulates of pure practical reason depend on the a priori object constructed by pure reason itself, and against these postulates theoretical reason has nothing to say, as they occupy a space it abdicates.

Thus the unity of reason is established not by the points of view of the two forms of reason being ordered by their perspectival relations to the (one) world, but by the harmony and full satisfaction of the legitimate claims of theoretical and practical reason as articulated in the form and structure of the two points of view. Reason supplies its own unity through a critique of itself: the aim of critique is precisely to establish this unity.

5. Many will find this view unsatisfactory. It may appear to give a merely pragmatic order of adjustment, almost a judicial settlement, as if the unity of reason is established by the court of reason—the supreme court of critique—arranging a peace between the disputing interests of reason itself. To say this would be a mistake, for there is no balancing of conflicting interests, and all of the legitimate claims of reason are fully met. Of course, many will have hoped for a unity modeled on the structure of the world itself, a unity already given for reason to discover. That is not the kind of unity Kant provides. As I have said, it is at this point that he breaks with the tradition of philosophy and theology up to his day.

Kant views philosophy as defense, not as apology in the traditional sense of Leibniz, but as the defense of our faith in reason and of the reasonable faith that sustains it. While we cannot give a theoretical proof of the possibility of freedom, it suffices to assure ourselves that there is no such proof of its impossibility; and the fact of reason then allows us to assume it (*KP* 5:94). If the legitimate claims of theoretical and practical reason are both reconciled in one constitution of reason, and if that constitution allows due place for mathematics and science, for morality and practical faith, and for our other fundamental interests as reasonable and rational persons, then, for Kant, the aims of the critique of reason are achieved.

It is essential to see that Kant is not presenting an argument that the beliefs of reasonable faith (in either form) are true by the criteria of empirical and scientific truth; it is not his intention to lay out evidence aimed at making a convincing theoretical case. He presents instead considerations showing why we are entitled to affirm those beliefs and why our doing so does not infringe the legitimate claims of theoretical reason, although, to be sure, the pretensions of the dogmatisms of empiricism and of pure reason are humbled, and both must give way to the intellectual virtues of modesty and tolerance.[7] Our affirming these beliefs springs from our moral sensibility, our devotion to the moral law, and answers to the needs of our practical reason. Kant's doctrine is a defense of reasonable faith, and, more generally, of what he sees as the fundamental interests of humanity.

7. See, for example, section 3 of Chapter 2 of Book 2 of the *Dialectic* (*KR* B490–504).

Hegel

HEGEL I

His *Rechtsphilosophie*

§1. Introduction

1. I begin by recalling how we have proceeded. With each writer—Hume, Leibniz, and Kant—I have tried to bring out what is distinctive in their approach to moral philosophy, why they were moved to write the texts we read, and what they hoped to accomplish. These texts have much to teach us, and knowing these works puts before us possibilities of thought vastly different from those we would normally be aware of. We don't study them in the hope of finding some philosophical argument, some analytic idea that will be directly useful for our present-day philosophical questions in the way they arise for us. No, we study Hume, Leibniz, and Kant because they express deep and distinctive philosophical doctrines.

2. In discussing Hegel (1770–1831), I have much the same aim.[1] I focus

---

1. Of Hegel's works, some of the main ones are *Hegel's Logic*, trans. William Wallace (Oxford: Oxford University Press, 1975), a translation of Part I of the *Encyclopedia* of 1817, revised 1827 and 1830; *Hegel's Philosophy of Mind*, trans. William Wallace and A. V. Miller (Oxford: Oxford University Press, 1971), a translation of Part III of the *Encyclopedia; Lectures on the Philosophy of World History*, Introduction, trans. H. B. Nisbet (Cambridge: Cambridge University Press, 1975); *The Phenomenology of Spirit (Geist)* (1807), trans. A. V. Miller (Oxford: Oxford University Press, 1977); *The Philosophy of Right* (1821), trans. H. B. Nisbet, ed. Allen Wood (Cambridge: Cambridge University Press, 1991); *Science of Logic* (1812–1816), trans. A. V. Miller (London: Unwin, 1969); *Hegel's Political Writings*, trans. T. M. Knox, with an introductory essay by Z. A. Pelczynski (Oxford: Oxford University Press, 1964). The following secondary texts are valuable among others: Michael Inwood, *A Hegel Dictionary* (Oxford: Blackwell, 1992); Frederick Beiser, ed., *The Cambridge Companion to Hegel* (Cambridge: Cambridge University Press, 1993); Allen Wood, *Hegel's Ethical Thought* (Cambridge: Cambridge University Press, 1990); Michael Hardimon, *Hegel's Social Philosophy* (Cambridge: Cambridge University Press, 1994); Shlomo Avineri, *Hegel's Theory of the Modern State* (Cambridge: Cambridge University Press, 1972).

on what Hegel added and on what is special about his contribution. With this in mind, I look, all too briefly, at his *Philosophy of Right* (1821) (hereafter *PR*). This work contains his moral philosophy and his distinctively institutional idea of ethical life *(Sittlichkeit)*, and explains how it connects with his view of persons as rooted in and fashioned by the system of political and social institutions under which they live. These are among Hegel's important contributions to moral philosophy. Regrettably, I say almost nothing about his metaphysics. I believe that most of his moral and political philosophy can stand on its own. Undeniably much is lost; at places in *PR*, and in the *Lectures on the Philosophy of World History*, the metaphysics comes to the fore. Hegel's ultimate explanation of the course of the world, and of the historical transitions from one epoch to another, is found in what he calls Spirit or Mind *(Geist)*. A true metaphysician, he believes that *reality is fully intelligible*—which is the thesis of absolute idealism—and so it *must* answer to the ideas and concepts of a reasonable and coherent categorial system. This system is laid out step by step in the *Science of Logic* (1812–1816). These fundamental matters I leave aside.

I interpret Hegel as a moderately progressive reform-minded liberal,[2] and I see his liberalism as an important exemplar in the history of moral and political philosophy of the *liberalism of freedom*.[3] Other such exemplars are Kant and, less obviously, J. S. Mill. (*A Theory of Justice* is also a liberalism of freedom and learns much from them.) I shall look at how Hegel thought the concept of freedom was actually realized *in* the social world through political and social institutions at a particular historical moment. In this, Hegel rejects Kant's account of transcendental freedom, and with it Kant's understanding of both ethics and the role of moral philosophy. As we will see, many of the traditional ambitions of moral philosophy are to be brought within those of political philosophy, as Hegel understands it.

Today I am particularly concerned to explain what Hegel means in saying that "[t]he free will is the will that wills itself as the free will." This combines *PR* §§10 and 27, but I hope does not distort the sense. And what

2. Although not a radical, Hegel always regarded the French Revolution as a colossal and progressive historical event. A student reported in 1826 that a year never went by that he didn't drink a toast celebrating the anniversary of Bastille Day. See Wood, in his note to the translation by Nisbet, p. 397.

3. By this I mean that its *first* principles are principles of political and civic freedoms, and these principles have a priority over other principles that may also be invoked.

does Hegel mean by saying that this free will is incorporated and made manifest in the political and social institutions of the modern state? Without knowing exactly how and why, we can already see that this account of free will is going to be very different from Kant's, which we have just considered. Hegel's views on this matter constitute one of his most important contributions to moral and political philosophy.

§2. Philosophy as Reconciliation

1. I begin by noting Hegel's view of philosophy as reconciliation.[4] To see what that might mean, consider the fifth paragraph of the Preface (fifth counting Nisbet paragraphs in Allen Wood's edition): "The *truth* about *right, ethics, and the state* is as old as its public exposition and promulgation in *public laws,* and *in public morality and religion.* What more does this truth require inasmuch as thinking is not content to possess it in this proximate manner? What it needs is to be comprehended so that the content which is already rational in itself may also gain a rational form and thereby appear justified to free thinking. For such thinking does not stop at what is given . . . but starts out from itself and thereby demands to know itself as united in its innermost being with the truth."

The term "reconciliation"—the German *Versöhnung*—fits here because Hegel thinks that the most appropriate scheme of institutions for the expression of freedom already exists. It stands before our eyes. The task of philosophy, especially *political* philosophy, is to comprehend this scheme in thought. And once we do this, Hegel thinks, we will become reconciled to our social world. Now, to become reconciled to our social world does not mean to become resigned to it. *Versöhnung* and not *Entsagung*—resignation. It is not as if the existing social world is the best among a number of unhappy alternatives. Rather, reconciliation means that we have come to see our social world as a form of life in political and social institutions that realizes our essence—that is, the basis of our dignity as persons who are free. It will "thereby appear justified to free thinking."

2. So the role of political philosophy, as Hegel sees it, is to grasp the social world in thought and to express it in a form in which it can be seen by us to

4. Michael Hardimon, *Hegel's Social Philosophy: The Project of Reconciliation* (Cambridge: Cambridge University Press, 1994), p. 95. I have learned much from this book and draw from it here.

be *rational*. The word Hegel uses for "rational" here is *vernünftig*. As I have said in discussing Kant, this is an important term in German philosophy. It must not be mistaken for instrumental, or means-ends, or economic rationality. Often the English word "reasonable" is better. When in our reflections we understand our social world as expressing our freedom and enabling us to achieve it as we lead our daily life, we become reconciled to it. Philosophy in this role is not merely an academic exercise. It tells us something about ourselves; it shows us our freedom of will—that we have it through institutions, not in other ways. This understanding in turn makes a form of life real. The explanation is that a form of life is not fully made real or actual *(wirklich)* until it is made self-conscious. *Geist* only fully realizes itself in human thought and self-consciousness. So the form of the modern state, which in its political and social institutions expresses the freedom of persons, is not fully actual until its citizens understand how and why they are free in it. The work of political philosophy is to help them to understand that. It looks not to a world that ought to be that lies beyond the world (as Hegel thought Kant's philosophy did), but to a world before their eyes that actualizes their freedom.

Here Hegel is attacking Kant's idea of freedom at the deepest level. He takes Kant to think that our freedom raises us above all the contingencies of our human nature (our inclinations and needs), and above all the contingencies of our society and its history, and therefore that it is *possible* for us always to act from the moral law and to achieve a good will, albeit gradually, once we fully resolve to do so. This alleged transcendental freedom implies that all persons have an equal chance to attain the ideal of a person of good moral character (a good will), whatever their more particular fortunes in the world. We might say that Kant thinks God has arranged things so that we all equally have the power (or capacity) to work for our salvation. Hegel will deny that human freedom can be fully actualized apart from the appropriate social framework. It is only within a rational (reasonable) social world, one that by the structure of its institutions guarantees our freedom, that we can lead lives that are fully rational and good. And although no social world can guarantee our happiness, it is only within such a world that full happiness can be attained. Thus Hegel endorses the Pythagorean's advice: "When a father asked him for advice about the best way of educating his son in ethical matters, a Pythagorean replied, 'Make him the *citizen of a state with good laws*'" (PR §153).

3. This brings us to another level of Hegel's criticism of Kant. Hegel wants to avoid the ethics of *Sollen* and thereby to change the point of ethics—what it should try to do. The basic shift is found in the idea of *Sittlichkeit*. It is the location of the ethical, the whole ensemble of rational *(vernünftig)* political and social institutions that make freedom possible: the family, civil society, and the state.

Hegel regards Kant's ethics as trying to provide specific guidance for people in their particular situations in everyday life. This guidance is given in the form of testing their (sincere and rational)[5] maxims by the categorical imperative (CI) procedure. Using the CI-procedure provides the individual with detailed and clear answers. By contrast, Hegel wants us to find our moral compass in the institutions and customs of our social world itself, as these institutions and customs have been made part of us as we grow up into them and develop habits of thought and action accordingly. Kant would reject this view as incompatible with his ideal of autonomy. As Hegel sees the matter, Kant doesn't provide *real* autonomy. For this, we must belong to a *rational* (reasonable) social world that individuals on reflection can accept and be reconciled to as meeting their fundamental needs. Hegel wants to show that people can and do act freely when conducting themselves on the basis of habit and custom (assuming them to be reasonable on reflection). This condition is met in the modern world (in contrast to the ancient or the medieval world), in which social institutions must promote subjectivity, individuality, and particularity, or what Hegel refers to as substantiality (which covers all three).

Hegel's view of freedom is that only a substance can be fully free, and that a rational social world is a substance. Moreover, individuals can attain the fullest freedom available to them, as opposed to the misguided autonomy of Kant's ethics, only by becoming self-reflecting and endorsing accidents (as Hegel says) of a rational social world. The term "accidents" brings out that for Hegel, individuals cannot by themselves be substances, cannot be free on their own. Rather, they are accidents, as it were, of a substance—of a rational social world—and it is through *that* substance that they achieve their real freedom. Do not be antagonized by Hegel's use of the substance-accident terminology, although it is not entirely without fault and may

5. Here we must, of course, understand rational in Kant's sense as given by the hypothetical imperative, and not in Hegel's sense.

encourage misinterpretation. It is crucial to stress that it is only through the self-reflection of individuals, and only in their being reconciled to their (rational) social world and in their correctly seeing it as rational and living their lives accordingly, that the social world itself is brought to its full substantiality. So while rational social institutions are the necessary background for freedom and for individuals' real autonomy, the reflection, judgment, and rational (reasonable) conduct of individuals are necessary to bring about the substantiality and freedom of their social world.

Thus for Hegel, in contrast to Kant, the aim of the account of ethics as *Sittlichkeit* is not to tell us what we *ought* to do—we know that—but to *reconcile* us to our *real* social world and to convince us not to fix our thinking and reflection on an ideal social world. For when we contemplate an ideal social world, we are likely to dwell on our real social world's shortcomings and then to criticize and condemn it. Whereas what we need to do is to become reconciled to the real social world by gaining insight into its true nature as *rational;* to gain this insight, we need a philosophical account of that world, and eventually a philosophical conception of the world as a whole, including a philosophy of history.

4. Hegel's criticisms of Kant are of several kinds, some more fundamental than others. Having looked at two of the deeper criticisms, we should also note some that are less fundamental but more familiar. Having the deeper criticisms in mind, we can better understand the others. The most familiar is Hegel's claim that Kant's formal conception of morality is in some ways empty (PR §135).

Hegel does not hold that there is no content at all to Kant's moral doctrine. Certainly the CI-procedure rules out some things; Hegel doesn't contest this. Rather, he holds that the procedure doesn't provide us with all the content Kant claims it does. Moreover, what it does give us are not moral conclusions that we can properly be said to know: we do not attain moral knowledge through the CI-procedure. We attain moral knowledge only in what Hegel calls *Sittlichkeit.*

Further, the conclusions derived from the CI-procedure are not fixed and valid for *all* circumstances, as Kant seems to think. The reason is that in order to arrive at those conclusions in the first place, we have to assume certain contingent circumstances, take certain background conditions as given. Thus, in general, which maxims are accepted and which are rejected will depend on such factors. The specific duties that Kant claims to derive from the moral law—as stated in the general way in which Kant renders them—are more or less acceptable to Hegel. That is, he doesn't in general dispute the scheme of duties Kant professes to derive from the moral law. But Hegel thinks that Kant arrives at this content only because he presupposes in the background a rational social world; by assuming that background, Kant simply avoids the main questions. For Hegel, those questions are precisely questions about how to give a philosophical characterization of a rational social world.

At a second level, Hegel's criticism is that the kind of guidance Kant aims to give us is not adequate. The reason is that it does not meet our fundamental ethical needs, which are connected with how we stand toward our social world. Hegel thinks that what we need to know is when its institutions are rational and what is their point.

5. Hegel views Kant as moved by a desire for radical purity, by a desire to act from the moral law itself and by nothing else. It is this, he thinks, that lies behind Kant's distinction between prudence and morality and his account of the supremacy of the good will. Hegel thinks that the way we are supposed to view ourselves as moral agents in Kant's doctrine is both narrow and alienating.

(a) It is *narrow* because, first, it doesn't take account of the features of ourselves that we assume as members of our social world or of our particular community. And it is narrow because, second, on the level of motivation, it restricts far too much the kind of motives consistent with good moral character.

(b) It is *alienating* because the form of moral life that Kant's doctrine requires excludes so many of the desires and aspirations of everyday life and so greatly distances us from them that it alienates us from ordinary affairs. One might say that Hegel rejects Kant's distinction between prudence and morality: rather, he wants to allow that the aims of everyday life—those of love and friendship, family and association, and the rest, all pursued in their own terms from normal motives—are fully consistent with ethical life, with what he calls *Sittlichkeit*.

6. An essential aspect of Hegel's view is that a rational social world is not by any means a *perfect* world. Indeed, a rational social world has serious social problems that cause great human unhappiness and pain. He discusses

the problems of divorce, poverty, and war, among others. Thus Hegel writes (Preface, paragraph 14): "To recognize reason as the rose in the cross of the present and thereby to delight in the present—this rational insight is the *reconciliation* with actuality which philosophy grants to those who have received the inner call to *comprehend*."

Thus to be reconciled to our social world is not to think everything is just fine and everyone is happy. A reasonable social world is not a utopia. That is naive and foolish: there is no such world and there cannot be. Contingency and accident, misfortune, and bad luck are necessary elements of the world, and social institutions, no matter how rationally designed, cannot correct for them. However, a rational social order can provide for freedom and makes it possible for citizens to realize their freedoms. Their freedom *can* be guaranteed, and for Hegel freedom is the greatest good. Happiness cannot be guaranteed, though freedom furthers it by enabling us to achieve it, provided that we are fortunate and lead our lives wisely.

A difference between Hegel and Marx in this respect is that Hegel thinks that the citizens of a modern state are objectively free now, and their freedom is guaranteed by its political and social institutions. However, they are subjectively alienated. They tend not to understand that the social world before their eyes *is* a home. They do not grasp it as such, nor do they feel at home *(bei sich)* in it, nor do they accept and affirm it. By contrast, Marx thinks that they are both objectively and subjectively alienated. For him, overcoming alienation, both subjective and objective, awaits the communist society of the future after the revolution.

§3. The Free Will

1. Recall that we want to understand what Hegel means in saying, "The free will is the will that wills itself as the free will." Here we are concerned with §§5–30 in the Introduction. This part is very difficult, but it is where Hegel begins and what he takes as his starting point. But that is not our only reason for taking this up. Understanding what Hegel means here is necessary if we are to understand the importance of *Sittlichkeit* in general, and the role of civil society and right in the project of reconciliation.

Consider the concept of willing as the concept of being able to act for the sake of some end, an end that we identify with, or accept, as our own.

What elements, or moments as Hegel sometimes says, would we expect this concept to have? I take §§5–7 as a unit.

(a) Hegel starts in §5 with the element of pure indeterminacy. This is what we are left with by taking away every limit and every content that is present to our consciousness at any moment of time. Suppose these limits and contents are presented to you by nature or by your desires and impulses. Now, imagine that you do not have any of those desires and impulses. Hegel says in the lectures of 1824–25: "The human being can abstract from every content, make himself free of it, whatever is in my representation I can let it go, I can make myself entirely empty. . . . [H]e [the human being] can let go all bonds of friendship, love, whatever they may be" (see Wood, p. 398nn.). This is the will's pure thought of itself: "Das reine Denken seiner selbst." In the remark to §5, Hegel stresses, as Kant does, that thinking and willing are not two separate things but two aspects of one thing.

(b) In §6, Hegel indicates that, in willing, the self is in transition from this pure indeterminacy to the positing of determinacy: it gives itself content and an object. By this positing of something determinate, the self steps in principle into determinate existence. It has resolved its indeterminacy and has become something particular in seeking its content and obtaining its object.

(c) In §7, the concept of the will is said to be the unity of both the preceding elements. The will's content and object are reflected back into itself, and in this way brought to universality. It is, as Hegel says, individuality.

Taken together, §§5–7 characterize the will's capacity to determine itself from its pure indeterminacy and then to make those ends and aims its own, or, let's say, to identify itself with the ends it has adopted. In doing this, the will (or the self, if you like) knows—recall that it is thinking and willing together (§5)—that it could have adopted other ends and aims, that it must adopt some ends, and that it must identify with the ends it has adopted. It could have adopted other ends since it starts from pure indeterminacy; it must adopt some ends, else it remains empty and never steps into existence and realizes itself; and if it is truly to act, it must identify with, or adopt as its own, the ends it adopts.

2. At this point, we must discuss what content is appropriate for the concept of the free will. The concept of the free will is not simply that of a will that wills whatever it wants. Nor is a free will a will that simply adopts whatever desires and impulses it happens to have. Hegel follows

Kant in this respect. It comes as no surprise, then, that the concept of a free will is that of a will willing what is proper to a free will. So as a free will, the will must be self-determined and not determined by what is external to it. This leads Hegel to say in §10, as we noted before, "It is not until it has itself as its object that the will is for itself what it is in itself." And later he says, in §27: "The absolute determination . . . of the free spirit [see §21] is to make its freedom into its object—to make it objective both in the sense that it becomes the rational system of spirit itself and in the sense that this system becomes immediately actual [§26]. This enables the spirit to be for itself, as Idea, what the will is in itself. The abstract concept of the Idea of the will is in general *the free will which wills the free will* [*der freie Wille, der den freien Willen will*]." And then earlier in §23: "Only in freedom of this kind is the will *with itself* [*bei sich*], because it has reference to nothing but itself so that every relationship of dependence on something *other* than itself is thereby eliminated.—It is *true*, or rather it is *truth* itself, because its determination consists in being its existence [*Dasein*]—i.e., as something opposed to itself—what it is in its concept; that is, the pure concept, the pure concept of the will has the intuition of itself for its end and reality."

Well and good, but what does this mean, you say! As a start, let's say the following. The free will wills itself as the free will, first, when it wills a system of political and social institutions within which it can be free. But this is not enough. The free will wills itself as a free will when, second, in willing the ends of those institutions it makes their ends its own, and, third, when it is thereby willing a system of institutions within which it is *educated* to the concept of itself as a free will by various public features of the arrangement of those institutions, features which exhibit the concept of a free will (or of freedom). Note here the significance of education *(Bildung)*.

We always have to keep in mind that Hegel is not talking about individual wills as such; not about yours and mine. He is talking about the *concept* of the free will. This concept is an aspect of *Geist* and is actualized in the world throughout human history, where it takes, from one epoch to the next, a more appropriate form for the expression of the freedom of the will. For Hegel, a system of right is a realm of freedom made actual. He says in §29: "*Right* is any existent [*Dasein*] in general which is the *existence* of the *free will*. Right is therefore in general freedom, as Idea." (The German reads: "Dies, dass ein Dasein überhaupt Dasein des freien Willens, ist das Recht.")

On the basis of this, let's say that to justify a system of right—a system of political and social institutions including a scheme of rights—it is necessary to show that it is required for the expression of the free nature of the will. Thus in §30: "Right is something *utterly sacred,* for the simple reason that it is the existence [*Dasein*] of the absolute concept, of self-conscious freedom."

Hegel's claim in PR is that the system of institutions he describes is the system most appropriate—at this point in the historical development of spirit—for the expression and actualization of freedom. This being so, those institutions can be justified to the free will. This is Hegel's concept of justification, or of the legitimacy, of a system of institutions.

3. This is still somewhat unclear but things are getting clearer. We must avoid a mistaken thought as to what Hegel means in connecting the concept of a free will with a system of political and social institutions. First I quote from §156Z: "The ethical is not abstract like the good, but is intensely actual. The spirit has actuality and the individuals are its accidents. Thus, there are always only two possible viewpoints in the ethical realm: either one starts from substantiality, or one proceeds atomistically and moves upward from the basis of individuality. This latter viewpoint excludes spirit, because it leads only to an aggregation, whereas spirit is not something individual, but the unity of the individual and the universal."

The point here is this: on Hegel's view, we are not to start with given individuals who already desire freedom, or, indeed, who already understand what freedom means. The case is not as if people already desire—to take another example—pleasure, or the satisfaction of certain given natural interests, or that they already desire wealth and power over other people. If this were so, then one might figure out what the system of political and social institutions should be, assuming that these desires and aims were appropriate. It seems easy enough to suppose that we know what it means to desire pleasure or wealth, say, apart from any system of social institutions. Then we simply ask what system would be the best instrument, the most effective means, to fulfill those ends.

I take Hegel to say that with the concept of a free will willing itself as a free will, the case is different. In understanding ethical life, we must start from the historically given system of institutions themselves, from ethical life in its substantiality as we see it before our eyes. From this, we may infer that Hegel rejects the idea that the system of institutions is only a means to ethical life. He thinks that those institutions—to use a word now often used—constitute ethical life. Yet what is the force of "constitute" here? Rousseau and Mill thought that the institutions of freedom were good for their own sake, and not only as a means to happiness or welfare. And Kant, I believe, held that the principles of right constitute the scheme of human rights: a system of liberty in which the freedom of each can coexist with the freedom of everyone else. The justification of these principles has its basis in the moral law as a law of freedom and is entirely independent of the principle of happiness ("Theory and Practice" 79f.). But I think it fruitless to discuss Hegel's meaning further in this way. We have to return to the meaning of Hegel's text.

§4. Private Property

1. Earlier I quoted Hegel as saying that any kind of institutional embodiment of the concept of free will is what right is. The darkness of this remark can, I think, be dispelled only by looking at the details of how Hegel describes such institutions. We will only have time to look at the case of property. But before turning to property, a few words about the account of abstract right at §§34–40. First, an important point, one happily easy to understand. Recall that a system of right is to be justified in virtue of its making actual the concept of a free will that has itself as its object. And this implies that a system of right is not to be justified in virtue of its fulfilling people's needs or desires, or meeting their welfare. So a utilitarian justification is not appropriate in this case. As Hegel says in §37: "In formal right . . . it is not a question of particular interests, of my advantage or welfare, and just as little of the particular ground by which my will is determined, i.e., of my insight and intention."

Private property, then, is to rest on considerations of freedom, for freedom is the basis of our dignity and of right. In this, Hegel follows Kant, for whom this was true: the moral law is a law of freedom, and our having the capacity to act from that law is the basis of our dignity and makes us a member of the realm of ends.

2. By having personality, Hegel says, I am aware of myself as this person (§35). Of course, I am also moved by impulses and desires, and limited in my circumstances; yet I am, as a person, simply self-relation, and therefore

I know myself as having a will that is indeterminate and free. For I can suppose myself without the particular desires and impulses that move me, and I can imagine myself in other circumstances.

Now, as Hegel says in §36, personality involves the capacity for rights and constitutes the concept and the basis of the system of abstract and formal right. He then says, "The imperative of right is: '. . . *be a person and respect others as persons.*'"

But the particular desires and needs, while present in us, are not themselves part of personality as such—not part of its capacity for rights, or indeed of its capacity to have a free will. And so they are irrelevant to the explanation and justification of rights. The basic rights of personality do not depend on what our particular desires and needs are. At §38, Hegel says: "For the same reason of its abstractness, the necessity of this right is limited to the negative—not to violate personality and what ensues from personality. Hence, there are only *prohibitions of right*."

3. In regard to the system of private property, the question now is: How does the system of its rights conform to the two injunctions "to be a person and to respect the rights of others as persons; and do not infringe on personality and what it entails"? How exactly do the rights of property—to own it, to use it, and even to abuse it; to exclude others from it as well as to sell it—show respect for persons and embody the concept of the free will? We can point to three features of the system of private property that show respect for persons.

(a) We saw in discussing the concept of a free will that the will, and persons as having a free will, must resolve their indeterminacy and step into the external sphere in order to exist as Idea. Hegel repeats this at §41. Now what is external to mind is the thing: a thing is not something free, it is not personal, and it is without rights (§42). Whereas in the system of abstract right, persons have the right of putting their will into everything in the external sphere and of making it their own. The thing has no end in itself and derives its place and use from the will of its owner.

This is the absolute right of appropriation which man has over all 'things'.

Hegel's thought here seems to be this: When a system of right (of law and institutions) gives to all persons the right to own all things as things (which have no personality), and it does this in virtue of personality alone and so independently of the needs and desires of persons, then that system expresses the concepts of a free will, of the dignity of free persons as such, and of their superiority to all things.

(b) A second feature of the system of private property that Hegel thinks shows respect for persons is that persons as owners can do anything they want with their property, as long, of course, as it is consistent with respecting the rights of others as persons. We have fluctuating and changing desires and wants, which may influence how we use our property and exercise our rights, e.g., by selling it. Nevertheless, our property rights are based not on our desires and wants, but on our status as persons. This is clear from §45: "That I make something my own out of natural need, drive, and arbitrary will is the particular interest of possession. But the circumstance that I, as free will, am an object to myself in what I possess and only become an actual will by this means constitutes the genuine and rightful element in possession, the determination of *property*." And from the remark: "In relation to needs—if these are taken as primary—the possession of property appears as a means [to the satisfaction of needs]; but the true position is that, from the point of view of freedom, property, as the first *existence* [*Dasein*] of freedom, is an essential end for itself."

So it is as a free will that I have the right to own property; my needs and the fulfillment of my desires have nothing to do with it. The true position, as Hegel says, is that the system of property is justified as the most appropriate embodiment of freedom. The very system itself as expressing freedom is the substantive end.

(c) A third feature is that since persons are individuals, their property becomes objective to them as private property (§46). And similarly with their bodies (§48). If my body is to be the instrument of my person as having free will, I must take possession of it. I become objective to myself in my body. But from the point of view of others, I am in effect a free being in my body and my possession of it is immediate, a matter of course. So my body is the first embodiment of my freedom. We must all have some body; it is by our different bodies that we are distinguished from one another. Not to be allowed to own a body at all is to be killed. So somewhat similarly, not to be allowed to own any property at all (as were the guardians in Plato's *Republic*) is to suffer violation of the rights of personality. Such a violation is not of course as severe as to be deprived of a body altogether, but it is still a serious restriction of the exercise of personality in ways not required by the similar rights of others.

Thus we show respect for persons by showing respect for the integrity of their bodies and by honoring the precepts not to injure, not to harm, and of course not to enslave (which deprives others of their own direction of the use of their bodies). Similarly, we show respect for persons by respecting the property they have, whatever it is. Questions about how much people should have and about the equality of property fall elsewhere and are not matters of abstract right (§49).

4. So far I have been merely paraphrasing Hegel's view as I understand it, putting it in words clearer to me. I hope I have expressed it clearly enough and have not distorted it. The crucial point is that Hegel's reasoning seems to move strictly from what is required if a system of property—or any system of right—is to express freedom. Or more fully, if it is to express the concept of a free will that wills itself as a free will and thus takes itself as its object. It is this concept of a free will that is the basis of the concept of the person and of personality. I shall not consider whether Hegel presents an argument in the strict sense, or whether he is even trying to do so. To do that would be extremely difficult.

I shall, however, make a few general comments. Note first that Hegel leaves aside any appeal to the advantages of private property, either to individual persons or to society as a whole. He doesn't appeal to the desirable consequences to society of property in the long run. Nor does he appeal to what people might want to do with their property. In this respect, he is, as Kant was before him, radically opposed to a utilitarian or welfarist explanation and justification of a system of right. This is characteristic of a liberalism of freedom, as I explain further next time.

Less obviously, Hegel doesn't appeal to a psychological need of persons for private property, as if somehow they couldn't develop into free citizens unless private property were permitted. He will surely want at some point to take account of this need, but he won't appeal to it in the first instance. In the section on abstract right, the reasoning for private property turns on showing it to be the most appropriate expression of freedom. It is in this that we see the special feature of Hegel's doctrine. I shall not offer other examples, but the same pattern is seen throughout. I have dealt with the concept of the free will and of private property because its relative simplicity enables one to illustrate the main point.

§5. Civil Society

1. Recall that the three main institutions of ethical life are the family, civil society, and the state. The family is ethical life in its natural or immediate phase. In due course, its substantial unity gives way to civil society, which is an association of individuals in a universality that is only abstract or formal. Then civil society in turn is brought back to the substantial universal by the state and its constitutional powers. To be sure, civil society does not arise directly out of the family. The order of things here is conceptual, and historical only in Hegel's larger sense. What is important for us is this: systems of right, such as property, do not require civil society; rather, it is in and through the institutions of civil society, such as the free market, that awareness of freedom of the will *in* property is possible.

Civil society comprises three parts:

(a) The system of needs *(Bedürfnisse)*. This is the economy in which individuals exchange goods and services to fulfill their needs and wants, and these take new forms and develop as the economy progresses. Exchange comes to determine how needs are satisfied. Division of labor increases; individuals and families recognize that they are interdependent. Estates, or classes *(Stände)*, take form: an agricultural class, a business class, and a "universal" class of civil servants. With this, we have the rise of the modern economy.

(b) The administration of justice *(Rechtsflege)*. Abstract right is formulated in laws that are definite, promulgated, and known. This public aspect is an essential feature of law, which is framed to protect individuals from harm and injury. This is the new part. In civil society, "a human being counts as such because he is a human being, and not because he is a Jew, Catholic, Protestant, German, Italian . . ." (PR §209). The combination of self-sufficient individuals organized in a system of needs and the provision of security for their persons and property through a system of justice gives rise to, in Hegel's words, a "formal universality."

(c) The police *(Polizei)* and corporation *(Korporation)*. *Polizei* is from the

Greek *politiea* and its meaning is much wider than our word "police." In Hegel's day it covered not only law enforcement but also the fixing of the prices of necessities, the control of the quality of goods, the arrangements of hospitals, street lighting, and much else. Hegel has considerable discussion of the problems of civil society. He was distressed at the growth of poverty and the resentful *Pöbel* (rabble), but he offers no answer to it.

Hegel's corporation is not a trade union since it includes employers as well as employees. It also covers religious bodies, learned societies, and town councils. The role of corporations is to moderate the competitive individualism of the system of needs (the economy) and to prepare burghers for their lives as citizens of the state. Then civil society in turn is brought back to the substantial universal and a public life dedicated to it by the state and its constitutional powers. (Here I use Hegel's language in §157).

2. Hegel viewed his account of civil society as of great importance; this itself distinguishes him from other writers. Civil society, as he thought of it, was new to the modern state and characterized modernity itself. His view is distinctive in that he considers many aspects of what had been regarded as elements of the state as actually elements of civil society. See, for example, the above discussion of the judiciary, the police, and corporation. The *political* state is separate from civil society, while both together are the state in the wide sense (§267).

A contrast with Greek society may help. Hegel's conception of Greek society was that it had only two forms of ethical life: the family and the state or polis. It had no civil society. Although civil society comes before the state in the dialectical progression of concepts in *PR*, historically it came after the first forms of the state. Since Greek society lacked civil society, its members had no conception of themselves as persons with particular and separate interests that they viewed as their own and wanted to pursue. As a result, Hegel thinks they unreflectively identified themselves with their family or their polis. That is, they viewed themselves as members of a particular family and of a particular state, and they pursued the interests of these social forms untroubled by the hesitations of a conscience that takes account of more universal interests. This unreflective form of life inevitably becomes unstable and falls into decay upon the appearance of reflective thought.

Like many Germans of his day, Hegel was much attracted to classical

Greek culture, and he pondered deeply the reasons for its demise. It led him to pose one of his most basic questions, namely, how is it possible that a reflective form of ethical life can be stable? Of course, we can put this question more elaborately in terms of the free will that wills itself as free, but I forgo this. The point here is that civil society and its institutions have an important role in making possible a stable form of reflective social life.

3. Let's consider how this works with two institutions. One is the institution of the free market of the classical political economists whom Hegel read; the other is freedom of religion.

Hegel describes people in the market as pursuing their own interests and using one another as means to their own ends. So far all this sounds familiar. But while one principle of civil society is the concrete person—the person with particular ends, a mixture of wants and caprice—the other principle is the form of universality. He says:

> [A] particular end takes on the form of universality and gains satisfaction by simultaneously satisfying the welfare of others. Since particularity is tied to the condition of universality, the whole (of civil society) is the sphere of mediation in which all individual characteristics, all aptitudes, and all accidents of birth and fortune are liberated, and where the waves of all passions surge forth, governed only by the reason which shines through them. Particularity, limited by universality, is the only standard by which each particular [person] promotes his welfare. (§182 *Zusatz*)

What is the reason "shining through" and governing the waves of passion here? It is simply the laws of economics, supply and demand and all that, leading to an efficient allocation of social resources as it would be explained, say, by Adam Smith in his *Wealth of Nations* (1776). This is the form of universality appropriate to the relations between concrete persons pursuing their separate interests and particular ends. By reflecting on their relations to one another, the members of civil society become aware of their mutual interdependence, and this plays a role in leading them back to the universal aims of the state itself. (Other institutions in civil society are crucial here, in particular the corporations, in ways I mention next time.)

4. Hegel says that the great strength of the modern state is that it draws on (§185R) "the truly infinite power which resides solely in that unity which

allows the *opposition* within reason [*Vernunft*] *to develop to its full strength*, and has overcome it so as to preserve itself within it and *wholly contain it within itself.*" Or as Hegel says later (§260): "The principle of modern states has enormous strength and depth because it allows the principle of subjectivity to attain fulfillment in the *self-sufficient extreme* of personal particularity, while at the same time *bringing it back to substantial unity* and so preserving this unity in the principle of subjectivity itself."

As part of the explication of these ideas, appended to §270 is a long and complex remark on religion, which I can't begin to summarize here. Yet it needs to be stressed that if one aspect of the principle of subjectivity and particularity in civil society is the pursuit of one's interests in personal and private life, another aspect is the freedom of religion, and of all religion. In freedom of religion, we find a second way in which an institution of civil society makes possible a stable form of reflective social life.

The remark at §270 ends with the following:

> If the state is to attain existence [*Dasein*] as the *self-knowing* ethical actuality of spirit, its form must become distinct from that of authority and faith. But this distinction emerges only in so far as the Church for its part becomes divided within itself. Only then, [when it stands] above the *particular* Churches, can the state attain *universality* of thought as its formal principle and bring it into existence [*Existenz*]; but in order to recognize this, one must know not only what universality is *in itself,* but also what its *existence* [*Existenz*] is. Consequently, far from it being, or ever having been, a misfortune for the state if the Church is divided, it is *through this division alone* that the state has been able to fulfill its destiny [*Bestimmung*] as self-conscious rationality and ethical life. This division is likewise the most fortunate thing which could have happened to the Church and to thought as far as their freedom and rationality are concerned.

This is a good example of philosophy as reconciliation. For the early controversies over toleration in the sixteenth and seventeenth centuries show that it was nearly impossible then for most people to accept it. The division of Christendom seemed to them an utter disaster. They came to accept toleration as state policy only because they feared that endless religious war would destroy society. Whereas Hegel says that now, centuries later, once we see toleration and the separation of church and state as necessary to modern liberty—to the freedom of the free will that wills itself as free—we can become reconciled to it: we accept it.

The remark also contains a good example of what Hegel calls the cunning of reason *(die List der Vernunft)*.[6] Ironically, Martin Luther, one of the most intolerant of men, turns out to be an agent of modern liberty. This is an aspect of history that Hegel emphasized—that great men who had enormous effects on major events of history usually never understood the real significance of what they had done. It is as if they are used by a providential plan unfolding through time and embedded in the flow of events.

I have tried to indicate how in Hegel's account of the institutions of the modern state he aims to discern how their features express and constitute the different aspects of freedom, and how the intricacies of the text can often be given a reasonably clear sense. Unhappily I have not done enough to guard against misinterpretations of Hegel's view and to emphasize that he sees himself as describing the institutions of the modern state insofar as they are reasonable *(vernünftig)*. He doesn't mean to defend all existing aspects of these arrangements, and he certainly allows for bad and corrupt states and for human misery and anguish, not to mention the terrible sacrifices of war, the miseries of divorce, and the moral evils arising from the resentment and indignation of poverty. These last evils afflict what Hegel called "der Pöbel" (the rabble), the underclasses (defined by level of wealth and status and not by estate) of modern society, and for which he thinks there is no solution.[7] I have taken him to be laying out an ideal-typical system of institutions that he thinks *does* constitute modern freedom. It is a political and social world of real freedom but not one of pleasure and happiness. Achieving the latter is up to us.

6. In his lectures on world history, Hegel says: "[I]t is not the universal Idea which enters into opposition, conflict, and danger; it keeps itself in the background, untouched and unharmed, and sends forth particular interests of passion to fight and wear themselves out instead. It is what we may call *the cunning of reason* that it sets the passions to work in its service." See *Lectures on World History*, trans. H. B. Nisbet, Introduction by Duncan Forbes (Cambridge: Cambridge University Press, 1975), p. 89. It is in these lectures particularly that Hegel's philosophy of history and metaphysical view of the world are evident. See the discussion by Allen Wood of these matters in *Hegel's Ethical Thought*, chap. 13, which discusses the limits of ethics, concluding with Hegel's amoralism.

7. See Wood, *Hegel's Ethical Thought*, pp. 247–255.

HEGEL II

Ethical Life and Liberalism

§1. *Sittlichkeit:* The Account of Duty

1. Last time I said that Hegel was a moderately progressive reform-minded liberal, and that his liberalism is an important exemplar in the history of moral and political philosophy of the *liberalism of freedom*. I emphasized two ideas: philosophy as reconciliation, and the role of *Sittlichkeit* as the location of the ethical: the whole ensemble of rational social institutions that make freedom possible. Today, after a brief review of Hegel's account of the freedom of the will and the nature of our duties as free persons, we will take up the third component of ethical life: the State. It is here that we will most clearly see the elements and purpose of Hegel's liberalism. We will also look at two areas where Hegel seems to depart from traditional liberalism: his doctrine of war and its role in the life of states, and his legacy as a critic of liberalism.

2. I begin by recalling a main point from last time. It is the one that I referred to as the main thesis: that the free will wills itself as the free will. I suggested that this dark saying means the following four things.

First, that the free will wills a system of political and social institutions within which the free will can be free. Here institutions are understood as forms of life as lived by human beings.

Second, that the free will wills the ends of this system of political and social institutions, and it wills these ends as its own.

Third, that the free will is educated to the concept of itself as a free will by various public features of this system of institutions.

Fourth, that these various public features that thus educate the free will are themselves features that fully express the concept of a free will.

We need all four of these conditions. Each is important, and a strict interpretation of the fourth is vital. What is meant by an institution expressing the concept of a free will as a free will I explained by discussing at some length the concept of the free will itself and then considering as an illustration how the right of private property could be seen as expressing its freedom. We must also distinguish between a system of political and social institutions understood, on the one hand, as an abstract structure that can be described by certain principles and precepts, by its various powers and agencies, and on the other hand, as lived forms of life animated by people in the world. It is as such lived forms of life that institutions are to be understood here.

3. The general description of ethical life *(Sittlichkeit)* is given by the main thesis we have reviewed. It is a system of political and social institutions that expresses and makes actual in the world the concept of freedom. Hegel says (§142), "Ethical life is accordingly *the concept of freedom which has become the existing world and the nature of self-consciousness.*"

This system of institutions is described in the third part of *PR* and is quite complicated; all readers of Hegel come across passages they can't figure out, even if the main lines are reasonably clear. The description runs from §142 through §320, and concludes with the sovereignty of the state vis-à-vis other states and the international realm. I note Kant's social contract doctrine as a third alternative falling between the two Hegel suggests in §156 *Zusatz*, between his own theory and Hobbes's so-called individualistic atomism. We will return to this.

4. First, I mention an important contrast with Kant's understanding of duty. As we have seen, Kant views the duties of justice and of virtue as given by the moral law as we know it via the categorical imperative and the procedure for applying it. The duties of justice restrict the means we can use to advance our ends, while the duties of virtue specify obligatory ends to which we must give some weight. Hegel's view is markedly different. In Kant's sense, Hegel has no doctrine of duties at all. His account of *Sittlichkeit* describes various forms of political and social life. These forms,

Hegel says, are not alien to the subject; rather, "the subject bears spiritual witness to them as to its own essence, which it has in its self awareness and lives as in its element . . . a relationship which is immediate and closer to identity than even [a relationship of] faith or trust" (§147). And he continues: "The ethical theory of duties . . . therefore consists in that systematic development of the circle of ethical necessity which follows here in *Part Three*. . . . The difference between its presentation here and the form of a *theory of duties* [i.e., Kant's] lies solely in the fact that the following account merely shows that the ethical determinations are necessary relations, and does not proceed to add in every case 'this determination is therefore a duty of human beings.' "

Duties are implicit in the account of the institutional background and so there is no need for such an addition. For Hegel, duty appears as a restriction only to indeterminate subjectivity or to natural will (the will given by our natural wants). So to a free will that wills itself as a free will, the institutions of ethical life express its essence as such a will and disclose in their duties the individual's liberation *(Befreiung)* (§149).

(a) We find liberation from dependence on mere natural impulse, or from the dejection or depression *(Gedrückheit)* we experience in having to dwell by moral reflection on what in general ought to be and might be; and

(b) We find liberation from indeterminate subjectivity and the failure to reach an objective determinacy while remaining devoid of actuality. By contrast, in our duties as given by the forms of ethical life, we acquire, as individuals, our substantial freedom.

5. So in a reasonable and vibrant ethical life, it is easy to say what our more concrete duties are, and what we must do to be virtuous. All we have to do is to follow the well-known and explicit precepts of our situation: to ask ourselves what are our duties, say, as husband or wife, or instructor or student, and the rest (§150). Virtue, then, is rectitude *(Rechtschaffenheit)*: it is having the general character that may be demanded of us by the forms of life of *Sittlichkeit*, in a word, by our station and its duties. The various aspects of rectitude may be called virtues. In a developed ethical order, where the appropriate system of ethical relations has been developed in forms of life, virtue in the proper sense of the word (§150R) "has its place and actuality only in extraordinary circumstances, or where the above relations come into collision."

In such an order, once we have acquired a sense of its institutions, we can often resolve collisions of obligation that arise, although some may have no clear answer. (Consider the conflict in Sophocles between Creon and Antigone.) Yet a developed ethical order may manage to avoid serious collisions most of the time so that they will be exceptional. Modern life, Hegel thinks, has little place or need for the heroism of virtue. That is one of its merits, an aspect of our freedom.

I have mentioned Hegel's account of moral duties (§§147–150, 207) and how they are given by the forms of ethical life first in order to show his emphasis on the fundamental role of political and social institutions. Giving an account of those institutions as forms of life must come first. This approach contrasts sharply with Kant's, which starts with the moral law. We also need to see Hegel as saying that when our duties are given by ethical life as expressing freedom, those duties so understood are an aspect of our freedom, of our liberation, as he says. As individuals we know our place in the social world; we are fulfilled, and gain our happiness, by doing our duties well, by being a good husband or wife, father or mother, and so on. In the forms of life of ethical life, there is no essential conflict between duty and happiness or between duty and inclination. Part of Kant's error is to think that there may be.

§2. *Sittlichkeit:* The State

1. I have said that Hegel stands in the liberal tradition and expresses what may be called a liberalism of freedom. In Hegel's rendition of the view, freedom is understood as a system of political and social institutions that guarantee and make possible citizens' basic freedoms. However, Hegel's political doctrines have been, until quite recently, badly misinterpreted. For a long time, *PR* was read as an attempted justification of the Prussian state in 1820 or later; Hegel has even been associated with German imperialism and the Nazis. Yet there were always writers ("the Hegelian center") who insisted that Hegel was a moderate liberal and defender of the modern constitutional state. In the last fifty years or so, this has become the general opinion of the English-language literature on Hegel.

Under the reform administration of Chancellor Hardenberg, King

Friedrich Wilhelm III of Prussia promised in 1815 to give a written constitution to his nation, but in 1819 the political victory of the conservatives made sure that the promise would not be kept. Earlier that year, Hardenberg and the progressive interior minister Wilhelm von Humboldt had drawn up constitutional plans for a bicameral estates assembly, plans that are similar to Hegel's own. Under the existing law, only the hereditary nobility was able to join the Prussian officer corps and to serve in the higher level of the civil service, which staffed the government (what Hegel called the political state [PR §257]). Whereas in Hegel's *vernünftig* state, all citizens are eligible for military command and the civil service (PR §271, note 2; §277, note 1; §291, note 1). Hegel's state resembles not the Prussia of 1820 but the Prussia that would have been had the reformers won over the conservatives.[1]

2. The main elements of Hegel's state, beginning with constitutional law, are these. The state is not founded on contract as are the commercial transactions of civil society. It was not formed by an original contract, nor is it to be judged by how well it fulfills an imagined original contract with its citizens (PR §§75, 258). The state is not an institution for satisfying the already given antecedent needs and wants of so-called atomistic individuals, that is, individuals as described apart from their place in a system of basic institutions. What makes us fully developed persons is being citizens of a rational state: "The rational destiny of human beings is to live with a state" (PR §75A). The states make one a *citoyen* and not simply a *Bürger*.

The constitution of the state has three elements or powers.

(a) The monarchy provides the *individual* element. The office is hereditary, which Hegel thinks avoids caprice and eliminates any contractual as-

---

1. For the story of constitutional politics in Prussia in these years, see James Sheehan, *German History, 1770–1866* (Oxford: Clarendon Press, 1989). A memorandum by Hardenberg in 1807 gives an idea of the German reformers' hopes. Hardenberg defined the purpose of reform as "a revolution in the positive sense, one leading to the ennoblement of mankind, to be made not through violent impulses from below or outside, but through the wisdom of the government. . . . Democratic principles in a monarchical government—that seems to me the appropriate form for the spirit of the age to go." Sheehan comments that by "democratic," Hardenberg meant economic freedom and social emancipation, the opening of careers to all men of talent, religious toleration and civil liberty for Jews, freedom of opinion and education. As for the citizens' taking part and having an active role in democratic institutions, he seems to have been unconcerned with or uncertain about representative institutions. Freedom meant freedom for individuals in the economic and social realm—Hegel's civil society—with public affairs and foreign policy conducted by the state and its administration, to which citizens could belong (p. 305).

pects that may arise from election. Although the Monarch has the final decision in the appointment of executives and in state acts such as the declaration of war, the Monarch is always guided by expert advice. "[T]he objective part belongs to the law alone, and the Monarch's part is merely to set to the law the subjective 'I will'" (*PR* §280A). This yields a constitutional monarchy.

(b) The executive or governmental power is the *particular* element, since it brings the particular under the universal (*PR* §287). It applies the law and decisions of the Monarch to particular cases. It is composed of the civil service, the judiciary, the police, and much else. All these positions are open to all (male) citizens of talent, one of the reforms Hegel supported.

(c) Next is the legislature, which is the *universal* element (*PR* §§289–320). The people as a whole—but not the peasants or workers, or in those days women, whose place was in the family (*PR* §166)—are represented in this part of the state. Moreover, the citizens are represented not as atomistic individuals but as members of the Estates. Hegel lists three estates: (i) the hereditary landed gentry, who sit as individuals in the upper house; (ii) the business class; and (iii) the universal class of civil servants (which in Prussia included teachers and professors at universities). Representatives to the second two estates are elected as members of the respective corporations to which they belong. In this way, as we shall see, Hegel hopes to moderate the free market and to make it serve the purpose of universal ends.

3. I begin with a rather long quotation from *PR* §260 (the first section of "Constitutional Law") and then comment on it:

[a] The state is the actuality of concrete freedom. But concrete freedom requires that personal individuality [*Einzelheit*] and its particular interests should reach their full *development* and gain *recognition of their right* for itself (within the family and civil society),

[b] and also that they should, on the one hand, *pass over* of their own accord into the interest in the universal, and on the other, knowingly and willingly acknowledge this universal interest even as their own *substantial spirit,* and *actively pursue it* as their *ultimate end.*

[c] The effect of this is that the universal does not attain validity or fulfillment without the interest, the knowledge and the volition of the

particular, and that individuals do not live as private persons merely for these particular interests without at the same time directing their will to a universal end [*in und für das Allgemeine wollen*] and acting in conscious awareness of this end.

[d] The principle of modern states has enormous strength and depth because it allows the principle of subjectivity to attain fulfillment in the *self-sufficient extreme* of personal particularity, while at the same time *bringing it back to substantial unity* and so preserving this unity in the principle of subjectivity itself.

If we understand this important paragraph, we should be able to understand the rest. I have divided it into parts and remark on them separately.

(a) The state as a whole is the framework of basic political and social institutions that, together with the family and civil society, enable citizens, who are members of the state, to attain their freedom. (It is useful to distinguish what Hegel calls the "political state" [the government and its bureaucracy] from the "external state" [the rest of the framework of institutions].) That is what Hegel means by calling the state the actuality of *concrete* freedom. It is concrete freedom because it enables *individuals* to fulfill their *particular* interests as these interests have developed within the limits allowed by the rights and duties specified in family and civil society and protected by the rule of law.

(b) Unless we understand Hegel's terminology, the next part is very mysterious. What does it mean for interests to pass over of their own accord into the universal? It means that in one's capacity of being a citizen, as opposed to a *Bürger*, one understands that society is held together not simply by the satisfaction of particular interests but by a sense of reasonable order, and that it is regulated by, let's say, a common-good conception of justice, which recognizes the merits of the claims of all sectors of society. What raises human life above the workaday *bürgerliche* world is the recognition of the universal interest of all citizens in participating in and maintaining the whole system of political and social institutions of the modern state that makes their freedom possible. Citizens knowingly and willingly acknowledge this universal (collective) interest as their own, and they give it the highest priority. They are ready to act for it as their ultimate end. This is the goal of the project of *reconciliation*.

(c) For Hegel, this universal interest attains neither its validity nor its fulfillment without the interest, the knowledge, and the acceptance of individual citizens in civil society. They do not live simply as private persons absorbed in and concerned with only their particular interests. For at the same time, citizens are concerned with the universal end—as guided by a common-good conception of justice—and their will as *citizens* is directed to this end ("in und für das Allgemeine wollen") and acting in the full conscious awareness of this end.

(d) Hegel believed that the fact that the modern constitution allowed for full freedom in civil society gave enormous strength to the state, provided that the universal (collective) interest of citizens was recognized and given priority by them in their political life. The result is a revolution in Hardenberg's sense, "one leading to the ennoblement of mankind, to be made not through violent impulses from below or outside, but through the wisdom of the government. . . . Democratic principles in a monarchical government—that seems to me the appropriate form for the spirit of the age to go." As we saw earlier, by this economic freedom and social emancipation, Hardenberg meant the opening of careers to all men of talent, religious toleration and civil liberty for Jews, and freedom of opinion and education. Where Hegel differs from Hardenberg is in allowing more room for the citizens to take part and have an active role in representative democratic institutions.

4. Hegel's preferred scheme of voting is not what we would expect. He thinks that people take a more reasonable and knowledgeable interest in political life when they are represented by estates, corporations, and the associations to which they belong and whose members share their occupations and tasks in civil society. Whereas in the liberal scheme, where each citizen has one vote, citizens' interests tend to shrink and center on their private economic concerns, resulting in a loss both to themselves and to the ties of community in political society. Thus Hegel rejects the idea of "one person, one vote" on the grounds that it expresses the democratic and individualistic idea that each person, as an atomic unit, has the basic right to participate equally in political deliberation.[2] By contrast, in the well-ordered

2. *Philosophy of Right* (1821), §308. Hegel's main objection to the idea of direct suffrage in the Constitution of Württemberg presented by the liberal king in 1815–16 is found in part in the following passage from the essay of 1817, "The Proceedings of the Estates Assembly in the Kingdom of Würt-

rational state, as Hegel presents it in *PR*, persons belong first to estates, corporations, and associations. Since these social forms represent the rational interests of their members in what Hegel views as a just consultation hierarchy (described in that work), some persons will take part in politically representing these interests in the consultation process, but they do so as members of estates and corporations and not as individuals.

We must understand Hegel's voting scheme as having the purposes of moderating the influence of the competitive market and aspirations of the business class on the political process and ensuring public policies that would work for the universal interest, the common good of the state as a whole. He thought it was necessary to embed the economy in surrounding arrangements of public regulation and support, and to establish ways of encouraging noncompetitive values. The modern industrial economy would otherwise be a danger to and corrupt political and civil life. His constitutional scheme with its three estates no doubt strikes us as quaint and out of date, and teaches us little. But does a modern constitutional society do any better? Certainly not the United States, where the purchase of legislation by "special interests" is an everyday thing.

5. In §§315–318, Hegel discusses the role of public opinion. The views in his earlier political writings are more optimistic than those in *PR*, but Hegel never abandons the idea that public opinion must be consulted and that in the assembly of the Estates the government should have a working majority. Hegel wrote before political parties in our sense had formed and had become an essential part of politics. For him, parties were particular groups of politicians in the Estates expressing various interests.

Public opinion has two important roles. One is to bring to the attention of the government grievances and wishes of the electorate, thereby provid-

---

temberg, 1815–1816": "The electors appear otherwise in no bond or connexion with the civil order and the organization of the state. The citizens come to the scene as isolated atoms, and the electoral assemblies as unordered inorganic aggregates; the peoples as a whole are dissolved into a heap. This is a form in which the community should never have appeared at all in undertaking any enterprise; it is a form most unworthy of the community and most in contradiction with its concepts as a spiritual order. Age and property are qualities affecting only the individual himself, not characteristically constituting his worth in the civil order. Such worth he has only on the strength of his office, his position, his skill in craftsmanship which, recognized by his fellow citizens, entitles him accordingly to be described as master of his craft" (p. 262 in *Hegel's Political Writings*, trans. T. M. Knox, with an introduction by Z. A. Pelczynski [Oxford: Clarendon Press, 1964]).

ing the government with a fuller understanding of what is on people's minds and of their more urgent needs and difficulties. The other role of public opinion is to bring the government's problems and views to the citizenry, so that citizens acquire a political sense and a knowledge of what the government's decisions and policies are based on. This give-and-take occurs in the debates in the assembly of the Estates.

Hegel regards the discussions in the Estates as deliberative: that is, the reasons offered on all sides should be seen as arguments. Both the ministers of the government, who must regularly appear in the Estates, as well as the elected members are viewed as possibly changing their minds in response to rational considerations. This requires that representatives be free agents and not delegates, and that the meetings of the Estates be public.

> If the Estates hold their assemblies in public, they afford a great public spectacle of outstanding educational value to the citizens, and it is from this above all that the people learn the true nature of their interests. . . . [I]t is only in such assemblies that those virtues, abilities, and skills are developed which must serve as models [for others]. These assemblies are, of course, tiresome for ministers, who must themselves be armed with wit and eloquence if they are to counter the attacks which are here directed against them. Nevertheless, such publicity is the most important means of education as far as the interests of the state in general are concerned. In a nation where this publicity exists, there is a much more lively attitude towards the state than one where the Estates have no assembly, or where such assemblies are not held in public. (PR §315A)

This is a strong statement of the educative role of political life in fashioning a lively and informed public opinion, which left to itself is a mix of truth and error.

§3. *Sittlichkeit:* War and Peace

1. I have said that Hegel should be counted in the liberal tradition. However, there are certain elements in his doctrine that raise doubts. One of these is his doctrine of war and its role in the life of states. Since Montesquieu,

writers in the liberal tradition have often held that constitutional democracy combined with commerce and trade would lead to peace among nations. Kant's "Perpetual Peace" (1795) shows the way. But Hegel rejects this idea.

The role of what Hegel calls "the Military Estate" (*PR* §327) is to defend the state in war against other states. Its characteristic virtue is valor, a formal virtue, because it is the highest abstraction of freedom from all particular ends, pleasure, and life. This virtue expresses the fact that the military must be prepared to sacrifice itself if need be for the defense of the state. Hegel accepts the Christian idea that a state should go to war only in self-defense; he rejects war for conquest and glory (*PR* §326).[3] As for the conduct of war, he says the war must not be waged against the civilians or institutions of the foreign state, nor may it be waged in a way that makes the establishment of a just peace more difficult. He says (*PR* §338): "War accordingly entails the determination of international law *(Völkerrecht)* that it should preserve that possibility of peace—so that, for example, ambassadors should be respected and war should on no account be waged either on internal institutions and the peace of private and family life, or on private individuals."

There is no difference here with traditional liberalism on the justification of war in self-defense of the system of modern freedom the state sustains and makes possible.

2. In *PR* §324, Hegel may appear to deny a liberal society a right to war when he says that it is "the substantial duty of individuals—their duty to preserve this substantial individuality—that is, the independence and sovereignty of the state—even if their own life and property, as well as their opinions and all that naturally falls within the province of life, are endangered or sacrificed. It is a grave miscalculation if the state, when it requires this sacrifice, is simply equated with civil society, and if its ultimate end is seen merely as the *security of the life and property* of individuals." (On the social contract view of the state, see §258 including *Zusätze* and addition.)

I interpret Hegel here not as rejecting a liberal society's right to engage in war in self-defense but rather as saying that when it does so, the ultimate

3. In §326, Hegel disapproves of aggressive war against other states. He says, "If the entire state thus becomes an armed power and is wrenched away from its own internal life to act on an external front, the war of defense becomes a war of conquest."

end of the political society cannot reasonably be viewed as the security of the life and property of individuals *as individuals* in civil society.[4] That would be, as he says, a grave miscalculation. He is correct in saying this. However, only a very limited idea of a liberal society would see it as involving only relations of property and economy and the more material features of life. This limited idea is not true of a liberal society which contains churches, universities, the spiritual activities of art, religion, and philosophy. Hegel also gives a strong statement of and fully affirms toleration and liberty of conscience going beyond the views of his day (§270).

When a liberal society engages in a war in self-defense, it must do so to protect and preserve the freedom of its citizens and its democratic political institutions. Only then is it acting in accordance with a liberalism of freedom and engaging in war for the right reasons. Indeed, a liberal society cannot justly require its citizens to fight to gain economic wealth or to acquire natural resources, much less to win power and empire.[5] Trespass on citizens' liberty by conscription or other such practices in raising armed forces may be done, on a liberal political conception, only for the sake of liberty itself, that is, as necessary to defend constitutional democratic institutions and civil society's many religious and nonreligious traditions and forms of life.[6] In this way, liberal political institutions perform the work of bringing civil society back to the universal. Once again there is no conflict here with liberalism and the right to war only in self-defense.

3. Now we do come to an important difference with liberalism. This difference concerns the two traditional powers of sovereignty and why Hegel asserts them. One power is the state's right to go to war in the rational (not necessarily reasonable) pursuit of its own national interests—Clausewitz's pursuit of politics by other means. The other power is the state's internal autonomy: the state has full control over the population (including minorities), resources, and land within its own recognized territory. Hegel thinks these rights are essential aspects of the state conceived as a substantive individual, for he thinks that states, as spiritual substances,

---

4. This view of liberalism is from Hegel's seeing it as founded on its idea of the social contract. See *Philosophy of Right*, §§258, 281.

5. Of course, so-called liberal societies sometimes do this, but that only shows they are unjust in war.

6. See *A Theory of Justice*, pp. 380f.

require the recognition of other states, just as much as persons require the recognition of other persons (PR §331). This recognition by other states is part of the process whereby a state as a spiritual substance becomes and endures as a state.

A liberal conception of freedom will conflict with Hegel's view here in two ways. First, in order to establish reasonable norms of right and justice to govern international law, a liberal conception will deny that states have the two traditional powers of sovereignty: the right to war to pursue their own rational interests and the right of internal autonomy. To allow the first risks perpetuating war. To allow the second threatens basic human rights. A state is not at liberty to abuse its own people or minorities among them with impunity; serious cases may justify some kind of sanction, even intervention.

The second way in which a liberal doctrine of freedom will conflict with Hegel's view is by not accepting his idea of the state as a spiritual substance needing the recognition of other states as such substances. I shall not, however, discuss the idea of the state as a substance, except to say that a liberalism of freedom doesn't understand the state in this way. A state is simply a people living within an established framework of political and social institutions and making its political decisions through the agencies of its free constitutional government. A state as a political actor is a body of citizens, an electorate, organized by and acting through its political institutions.

Hegel's view of international relations is based on his seeing these relations as founded on treaties alone, with there being no superior power to enforce them (PR §§333–334). These treaties are marked by contingency and can be violated at any time should a state wish to do so, with the issue to be settled if necessary by war. While Hegel's *vernünftige* state engages in war only in self-defense, it needs its own military estate to defend it when attacked. For Hegel, war results from the necessarily *anarchistic* nature of the relations between states. By contrast, the liberal view, exemplified by Kant's "Perpetual Peace," sees the cause of war as rooted in the *internal* nature of states and not mainly in the anarchistic nature of their mutual relations. Going back to Montesquieu,[7] the liberal tradition has proposed

7. See *The Spirit of Laws* (1748), Bk. 20, Chapters 1 and 2.

the idea of a *democratic peace* and held that peace will reign between democratic and commercial peoples organized by their free constitutional governments and engaged in trade. They are peaceful among themselves since
they have no reasons for attacking one another. As constitutional states,
they insist on freedom of religion and liberty of conscience; they do not
seek to convert other nations to their dominant religion, if they have one.
Industry and commerce meet their social and economic needs. Like Hegel's
state, they engage in war only in self-defense.

§4. A Third Alternative

1. In *Zusatz* §156, Hegel says that "there are always only two possible viewpoints in the ethical realm: either one starts from substantiality, or one
proceeds atomistically and moves upward from the basis of individuality.
The latter viewpoint excludes spirit, because it leads only to an aggregation,
whereas spirit is not something individual, but the unity of the individual
and the universal."

I suggest that there is a third alternative. Hegel opposes his viewpoint
to one that starts with single individuals as atoms and builds up from them
as a basis. Then the state and its institutions are nothing over and above
the individuals they serve as a means. Hegel wants us to see the state as
a concrete whole—a whole articulated into its particular groups. The member of a state is a member of such groups; and when we are dealing with
the state, members are considered only as so characterized. The third alternative I have in mind is found in Rousseau and Kant. Earlier I said a bit
about Kant's political view in connection with his doctrine of reasonable
faith. So I briefly consider it here.

2. Kant's political thought contains these main ideas, among others:[8]

> the essential political role of free public reason;
> the idea of the social, or of the original, contract;
> the idea of citizens as co-legislative members of the state;

---

8. These elements of Kant's political thought are found in a set of political essays: "Universal
History" (1784), "What Is Enlightenment?" (1784), "Theory and Practice" (1793), "Perpetual Peace"
(1795), and "Contest of the Faculties" (1798).

the rejection of the principle of happiness as a criterion of basic public law;

the freedom of religion and the right to pursue our happiness
in our own way free of state interference, provided we respect the rights of others.

As for Kant's practical hopes, the content of his reasonable faith, he
looked forward to the day when mankind would be organized into a society
of societies, each of which has its own representative constitutional regime.
Each regime would be a member of a confederation of peoples joined together to prevent war first of all. Underlying this hope is Kant's belief that
a world state would be either a soulless despotism or else torn by civil war
as separate regions tried to gain autonomy, as well as his further belief that
democratic governments do not go to war with one another. A society of
peoples, all with constitutional regimes, would, he thought, be peaceful and
progressive in culture and the arts ("Perpetual Peace," Ak. VIII:367).

3. The key to seeing Kant's view as a third alternative lies in his interpretation of the social, or the original, contract. There are two crucial features
of this idea.

(a) The first feature is the special nature of the social contract. All contracts involve an agreement to pursue an end by joint effort or constraint
(as when I agree not to prevent you from advancing your end, and recip-
rocally, you agree not to prevent me from advancing mine). Here we do
not share these ends. The social contract, however, is a union of many
individuals—of all citizens—for a common end that they do all share ("Theory and Practice," Ak. VIII:289). Now this very same end is not only an
end they do share but an end that they ought to share. This is because
Kant thinks that the first decision we are obliged to make is to abandon
the state of nature and to unite with everyone else whom our actions may
influence in order to submit together to a system of public law that may
be enforced against us *(Metaphysik der Sitten,* I:§44). Thus a state is a union
of people under the principles of public right (§45).

(b) A second distinctive feature of the social contract is that it is an idea
of reason ("Theory and Practice" 8:297). One thing Kant means by this is
that we are not to search for such a contract in the past, or to worry about
whether there ever was one or what its terms were. None of those inquiries

is to the point, since the idea of this contract is an idea of reason and as such it is nonhistorical. We understand the social contract the right way when we understand it as the highest criterion of constitutional and basic law. As the highest criterion, it obliges every legislator to frame laws in such a way that they could have been produced by the united will of the whole people and so to have the consent of each subject in the general will. Kant says: "This is the touchstone of any public law's conformity with right. . . . [I]f a public law is so constituted that a whole people could not possibly give its consent to it, . . . it is unjust" (ibid.). And at another place: "for what the whole people cannot decide upon for itself, the legislator cannot decide for the people" (*MdS* 6:327–328).

4. As an example of the application of this principle, Kant says that the law cannot establish a certain class of subjects as a privileged and hereditary class ("Theory and Practice," 8:297), nor can it declare a religion the religion of the state with appropriate sanctioning powers (*MdS* 6:327–328). "No people can decide never to make further progress in its insight (enlightenment) regarding beliefs, and so never to reform its churches, since this would be opposed to humanity in their own persons and so to the highest Right of the people." Any such law would be invalid, since it would violate our descendants' rights by preventing them from making further progress in religious understanding.

The two distinctive features of the social contract mean that the contract formulates the highest principle in political matters, and honoring that principle fulfills the first duty that everyone has as a reasonable and rational person to enter into a social union with everyone else in which the rights of all citizens are guaranteed by the principles of right. Everyone has this duty. Thus in entering society by the social contract, each of us achieves the very same end, an end we all share and *ought* to share. Hence the first special feature of the contract. The second feature of the contract— its being the highest criterion of basic law—follows from what reasonable and rational persons could agree to as the test of basic law. This is enough of Kant's political doctrine to indicate that it is a third alternative. It is different from starting with single individuals as atoms independent from all social ties and then building up from them as a basis. And it does not use the idea of the state as spiritual substance and individuals as mere accidents of its substantiality; the state is the arena in which individuals can pursue their ends according to principles each can see are reasonable and fair.

§5. Hegel's Legacy as a Critic of Liberalism

1. Some writers think that among Hegel's important legacies for today are his criticisms of liberalism. Hegel's critical insights are indeed significant; it is less clear that liberalism, especially a liberalism of freedom, cannot recognize and account for them.

It is occasionally said of a liberal society that it has no universal, collective goal but exists only to serve the particular and private ends of its individual members, of what Hegel thinks of as civil society. A familiar example of this is found in Hobbes's political philosophy. In his state of nature, all persons have the private or personal end of their own happiness, or of their own security. These ends are, of course, not shared; they may be of the same *kind,* yet they are not the very same *end.* Hobbes's social contract establishing the sovereign does not involve a shared end, much less an end that everyone ought to share, except insofar as they are rational (as opposed to reasonable). Moreover, the state's institutions are a common end only in the sense that they are a means to each individual's separate happiness or security. Those institutions do not specify a form of public political life that is to be seen by citizens as right or just in itself and from which they are moved by their sense of justice to act. The society of *Leviathan* is a kind of *private society.* Hegel says of Hobbes's approach that "it excludes mind because it leads only to a juxtaposition." There is no real unity since the very same end is not publicly shared. This is one sense of atomic individualism.

As we have just seen, this criticism is not true of Kant. He supposes that all citizens understand the social contract as an idea of reason, with its obligatory shared end that they politically establish a social union. On his doctrine, citizens have the *very same end* of securing for other citizens, as well as for themselves, their basic constitutional rights and liberties. Moreover, this shared end is characterized by reasonable principles of right and justice; it is a form of political life that is reasonable and fair. It is to citizens' good, of course, that their rights and liberties are respected, yet respecting them is what citizens owe one another as the shared end of their republican regime. So much is true of any liberalism of freedom, whether that of Kant or J. S. Mill, or of *A Theory of Justice.* It is incorrect to say that in a liberalism of freedom the state has no publicly shared common ends but is justified entirely in terms of the private aims and desires of its citizens.

The tradition of the liberalism of freedom started at least with the Reformation and gives special priority to certain basic liberties: liberty of conscience and freedom of thought, liberties of persons and the free choice of vocation—freedom from slavery and serfdom—to mention several basic cases. Political liberalism is also a liberalism of freedom. Moreover, it assures all citizens adequate all-purpose means (primary goods) so that they can make intelligent use of the exercise of their freedoms. Their happiness, though, is not guaranteed, for that is a matter for citizens themselves. The liberalism of the (classical) utilitarians—Bentham, James Mill, and Sidgwick—is distinct from the liberalism of freedom. Its first principle is that of the greatest happiness summed over all individuals. If it confirms the liberal freedoms, it is a liberalism of *happiness;* yet if it doesn't confirm these freedoms, it is not a liberalism at all. Since its basic ideal is that of maximizing happiness, it is a contingent matter whether doing this will secure the basic freedoms.

2. A second criticism of liberalism is that it fails to see, what Hegel certainly saw, the deep social rootedness of people within an established framework of their political and social institutions. In this we do learn from him, as it is one of his great contributions. But I don't think that a liberalism of freedom is at fault here. *A Theory of Justice* follows Hegel in this respect when it takes the basic structure of society as the *first* subject of justice. People start as rooted in society and the first principles of justice they select are to apply to the basic structure. The concepts of person and society fit together; each requires the other and neither stands alone.

If citizens of a constitutional democracy are to recognize one another as free and equal, basic institutions must educate them to this conception of themselves, as well as exhibit and encourage this ideal of political justice publicly. This task of education is part of the role of a political conception. In this role, such a conception is part of the public political culture: its first principles are embodied in the institutions of the basic structure and appealed to in their interpretation. Acquaintance with and participation in that public culture is one way citizens learn that conception of themselves, a conception which, if left to their own reflections, they would most likely never form, much less accept and desire to realize.

Consider further how the various contingencies of social life affect the content of people's final ends and purposes, as well as the vigor and confidence with which they pursue them. We assess our prospects in life according to our place in society, and we form our ends and purposes in the light of the means and opportunities we can realistically expect. Whether we are hopeful and optimistic about our future, or resigned and apathetic, depends both on the inequalities associated with our social position and on the public principles of justice that society not merely professes but more or less effectively uses to regulate the institutions of background justice. Hence the basic structure of a social and economic regime is not only an arrangement that satisfies given desires and aspirations but also an arrangement that arouses further desires and aspirations in the future. This it does by the expectations and ambitions it encourages not only in the present but over a complete life as well.

Moreover, native endowments of various kinds (say, native intelligence and natural ability) are not fixed natural assets with a constant capacity. They are merely potential and cannot come to fruition apart from social conditions; and when realized, they can take but one or a few of many possible forms. Educated and trained abilities are always a selection, and a small selection at that, from a wide range of possibilities that might have been fulfilled. Among what affects their realization are social attitudes of encouragement and support, and institutions concerned with their early discipline and use. Not only our conception of ourselves and our aims and ambitions, but also our realized abilities and talents, reflect our personal history, opportunities and social position, and the influence of good and ill fortune. These kinds of reasons show our rootedness in society, as a reasonable liberalism fully recognizes.

3. A third criticism of liberalism is that it cannot account for the intrinsic value of institutions and social practices as such. As Hegel sees it, the good of these social forms must go beyond the fulfillment of the aims and desires of individuals, even though these aims are social: they are the aims of citizens, officeholders, and politicians, all engaged in maintaining their democratic institutions; they are the aims of composers, performers, and conduc-

tors, all engaged in carrying on the traditions of music; and similarly for indefinitely many other cases. But the achievement of such aims, while of course satisfying to individuals whose aims they are, is not the private good of individuals as such; that is presumably a good they could have apart from the appropriate social relationships.

Then what is meant in saying that Hegel holds that collective goods have a value not reducible to the good of individuals? Hegel is said to hold that what makes the state rational and what makes it an end in itself is the systematic identification of its institutions with the actualizing of the subjective freedom and the private good of individuals.

What is crucial here is what is meant by the good of individuals, the private good of individuals, and the private good of individuals as such. Do these mean the same thing? Let's say that they are not the same, and distinguish them as follows.

First, the good of individuals consists, in part at least, of the achievement of individuals' final aims of all kinds, including here especially their social and public aims as defined above, together with the satisfaction of these aspirations.

Next, we say that the private good of individuals is the achievement of their nonpublic final aims of various kinds, counting here as nonpublic their aims as members of families, as husbands and wives, as sons and daughters. We consider the family and certain other institutions as nonpublic, which is not to say they are not subject to moral and legal constraints.

Finally, the private good of individuals as such is the good of individuals regarded purely individualistically, or singly: say, in terms of an individual's overall happiness, perhaps but not necessarily viewed hedonistically.

Granting that the liberal tradition can and indeed does allow for the good of individuals of all these kinds (especially the first), there is not so far any conflict between it and Hegel's view. As a scheme of free institutions, the basic structure of liberal institutions provides for the achievement of final aims of all these kinds; and this is what makes the state rational and an end in itself.

Hegel is not denying the tautology that collective goods also have value because they have a value for individuals. So if we construe collective goods as things like institutional states of affairs—say, the scheme of free institutions itself—that benefit individuals generally, then again there is no conflict with the liberal tradition. For liberalism recognizes that individuals as citizens and politicians may, in view of their final aims, strive to establish a scheme of free institutions for its own sake. Doing so fulfills their desire for public justice, their devotion to the ideal of democracy. Surely Hegel is not saying the liberal tradition recognizes no such aspirations. Their success in realizing this aspiration settles how far they realize their good (socially and institutionally defined).

4. Hegel claims that what has the most value for individuals, what actualizes their freedom most completely, is the pursuit of a universal or collective end, not the pursuit of their own private ends as such. But the liberal tradition does not in general deny this. What it does deny is that the greatest good of human beings generally is realized in politics, as in the public life of the Greek polis. Rather, liberalism stresses other great collective values, those of science, art, and culture, or those of the private and personal life, those of affection, friendship, and love.

5. I think we have still to get at the root of Hegel's view, since the alleged conflict with liberalism seems so far not to exist. The criticisms we have canvassed depend on a mistaken conception, actually a parody, of liberalism. So I try another tack.

The root of Hegel's view is found in his conceptions of history, *Geist*, and the role of reason in philosophical reflection. Hegel often characterizes the greatness of great historical figures in terms of their contribution to the progressive development of the institutional structure of human social life. The actions of historical agents over time unintentionally realize great social transformations that philosophy, looking back after the fact, understands in terms of the cunning of reason. Great figures seek their own narrow ends, yet unknown to them they serve the realization of *Geist*. Hegel often speaks of the fate and suffering of individuals in a way that cannot but strike us as callous and indifferent. They get used up in the course of history as so much material; they come and go as transient and fungible parts of institutions and culture. Yet the social framework remains and manifests the gains *Geist* has made in its goal of passing from substance to a subject fully conscious of itself, having articulated all its latent potentialities. This last is of higher, even of religious, importance and not simply of human importance. How are we to make sense of this?

Let's put the matter this way. There are three points of view. There is the point of view of humanity, the point of view of God, and the point of view of *Geist*. The idea of the point of view of *Geist* is the idea of a point of view that is at once human and divine, just as *Geist* is introduced as the mediation and reconciliation of the traditional concepts of God and humankind. *Geist* is not cruel and certainly not malicious. In the development of *Geist* from substance to subject, human beings suffer and die, not to be resurrected at the last day. But it's essential that social institutions be a framework to realize the good of individuals. Only so does *Geist* achieve its full expression in reasonable and rational social institutions. Only so can individuals become bearers of culture—of religion and philosophy, science and art—in the human awareness of which *Geist* itself achieves its conscious self-awareness. For Hegel, *Geist* achieves its highest self-awareness in religion, art, and philosophy only insofar as human beings can engage in and realize religion, art, and philosophy. The collective self-awareness of human beings in higher culture is that in which *Geist* achieves its fullest realization and complete manifestation. Whether they know it or not, human beings live in the service of the goal of *Geist*—a goal which is in some important sense their own. From the point of view of *Geist*, that is the higher value of human life and culture, not the values and goods as seen from the human point of view. These things are shown in Hegel's remarks about war and historical development.

But what is the point of view of *Geist*? It is not the point of view of the separate transcendent God of Christianity. For although Hegel thought of himself as a Lutheran, the whole point of his philosophical theology is to reject the idea of the radical otherness of God. Rather the self-consciousness of *Geist* is collective human self-consciousness over time, the self-consciousness expressed in different forms of human life in culture, and especially in art and religion and philosophy. Now, the highest form of human self-consciousness occurs in philosophy when it achieves the realization of absolute knowledge. So the point of view of *Geist* must be the point of view of the absolute knowledge achieved by philosophy in its highest and final stage of development. From that point of view, looking back on the whole course of history and culture, it must be possible for philosophy to see that the development of that history and culture is in itself the highest good, the good the realization of which individuals suffered and died for, and nations came and passed away—all for reasons unknown to them except insofar as they grasped the truths of philosophy itself, foreshadowed in art and religion. The good of individuals and peoples is indeed good, but not the highest good: not the highest good for the sake of which there is the world as we see it spread over time and space, and which makes the world intelligible to itself through and through.

What philosophical view is expressed in the point of view of *Geist* so that, when it looks back at the final and highest stage, it sees the whole course of history as good? I suppose there could be no answer to this except the answer that *Geist* sees that it is good, as it were, as a given fact. But this could not really be Hegel's answer, I think, because he is committed to the view that the world is fully intelligible through and through as a basic thesis of his idealism. So when *Geist* sees the world as good, it does so for a reason: what is this reason?

The reason, I believe, is that Hegel affirms the exacting standards Aristotle set up for the highest good: namely, that it be complete, desired only for its own sake, self-sufficient, and such that no added good could make it any better.[9] This complete, or perfect, good cannot be achieved by any human individual, or group, or nation, but it can be achieved by *Geist*—at once human and divine—over the whole course of world history.

This good is rooted in the potentialities of things and peoples. Good is achieved by the full expression of these potentialities in acts of various kinds. So when the potentialities of *Geist* reach their full expression in the world, *Geist*, in looking back in philosophy, brings them to self-consciousness and from the point of view of philosophy sees the course of history as itself good.

This good of the course of history as a whole is complete because all the potentialities of *Geist* have been realized and they express a reasonable and rational view of the whole, the outlines of which are given in Hegel's account of logic. The actualization of potentiality is desired for its own sake, the course of history as a whole is self-sufficient, and there is no added good that could make it any better: every potentiality has been expressed, everything reasonable and rational and good has been done. At last the true and the good are at peace in harmony.

9. This formulation I take from Gisela Striker, "Ataraxia: Happiness as Tranquillity," *Monist* (1990), 98.

APPENDIX

Course Outline: Problems in Moral Philosophy

In the Harvard University Catalogue of Courses this class is described as a study of Kant's moral philosophy, with some attention to Hume and Leibniz and, if time allows, to Hegel's criticisms of Kant. The outline of proposed lecture topics given below reflects this description, though it gives more attention to Hume than the description may suggest. As circumstances allow, there is some discussion of different approaches to moral philosophy and of how its problems may be seen to arise depending on writers' different points of view and on what they see as calling for philosophical reflection given the historical and cultural background of their day. While reading historically important works is but one approach to moral philosophy, we hope to gain some of its advantages.

A. *Hume*
 1. The *Treatise:* a fideism of nature and reason and passions
 2. His account of deliberation and of the role of reason
 3. His account of justice as an artificial virtue and the role of sympathy
 4. His critique of the Rationalists: Clarke and Cudworth
 5. His account of moral judgments: the judicious spectator

B. *Kant: The Moral Law*
 6. The *Grundlegung:* Preface and the argument of Part I
 7. The categorical imperative: the first (law of nature) formulation

8. The second (treating humanity as an end-in-itself) formulation
9. The third (universal legislation) formulation: relation of formulations
10. The realm of ends and the order of nature and other difficulties

C. *Leibniz*
11. Metaphysical perfectionism and his theory of truth
12. Spirits as free and rational substances
13. The *Theodicy* and the conception of freedom of the will

D. *Kant: The Fact of Reason (Das Faktum der Vernunft)*
14. The priority of right and the sequence of conceptions of the good
15. Moral constructivism and the reasonable and the rational
16. The fact of reason: texts and interpretation

E. *Kant: Philosophy as Defense*
17. The moral law as a law of freedom
18. Moral psychology of *Religion* I and *die freie Willkür*
19. The practical point of view and the unity of reason

F. *Hegel*
20. His official criticisms of Kant: what and how serious
21. His idea of ethical life *(die Sittlichkeit)* and of freedom
22. His implicit criticism of Kantian liberalism: what

G. *Texts*

Hume: *Treatise of Human Nature,* ed. P. H. Nidditch (Oxford: Oxford University Press, 1978).

Kant: *Groundwork of the Metaphysics of Morals,* trans. H. D. Paton (New York: Harper and Row, 1964); *Critique of Practical Reason,* trans. L. W. Beck (Indianapolis: Bobbs-Merrill, 1956); *Religion within the Limits of Reason Alone,* trans. T. M. Greene and H. H. Hudson (New York: Harper and Row, 1960); *Doctrine of Virtue,* trans. M. Gregor (New York: Harper and Row, 1964).

Leibniz: *Philosophical Essays,* ed. and trans. Roger Ariew and Daniel Garber (Indianapolis: Hackett, 1989).

Also recommended: Hegel, *Elements of the Philosophy of Right,* trans. H. B. Nisbet, ed. A. W. Wood (Cambridge: Cambridge University Press, 1991).

READINGS:

Hume: Lectures 1–2: *Treatise* II, iii, §§3–10; cf. §§1–2. Lecture 3: ibid., III, ii, §§1–6; II, i, §9. Lecture 4: ibid., III, i, §§1–2. Lecture 5: III, iii, §§1–6.

Kant: Lecture 6: *Grundlegung (Gr)*, Preface and Part I. Lectures 7–9: ibid., Part II; and with this *Critique of Practical Reason (KP)* Analytic: Chs. I, Ak. 18–41, and II, 67–71 (The Typic). Lecture 10: *Gr* II, Ak. 438ff.; *KP* Analytic: Ch. I, Ak. 43f.

Leibniz: Lecture 11: *Discourse on Metaphysics*, Garber #8 and #4, 6, 7, 9, 12. Lecture 12: Garber #11, 15, 25. Lecture 13: Garber #20, 28, 29.

Kant: Lecture 14: *KP* Analytic: Ch. II, Ak. 57–67. Lecture 15: *KP* Analytic: Ch. III, Ak. 71–89; and Doctrine of Method: Ak. 150–163. Lecture 16: texts to be given. Lecture 17: *KP* Analytic: Elucidation: Ak. 89–106; see also *KR* B560–586. Lecture 18: *Religion* (Rel), Bk. I, and *KP* Dialectic: Chs. I and II and §1: Ak. 106–114. Lecture 19: *KP:* Dialectic: §§2–9: Ak. 114–149.

Hegel: Lecture 20: *Philosophy of Right:* Intro., Abstract Right and Morality, §§1–141. Lecture 21: Ethical Life: The Family and Civil Society, §§142–256. Lecture 22: State and World History, §§257–360.

It should be mentioned that the lectures consist largely in examining texts and in trying to present a forceful but reasonably accurate interpretation of the doctrine they express. I shan't give Hume's view, say, and then proceed to criticize it to show how he could have done much better from a contemporary point of view. Some critical comments, yes, when sparing and fundamental, but we should be interested in understanding Hume (and the others), as wrongheaded as he may seem at times. One can say this of any author worthy of careful study and reflection, as the ones we read certainly are.

There will be a final examination, weekly sections, and written work summing to about 2,500–3,000 words.

INDEX

Rousseau, Jean-Jacques, 160, 204, 292, 340, 362
Rule, 54, 60–61, 64. *See also* Convention; Law

Satan, 295
Scanlon, T. M., 16n, 192n
Schiller, Johann Friedrich von, 180
Schlick, Moritz, 22
Schneewind, J. B., 10n
Scotus, Duns, 7
Self-conception: Kant, 16, 148; Hume, 86–87; and predispositions, 291–298; and self-knowledge, 202; and supremacy of reason, 205–207; and moral psychology, 304–305; and personality (Hegel), 340–343. *See also* Character; Predisposition; Rational agent
Self-interest / self-love / egoism, 32, 55, 59, 66–67, 99, 292
Shaftesbury, Earl of, 8n, 11
Sheehan, James, 353n
Sidgwick, Henry, 1, 2, 4, 46, 77, 97, 175, 176, 223, 238, 366
Sittlichkeit, 330, 333–336
Skepticism: and Hume, 22–24; epistemological, 22–23; pyrrhonism, 23; conceptual, 23; moral, 149. *See also* Philosophy as defense
Sleigh, Robert, 133
Smith, Adam, 8n, 21, 52, 84, 346
Smith, Ozzie, 112
Social contract, 363–366
Socrates, 1, 3
Sophocles (*Antigone*), 352
Spinoza, Baruch de, 11, 12, 106, 115, 124–127, 131, 134, 279
Spirits, 124–130
Spontaneity, 280–290, 301
Standpoints: two, 275–277, 322–325; as practical point of view, 309–310
State of nature, 57–58, 233–234

State, 352–358; powers of sovereignty, 360–361
Striker, Gisela, 371
Sturm, John Christopher, 126
Suarez, Francisco, 7, 8n, 75n
Sugden, Robert, 63n
Suicide, 192, 241
Sulzer, J. G., 144, 202
Sympathy, 59, 67, 84–88, 90–94, 99–102, 224

Talents, 154, 228, 367; positions open to (meritocracy), 354–356
Teleology, Kant's view distinguished from, 211, 222, 231
Themistocles, 39
Theoretical reason, 74–75, 82, 146–148, 263–266
Transcendental Deduction, 262–263, 267
Truth: Leibniz's account of, 114–122; and contingency, 119–121

Utilitarianism, 222
Utility, principle of, 97

Value, of the good will, 154–156, 209, 210–211, 224
Vasquez, Gabriel, 75n
Verdi, Guiseppe, 113
Virtue, 66, 109, 154–156, 178; artificial (Hume), 51–55, 57–58, 66; natural (Hume), 51–55; duties of (Kant), 185–187, 192, 208–209, 237; and Hegel, 352
Volition, principle of, 152–153, 177. *See also* Action; Maxim; Practical reason; Will
Voting, 356

Walpole, Sir Robert, 151n
War, 358–362